The Process of Schooling

The Open University
Faculty of Educational Studies

The Schooling and Society course team

Colin Brown (*staff tutor*)
Heather Cathcart (*course assistant*)
Ben Cosin (*unit author*)
Roger Dale (*unit author*)
Geoff Esland (*unit author*)
Ken Giles (*staff tutor/unit author*)
Martyn Hammersley (*unit author*)
Keith Harry (*liaison librarian*)
Richard Hoyle (*designer*)
Jack Jones (*staff tutor*)
Ken Little (*BBC*)

Madeleine MacDonald (*unit author*)
Donald Mackinnon (*unit author*)
Gill Mason (*editor*)
Edward Milner (*BBC*)
Robert Nicodemus (*IET*)
Maggie Preedy (*editor*)
Don Swift (*unit author*)
Vi Winn (*research officer*)
Peter Woods (*unit author*)
Ray Woolfe (*staff tutor/unit author*)

Reader prepared with the editorial assistance of Dawn Bramer

The Process of Schooling
A sociological reader

edited by

Martyn Hammersley
and Peter Woods
for the Schooling and Society Course
at The Open University

London and Henley
Routledge & Kegan Paul
in association with The Open University Press

6744

First published in 1976
by Routledge & Kegan Paul Ltd
39 Store Street,
London WC1E 7DD and
Broadway House,
Newtown Road,
Henley-on-Thames,
Oxon RG9 1EN
Set in Monotype Times by
Kelly, Selwyn & Co., Melksham, Wiltshire
Printed in Great Britain by
Billing & Sons Ltd, Guildford, London and Worcester

ISBN 0 7100 8495 1 (c)
0 7100 8496 X (p)

Contents

Acknowledgments vii

Introduction 1

Section I Theoretical and methodological orientations 11

1 The methodological position of symbolic interactionism 12
H. Blumer

2 Professions in process 19
Rue Bucher and Anselm Strauss

3 Signification 27
D. Matza

4 Making a lesson happen: an ethnomethodological analysis 33
George C. F. Payne

5 Subcultural conflict and working-class community 41
Phil Cohen

6 The elasticity of evil: changes in the social definition of deviance 48
Albert K. Cohen

7 Problems of sociological fieldwork: a review of the methodology of 'Hightown Grammar' 55
Colin Lacey

Section II The organization of teaching 67

8 The teacher in the authority system of the public school 68
Howard S. Becker

9 The career of the Chicago public schoolteacher 75
Howard S. Becker

10 The craftsman teachers 81
H. Gracey

11 Teaching and learning in English primary schools   86
Ann C. Berlak, Harold Berlak, Naida Tushnet Bagenstos and Edward R. Mikel

12 The child as conversationalist: some culture contact features of conversational interactions
between adults and children   98
Matthew Speier

13 The mobilisation of pupil attention   104
M. Hammersley

14 Ad hocing in the schools: a study of placement practices in the kindergartens of two schools   116
K. C. W. Leiter

15 Assessing children's school performance   126
Hugh Mehan

16 Mock-ups and cock-ups: the stage-management of guided discovery instruction   133
Paul Atkinson and Sara Delamont

17 Cue-consciousness   143
C. M. L. Miller and M. Parlett

Section III   Pupil cultures   151

18 The Sisterhood   152
Audrey M. Lambart

19 Interaction sets in the classroom: towards a study of pupil knowledge   160
Viv Furlong

20 The meaning of 'trouble'   171
Elizabeth Rosser and Rom Harré

21 Having a laugh: an antidote to schooling   178
Peter Woods

22 The class significance of school counter-culture   188
Paul Willis

23 Reactions to labelling   201
David H. Hargreaves

24 Physical context influences on behavior: the case of classroom disorderliness   208
Robert A. Stebbins

25 The delniquent school   217
David Reynolds

Index   231

Acknowledgments

The Open University and the publishers would like to thank the following for permission to reproduce copyright material. All possible care has been taken to trace ownership of the selections included and to make full acknowledgment for their use.

Reading   1, 3   Reprinted by permission of Prentice-Hall, Inc., © 1969.

2   By permission of the authors and The University of Chicago Press, 1961.

4, 12, 13, 18, 21, 23   © Routledge & Kegan Paul Ltd, 1976.

5   By permission of Phil Cohen, 1972.

6   By permission of Professor Cohen and Basil Blackwell, publisher, 1974.

7   By permission of Professor Lacey and Routledge & Kegan Paul Ltd, 1976.

8   By permission of H. S. Becker and the American Sociological Association, 1953.

9   By permission of H. S. Becker and The University of Chicago Press, 1952.

10   By permission of Harry L. Gracey and The University of Chicago Press, 1972.

11   By permission of the authors and The University of Chicago Press, 1975.

14   By permission of Dr Leiter and Academic Press, Inc., 1974.

15   Copyright © 1973 by John Wiley & Sons, Inc., reprinted by permission.

16   By permission of Croom Helm Ltd, publishers.

17   By permission of the authors and the Society for Research into Higher Education, 1974.

19   By permission of John Wiley & Sons Ltd.

20, 22, 25   © The Open University, 1976.

24   By permission of Sage Publications Ltd, Beverly Hills and London, 1973.

Introduction

The articles in this volume are set reading for the Open University course 'Schooling and Society'.[1] This collection is in many ways a successor to 'School and Society',[2] the Reader produced to accompany a previous OU course of the same name and now reissued in a revised edition to serve this course. The main aim of that book was to present new sociological ways of thinking about schooling, particularly focusing on the ways in which the relevant actors construct the various aspects of 'schooling' through their interactions. The papers included in this Reader largely represent work which started from this new thinking and attempted to use it in doing ethnographic studies of schools. In the process the original perspective has been broadened and deepened, both theoretically and methodologically.

The sociology of education in Britain largely dates from the early 1950s.[3] Theoretical and methodological orientations in this field have paralleled those in sociology as a whole, though with a time-lag and refracted through particular policy concerns. Thus in the fifties most of the work was centrally concerned with the question of equality of educational opportunity and was informed by theoretical perspectives within the structural functionalist-empirical social research axis dominant in sociology at the time.[4]

In the fifties the number of sociologists, and particularly the number of sociologists working in the field of sociology of education in Britain, was rather small. With the 1960s, however, came a rapid expansion of sociology not just in the universities but also in colleges of education. There was an accompanying broadening of topic in the field, in particular the application to educational institutions of ideas from two fast-growing areas of sociology: organisation theory[5] and role theory.[6] However, also in this decade, the structural functionalist-empirical social research paradigm began to break up. The result was recruitment, especially of younger sociologists—of whom there was an increasing number—to what, in Britain, had been minor or nonexistent traditions: interactionism, phenomenological sociology, ethnomethodology and varieties of Marxism.[7]

The breakdown in the structural functionalist-empirical social research paradigm and the revival or emergence of these other forms of sociology began to affect the sociology of education in Britain towards the end of the 1960s. The most important signs of this change were the appearance of M. F. D. Young (ed.), *Knowledge and Control*[8] and the production of the OU E282 'School and Society' course in 1971. Events internal to sociology, themselves no doubt related to broader social trends, were reinforced in the field of education by political concerns deriving from student militancy and radical criticism of schools and schooling across the Atlantic.[9] Hence the new sociological approaches to education frequently also involved redefinition of policy interests away from a concern with selection in itself and towards critique of the whole society, and also towards communication with 'radical' teachers rather than with policymakers.

As with all oppositional movements, the 'new sociology of education'[10] frequently caricatured the old, and was itself an amalgam of at least partially conflicting political, theoretical and methodological elements. With time, of course, the amalgam has begun to show signs of disintegrating. Initially the stress was very much on the social construction of the social world through interpretation and action, drawing particularly on interactionism and phenomenological sociology. In other words, the active potential of men was stressed. Previous work was rejected for what was regarded as an overemphasis on the determining effect of social systems on thought and action and for its assumption of universal validity regarding what were culturally specific and socially constructed phenomena such as 'teaching', 'rationality', 'science', 'English' being imposed on pupils who already possessed their own culture.[11] Stress was placed on the frameworks of meaning constructed by actors in terms of which they interpreted the world and on the basis of which they acted in the world, rather than on structural and cultural constraints. Thus there was analysis of the assumptions underlying different versions of teaching with an attempt to show that they denied the active character of understanding and the cultural competence of pupils, relegating the latter to a passive role.[12] There was also rejection of the common sociological view that 'erroneous' beliefs must be causally explained, whereas beliefs the analyst believes to be true are believed because they *are* true. All beliefs and actions —even those regarded as deviant or weird—were instead assumed to be rational, to be the product of competent reasoning. Thus pupils' views were no longer to be dismissed as a product of unintelligence, home background or even pupil subcultures when they differed from official school views, but were to be explored for their rationality in the situation, and perhaps beyond.

More recently there has been a swing back towards an emphasis on the determining effects of social systems, particularly of the capitalist system, and criticism of earlier statements which implied that change could occur if teachers changed the conceptions of teaching on which they operated.[13] Rather than actors' perspectives and actions being seen as emerging out of interaction, they are now seen as being the products of social structural forces, either directly, or mediated by the cultural hegemony of the ruling class. In those versions of this tendency close to a neo-Hegelian Marxist position, the stress on the knowledge which underlies actors' constructions, is retained, but this knowledge is now seen as the product and reproducer of alienation.[14]

The change of direction experienced by the sociology of education at the beginning of this decade opened up a wide range of topics for investigation which had hitherto been invisible or regarded as uninteresting or trivial by sociologists and/or which had been the concern of other disciplines. They all centred on the twin concerns of action and knowledge. The nature of teachers' perspectives and of classroom interaction as a process, for instance, which had previously been studied by educationists concerned with improving teaching, became an important area of research for sociologists. With the interactionist stress on the emergent nature of interaction and the importance of situation rather than background as the source of motivation, the classroom became not just a place where social structural and cultural forces were played out, but a situation with explanatory significance for pupil action, where the contingencies of interaction could lead to different outcomes for pupil belief and action. Similarly, teaching came to be seen not as a natural, normal activity not requiring investigation but as a term covering different kinds of possible orientation and operation by teachers, built on different assumptions about the nature of man and

society and having different consequences for pupils. A second area opened up, this time one which had previously been almost totally neglected, was pupil perspectives and strategies. Pupil perspectives became a legitimate topic of enquiry in themselves, as a form of culture, rather than simply one variable in the explanation of working-class failure in schools.[15] In other words, pupil orientations became important not *just* because they mediated the effects of the organisation of schools and the actions of teachers but also because their exploration could show the rationality or intellectual competence of those dismissed as ignorant or incompetent by 'culturally imperialistic' schools. A number of topics, loosely collected under the title of the 'hidden curriculum', also became a central issue. Instead of school achievement being taken to be the product of some mysterious 'intelligence', people began to ask: What exactly are pupils required to learn or to achieve in school? The obverse of this was also posed at the same time: Is there something else besides the official curriculum that is learned? In reply to these questions it was suggested that perhaps the most significant requirement of pupils that pervaded their learning was conformity.[16] Again, like teaching, curriculum became an area not simply open to the prescriptive interests of educationists but a topic fit for sociological enquiry. It was seen not as something legislated by the nature of knowledge but rather as the product of struggle between groups promoting different subjects or different conceptions of a particular subject, and also as reflecting the class structure of the society, the status hierarchy of subjects mirroring the status legitimations of the most powerful forces in the society.[17] Curriculum was to be studied as an important element of 'what passes for education' in schools and to be studied in light of the social structural and cultural constraints operating on educational institutions. Lastly, instead of sociologists accepting the psychologists' conceptions of intelligence and arguing about how much of it was determined by environmental factors, the focus became the conceptions of intelligence embedded in the practices in which and by which 'intelligence' was assessed.[18]

However, the new ideas thrown up in the late sixties and early seventies are not solutions or full-blown alternatives to previous sociology of education. They are rather correctives, and complement previous work. Furthermore, in their present form, they constitute only the barest beginnings, and thus require theoretical development and empirical exploration and validation. In this reader we have collected together articles referring to one particular area in the sociology of education: that concerned with processes of social interaction internal to the school.[19] We claim no necessary explanatory priority for this area. Nevertheless it is a crucial one where the operation of explanatory factors has to be demonstrated and which therefore requires close description. Thus if we adopt the hypothesis that the education system is structured so as to produce employees adapted to their destinations in various occupational locales,[20] then we need to trace out the constraints operating directly on schools, the nature of the diverse intra-school processes which shape pupils, and pupils' responses to these forces in order to check out, refine, and fill out this potential explanation.[21]

We would also argue that intra-school processes do have some *explanatory* significance. We necessarily approach this field from a particular theoretical stance which can loosely be described as interactionist. Therefore we would argue that what occurs in any process of interaction is never fully determined by social structural or cultural forces, even though we recognise that such forces do operate to constrain considerably the possibilities of thought and action. Actors always possess some degree of autonomy, however limited, both in relation to how they see and evaluate the world and in the lines of action that can be taken in the situations facing them. Social structures and cultures emerge out of and are sustained and changed by social interaction, though this is by no means to say that there are no structural and cultural constraints on the process and outcome of interaction between *particular* occasions. This adoption of 'soft determinism'[22] forces greater stress than would normally be laid in more deterministic approaches on the ways in which people make and display sense and significance. Nevertheless it must be stressed that this is only a matter of degree. It seems to us that few sociologists would argue for the existence of full determinism or absolute freedom of action. Opinions differ largely regarding the degree of constraint operating on different actors in particular situations.

Despite this theoretical base we recognise the weak spots in much interactionist work: the almost axiomatic cultural pluralism,[23] the tendency to neglect social structures, the frequently superficial treatment of consciousness and of the question of social order, and the rather naive outright rejection of 'positivist' methodological techniques that sometimes occurs. Thus we have included in the Reader articles which we feel consciously or unconsciously develop interactionism so as to deal with these issues. Thus besides classic interactionist pieces (Blumer, Becker, Bucher & Strauss, Matza) and recent interactionist ethnography in schools (Atkinson & Delamont, Berlak, Bagenstos & Mikel, Furlong, Stebbins, Hargreaves, Gracey, Harré & Rosser, Miller & Parlett, Woods, and Hammersley), there are also articles representing various forms of ethnomethodology (Speier, Payne, Mehan and Leiter) as well as others which bridge traditions theoretically and/or methodologically (Lacey, Lambart, P. Cohen, A. K. Cohen, Willis, and Reynolds).

The first section consists of articles included for their general theoretical and methodological significance. The other two sections represent work relevant to two substantive areas: teaching and the organisation of classroom interaction, and pupil cultures.

Blumer's article is the classic statement of the symbolic interactionist position with regard to methodology; it underwrites much of the work in this volume. He urges us, as social scientists, to stay faithful to the empirical world and not to reify methods. He reminds us of the fluidity, and of the emergent and negotiative character, of social interaction which brings interactionists to focus on process and experience.[24]

> Rather than viewing behaviour as a simple 'release' from a pre-existing psychological structure (such as drives, personalities, emotions or attitudes) or as a consequence of an external coercion by social 'facts' (cultures, structures, organizations, roles, power), the interactionist focuses upon emergence and negotiation—the processes by which social action (in groups, organizations or societies) is constantly being constructed, modified, selected, checked, suspended, terminated and recommenced in everyday life. Such processes occur both in episodic encounters and in longer-lasting socialization processes over the life history.

In stating the 'purist' case for viewing large-scale organisation as something to be 'seen, studied, and explained in terms of the process of interpretation engaged in by the acting participants', Blumer reminds us of areas of common interest that might be informed by such an approach.

Bucher and Strauss show the relevance of this interactionist or processual perspective to action of and in collectivities by applying it to an area of sociology which was, and to some extent still is, dominated by structural functionalist approaches. They show that an important assumption of the latter is defective. Rather than being a community agreed on purposes, theories and methods whose actions are governed by consensual norms, even the medical profession is riven with segments or factions promoting different perspectives, competing to gain control of the master institutions of the occupation: professional associations, journals, etc. In other words, a central though previously unremarked aspect of professional life is conflict between groups promoting different interests and conceptions of the occupational task. Thus Bucher and Strauss show that the nature of work tasks and the methods to be used to deal with them are not somehow given in the nature of the world but rather are constructed, argued and struggled over, and that this is as true of occupations claiming high status and massive expertise vis-à-vis clients as of occupations enjoying less autonomy.

David Matza expounded a similar interactionist philosophy in his book *Becoming Deviant*, though this time the focus is much more on individual subjectivity. 'Naturalism', in Matza's sense, urges that we remain true to the phenomena under study:[25]

Man participates in meaningful activity. He creates his reality, and that of the world around him, actively and strenuously. Man naturally— not supernaturally—transcends the existential realms in which conceptions of cause, force and reactivity are easily applicable. Accordingly, a view which conceives of man as an object, methods that probe human behaviour without concerning themselves with the meaning of that behaviour, cannot be regarded as naturalist.

The rest of his book is devoted to drawing out the implications of this for the study of deviance. The extract included in the reader illustrates the centrality of the actor and the pay-off of a sustained focus on meaning in an area of deviance theory—labelling (which Matza terms 'signification')—which has been criticised for neglecting the part played by the actor. As P. K. Manning notes, it is 'this focus on *the inner life* that makes this book very nearly the end of the phenomenological quest.'[26]

The article by George Payne illustrates a somewhat different direction of development of or out of inter-actionism: ethnomethodology.[27] After providing a general account of ethnomethodology, the study of the methods by which members produce a recognisable social world, Payne goes on to illustrate just what ethnomethodological analysis looks like in practice, through explicating the means by which members produce and make sense of the first few utterances of a lesson *as those of a lesson*. Instead of recommending the investigation of individual subjectivities in depth, as Matza does, ethnomethodology proposes the investigation of the shared methods which must underlie the production of the social world, given the fact that the world is *intersubjective*. While individual actors may make idiosyncratic sense of any pheno-menon, that sense will usually be understandable to others, hence it must have been produced by shared methods. Not only must the social world therefore be produced by such methods but the only way in which the analyst can avoid producing members' glosses of the world, that is producing accounts that are *of* rather than *about* the society, is to investigate those methods by which he and all members of the society interpretively produce that society. On this basis, ethnomethodologists are particularly critical of any approaches such as that of interactionism[28] that claim to be able to get at individual subjectivities. They argue that all that can be produced are members' accounts of such subjectivities, accounts relying on common resources of the culture to which both analyst and participant belong. Only study of members' methods, they argue, provides any analytic leverage and produces an account of the production of the social world.

Phil Cohen's paper marks quite a different direction of development of interactionism focused on, but not limited to, the field of youth subcultures. He relates some subcultures, in origin and content, to the broader and more basic class structure and culture of the wider community in which they arose. He argues that changes in the kinship system, the ecological setting and the structure of the local economy under-mined the strength of the working-class community in London's East End. Cohen traces the impact of these developments on the young. Some met them with an attempted 'ideological solution' to the central paradox of the traditional working class: traditional puritanism and the new ideology of consumption.

Mods, Parkers, Skinheads, Crombies, all represent, in their different ways, an attempt to retrieve some of the socially cohesive elements destroyed in their parent culture, and to combine these with elements selected from other class fractions, symbolising one or other of the options confronting it.

Cohen's paper has stimulated much empirical work[29] which features prominently interactionist interests and techniques (for example in the attention given to the actor, and to meaning and the use of participant observation) but working them through analysis of the general structural setting.

Albert Cohen also offers a conceptual schema which incorporates societal and individual elements, but with rather different implications. He relates changing social definitions of deviance to identity theory. Identities, of individuals and collectivities, can be enhanced by 'creating new scales of virtue' or de-fended by contracting the definition of, or 'normal-ising', deviance.[30] 'Generation gap' theories have been less popular in the more political climate of the 1970s. Cohen, however, retains the notion of a 'generation gap', but it is a 'moving' one, the old continually under pressure to legitimate the erstwhile deviant behaviour of the young. He provides a means of conceptualising the enormous changes in the societal moral order over the past generation, which cross-cuts the class structure and which bears on the more general youth culture, as compared with the more specific working-class subcultures featured in Phil Cohen's paper.

An area often neglected in research reports is that which comes between theory and the products of research: questions of why we undertake research, how we come by our intellectual persuasions, what research techniques we adopt and why, what problems we meet in the course of research and how we resolve them. However, if we carry Blumer's tenet to its logical conclusion, the researcher's own position, background assumptions and aims need to be expli-cated. This Colin Lacey does, and casts new light on his study of Hightown Grammar.[31] His discussion of problems of bias and role conflict displays the evaluative, interpretational and interactional pro-cesses involved in research, while his account of how he came to combine methods and integrate them into the analysis deals with a particularly difficult problem encountered by many fieldworkers.

The second section of the Reader is concerned with work focusing on the nature of teaching activities in the context of classroom interaction, an area in which, until fairly recently, there was very little sociological work. This area is only just now beginning to be staked out and explored, much of the research still being very much 'in progress'. The two articles by Becker, along with his 'Social-Class Variations in the Teacher-Pupil Relationship' which is reprinted in the revised edition of the *School and Society* Reader, are the product of one of the earliest pieces of inter-actionist work on education (though Willard Waller's book *The Sociology of Teaching*[32] may be seen as a precursor). Becker's work is interactionist in the way that he attempts to elicit from the teachers their perceptions of the situations facing them and the ways in which they attempt to deal with these situations rather than, as much previous and subsequent work has done,[33] focusing on teachers' social backgrounds and training or their personalities.[34] While Becker's research method was not that of participant observation his interviews appear to have been relatively open-ended, allowing the respondents to express their views of the world, minimising the interviewer's imposition of his own frameworks on the teachers, and allowing him to follow up any 'leads' as they arose.[35]

> The interviews were oriented around the general question of the problems of being a teacher and were not specifically directed towards discovering feelings about social-class differences among students. Since these differences created some of the teachers' most pressing problems they were continually brought up by the interviewees themselves.

Furthermore, he tried to keep the focus on specific events, not seeking to elicit general attitude statements whose relationship to what was actually done in the situation might be obscure. Becker's central concern is the constraints operating on teachers in the situations in which they work and the strategies by which they seek to deal with these problems: movement to a 'better' school, setting up barriers against parents, sanctioning the head, and the typing and differential treatment of pupils.

Gracey also focuses on the constraints operating on teachers, but via a different method. He contrasts the 'progressive' ideology of some of the teachers in the American elementary school he studied with the way in which they did organise social interaction in their classrooms. In the extracts included here he displays, through description of classroom activity and reporting the comments of one of the teachers, how, to various degrees and in various ways, she compromised her ideal classroom organisation in order to cope with the bureaucratic structure in which she must operate. He also notes that the major solution adopted to deal with the frustrations involved in such compromises is to get out of the classroom, either by upward mobility within the education system or by leaving it altogether.

The article by Berlak and her colleagues takes up this issue of compromises in order to demonstrate that the common descriptions of English primary school classrooms as unstructured are inaccurate, deriving from superficial investigation. This is a good illustration of the importance of undertaking intensive ethnographic investigation. These authors show that the different classrooms they studied all involved a trade-off between the polarities usually taken to characterise the differences between 'traditional' and 'progressive' teaching. They argue that these trade-offs are made differently on different occasions according to such considerations as the 'type' of pupil involved. However, whereas Gracey attributes the need for the compromises largely to the bureaucratic structure in which the teachers had to work, as do his teachers themselves, in this paper it is explained in terms of the diversity of belief about how children should be treated in society generally, among teachers and even within each teacher. Compromise between the 'traditional' and 'progressive' poles is unavoidable because of the culturally pluralistic nature of modern societies.

With Matthew Speier, we move to a rather deeper theoretical level to look at the structure of social interaction. While he is specifically talking about interaction in households, the notion of interactional rights which he elaborates is central to any study of interaction, and the more specific findings are also relevant to teacher-pupil relationships. Speier grounds his analysis in a view of adult-child interaction as cross-cultural in nature. This is an interesting re-working of the 'generation gap' theories mentioned earlier, which constitute a competing account to that in terms of class cultures.[36]

The notion of the cross-cultural character of teacher-pupil interaction, whether the cultures are class or generational, provides an important though not the only or an exclusive explanation for the salience of a concern with control in the orientations of teachers. Hammersley subjects classroom inter-action to description and analysis, focusing on one aspect of teachers' concern with control. He implicitly uses the notion of interactional rights, but argues that 'rights' have to be established and continually main-tained. The article discusses the techniques used by the teachers in one school to establish and maintain 'proper' attention and, in particular, those which involved 'strategic action'. The purpose of the analysis is to lay the foundations for an account of what 'good behaviour', 'intelligence', 'school achievement', etc., mean as well as to provide one of the bases for explaining pupil perspectives and actions.

The articles by Leiter and Mehan involve a similar focus, but instead of dealing with the classroom setting, are concerned with testing situations. Leiter concentrates on the procedures and typifications by which kindergarten teachers assign pupils to different classes. One element of his approach is a stress on the contingent, achieved character of the interviews used to assess children: that the teachers do not, and could not, simply follow an interview schedule because, if they did, interaction in the interview would break down. They therefore use various strategies to keep interaction going and to get through the schedule: leading questions, expansions of pupil talk, etc. The implication of this, of course, is that pupils are not being subjected to standard treatment. Their differential responses may be as much a product of variation in the behaviour of the tester as of any of their own features such as 'ability'. Leiter goes on to show how a pupil's performances are interpreted through assumptions as to the type of pupil he is, in which are embedded theories of human behaviour, and which have implications for which class he should be placed in. Mehan develops this line by pointing to the complex problems of interpretation involved in deciding what a pupil's answer to the question is, and also to how competent reasoning can produce 'wrong' answers and faulty reasoning produce 'right' answers. What is being indicated is the achieved character of interviews, the interpretive and interactional complexities that underlie any 'results'.

Atkinson and Delamont focus on the teaching situation and point to the contingencies of interaction and the interpretive processes involved in 'discovery' methods in science teaching in schools and bedside teaching in medicine. They show that rather than being identical with the 'real thing', discovery methods and bedside teaching simulate only certain aspects of 'doing science' and 'hot medicine'; and moreover that pupil and student learning depend on the recognition by students of the artificiality of the situation, as it does under 'traditional' teaching. They show that interaction in these circumstances can be usefully conceptualised as an information game which involves covering and uncovering moves on the part of teachers. Learning is still managed, the teacher is still arbiter of 'right answers' or 'right approaches', though now this teacher decision-making is implicit rather than explicit.

In the final article of this section Miller and Parlett point to the importance of cue-taking in examinations. They display the differences between students in the ways in which they orient to cues. Some are 'cue-deaf', taking no note of cues, apparently unaware of their existence or importance, whereas some organise their work on the basis of what cues they pick up, and others actively seek cues in their interactions with staff. The significance of cues in exams is similar to that of the devices used by testers discussed by Leiter and Mehan. What is actually being measured is, at least in part, rather different from what it is officially claimed is being measured.

The final section is concerned with certain aspects of pupil cultures. The standard texts of the late sixties and early seventies, especially those of Hargreaves and Lacey,[37] focused on the broad division they discovered between pupils involved in a pro-school culture on the one hand and an anti-school culture on the other; and

they examined the processes by which these cultures came into being. Hargreaves and Lacey pointed to the processes of differentiation, by which the pupils were assessed, allocated and divided up by the school's formal structure, and 'polarisation', in which the pupils reinforced the separation so that those at either end of the school status system grew closer together and demarcated themselves more sharply from the other group. However, while Hargreaves and Lacey recognised that there are many kinds of pupil cultures, they failed to deal with this diversity in their analyses. They did not give pre-eminence to pupil views and categories, though they gave them far more consideration than any other writers on the subject up to that time; neither did they explore the connection these cultures might have had with social class groupings.

The first five articles in Section III explore aspects of these three points. Lambart's paper is of especial interest since her research was part of that broader study of schools in Manchester to which Hargreaves and Lacey contributed. Her 'Sisterhood' is an interform grouping that cannot be explained by the usual factors, but owes something to the interweaving of the formal and informal structure of the school, and also to home situation and area of residence. It is also notable for its members' higher than average rates of achievement, despite a higher than average rate of deviancy. Her work is an illustration in practice of the complexity to which Hargreaves and Lacey often refer, but tend to gloss over, and of the ways in which their rather simplistic general categories of pro- and anti-school cultures need to be developed.

This is taken much further by Furlong, who criticises the narrowness of the view which sees interaction as the product solely of group membership. Interaction does not just 'happen', but is constructed by individuals. One interacts with many people in the course of a day, and one's behaviour is tailored to the context of particular groupings. Furlong's analysis from an interactionist approach takes us into a position where we can view the action from inside the scene, based on pupil knowledge and experience. From here we see a different kind of pupil association—emergent, negotiative, changing— which casts light on the considerable fluctuations in behaviour which we know occur.

Pupils' constructions are largely new territory, though there have been many representations of them through secondary filters. Too often they have been represented or studied in official terms and within official categories as 'succeeding' or 'failing', 'choosing options', 'misbehaving', or 'coming from a poor home'. Deviant behaviour has been viewed as chaotic, disorganised, aimless, as in the popular pupil activity of 'mucking about'. But this might be only a small piece, or even a misrepresentation, of their world. Rosser and Harré make this clear. Using what they term an 'ethogenic' approach, which bears similarities to other interactionist positions discussed above, they uncover rather different accounts of classroom processes from those informed by official rhetoric, and give an indication of the implications for the education system as a whole. They suggest, for example, that the current practical issue of 'disorder in our schools' as perceived by teachers might turn out to owe more to depersonalisation caused by the institution than to extra-school factors, if we take pupils' views into account.

That many children are bored in schools, particularly secondary schools, seems incontestable. Woods sees the life-style of one particular group of pupils in the school he studied as largely a reaction to this condition. Analysing the 'laughter' which is the essential element in their school life, he sees much seemingly aimless 'mucking about' in this light, while other forms of laughter might be more subversive. Woods demonstrates how these reactions differ between groups, which develop their own rules and norms, and also differ in response to different teacher strategies. The implications of this are that individual teachers do have considerable power to affect such outcomes.

However, such influence always operates within certain more general structural and cultural constraints. Paul Willis's paper, which owes something both to interactionist and to the more structural approach of Phil Cohen, makes this clear. The anti-school culture is related to the parent culture, and in this case particularly to 'shop floor' culture. There is a consistency between aspects of the latter and of some pupil cultures, especially in their devices for 'getting by', in, for example, counteracting boredom. Willis emphasises the liveliness and richness of working-class culture and its necessity for working-class survival.[38] Attempts to crush it or otherwise change it, for example by well-intended schemes to 'provide for' 'deprived' pupils, are therefore misguided and potentially damaging. In many respects the culture is a palliative to the problems that come to them as a consequence of their position in the class structure. By this reckoning, real change can come only via a change in their relationship to the processes of production which would alter the class structure as a whole.

The last three articles are specifically concerned with school deviance. Hargreaves, Hester and Mellor have begun the work of examining teacher rule-construction, the labelling of actions and the typing of pupils by teachers.[39] In this volume, Hargreaves suggests factors in the pupil response which might contribute to the definition of deviance, and also illustrates, in a school context, how the societal reaction works—through, for example, secondary deviation and stigmatisation. The construction of deviant identities and the formation of deviant sub-cultures are viewed as part of a potential chain reaction.

Stebbins looks at disorder in classrooms from yet another view, that is in relation to their physical and temporal conditions, and argues for the centrality of these conditions as compared with cultural factors. Interactionist concern with, for example, the definition of the situation, and the emergence of the problem during observation is again in evidence. The sharp contrast between the physical properties and behaviour attending the classrooms of the Kingston school on the one hand and the St John's school on the other throws into relief the possible implications of the spatial and temporal dimensions. Stebbins recounts this against the background of a rudimentary theory of the influence of physical context on behaviour. In the age of the 'open-plan school' and the 'integrated day', his particular examples are of especial interest.

Theoretically we have long suspected that the schools themselves—ideologically, pedagogically, organisationally—must play a considerable role in the creation of deviance. As 'moral entrepreneurs' and labellers, teachers are the arbiters of right and wrong. But, more than this, they differ among and within themselves in their definitions of, concern about, and treatment of pupil deviance. The work of Power and Phillipson testifies to this.[40] David Reynolds's research is the latest in this line of investigation. Here he shows large differences in deviancy rates between schools that can be accounted for only by intra-school factors, and presents some of his analysis of these factors.

This collection as a whole captures the drift of our own interests in theory, method and content in a particular field. These represent a meeting of various traditions and approaches. Based broadly in Blumer-type interactionism, our position recognises both the autonomy of the moment and the range of choices open to the actor in any situation, *and* the existence and influence of social structures which not only constrain but also make possible particular activities. It is concerned with the analysis of micro-situations, such as pieces of conversation, and with the macro-societal context in which they occur. It is interested in the thoughts, values and feelings of the actor as an individual and in the structure and operation of collectivities of various kinds. It recognises actors' accounts but also the necessity for analytic concepts. It realises the political nature of all interaction but is also aware of the routine everyday character of much interaction and the underlying understandings which envelop and cross-cut conflicting groups. On the whole it favours participant observation, which is the only means for us to get anywhere near Matza's naturalism, but does not turn its back on quantitative techniques as additional methodological devices. Several articles here display this kind of eclecticism; unsurprisingly, for that is in the spirit of fieldwork.

The book is an amalgam of established and new articles, the former representing theoretical bases and the latter recent and current research at various stages of completion which has largely been inspired by them. Thus it is not a conclusion or definitive pronouncement but a snapshot of a moving process that represents the key elements of a position within a debate at one point in time. Wherever this dynamic leads us, we hope this Reader offers a glimpse of the illumination sociology can cast on school processes, many of which have for too long been taken for granted, ignored or simply not seen or identified.

Notes

1 E202, a second level course.
2 School and Society Course Team, Routledge & Kegan Paul, 1971.
3 For discussion of work prior to this, see J. Floud and A. H. Halsey, 'The sociology of education: a trend report and bibliography', *Current Sociology*, 7 (3), 1958, 165–233.
4 Structural functionalism is a theoretical perspective having its roots in early nineteenth-century French and German thought, developed by Emile Durkheim in his work on the division of labour and on religion and first systematised and applied by British social anthropologists in their studies of 'primitive societies'. This perspective became dominant in American sociology in the 1950s via the work of Talcott Parsons and several generations of his students. Briefly, this is a theory which views societies as systems made up of parts, each of which performs a particular function for the operation of the whole. The structure of any institution is seen as being determined by the function it performs in the society of which it forms a part. Empirical social research also has its origins in the nineteenth century in the work of the moral statisticians. It was further developed in Germany in the early part of this century and became a major tradition in a number of centres in America in the fifties, the major figure being Paul. F. Lazarsfeld. This tradition is centrally concerned with large-scale surveys of attitudes and the variables explaining the distribution of attitudes. Whereas structural functionalism, in its American version, was little concerned with methodology, empirical social research displays what some regard as an obsession with methodological issues. Towards the end of the 1950s these two traditions became more and more interpenetrated, combined in the work of individual authors and co-ordinated in research teams.
5 Organisation theory is a substantive area of sociology which studies the structure and operation of organisations, usually—though not necessarily or entirely—private, business organisations. The practical management applications are obvious and have been an important shaping factor on the growth in this area. For a discussion and evaluation of organisation theory from an interactionist point of view, see D. Silverman, *The Theory of Organisations*, Heinemann, 1970. On the application of organisation theory to the study of educational institutions see B. Davies, 'On the contribution of organisational analysis to the study of educational institutions', in Richard Brown (ed.), *Knowledge, Education and Cultural Change*, Tavistock, 1974.
6 The concept of role has been used in myriad ways but, in our terms, refers to the activities a person adopting a particular social identity, occupational or otherwise, claims the right to engage in and/or is expected by others to carry out. For criticism of the concept of role, drawing on teaching as an example, see M. Coulson, 'Role: a redundant concept in sociology?', in J. A.

Acknowledgments

The editors would like to thank Dawn Bramer, Heather Cathcart, Pat O'Farrell and Marion Richards for their considerable help in preparing this volume.

Jackson (ed.), *Role*, Sociological Studies 4, Cambridge University Press, 1972. For a discussion of many of the applications of this concept to educational institutions, see G. Grace, *Role Conflict and the Teacher*, Routledge & Kegan Paul, 1972.
7 Interactionism is a sociological tradition, American in origin, dating from the early twentieth century, and deriving particularly from the work of G. H. Mead. It was further developed by the Chicago School of the 1930s and 1940s, notably in their ethnographic studies of various aspects of Chicago life. There was a resurgence of interest in America in this perspective in the 1960s, again focused on the University of Chicago. The stress here is on the partial independence from social structural, cultural and psychological forces of the sense people make of the world and of action based on such perspectives (G. H. Mead, *Mind, Self and Society*, University of Chicago Press, 1934. For a description of the original Chicago School from a neo-Chicagoan position see D. Matza, *Becoming Deviant*, Prentice Hall, 1969). Sociological work inspired by phenomenology, a philosophical tradition founded by Edmund Husserl, is a fairly recent phenomenon of which the best-known exponents are Alfred Schutz and Berger and Luckmann. These authors are concerned with the knowledge and assumptions which must be possessed and acted on by people in order for the social world to exist. Their project is to explicate this knowledge, which is not given in consciousness but rather is taken for granted by all of us in our everyday lives (see for instance A. Schutz, *Collected Papers*, Martinus Nijhoff, 1971, vols 1 and 2, and P. L. Berger and T. Luckmann, *The Social Construction of Reality*, Penguin, 1967). Ethnomethodology is in one sense a brand of phenomenological sociology since it has certainly drawn on phenomenology, though there are other important sources in Goffman's interactionism and the work of the philosopher Wittgenstein. However, in other ways ethnomethodology constitutes a much more radical break with previous sociology than do other forms of phenomenological sociology. Thus the latter see themselves as providing a sounder basis for the investigation of the traditional sociological issues, whereas ethnomethodology proposes an entirely different sociological enterprise: the study of the methods by which people interpret and display the social world as having the recognisable features it appears obviously to have. As in phenomenological sociology and interactionism, there is a focus on the ways in which people construct the social world through their interpretations and actions, but here the stress is on the discovery of methods, formal devices which it is argued must underlie this construction, rather than on substantive, context-bound knowledge (see R. Turner (ed.), *Ethnomethodology*, Penguin, 1974). There are almost as many versions of Marxism as there are of sociology, and this tradition also has its origins in the nineteenth century. Like ethnomethodology,

Marxism partly stands outside of sociology as an alternative enterprise, despite many attempts to incorporate it into sociology. The tradition stems of course from the work of Karl Marx and much Marxist work has been devoted to close study of his writings. Marx stresses the dialectical nature of the development of societies, which he sees as leading to the realisation of man's species-specific nature; that is, the realisation of the ideals of the French Enlightenment. The motor of societal development is a struggle between social classes which are integral to particular modes of production. Class conflict is caused by contradictions between developing forces of production and the continued existence of social relations of production once suited to but now hampering the further development of the forces of production. However there have been important disagreements over the interpretation of Marx's work among Marxists, the most significant contemporary one being over the extent to which the Hegelian philosophy of history forms the basis for Marx's later work. The neo-Hegelians such as the Frankfurt School believe that it does, the Althusserians see a break in Marx's work which divides his Hegelian early work from his later scientific writings. (For an account of Marx (and Durkheim and Weber), see A. Giddens, *Capitalism and Modern Social Theory*, Cambridge University Press, 1971. On the Frankfurt School, see M. Jay *The Dialectical Imagination*, Heinemann, 1973. For the Althusserian approach to the study of educational institutions, see L. Althusser, 'Ideology and ideological state apparatuses', in B. R. Cosin (ed.), *Education: Structure and Society*, Penguin, 1972.)

8 Macmillan, 1971.

9 We are referring to the work of writers such as Holt, Kohl, Dennison, Illich.

10 This term derives from D. Gorbutt: 'The new sociology of education', *Education for Teaching*, no. 89, autumn 1972, 3–11.

11 See for instance M. F. D. Young, Introduction to *Knowledge and Control*, and N. Keddie (ed.), *Tinker, Tailor: the Myth of Cultural Deprivation*, Penguin, 1973.

12 See for instance G. Esland, 'Teaching and learning as the organisation of knowledge', in M. F. D. Young, op. cit.

13 See G. Whitty, 'The experience of social studies', in P. E. Woods and M. Hammersley (eds), *School Experience*, Croom Helm (forthcoming). One of the companion volumes to this collection, I. R. Dale, G. Esland and M. MacDonald (eds), *Schooling and Capitalism: a Sociological Reader*, Routledge & Kegan Paul, 1976, illustrates this trend.

14 For instance M. F. D. Young, 'School science: innovations or alienation?', in P. E. Woods and M. Hammersley, op. cit.

15 Despite their stress on the partial autonomy of school processes from the impact of the class structure, Hargreaves and Lacey did not really explore pupil perspectives. See D. H. Hargreaves, *Social Relations in a Secondary School*, Routledge & Kegan Paul, 1967, and C. Lacey, *Hightown Grammar*, Manchester University Press, 1970.

16 Prior to this, the issue of socialisation in schools had been tackled largely within a structural functionalist framework. See for instance T. Parsons, 'The school class as a social system', in A. H. Halsey, Jean Floud and C. A. Anderson (eds), *Education, Economy and Society*, Free Press, 1961.

17 See for instance M. F. D. Young, 'An approach to the study of curricula as socially organized knowledge', in Young, op. cit.

18 See for example P. Squibb, 'The concept of intelligence: a sociological perspective', *Sociological Review*, 21(1), 1973, 147–66.

19 Dale, Esland and MacDonald, op. cit., adopts a complementary focus.

20 See S. Bowles and H. Gintis, *Schooling in Capitalist America*, Routledge & Kegan Paul, 1976.

21 For an attempt to do this, see E. B. Leacock, *Teaching and Learning in City Schools*, Basic Books, 1969.

22 D. Matza, *Delinquency and Drift*, Wiley, 1964.

23 That is the argument that modern societies are made up of a collection of distinct cultures each having its own conception of the world, values, norms, etc. While we accept that this is in one sense quite correct there has been a tendency to see conflict as necessarily *cultural* rather than as, for instance, conflict over interests, and a tendency to neglect the existence of more basic cultural *resources* shared by the different cultures or subcultures within a society.

24 K. Plummer, *Sexual Stigma*, Routledge & Kegan Paul, 1975, p. 13.

25 Prentice-Hall, 1969, p. 8.

26 'On deviance', *Contemporary Sociology*, 2(2), 1973, p. 125.

27 We are not suggesting that historically ethnomethodology grew out of interactionism (though there is some truth in that) but rather that it can be seen as a development of one element in interactionism.

28 Though in fact they are critical of all sociology.

29 Some of which is reported in University of Birmingham, Centre for Contemporary Cultural Studies, *Resistance through Rituals, Working Papers in Cultural Studies*, no. 7–8, summer 1975; a set book for the Schooling and Society course.

30 This is a development of his previous work on delinquency (see A. K. Cohen, *Delinquent Boys*, Free Press, 1955).

31 op. cit.

32 Wiley, 1967 (first published in 1932).

33 For a review of this work, see A. Morrison and D. McIntyre, *Teachers and Teaching*, Penguin, 1969.

34 This is not to say that the backgrounds or personal strategies of teachers are unimportant but that they become relevant after teachers' perceptions and occupational strategies have been described and related to the situations facing them and the groups in which they are presently interacting. Furthermore, the interest in background should be in terms of the sedimentation of experience rather than as *simply* a source of variables to be correlated with aspects of present behaviour.

35 H. S. Becker, 'Social-Class Variations in the Teacher-Pupil Relationship', in the second edition of the *School and Society* Reader.

36 Though this is by no means to say that these accounts are mutually exclusive.

37 See titles in n. 15.

38 Compare the cultural deprivation literature. See, for example, Schools Council Working Paper 27, *Cross'd with Adversity*, Evans/Methuen Educational, 1970. For commentaries on this literature see C. A. Valentine, *Culture and Poverty*, University of Chicago Press, 1968.

39 D. H. Hargreaves, S. K. Hester and F. J. Mellor, *Deviance in Classrooms*, Routledge & Kegan Paul, 1975.

40 M. Power *et al.*, 'Delinquent schools?', *New Society*, 19 October 1967; C. M. Phillipson, 'Juvenile delinquency and the school', in W. G. Carson and P. Wiles (eds), *Crime and Delinquency in Britain*, Martin Robertson, 1971.

Section I Theoretical and methodological orientations

1 The methodological position of symbolic interactionism

H. Blumer

(. . .) The proper picture of empirical science, in my judgment, is that of a collective quest for answers to questions directed to the resistant character of the given empirical world under study. One has to respect the obdurate character of *that* empirical world—this is indeed the cardinal principle of empirical science. Empirical science pursues its quest by devising images of the empirical world under study and by testing these images through exacting scrutiny of the empirical world. This simple observation permits us to put the topic of methodology in proper focus. Methodology refers to, or covers, the principles that underlie and guide the full process of studying the obdurate character of the given empirical world. There are three highly important points implied by this conception of methodology: (1) methodology embraces the entire scientific quest and not merely some selected portion or aspect of that quest; (2) each part of the scientific quest as well as the complete scientific act, itself, has to fit the obdurate character of the empirical world under study; therefore, methods of study are subservient to that world and should be subject to test by it; and (3) the empirical world under study and not some model of scientific inquiry provides the ultimate and decisive answer to the test. I wish to elaborate each of these three points.

(. . .) All of these components are essential to scientific study and all of them need to be analyzed and respected in developing the principles of methodology. To understand this matter, let me identify the more important parts of scientific inquiry, parts that are indispensable to inquiry in empirical science.

(a) *The Possession and Use of a Prior Picture or Scheme of the Empirical World under Study.* As previously mentioned, this is an unavoidable prerequisite for any study of the empirical world. One can see the empirical world only through some scheme or image of it. The *entire act* of scientific study is oriented and shaped by the underlying picture of the empirical world that is used. This picture sets the selection and formulation of problems, the determination of what are data, the means to be used in getting data, the kinds of relations sought between data, and the forms in which propositions are cast. In view of this fundamental and pervasive effect wielded on the entire act of scientific inquiry by the initiating picture of the empirical world, it is ridiculous to ignore this picture. The underlying picture of the empirical world is always capable of identification in the form of a set of premises. These premises are constituted by the nature given either explicitly or implicitly to the key objects that comprise the picture. The unavoidable task of genuine methodological treatment is to identify and assess these premises.

(b) *The Asking of Questions of the Empirical World and the Conversion of the Questions into Problems.* This constitutes the beginning of the act of inquiry. It is obvious that the kind of questions asked and the kind of problems posed set and guide the subsequent lines of inquiry. Accordingly, it is highly important for the methodologist to examine carefully and appraise critically how problems are selected and formulated. Superficiality, humdrum conventionality, and slavish adherence to doctrine in the selection and setting of problems constitute a well-known bane in empirical science.

(c) *Determination of the Data to be Sought and the Means to be Employed in Getting the Data.* Obviously, the data are set by the problem—which indicates the importance of being sure of the satisfactory character of the problem. Even though set by the problem, the data need to be constantly examined to see if they require a revision or rejection of the problem. Beyond this, it is important to recognize that the means used to get the data depend on the nature of the data to be sought. A reverse relation of allowing the method used in securing data to determine the nature of the data

Source: *Symbolic Interactionism: Perspective and Method,* Englewood Cliffs, Prentice-Hall, 1969, pp. 21–60.

vitiates genuine empirical inquiry. These few observations suggest the clear need for careful and critical consideration of how data are to be determined and collected.

(d) *Determination of Relations Between the Data.* Since the establishment of connections between the data yield the findings of the study, it is highly important to be aware of how such connections are reached. This is true whether one arrives at the connections through judicious reflection on what one conceives might be significant relations or whether one relies on a mechanical procedure such as factorial analysis or a scheme of computer correlation.

(e) *Interpretation of the Findings.* This terminal step carries the scientist beyond the confines of the problem he has studied, since in making interpretations he has to relate his findings to an outside body of theory or to a set of conceptions that transcend the study he has made. This important terminal step particularly merits methodological scrutiny in the case of social and psychological science. It is at this point, speaking metaphorically, that new cards may be slipped into the deck, conferring on the interpretation an unwarranted 'scientific' status merely because the preceding steps of the study have been well done. The outside body of theory or set of conceptions used to frame the interpretation may be untested and may be false.

(f) *The Use of Concepts.* Throughout the act of scientific inquiry concepts play a central role. They are significant elements in the prior scheme that the scholar has of the empirical world; they are likely to be the terms in which his problem is cast; they are usually the categories for which data are sought and in which the data are grouped; they usually become the chief means for establishing relations between data; and they are usually the anchor points in interpretation of the findings. Because of such a decisive role in scientific inquiry, concepts need especially to be subject to methodological scrutiny. (. . .)

(2) Recognizing that methodology embraces all of the important parts of the act of scientific inquiry, I wish now to state and stress a point of even greater importance for methodology. Every part of the act of scientific inquiry—and hence the full act itself—is subject to the test of the empirical world and has to be validated through such a test. Reality exists in the empirical world and not in the methods used to study that world; it is to be discovered in the examination of that world and not in the analysis or elaboration of the methods used to study that world. Methods are mere instruments designed to identify and analyze the obdurate character of the empirical world, and as such their value exists only in their suitability in enabling this task to be done. In this fundamental sense the procedures employed in each part of the act of scientific inquiry should and must be assessed in terms of whether they respect the nature of the empirical world under study—whether what they signify or imply to be the nature of the empirical world is actually the case. Thus the underlying scheme of the empirical

world used in the act of scientific inquiry needs to be critically examined to see whether it is true; the problems set for study need to be critically studied to see whether they are genuine problems *in the empirical world*; the data chosen need to be inspected to see if in fact they have in the empirical world the character given to them in the study; similarly, the empirical world has to be examined, independently of the study, to see if the relations staked out between the data are found in their asserted form; the interpretations of the findings, particularly since they arise from sources outside the study, need to be given empirical testing; and the concepts used throughout the course of the study are in special need of scrutiny to see if they match in the empirical world what they purport to refer to. Nothing less than this is called for in methodological treatment.

(. . .) Current methodology gives no encouragement or sanction to such direct examination of the empirical social world. Thus, a diligent effort, apart from the research study one undertakes, to see if the empirical area under study corresponds in fact to one's underlying images of it, is a rarity. Similarly, a careful independent examination of the empirical area to see if the problem one is posing represents meaningfully what is going on in that empirical area is scarcely done. Similarly, an independent careful examination of the empirical area to see if what one constructs as data are genuinely meaningful data in that empirical area is almost unheard of. Similarly, a careful identification of what one's concepts are supposed to refer to, and then an independent examination of the empirical area to see if its content sustains, rejects, or qualifies the concept, are far from being customary working practices. And so on. (. . .)

(3) It is no wonder that the broad arena of research inquiry in the social and psychological sciences has the character of a grand display and clash of social philosophies. Instead of going to the empirical social world in the first and last instances, resort is made instead to a priori theoretical schemes, to sets of unverified concepts, and to canonized protocols of research procedure. These come to be the governing agents in dealing with the empirical social world, forcing research to serve their character and bending the empirical world to their premises. If this indictment seems unwarranted I merely call attention to the following: the array of conflicting schemes as to the nature and composition of human society and the conspicuous ease with which the adherents of each scheme 'validate' the scheme through their own research; the astonishing fact that the overwhelming proportion of key concepts have not been pinned down in their empirical reference in the proper sense that one can go to instances in the empirical world and say safely that this is an instance of the concept and that is not an instance (try this out with such representative concepts as mores, alienation, value, integration, socialization, need-disposition, power, and cultural deprivation); the innumerable instances

of scholars designing and pursuing elegant schemes of research into areas of social life with which they have little if any familiarity; and an endless parade of research studies that consist of no more than applying an already devised instrument, such as a scale or test, to a different setting of group life. Without wishing to be overly harsh, I believe one must recognize that the prevailing mode in the social and psychological sciences is to turn away from direct examination of the empirical social world and to give preference, instead, to theoretical schemes, to preconceived models, to arrays of vague concepts, to sophisticated techniques of research, and to an almost slavish adherence to what passes as the proper protocol of research inquiry. (. . .)

(. . .) [At this point,] I find it necessary to make clear what I mean by the exhortation to turn to a direct examination of the empirical social world.

Let me begin by identifying the empirical social world in the case of human beings. This world is the actual group life of human beings. It consists of what they experience and do, individually and collectively, as they engage in their respective forms of living, it covers the large complexes of interlaced activities that grow up as the actions of some spread out to affect the actions of others; and it embodies the large variety of relations between the participants. This empirical world is evidenced, to take a few examples, by what is happening in the life of a boy's gang, or among the top management of an industrial corporation, or in militant racial groups, or among the police confronted by such groups, or among the young people in a country, or among the Catholic clergy, or in the experience of individuals in their different walks of life. The empirical social world, in short, is the world of everyday experience, the top layers of which we see in our lives and recognize in the lives of others. The life of a human society, or of any segment of it, or of any organization in it, or of its participants consists of the action and experience of people as they meet the situations that arise in their respective worlds. The problems of the social and psychological sciences necessarily arise out of, and go back to, this body of ongoing group life. This is true whether the problems refer to what is immediately taking place, as in the case of a student riot, or to the background causes of such a riot, or to the organization of institutions, or to the stratified relations of people, or to the ways in which people guide their lives, or to the personal organization of individuals formed through participation in group life. Ongoing group life, whether in the past or the present, whether in the case of this or that people, whether in one or another geographical area, is the empirical social world of the social and psychological sciences.

Several simple yet highly important observations need to be made with regard to the study of this world. The first is that almost by definition the research scholar does not have a firsthand acquaintance with the sphere of social life that he proposes to study. He is rarely a participant in that sphere and usually is not in close touch with the actions and the experiences of the people who are involved in that sphere. His position is almost always that of an outsider; as such he is markedly limited in simple knowledge of what takes place in the given sphere of life. (. . .)

This leads me to a second simple observation, namely, that despite this lack of firsthand acquaintance the research scholar will unwittingly form some kind of a picture of the area of life he proposes to study. He will bring into play the beliefs and images that he already has to fashion a more or less intelligible view of the area of life. In this respect he is like all human beings. Whether we be laymen or scholars, we necessarily view any unfamiliar area of group life through images we already possess. We may have no firsthand acquaintance with life among delinquent groups, or in labor unions, or in legislative committees, or among bank executives, or in a religious cult, yet given a few cues we readily form serviceable pictures of such life. This, as we all know, is the point at which stereotyped images enter and take control. All of us, as scholars, have our share of common stereotypes that we use to see a sphere of empirical social life that we do not know. In addition, the research scholar in the social sciences has another set of pre-established images that he uses. These images are constituted by his theories, by the beliefs current in his own professional circles, and by his ideas of how the empirical world must be set up to allow him to follow his research procedure. No careful observer can honestly deny that this is true. We see it clearly in the shaping of pictures of the empirical world to fit one's theories, in the organizing of such pictures in terms of the concepts and beliefs that enjoy current acceptance among one's set of colleagues, and in the molding of such pictures to fit the demands of scientific protocol. We must say in all honesty that the research scholar in the social sciences who undertakes to study a given sphere of social life that he does not know at first hand will fashion a picture of that sphere in terms of pre-established images.

(. . .) The empirical social world consists of ongoing group life and one has to get close to this life to know what is going on in it. If one is going to respect the social world, one's problems, guiding conceptions, data, schemes of relationship, and ideas of interpretation have to be faithful to that empirical world. This is especially true in the case of human group life because of the persistent tendency of human beings in their collective life to build up separate worlds, marked by an operating milieu of different life situations and by the possession of different beliefs and conceptions for handling these situations. One merely has to think of the different worlds in the case of a military elite, the clergy of a church, modern city prostitutes, a peasant revolutionary body, professional politicians, slum dwellers, the directing management of a large industrial corporation, a gambling syndicate, a university faculty, and so on endlessly. The modes of living of such groups, the parade of situations they must handle, their institutions and their organizations, the relations between their members, the views and images through which they see their worlds, the personal organizations formed by their members—all these and more reflect their different empirical worlds. (. . .)

We should add that ongoing group life, whether in its entirety or in any of its spheres, takes place, as far as our perceptions of it are concerned, on different levels. The person who perceives nothing of it can know essentially nothing of it. The person who perceives it at a great distance, seeing just a little bit of it, can have correspondingly only a limited knowledge of it. The person who participates in it will have a greater knowledge of it, although if he is a naïve and unobservant participant his knowledge may be very restricted and inaccurate. The participant who is very observant will have fuller and more accurate knowledge. But there are levels of happening that are hidden to all participants. If we view the process of ongoing group life in this way, as I believe we are compelled to do, the study of such group life requires us to expand and deepen our perception of it. This is the direction of movement if we wish to form an accurate knowledge of it—movement from ignorance or an uninformed position to greater and more accurate awareness of what is taking place. The metaphor that I like is that of lifting the veils that obscure or hide what is going on. The task of scientific study is to lift the veils that cover the area of group life that one proposes to study. The veils are not lifted by substituting, in whatever degree, preformed images for firsthand knowledge. The veils are lifted by getting close to the area and by digging deep into it through careful study. Schemes of methodology that do not encourage or allow this betray the cardinal principle of respecting the nature of one's empirical world. (. . .)

Granted that human group life has the character that is stated by the premises of symbolic interactionism, (. . .) [I wish to] point out several of the more important methodological implications of the symbolic interactionist's view of human group life and social action. I want to consider such implications in the case of each of four central conceptions in symbolic interactionism. These four central conceptions are: (1) people, individually and collectively, are prepared to act on the basis of the meanings of the objects that comprise their world; (2) the association of people is necessarily in the form of a process in which they are making indications to one another and interpreting each other's indications; (3) social acts, whether individual or collective, are constructed through a process in which the actors note, interpret, and assess the situations confronting them; and (4) the complex interlinkages of acts that comprise organization, institutions, division of labor, and networks of interdependency are moving and not static affairs. I wish to discuss each of these in turn.

(1) The contention that people act on the basis of the meaning of their objects has profound methodological implications. It signifies immediately that if the scholar wishes to understand the action of people it is necessary for him to see their objects as they see them. Failure to see their objects as they see them, or a substitution of his meanings of the objects for their meanings, is the gravest kind of error that the social scientist can commit. It leads to the setting up of a fictitious world. Simply put, people act toward things on the basis of the meaning that these things have for them, not on the basis of the meaning that these things have for the outside scholar. Yet we are confronted right and left with studies of human group life and of the behavior of people in which the scholar has made no attempt to find out how the people see what they are acting toward. This neglect is officially fostered by two pernicious tendencies in current methodology: (1) the belief that mere expertise in the use of scientific techniques plus facility in some given theory are sufficient equipment to study an unfamiliar area; and (2) the stress that is placed on being objective, which all too frequently merely means seeing things from the position of the detached outside observer. We have multitudes of studies of groups such as delinquents, police, military elites, restless students, racial minorities, and labor unions in which the scholar is unfamiliar with the life of the groups and makes little, if any, effort to get inside their worlds of meanings. We are compelled, I believe, to recognize that this is a widespread practice in the social sciences.

To try to identify the objects that comprise the world of an individual or a collectivity is not simple or easy for the scholar who is not familiar with that world. It requires, first of all, ability to place oneself in the position of the individual or collectivity. This ability to take the roles of others, like any other potential skill, requires cultivation to be effective. By and large, the training of scholars in the social sciences today is not concerned with the cultivation of this ability nor do their usual practices in research study foster its development. Second, to identify the objects of central concern one must have a body of relevant observations. These necessary observations are rarely those that are yielded by standard research procedure such as questionnaires, polls, scales, use of survey research items, or the setting of predesignated variables. Instead, they are in the form of descriptive accounts from the actors of how they see the objects, how they have acted toward the objects in a variety of different situations, and how they refer to the objects in their conversations with members of their own group. The depiction of key objects that emerge from such accounts should, in turn, be subject to probing and critical collective discussion by a group of well-informed participants in the given world. This latter procedure is a genuine 'must' to guard against the admitted deficiencies of individual accounts. Third, as mentioned in earlier discussion, research scholars, like human beings in general, are slaves to their own pre-established images and thus are prone to assume that other people see the given objects as they, the scholars, see them. Scholars need to guard against this proneness and to give high priority to deliberate testing of their images. (. . .)

(2) Symbolic interactionism sees group life as a process in which people, as they meet in their different situations, indicate lines of action to each other and interpret the indications made by others. This means, obviously, that their respective lines of behavior have to be built up in the light of the lines of action of the others with whom they are interacting. This adjustment of developing acts to each other takes place not merely between individuals in face-to-face association but also between collectivities such as industrial corporations or nations who have to deal with one another, and occurs also in the case of any one of us who gives consideration to the judgment of an outside audience or community in guiding his line of action. This need of adjusting to the lines of action of others is so evident in the simplest observations that I find it difficult to understand why it is so generally ignored or dismissed by social scientists.

The methodological implications of the premise are very telling. First of all, it raises the most serious question about the validity of most of the major approaches to the study and analysis of human group life that are followed today—approaches that treat social interaction as merely the medium through which determining factors produce behavior. Thus, sociologists ascribe behavior to such factors as social role, status, cultural prescription, norms, values, reference group affiliation, and mechanisms of societal equilibrium; and psychologists attribute behavior to such factors as stimuli configurations, organic drives, need-dispositions, emotions, attitudes, ideas, conscious motives, unconscious motives, and mechanisms of personal organization. Social interaction is treated as merely the arena in which these kinds of determining factors work themselves out into human action. These approaches grossly ignore the fact that social interaction is a formative process in its own right— that people in interaction are not merely giving expression to such determining factors in forming their respective lines of action but are directing, checking, bending, and transforming their lines of action in the light of what they encounter in the actions of others. In setting up studies of human group life and social action there is need to take social interaction seriously. It is necessary to view the given sphere of life under study as a moving process in which the participants are defining and interpreting each other's acts. It is important to see how this process of designation and interpretation is sustaining, undercutting, redirecting, and transforming the ways in which the participants are fitting together their lines of action. Such a necessary type of study cannot be done if it operates with the premise that group life is but the result of determining factors working through the interaction of people. Further, approaches organized on this latter premise are not equipped to study the process of social interaction. A different perspective, a different set of categories, and a different procedure of inquiry are necessary.

A second important methodological implication that comes from seeing that human interaction is a process of designation and interpretation is the lack of warrant for compressing the process of social interaction into any special form. Such compression is an outstanding vice in social science, both past and present. We see it exemplified in the quaint notion that social interaction is a process of developing 'complementary expectations'—a notion given wide currency by Talcott Parsons and serving as the basis of his scheme of human society as a harmoniously disposed social system. We see it illustrated, also, in the contrary premise that human society is organized basically in terms of a conflict process. We see it, still further, in the current popular view that human interaction follows the principles of 'game theory.' Anyone who observes social interaction with open eyes should readily recognize that human participants, both individually and collectively, meet each other's actions in diverse and varying forms. Sometimes they cooperate, sometimes they conflict with each other, sometimes they are tolerant of each other, sometimes they are indifferent to each other, sometimes they follow rigid rules in their interaction, and sometimes they engage in a free play of expressive behavior toward one another. To see all human interaction (and accordingly human society) as organized in the form of some special type of interaction does violence to the variety of forms that one can see if he wants to look. The very fact that human beings make indications to one another and interpret each other's indications in the light of the situation in which they are acting should make clear that the process of social interaction is not constrained to any single form. The task of the research scholar who is studying any sphere of social life is to ascertain what form of interaction is in play instead of imposing on that sphere some preset form of interaction. The identification of the kind of interaction that is in play is not achieved, except by chance, when the study itself presupposes a special form of interaction. A different investigating procedure is required. It is my experience that the interaction usually shifts back and forth from one to another form, depending on the situations that are being met by the interacting parties. Whatever be the case, the form of the social interaction is a matter for empirical discovery and not a matter to be fixed in advance.

(3) The view of social action held by symbolic interaction leads to a number of significant methodological consequences. Symbolic interactionism sees social action as consisting of the individual and collective activities of people who are engaged in social interaction—that is to say, activities whose own formation is made in the light of the activity of one another. Such activity makes up the ongoing social life of a human group, whether the group be small as

a family or large as a nation. It is from the observation of social action that we derive the categories that we use to give conceptual order to the social makeup and social life of a human group—each one of such categories stands for a form or aspect of social action. Thus, a chief, a priest, a social role, a stratification arrangement, an institution, or a social process such as assimilation stands for a form or aspect of social action; the category is meaningless unless seen and cast ultimately in terms of social action. In a valid sense social action is the primary subject matter of social science, the subject matter from which it starts and to which it must return with its schemes of analysis. Hence, an accurate picture and understanding of social action is of crucial importance.

A part of this picture of social action as seen by symbolic interactionism has already been sketched in the immediately foregoing discussion of social interaction; that is, social action must be seen as necessarily taking place within the process of social interaction. The other part of the picture refers to the activity of the participant in social interaction, whether the participant be an individual or a collectivity. In other words, there is need to see social action in terms of the actor since it is only actors who act. It is the position of symbolic interactionism that the social action of the actor is *constructed* by him; it is not a mere release of activity brought about by the play of initiating factors on his organization. In this sense, as explained earlier, symbolic interactionism sees social action in a markedly different way from that of current social and psychological science. The actor (let me deal with the individual actor first) is seen as one who is confronted with a situation in which he has to act. In this situation, he notes, interprets, and assesses things with which he has to deal in order to act. He can do this by virtue of being able to interact or communicate with himself. Through such self-interaction he constructs his line of action, noting what he wants or what is demanded of him, setting up a goal, judging the possibilities of the situation, and prefiguring his line of action. In such self-interaction he may hold his prospective act in suspension, abandon it, check it at one or another point, revise it, or devise a substitute for it. Symbolic interactionism declares that this is the way in which the human being engages in his social action. (. . .)

The same sort of picture exists in the case of the social action of a collectivity, such as a business corporation, a labor union, an army, a church, a boy's gang, or a nation. The difference is that the collectivity has a directing group or individual who is empowered to assess the operating situation, to note different things that have to be dealt with, and to map out a line of action. The self-interaction of a collectivity is in the form of discussion, counseling, and debate. The collectivity is in the same position as the individual in having to cope with a situation, in having to interpret and analyze the situation, and in having to construct a line of action.

The premise that social action is built up by the acting unit through a process of noting, interpreting, and assessing things and of mapping out a prospective line of action implies a great deal as to how social action should be studied. Basically put, it means that in order to treat and analyze social action one has to observe the process by which it is constructed. This, of course, is not done and cannot be done by any scheme that relies on the premise that social action is merely a product of pre-existing factors that play on the acting unit. A different methodological stance is called for. As opposed to an approach that sees social action as a product and then seeks to identify the determining or causative factors of such action, the required approach is to see the acting unit as confronted with an operating situation that it has to handle and vis-à-vis which it has to work out a line of action. The acting unit is lifted out of a position of being a neutral medium for the play of determining factors and is given the status of an active organizer of its action. This different stance means that the research scholar who is concerned with the social action of a given individual or group, or with a given type of social action, must see that action from the position of whoever is forming the action. He should trace the formation of the action in the way in which it is actually formed. This means seeing the situation as it is seen by the actor, observing what the actor takes into account, observing how he interprets what is taken into account, noting the alternative kinds of acts that are mapped out in advance, and seeking to follow the interpretation that led to the selection and execution of one of these prefigured acts. Such an identification and analysis of the career of the act is essential to an empirical understanding of social action—whether it be juvenile delinquency, suicide, revolutionary behavior, the behavior of Negro militants, the behavior of right-wing reactionary groups, or what not. (. . .)

(4) Finally, I want to say something about the methodological consequences of the way in which symbolic interactionism looks upon the large or so-called molar parts or aspects of human society. These large parts or aspects constitute what have been traditionally the major objects of sociological interest—institutions, stratification arrangements, class systems, divisions of labor, large-scale corporate units and other big forms of societal organization. The tendency of sociologists is to regard these large complexes as entities operating in their own right with their own dynamics. Each is usually seen as a system, composed of given parts in interdependent arrangement and subject to the play of mechanisms that belong to the system as such. Structural functionalism, which is so popular today, is a good example (although only one example) of this view. Under the general view, the participants in the given unit of societal organization are logically merely media for the play and expression of the forces or mechanisms of the system itself; one turns to such forces

or mechanisms to account for what takes place. The given societal organization is likened to a huge machine or organism (I do not say this invidiously) in that its behavior and the behavior of its parts are to be explained in terms of the principles of operation of the societal organization itself.

Symbolic interactionism sees these large societal organizations or molar units in a different way. It sees them as arrangements of people who are interlinked in their respective actions. The organization and interdependency is between such actions of people stationed at different points. At any one point the participants are confronted by the organized activities of other people into which they have to fit their own acts. The concatenation of such actions taking place at the different points constitutes the organization of the given molar unit or large-scale area. A skeletalized description of this organization would be the same for symbolic interactionism as for the other approaches. However, in seeing the organization as an organization of actions symbolic interactionism takes a different approach. Instead of accounting for the activity of the organization and its parts in terms of organizational principles or system principles, it seeks explanation in the way in which the participants define, interpret, and meet the situations at their respective points. The linking together of this knowledge of the concatenated actions yields a picture of the organized complex. Organizational principles or system principles may indeed identify the limits beyond which there could be no concatenation of actions, but they do not explain the form or nature of such concatenations. True, a given organization conceived from organizational principles may be imposed on a corporate unit or corporate area, as in the case of a reorganization of an army or an industrial system, but this represents the application of somebody's definition of what the organization should be. What happens in the wake of such application is something else, as we well know from striking examples in recent times. The point of view of symbolic interactionism is that large-scale organization has to be seen, studied, and explained in terms of the process of interpretation engaged in by the acting participants as they handle the situations at their respective positions in the organization. Such study, it may be noted, would throw a great deal of light on a host of matters of concern to the organizational theorist or to the system analyst—problems such as morale, the functioning of bureaucracy, blockage in effective communication, corruption and ranges of bribery, 'exploiting the system,' favoritism and cliquishness, the rise (and decline) of oligarchic control, the disintegration of the organization, or the infusion of new vigor into the organization. A knowledge of large-scale organizations and complexly organized areas is to be sought in the examination of the life of such organizations and areas as represented by what the participants do. This does not mean, as current phraseology would put it, turning from the molar to the minuscule; it means studying the molar in terms of its empirical character of being an interlinkage of action.

The shaping of inquiry to a study of what is done by the people comprising a complex organization or a complexly organized area sets no methodological problems for symbolic interactionism that are different from those discussed above. What is needed is the same type of exploratory and inspection procedure previously outlined. I would like to add, however, two noteworthy points that bear on the shift from seeing organization as a self-contained matter with its own principles to seeing it as an interlinkage of the activities of people.

One of these points refers to what I commented on earlier in indicating that stable and recurrent forms of joint action do not carry on automatically in their fixed form but have to be sustained by the meanings that people attach to the type of situation in which the joint action reoccurs. This observation applies to large-scale organization. Beneath the norms and rules that specify the type of action to be engaged in at any given point in the organizational complex there are two concurrent processes in which people are defining each other's perspectives and the individual, through self-interaction, is redefining his own perspective. What takes place in these two processes largely determines the status and the fate of the norms or rules; the rules may still be observed but the observance may be weak or hollow, or, contrariwise, reinforced or invested with greater vigor. Such shifts in the support of norms and rules are something other than applying sanctions or neglecting to apply them. They point to a separate area of happening in the interaction between people. Scholarly study or analysis of organization cannot afford to ignore the process of interaction between people that is responsible for sustaining organization as well as for affecting it in other ways.

The other point is a reminder of the need to recognize that joint action is temporarily linked with previous joint action. One shuts a major door to the understanding of any form or instance of joint action if one ignores this connection. The application of this general point to the topic of large-scale societal organization is particularly in order. There is a noticeable neglect of this historical linkage by organizational theorists and system analysts in both their formulation of principles and their research. The complex organization or the complexly organized area is cut off by them, so to speak, from the background out of which it grew. This can only lead to misrepresentation. The designations and interpretations through which people form and maintain their organized relations are always in degree a carry-over from their past. To ignore this carry-over sets a genuine risk for the scholar. On this point the methodological posture of symbolic interactionism is to pay heed to the historical linkage of what is being studied. (. . .)

2 Professions in process[1]
Rue Bucher and Anselm Strauss

The 'process' or 'emergent' approach to the study of professions developed in the following pages bears considerable resemblance to a common-sense point of view. It utilizes common language to order the kinds of events that professionals informally discuss among themselves—frequently with great animation. It is even used by sociologists in their less professional moments when they are personally challenged by their own colleagues or by persons from other fields. What is different here is that we shall take the first steps toward developing an explicit scheme of analysis out of these commonplace materials. In addition, it will become apparent that this approach differs from the prevailing 'functionalism' because it focuses more pointedly upon conflicting interests and upon change.

Functionalism sees a profession largely as a relatively homogeneous community whose members share identity, values, definitions of role, and interests.[2] There is room in this conception for some variation, some differentiation, some out-of-line members, even some conflict; but, by and large, there is a steadfast core which defines the profession, deviations from which are but temporary dislocations. Socialization of recruits consists of induction into the common core. There are norms, codes, which govern the behavior of the professional to insiders and outsiders. In short, the sociology of professions has largely been focused upon the mechanics of cohesiveness and upon detailing the social structure (and/or social organization) of given professions. Those tasks a structural-functional sociology is prepared to do, and do relatively well.

But this kind of focus and theory tend to lead one to overlook many significant aspects of professions and professional life. Particularly does it bias the observer against appreciating the conflict—or at least difference—of interests within the profession; this leads him to overlook certain of the more subtle features of the profession's 'organization' as well as

Source: *American Journal of Sociology*, 66, January 1961, pp. 325–34.

to fail to appreciate how consequential for changes in the profession and its practitioners differential interests may be.

In actuality, the assumption of relative homogeneity within the profession is not entirely useful: there are many identities, many values, and many interests. These amount not merely to differentiation or simple variation. They tend to become patterned and shared; coalitions develop and flourish—and in opposition to some others. We shall call these groupings which emerge within a profession 'segments.' (Specialties might be thought of as major segments, except that a close look at a specialty betrays its claim to unity, revealing that specialties, too, usually contain segments, and, if they ever did have common definitions along all lines of professional identity, it was probably at a very special, and early, period in their development.) We shall develop the idea of professions as loose amalgamations of segments pursuing different objectives in different manners and more or less delicately held together under a common name at a particular period in history.

Our aim in this paper, then, is to present some initial steps in formulating a 'process' model for studying professions. The model can be considered either as a supplement of, or an alternative to, the prevailing functional model. Some readers undoubtedly will prefer to consider the process model as supplementary. If so, then there will be a need for a further step, that is, for a transcending model. But we ourselves are concerned here only with sketching the outlines of a process approach, suggesting a few potentially useful concepts, and pointing to certain research problems that flow from our framework and concepts.

Organized medicine

Medicine is usually considered the prototype of the professions, the one upon which current sociological conceptions of professions tend to be based; hence, our illustrative points in this paper will be taken from medicine, but they could just as pertinently have come from some other profession. Of the medical profession as a whole a great deal could be, and has been, said: its institutions (hospitals, schools, clinics); its personnel (physicians and paramedical personnel); its organizations (the American Medical Association, the state and county societies); its recruitment policies; its standards and codes; its political activities; its relations with the public; not to mention the profession's informal mechanisms of sociability and control. All this minimal 'structure' certainly exists.

But we should also recognize the great divergency of enterprise and endeavor that mark the profession; the cleavages that exist along with the division of labor; and the intellectual and specialist movements that occur within the broad rubric called 'organized medicine.' It might seem as if the physicians certainly share common ends, if ever any profession did. When backed to the wall, any physician would probably agree that his long-run objective is better care of the patient. But this is a misrepresentation of the actual values and organization of activity as undertaken by various segments of the profession. Not all the ends shared by all physicians are distinctive to the medical profession or intimately related to what many physicians do, as their work. What is distinctive of medicine belongs to certain segments of it—groupings not necessarily even specialties—and may not actually be shared with other physicians. We turn now to a consideration of some of those values which these segments do *not* share and about which they may actually be in conflict.

The sense of mission It is characteristic of the growth of specialties that early in their development they carve out for themselves and proclaim unique missions. They issue a statement of the contribution that the specialty, and it alone, can make in a total scheme of values and, frequently, with it an argument to show why it is peculiarly fitted for this task. The statement of mission tends to take a rhetorical form, probably because it arises in the context of a battle for recognition and institutional status. Thus, when surgical specialties, such as urology and proctology, were struggling to attain identities independent of general surgery, they developed the argument that the particular anatomical areas in which they were interested required special attention and that only physicians with their particular background were competent to give it. Anesthesiologists developed a similar argument. This kind of claim separates a given area out of the general stream of medicine, gives it special emphasis and a new dignity, and, more important for our purposes, separates the specialty group from other physicians. Insofar as they claim an area for themselves, they aim to exclude others from it. It is theirs alone.

While specialties organize around unique missions, as time goes on segmental missions may develop within the fold. In radiology, for example, there are groups of physicians whose work is organized almost completely around diagnosis. But there is a recently burgeoning group of radiologists whose mission is to develop applications of radiation for therapeutic purposes. This difference of mission is so fundamental that it has given rise to demands for quite different residency training programs and to some talk of splitting off from the parent specialty. In pathology—one of the oldest medical specialties, whose traditional mission has been to serve as the basic science of medicine with relatively little emphasis upon clinical applications—lately a whole new breed of pathologists has come to the fore, dedicated to developing pathology as a specialized service to clinical practitioners and threatening those who cling to the traditional mission.

The split between research missions and clinical practice runs clear through medicine and all its specialties. Pediatrics has one of the most rapidly growing fields of practice, but it has also attracted a number of young people, particularly at some centers in the Northeast, specifically for research. They are people who have no conceptions of themselves as family pediatricians at all; they are in this field because of what they can do in the way of research. In the two oldest specialties, surgery and internal medicine, one finds throughout the literature considerable evidence of this kind of split. One finds an old surgeon complaining that the young men are too much interested in research, and in internal medicine there are exhortations that they should be doctors, not scientists. This latter lament is particularly interesting in view of the traditional mission of the internist to exemplify the finest in the 'art of medicine': it is a real betrayal when one of them shows too much interest in controlled research.

Work activities There is great diversity in the tasks performed in the name of the profession. Different definitions may be found between segments of the profession concerning what kinds of work the professional should be doing, how work should be organized, and which tasks have precedence. If, for example, the model physician is taken as one who sees patients and carries out the diagnosis and treatment of illness, then an amazing variety of physicians do not fit this model. This diversity is not wholly congruent with the organization of practice by medical specialties, although there are certain specialties—like pathology, radiology, anesthesiology, and public health—whose practitioners for the most part do not approach the model. Within a core specialty like internal medicine there are many different kinds of practice, ranging from that of a 'family doctor' to highly specialized consultation, a service to other doctors. These differences in the weights assigned to elements of practice do not begin to take into account the further diversity introduced when professionals assign different weights to such activities as research, teaching, and public service.

This point can be made more clearly by considering some of the different organizations of work activities that can be found within single specialties. The people who organize their work life as follows all call themselves 'pathologists': (a) time nearly equally divided between research and teaching, with little or no contact with patient care; (b) time divided (ideally) equally between research, teaching, and diagnostic services to other doctors; (c) administration of a hospital service, diagnostic services and consultations with other physicians, and educational activities. (The objects of educational activities are not only medical students and residents but other practitioners of the hospital. These pathologists may also actually examine patients face-to-face and consult on a course of treatment.)

Again, consider the radiologist. There is considerable range in the scope and kind of practice subsumed under radiology. The 'country radiologist' tends to function as an all-round diagnostic consultant, evaluating and interpreting findings concerning a broad spectrum of medical conditions. In the large medical center the diagnostic radiologist either does limited consultation concerning findings or else specializes in one area, such as neurological radiology or pediatric radiology. Then there is the radiologist whose work is not primarily diagnostic at all but involves the application of radiation for therapeutic purposes. This man may have his own patients in course of treatment, much like an internist or urologist.

These illustrations suggest that members of a profession not only weigh auxiliary activities differently but have different conceptions of what constitutes the core—*the most characteristic professional act*—of their professional lives. For some radiologists it is attacking tumors with radiation; for others it is interpreting X-ray pictures. For many pathologists it is looking down the barrel of a microscope; for others it is experimental research. A dramatic example of the difference in characteristic professional acts is to be found in psychiatry, which for many of its practitioners means psychotherapy, an intricate set of interactions with a single patient. This is what a psychiatrist does. Yet many practitioners of psychiatry have as little face-to-face interaction with a patient as possible and concentrate upon physical therapies. Still others may spend a good deal of their time administering or directing the activities of other people who actually carry out various therapies.

Not all segments of professions can be said to have this kind of core—a most characteristic activity; many are not so highly identified with a single work activity. But, to the extent that segments develop divergent core activities, they also tend to develop characteristic associated and auxiliary activities, which may introduce further diversity in commitment to major areas, like practice, research, or public health.

Methodology and techniques One of the most profound divisions among members of a profession is in their methodology and technique. This, again, is not just a division between specialties within a profession. Specialties frequently arise around the exploitation of a new method or technique, like radiology in medicine, but as time goes by they may segmentalize further along methodological perspectives. Methodological differences can cut across specialty—and even professional—lines with specialists sharing techniques with members of other specialties which they do not share with their fellows.

Insofar as these methodological differences reflect bitter disagreements over the reality that the profession is concerned with, the divisions are deep indeed, and communication between the factions is at a minimum. In psychiatry the conflict over the biological versus the psychological basis of mental illness continues to produce men who speak almost totally different languages. In recent years the situation has been further complicated by the rise of social science's perspectives on mental illness. Focusing upon different aspects of reality, psychiatrists of these various persuasions do different kinds of research and carry out various kinds of therapy. They read a variety of journals, too; and the journals a man reads, in any branch of medicine, tend to reflect his methodological as well as his substantive interests.

Social scientists must not suppose that, since psychiatry is closer in subject matter to the social sciences, it is the only branch of medicine marred by bitter methodological disputes (we do not mean to imply that such disputes ought to be avoided). Pathologists are currently grappling with methodological issues which raged in some of the biological sciences, particularly anatomy, some years ago. The central issue has to do with the value of morphology, a more traditional approach which uses microscopic techniques to describe the structure of tissues, as against experimental approaches based upon more dynamic biochemical techniques. While the proponents of the two methodologies appear to understand each other somewhat better than do the psychiatrists, they still do not wholly appreciate each other: the morphologists are disposed to be highly defensive, and the experimentalists a little embarrassed by the continued presence of those purely morphologically inclined. Then, in the primarily clinical specialties, those combining medical and surgical techniques offer their own peculiar possibilities for dispute. Men can differ as to how highly they value and emphasize the medical or surgical approach to treatment; for example, an older urologist complained in a journal article that the younger men in the field are 'knife-happy.' An analogous refrain can be heard among clinicians who frown upon too great a dependence upon laboratory techniques for diagnosis and accuse many of their colleagues of being unable to carry out a complex physical examination in the grand clinical manner.

Clients Characteristically, members of professions become involved in sets of relationships that are distinctive to their own segment. Wholly new classes of people may be involved in their work drama whom other segments do not have to take into account. We shall confine ourselves for the moment to considering relationships with clients.

We suspect that sociologists may too easily accept statements glorifying 'the doctor-patient relationship' made by segments of the medical profession who have an interest in maintaining a particular relationship to patients. In actuality, the relationships between physicians and patients are highly varied. It does appear that an image of a doctor-patient relationship pervades the entire medical profession, but it is an image which, if it fits any group of physicians in its totality, comes closest to being the model for the general practitioner or his more modern counterpart, the family-practice internist. It seems to set an ideal for other physicians, who may incorporate whatever aspects of it are closest to their own working conditions into an image of the doctor-patient relationship peculiar to their own segment.

Specialties, or segments of specialties, develop images of relationships with patients which distinguish them from other medical groupings. Their own sense of mission and their specialized jobs throw them into new relationships with patients which they eventually formulate and refer to in idealized ways. Moreover, they do not simply define the relationship, but may highly elaborate a relation which this particular kind of doctor, and this kind alone, can have with patients. The pediatricians, for example, have created an image of family practitioner to whom not only the child but the parents and the whole family group surrounding the sick child are patients. According to a spokesman of the pediatricians, the peculiar involvement of parents in the illness of the child creates the conditions under which the pediatrician can evolve his relationship to the family unit. Something similar exists in psychiatry, where it is not the mentally ill patient who may be regarded as the sole or even main client but the family. It is probably in psychiatry, too, that the most highly elaborated doctor-patient relationships exist, since the psychotherapeutic practitioner uses his relationship to patients as a conscious and complex therapeutic tool. The most significant point here is that the young psychiatrist, learning the art of psychotherapy, has to unlearn approaches to the patient that he acquired in medical school.

In addition, there are the physicians who only in a special sense can be said to have patients at all. We are likely to think of pathologists, anesthesiologists, and radiologists as doctors without patients: they may have little or no contact with patients, but they do have a relationship to them. The pathologist practicing in a hospital has a well-developed set of obligations to the patient whom he may never confront, and interest groups among the pathologists are concerned with making the lay public aware of the functions of the pathologist behind the scenes. Practitioners in all three of these specialties appear to be concerned with defining their own relationship to patients.

Colleagueship Colleagueship may be one of the most sensitive indicators of segmentation within a profession. Whom a man considers to be his colleagues is ultimately linked with his own place within his profession. There is considerable ambiguity among sociologists over the meaning of the term 'colleague.' Occasionally the word is used to refer to co-workers, and other times simply to indicate formal membership in an occupation—possession of the social signs. Thus, all members of the occupation are colleagues. But sociological theory is also likely to stress colleagueship as a brotherhood. Gross, for example, writes about the colleague group characterized by *esprit de corps* and a sense of 'being in the same boat.' This deeper colleague relationship, he says, is fostered by such things as control of entry to the occupation, development of a unique mission, shared attitudes toward clients and society, and the formation of informal and formal associations.[3]

This conception of colleagueship stresses occupational unity. Once entry to the occupation is controlled, it is assumed that all members of the occupation can be colleagues; they can rally around common symbols. However, the difficulty is that the very aspects of occupational life which Gross writes about as unifying the profession also break it into segments. What ties a man more closely to one member of his profession may alienate him from another: when his group develops a unique mission, he may no longer share a mission with others in the same profession.

Insofar as colleagueship refers to a relationship characterized by a high degree of shared interests and common symbols, it is probably rare that all members of a profession are even potentially colleagues. It is more feasible, instead, to work with a notion of circles of colleagueship. In the past, sociologists have recognized such circles of colleagueship, but from the viewpoint of the selective influence of such social circumstances as class and ethnicity. The professional identity shared by colleagues, though, contains far more than the kinds of people they desire as fellows. More fundamentally, they hold in common notions concerning the ends served by their work and attitudes and problems centering on it. The existence of what we have called segments thus limits and directs colleagueship.

Identification with segments not only directs relationships within a profession but has a great deal to do with relations with neighboring and allied occupations. We might use the term 'alliances' to distinguish this phenomenon from colleagueship within a profession. Alliances frequently dramatize the fact that one branch of a profession may have more in common with elements of a neighboring occupation than with their own fellow professionals. For example, experimentally minded pathologists consult and collaborate with biochemists and other basic scientists, while pathologists oriented toward practice make common cause with clinicians of various specialties.

Interests and associations To what extent, and under what conditions, can we speak of professionals as having interests in common? (Here we mean 'interests' in the sense of fate, not merely that they are 'interested in' different matters.) Sociologists have been overlooking a very rich area for research because they have been too readily assuming unity of interest among professionals. That interests do diverge within a profession is clear enough when the observer looks for it; not only may interests run along different lines, but they may be, and frequently are, in direct conflict.

Pathologists present a particularly striking illustration of conflict of fateful interest between segments of a specialty. The practitioner pathologists are intent upon promulgating an image of the pathologist that undermines the identity of the research-oriented pathologist. The more the practitioners succeed in promoting the notion of the pathologist as a person who performs invaluable services to the clinician, and succeeds in enlarging the area of service, the more do the pathologists who want to do research have to ward off demands from their institutions for more and more service. Fee-splitting in surgery is an example of another kind of conflict of interest: many surgeons can make a living only by engaging in fee-splitting relationships. The more successful surgeons who dominate the professional associations see the practice as tarnishing the reputation of the specialty as a whole and attempt to discredit it in codes of ethics, but they cannot, and even dare not, attempt to stamp it out.

Probably the areas in which professionals come most frequently into conflicts of interest are in gaining a proper foothold in institutions, in recruitment, and in relations with the outside. Here there are recurrent problems which segments and emerging specialties have with their fellow professionals. In order to survive and develop, a segment must be represented in the training centers. The medical-school curriculum today is crowded as the medical specialties compete for the student's time and attention, seeking to recruit or, at least, to socialize the budding professional into the correct attitudes toward themselves. (Some specialties regard themselves as having so little lien on the student's time that they use that time primarily, in some medical schools, to impress upon him that only specialists can safely do certain procedures—in short, how important and necessary is the particular specialty of the instructor.)

Then, too, segments require different understandings, even different contractual relations, with clients and institutions. Many a professional association has arisen out of just such conflicts as this. In the 1920s there was a great deal of ferment between the rising specialty of pediatrics and the American Medical Association over governmental ventures into child health legislation, the pediatricians favoring the Shepherd-Towner Act. The pediatricians, recognizing a need for an organization which would represent their own interests independent of the American Medical Association, eventually formed the American Academy of Pediatrics. The big professional associations in the specialty of pathology are all dominated by, and exist for, practitioners in pathology. Therefore, when leading research-oriented pathologists recently became concerned with increasing research potential in the field, and incidentally with capturing some of the funds which the National Institutes of Health were dispensing to pathology, they formed committees especially for this purpose to function as temporary associations. Recently, a Society of Medical Psychiatry has been formed, undoubtedly in response to the growing power of psychoanalytic psychiatry and to the lessening importance, in many academic settings, of somatic psychiatrists.

Looking at professional associations from this perspective, it seems that associations must be regarded in terms of just whose fateful interests within the profession are served. Associations are not everybody's association but represent one segment or a particular alliance of segments. Sociologists may ask of medicine, for example: Who has an interest in thinking of medicine as a whole, and which segments take on the role of spokesmen to the public?

Spurious unity and public relations There remain to be considered the relations of professions to the lay public and the seeming unity presented by such arrangements as codes of ethics, licensure, and the major professional associations. These products of professional activity are not necessarily evidence of internal homogeneity and consensus but rather of the power of certain groups: established associations become battlegrounds as different emerging segments compete for control. Considered from this viewpoint, such things as codes of ethics and procedures of certification become the historical deposits of certain powerful segments.

Groups that control the associations can wield various sanctions so as to bring about compliance of the general membership with codes which they have succeeded in enacting. The association concerned with the practice of pathology, for example, has recently stipulated specific contractual relations which the pathologist should enter into with his hospital and is moving toward denying critical services of the association to non-complying members—despite the fact that a goodly proportion of practicing pathologists neither have such contractual relations nor even consider them desirable. But more or less organized opposition to the code-writing of intrenched groups can lead to revision of codes from time to time. Changes occur as the composition of critical committees is altered. Thus, since the clinically oriented pathologists have gained power, they have succeeded in making certification examinations more and more exacting along applied lines, making it steadily more difficult for young pathologists trained for research to achieve certification. Certification procedures thus shift with the relative power of segments, putting a premium on some kinds of training and discriminating against others.

Those who control the professional associations also control the organs of public relations. They take on the role of spokesmen to the public, interpreting the position of the profession, as they see it. They also negotiate with relevant special publics. The outsider coming into contact with the profession tends to encounter the results of the inner group's efforts; he does not necessarily become aware of the inner circle or the power struggles behind the unified front. Thus, in considering the activities of professional associations the observer must continually ask such questions as: Who handles the public and what do they represent? Whose codes of ethics are these? What does the certification stand for? We should also ask, wherever a profession seems to the general public to be relatively unified, why it seems so—for this, too, is a pertinent problem.

Segments as social movements

Our mode of presentation might lead the reader to think of segments as simple differentiation along many rubrics. On the contrary, the notion of segments refers to organized identities. A position taken on one of the issues of professional identity discussed above entails taking corresponding positions along other dimensions of identity. Segments also involve shared identities, manifested through circles of colleagueship. This allows one to speak of types of pathologist or types of pediatrician—groups of people who organize their professional activity in ways which distinguish them from other members of their profession.

Segments are not fixed, perpetually defined parts of the body professional. They tend to be more or less continually undergoing change. They take form and develop, they are modified, and they disappear. Movement is forced upon them by changes in their conceptual and technical apparatus, in the institutional conditions of work, and in their relationship to other segments and occupations. Each generation engages in spelling out, again, what it is about and where it is going. In this process, boundaries become diffuse as generations overlap, and different loci of professional activity articulate somewhat different definitions of the work situation. Out of this fluidity new groupings may emerge.

If this picture of diversity and movement is a realistic description of what goes on within professions, how can it be analyzed? As a beginning, the movement of segments can fruitfully be analyzed as analogous to social movements. Heretofore, the analysis of social movements has been confined to religious, political, and reform movements, to such problems as the conditions of their origin, recruitment, leadership, the development of organizational apparatus, ideologies, and tactics. The same questions can be asked of movements occurring within professions. Professional identity may be thought of as analogous to the ideology of a political movement; in this sense, segments have ideology. We have seen that they have missions. They also tend to develop a brotherhood of colleagues, leadership, organizational forms and vehicles, and tactics for implementing their position.

At any one time the segments within a profession are likely to be in different phases of development and engaging in tactics appropriate to their position. In pathology, for example, the clinically oriented segment, which one of its antagonists termed 'evangelistic' and which is still expanding, has already created strong organizations, captured many academic departments, promulgated codes of ethics, and is closing in on the battle to secure desirable status for pathologists in hospitals. The more scientifically oriented segment, on the other hand, finds itself in a somewhat defensive position, forced to reaffirm some aspects of its identity and modify others and to engage in tactics to hold its institutional supports. Possibly the acme for some expanding segments is the recognized status of specialty or subspecialty. Certainly, this is the way specialties seem to develop. But the conditions under which segments will become formal specialties is in itself a fascinating research problem. (So also is the whole question of relative development, degree of change, influence, and power —matters expressively alluded to when professionals speak of 'hot' areas and dead ones.)

We have said that professions consist of a loose amalgamation of segments which are in movement. Further, professions involve a number of social movements in various kinds of relationship to each other. Although the method of analysis developed for studying political and reform movements provides a viewpoint on phenomena of professional life neglected in contemporary research, some differences must be noted between professional movements and the traditional subject matter of analysis. First of all, professional movements occur within institutional arrangements, and a large part of the activity of segments is a power struggle for the possession of them or of some kind of place within them. Second, the fates of segments are closely intertwined: they are possibly more interdependent and responsive to one another than are other kinds of movements. It is probably impossible to study one segment in movement adequately without taking into account what is happening to others. Third, the leaders are men who recognize status within the field, operate from positions of relative institutional power, and command the sources of institutionalized recruitment. Finally, it must be pointed out that not all segments display the character of a social movement. Some lack organized activities, while others are still so inchoate that they appear more as a kind of backwash of the profession than as true segments.

In any case, the existence of segments, and the emergence of new segments, takes on new significance when viewed from the perspective of social movements within a profession. Pockets of resistance and embattled minorities may turn out to be the heirs of former generations, digging in along new battle lines. They may spearhead new movements which sweep back into power. What looks like backwash, or just plain deviancy, may be the beginnings of a new segment which will acquire an institutional place and considerable prestige and power. A case in point is that of the progenitors of the clinical pathologists, who today are a threat to the institutional position of research-oriented pathologists but who were considered the failures, or poor cousins, of the specialty thirty years ago.

We have indicated what new kinds of research might originate from the conception of professions that we have presented. However, this perspective has implications for several quite traditional areas of research.

1 *Work situation and institution as arenas* The work situation and the institution itself are not simply places where people of various occupations and professions come together and enact standard occupational roles, either complementary or conflicting. These locales constitute the arenas wherein such roles are forged and developed. Work situation and institution must be regarded in the light of the particular professional segments represented there: where the segments are moving and what effect these arenas have on their further development. Since professions are in movement, work situations and institutions inevitably throw people into new relationships.

2 *Careers* The kinds of stages and the locales through which a man's career moves must be considered in terms of the segment to which he 'belongs.' Further, the investigator must be prepared to see changes not only in stages of career but in the ladder itself. The system that the career is moving through can change along the way and take on entirely new directions. The fate of individual careers is closely tied up with the fate of segments, and careers that were possible for one generation rarely are repeatable for the next generation.

3 *Socialization* An investigator should not focus solely upon how conceptions and techniques are imparted in the study of socialization; he should be equally interested in the clash of opinions among the socializers, where students are among the prizes. Segments are in competition for the allegiance of students: entire schools as well as single departments can be the arena of, and weapons in, this conflict. During their professional training, students pick their way through a maze of conflicting models and make momentous commitments thereby.

4 *Recruitment* The basic program of recruitment probably tends to be laid down by powerful segments of the profession. Yet different segments require different kinds of raw material to work upon, and their survival depends upon an influx of candidates who are potential successors. Thus, recruitment can be another critical battleground upon which segments choose candidates in their own image or attempt to gain sufficient control over recruitment procedures to do so. Defection by the recruited and recruiters, by the sponsored and the sponsors, is also well worth studying, being one way that new careers take form.

5 *Public Images* We have seen that images beamed to the public tend to be controlled by particular segments of the profession. However, sometimes segments reject these public images as inappropriate —either to themselves, specifically, or to the profession at large. If only the former, then they may require that the public acquire specialized images for themselves. In any case, segments from time to time must engage in tactics to project their own images to the public. The situation is more complicated when the whole profession is considered as a public for particular specialties or for segments of specialties. Segments may be at pains to counteract the images which other people in the profession have of them, and attempt to create alternative images.

6 *Relations with other professions* Different segments of the profession come into contact with different occupations and professions. They might have quite special problems with other occupations which they do not share with other members of their profession. In considering the handling of relations with other professions, it is thus necessary to ask such questions as: Who in the profession is concerned with this problem and what difference does it make to them? Who does the negotiating and in what ways?

7 *Leadership* Most leadership is associated less with the entire profession than with restricted portions of it. Certainly, it is linked with intellectual movements, and with the fates and fortunes of certain segments. Leadership, strategies, and the fates of segments deserve full focus in our studies of professionalization.

Notes

1 The intellectual origins of this scheme of analysis are both our own research and various writings of our predecessors and colleagues. Its specific ideas occurred to us when Miss Bucher, several years ago, had occasion to analyze a number of specialty journals and interview a sample of pathologists. Since then we have both been engaged in a study which brings us much information about psychiatrists and psychiatric nurses in Chicago, and we have had available also Everett C. Hughes's interviews with the medical staff at the University of Kansas medical school. The writings to which we are most indebted are those of Everett Hughes on work and professions (cf. *Men and Their Work*, Chicago, Free Press, 1958) and the symbolic-interaction position in social psychology (cf. George Herbert Mead's *Mind, Self, and Society*, University of Chicago Press, 1934).

Because the materials on occupations, work, and professions are well known and readily available, we have not cited all references to pertinent literature; the files of various specialty journals in all the professions are useful to anyone interested in further illustrations.

2 Cf. William J. Goode, 'Community within a community: the professions', *American Sociological Review*, 20 (1957), 194–200.
3 Edward Gross, *Work and Society* (New York, Thomas Y. Crowell, 1958), pp. 223–35.

3 Signification
D. Matza

Apprehension: being selected

To become deviant is to embark on a course that justifies, invites or warrants intervention and correction. By definition, then, to deviate is to run the risk of apprehension. Not an empirical proposition, the relation between deviation and societal reaction is incontestable. The relation exists in the very meaning of deviation. If no reminder of the correct path is justified, no arrest warranted, a path has not been strayed from; one simply not so well-worn has been taken. Thus, deviation is actionable activity.[1] Inherent in the very conception of deviation is a double reality. Right in the deviation is a warrant to be told *not* to in whatever terms and tone righteous authority chooses to speak. That is the meaning of deviation—what distinguishes it from merely 'being different.'[2] As real as the behavior itself, the warrant to be corrected may not appear very real to the subject—not until it is made to materialize before his very eyes. But elsewhere —in organized institutions—the reality of warranted correction is already quite concrete. And there too, it never exists separate from the reality it seeks to control and correct. Without each other, the two elements of deviation—infraction and reaction—suffer a loss of meaning.

The relevance of signification for becoming deviant may be introduced by considering its various meanings. A first meaning of signification, to be *registered*, is roughly equivalent to being labeled, defined or classified. It refers to the event or process of assigning persons to categories, usually as a result of demonstrating that someone has actually done something 'wrong.' Secondly, signifying implies a 'putting down' or derogation as in the term stigmatizing. This sense of signifying is part of the vernacular of slum Negroes, as indicated for instance in the many versions and widespread knowledge of 'signifying monkey.' In this

Source: *Becoming Deviant*, Prentice-Hall, 1969, pp. 155–65.

meaning, signifying refers to baiting, teasing, humiliating or exposing another on the basis of presumed deficiencies or airs.[3] Signifying ranges wide in many sections of the Negro ghetto. The term may refer to a store-front preacher signifying a backsliding member of his congregation or it may equally refer to the barbed rhymes by which slum youth playfully derogate each other. This meaning is important since it clearly denotes what might otherwise be taken for granted or obscured: the registration of a subject as deviant is an act of derogation, even if warranted. Unwarranted, it is defamation of character, a pursuit itself deemed sufficiently harmful and dangerous as to be usually both criminal and civilly actionable. The view that the registration of persons as deviant is serious, consequential and derogatory receives full confirmation in law and common sense.

The final meaning is perhaps the deepest. To signify is to *stand for* in the sense of representing or exemplifying. An object that is signified, whether it be man or thing, is rendered more meaningful. To be signified a thief does not assure the continuation of such pursuits; but it *does* add to the meaning of a theft in the life of the perpetrator, and it does add to the meaning of that person in the eyes of others. To make someone or something stand for yet something else is an act of genuine creation requiring an investment of meaning. Thus, signifying makes its object more significant—as we might expect. The object enjoys— or suffers—enhanced meaning. To be signified a thief is to lose the blissful identity of one who among other things happens to have committed a theft. It is a movement, however gradual, toward being a thief and representing theft. The two movements are intimately related; without a population selected and cast as thieves, we might have to look everywhere to comprehend the prevalence of theft. The casting comes first. Its consequence is to provide a working account of the prevalent level of theft—and to thus safeguard most of us from suspicion and interference. In that sense, those selected and then cast as thieves come to represent the enterprise of theft.

Being cast

The *activity* of signification distinguishes it from the natural selection of traits exerted by a milieu over resident species. Darwin's principle of selection illuminated a process in nature that was blind, fortuitous or without purpose. In that limited sense, the natural selection in the organic realm is *passive*. Without motive, it maintains consequence. That is one of the reasons the principle is so intriguing and Darwin's apprehension of it so startling.

The human selection of persons to be cast in one part or another is not blind, fortuitous or without purpose. No less natural than selection in the organic realm, human selection develops along different lines. The irony of direction (evolution is a direction) produced by no intention whatsoever is replaced by one that is less bold. In Darwin's natural selection evolution occurs without Author. Human selection restores active authority to a central place, but an irony is maintained. Being merely human, he who casts another as deviant may intend something quite different or if conscious of his activity may view it as inconsequential, as *following* the formation of character rather than contributing to it. In the human realm, the irony of selection is that it is done with good intentions; not with no intentions whatsoever. Self-deception, bad faith, the limitations of perspective and short-sightedness replace the fully blind forces of nature. Motive restored, consequence becomes more devious.

To be cast a thief, a prostitute, or more generally, a deviant, is to further compound and hasten the process of becoming that very thing. But the compounding implicit in being called something, cast as that, or even treated as one who is that thing would not be so very meaningful if the subject—in this case, the object of signification—were not already rehearsed in being more deviant than, externally considered, he apparently is. Because of ban, and his collaboration with *its* logic, more of the subject's character may be devoted to deviation than he could have reckoned initially. He has to be devious in order to be deviant. Consequently, he becomes prepared for a more stunning spread. Though here too the subject must collaborate, he is now as well situated as could be imagined to begin conceiving himself in the terms of the signifier. That the signifier conceives him in that way is readily understandable once we appreciate that the conception is a workaday simplification. More difficult to understand is why the subject would be willing to concur in such a simplification. Let us briefly consider what the signifier does and why. Then we may turn to the more difficult matter of the subject's possible collaboration.

No relentless Javert, the agent of signification need only perform his limited duty in a professional (it used to be called officious) manner to provide *terms of identity*. Unless he is malicious—something that is possible but hardly entertaining when developing irony and hardly noteworthy when describing human behavior—the signifier when developing and refining these terms of identity does not mean them for the eyes or ears of the deviant subject and does not intend them as caricatures. He means them for himself and others involved in the duties of signification. He intends them as routine notations and observations by which his work may be expedited. As such, the signifier's terms of identity, like those developed in any bureaucracy, bear the signature of limited perspective and the stipulation of convenient simplification. Why blame me, the signifier might well ask, when the otherwise attentive deviant subject has remained unattentive to both signature and stipulation. The terms of identity are not intended as ontological statements regarding the essential condition of the signified subject. To say or note of someone that 'he is a thief' or, even stronger, 'he's just a plain drunk' certainly sounds exhaustive; but in context the statements refer to the limited aspect of being that is of direct relevance to a bureau assigned limited duties. The designation reflects the intentionally limited perspective *of the signifying agent*. Routine, and made for convenience rather than profound assessments of character, such simplifications are rather like the employment counselor's observation, 'he's a public relations type.' Thus, the terms of identity contain an ellipsis. Obscured from view, the modifications may remain inoperative. Consequently, the deviant subject may easily take the terms of identity out of their intended context. He may fail to realize that, though invited to his apprehension, arraignment, trial and other formal processes considering him, still he is in many ways an interloper in them. Like the patient on a ward, the young child among adults, or the stranger at his trial, he may become shop-talk in his very presence. In that way, he easily overhears the elliptical statement of his character.[4]

Additionally, of course, the same statements may be uttered directly as accusation or denunciation. If malice and sadism did not exist, impatience and the flaring of temper would suffice, as even parents know, to provide the most sweeping derogations of character in terms that at the very least are easily equated or confused with those of identity. These displays occur, and are quite useful in augmenting terms of identity less directly provided.

Whatever the reasons for providing terms of identity, a more difficult question remains: why would the signified subject collaborate in widening the meaning of his deviant acts; why go along with a spread that confuses or equates the things he sometimes does with what he is? To attempt answering that question, we must first appreciate that often enough he does *not*; with that fact taken for granted, a few possibilities may be considered. The possibilities may be ranged according to the measure of subjective complicity, the extent to which the subject collaborates in absorbing the terms of deviant identity. At the extreme of non-complicity is the possibility of being excluded from occasions and circles providing competing and conventional terms of identity. At the opposite extreme—that of subjective complicity—are two subtle matters; one having to do with the equivocal language of identity, the other with a built-up equivocation at the time of next commission. Between the two is the frequent tendency of the subject to concede that a display of authority is, after all, authoritative.

Exclusion

Without access to the occasions and circles in which various identities are realistically embedded, the chances of continuing to conceive oneself in their terms, or to do so anew grow small. Continued identification in the face of exclusion depends on fantasy, not an unimportant phenomenon but something which even in the most fertile imagination requires the eventual refueling of experience. Thus, the consequence of exclusion—minimizing the chances of competing terms of identity—is easily recognized and almost taken for granted. That exclusion occurs due to past deviations is hardly debatable. If one is sceptical regarding the methods of social research, he may suit himself and inquire into the specifications for entry into many colleges and universities, the U.S. military service, a great many jobs and marital—as well as trade—unions.[5] This does not deny the persistence, perhaps even the growth of an enlightened attitude that gives past sinners a chance to redeem themselves. Many organizations devote themselves to precisely that aim. Nonetheless, gross exclusion persists. And, as Goffman has striven to show, devotion to the care or cause of the stigmatized sophisticates exclusion but does not remove it.[6]

Thus, the gross exclusion suggested by Becker is augmented by the more bewildering and subtle forms recounted by Goffman. For a man to refuse a homosexual a job seems cruel and unduly vengeful, something limited to practicing Neanderthals. But to refuse him a place next to me in a shower—now, there is something that even a committed civil libertarian might fail to take issue with. Unfortunately, the apparently reasonable exclusion may be just as effective—though in a different way—as the unreasonable form in establishing the deviant terms of identity. Gross exclusion withers the possibility of ancillary identities. Reasonable exclusion speaks to a narrower and more pertinent issue.

The basis for gross exclusion, according to Becker, is in the tendency to regard the new, deviant status of the subject as controlling or overriding. It is treated by others as central or essential, not as peripheral. After apprehension, Becker suggested:[7]

One will be identified as a deviant first, before other identifications are made. The question is raised: 'what kind of person would break such an important rule?' And the answer is given: 'one who is different from the rest of us, who cannot or will not act as a moral human being and therefore might break other important rules.' The deviant identification becomes the controlling one.

Because of the fear that he 'therefore might break other important rules,' the exclusion pointed to by Becker goes far beyond what might be deemed reasonable. It covers almost all aspects of the deviant subject's life. Since other aspects are affected in a negative fashion, the possibility of maintaining the primacy of ancillary identities—ones having little relation to the fact of deviation—is reduced. The possibility of figuratively saying, 'I am a thief but also a pretty good husband' is sharply reduced by a notification that one's wife plans to divorce him; so too is the possibility of figuratively saying 'I am homosexual but a very successful businessman' by being discharged from *that* responsibility. As the competition of ancillary status is reduced, the deviant identity may come to be controlling for the subject too. Becker concluded:[8]

Treating a person as though he were generally rather than specifically deviant produces a self-fulfilling prophecy. It sets in motion several mechanisms which conspire to shape the person in the image people have of him. . . . One tends to be cut off, after being identified as a deviant, from participation in more conventional groupings. . . . In such cases, the individual finds himself deviant in these areas as well. The homosexual who is deprived of a 'respectable' job by the discovery of his deviance may drift into unconventional marginal occupations where it does not make so much difference.

If Becker's implicit villain is a garden-variety bigot, Goffman's in *Stigma*—and in most of his writings—is the liberal professional, willing to accept the stigmatized on the condition that those bearing stigma accept themselves as they exist in his eyes. The acceptance is conditional on the tacit agreement that certain limited exclusion is in the best interests of all concerned. Henceforth, if all goes well, the limited exclusions take on the character of being reasonable. But for that very reason, they testify in a very pointed and one-sided way when considered in light of the issue of specific identity. This issue of specific identity is much narrower than that of primacy among competing identities. The more rudimentary issue of whether I am a thief or not replaces the question of whether my identity as thief or good husband is to predominate.

Consider a most reasonable of reasonable exclusions—that of a one-legged man excluded from a company of dancing two-legged women. Everyone has difficulty: the man feels put down, the women awkward and embarrassed; the entire enterprise of dancing suffers.

Equally important, the enterprise of one-legged men accepting themselves as they are is interfered with. Nothing especially surprising follows from this exclusion. One-legged persons are reminded that they are one-legged. It is as simple as that. The trouble is that most other issues of specific identity are not quite that simple and that nevertheless the logic of reasonable exclusion prevails.

Consequently, known thieves may be provided jobs, allowed wives and children—but not bonded. Equally reasonable is the exclusion of known homosexuals from my shower, of known pederasts from the company of my children, of known cheats from the dignity of my professional absence during exams. Reasonable exclusion has the general feature of testifying to the issue of specific identity. It points the subject to a conclusion steadily permanent in the case of one-legged men (though even there over-drawn), but unquestionably premature and untenable in most other cases. Both thief and not thief, as all thieves are, his identity *as* thief is *intensified* by reasonable exclusion. In gross exclusion, that identity is *extended* until it predominates over ancillary identities.

Thus exclusion, whether gross or reasonable, tends to focus the deviant subject's attention on the terms of identity initially provided by the agent of signification during apprehension. Though meaning different things, both forms of exclusion testify to the same conclusion: he *is* a thief. As in most forms of exclusion, the subject need hardly collaborate for the appropriate lesson to be drawn. All that really matters is that occasions and circles which sustain competing identities be inaccessible to him. Such a method of inculcating the terms of deviant identity does not require the subject's presence; other methods do.

The display of authority

Until apprehension, the deviant subject exists in an abstract relation with organized authority. The warrant to be stopped or arrested is there, alongside the activity of deviation. However, real organized authority lacks a certain substance. When it finally materializes—if it does—its appearance is likely to include some elements of surprise. Partly because he is usually taken without warning, and partly because a most notable feature of authority is quite superficial—right there on its face—the deviant subject is likely to experience the shock of concrete discovery. Of course, the shock of concrete discovery is familiar enough. Not especially connected with new knowledge, the shock derives from the sense or appearance of discovery associated with a shift from abstract to concrete understanding.[9] The increment of understanding is in intensity; little is added to extent. Consequently, the subject may grow reluctant to publicize what, after all, 'everybody knows.' Having been reminded a few times that he is rather retarded in mastering the self-evident, the subject learns to keep to himself the way in which he managed to grasp the knowledge about which he is most certain. And reminding others of their retardation, he contributes to the collective process by which the difference between abstract and concrete understanding is suppressed and lost from view. To appreciate the impact of authority, that difference must be made explicit.

Until being signified, the deviant subject does not concretely understand the reality of organized authority; just as he did not understand the reality of deviation until affiliation. Understood abstractly, the most superficial features of authority appear of little or no account. Experienced and understood concretely, they are the most compelling features. They are what stand before the deviant subject when a figure of authority takes him by surprise. Shocked, he will rediscover what everyone claims to have known all along—that in several respects, authority is terribly authoritative.[10]

Being authoritative is the most superficial feature of authority. Dressed that way, rehearsed or trained in its tone of voice, inculcated in its posture and very demeanor, explicitly taught and henceforth conscious of its essential part in commanding respect, the agent of signification appears. Being authoritative is his display in a world that a moment before existed without so imposing and arresting a presence. That display may subsequently become familiar to the subject—and thus devoid of shock and consequence. It becomes devoid when the subject grows innured, accustomed, or even weary of it—but that is just another way of saying that authority has already made its imprint. Dressed properly and acting his part, the personification of authority, whether policeman, judge, or someone less notable, impresses; by being impressive, he helps a bit to cast the subject in his deviant part.

A main purpose of the entire display of authority is to convince the apprehended subject of the gravity of what he has done—to restore the *unity of meaning* that Hobbes correctly saw as basic to the kind of order imposed by Leviathan. In that unity of meaning, it is not enough that the subject concur in assessing his behavior as wrong; equally important is an attitude of gravity. The authoritative display aims at the creation of an attitude of gravity toward what he has done—within the deviant subject. Needless to say, perhaps, it is a bit difficult to add gravity without making more of something that has been done than it appeared the moment before. To attain a unity of meaning regarding the gravity of deviation, authority adds meaning to that previously envisaged by the subject. In shocked discovery, the subject now concretely understands that there are serious people who really go around building their lives around his activities—stopping him, correcting him, devoted to him. They keep records on the course of his life, even develop theories about how he got to be that way. So confident are they of their unity with the rest of society, so secure of their essential legitimacy, that they can summon or command his presence, move him against his will, set terms on which he may try to continue living in civil society, do, in short, almost anything of which only the mightiest of men are capable. What enormity has the deviant subject managed to uncover? Only the concrete reality of Leviathan, armed with an authority more potent than his own.

Pressed by such a display, the subject may begin to add meaning and gravity to his deviant activities. But he may do so in a way not especially intended by agents of the state. Their aim was to impress upon him the unity of society, their method to utilize the bare surface of authority. Faced with the appearance of authoritative being, the deviant subject may join society in seeing that what he had done could not be taken lightly, that instead it was a matter of consider-able gravity. And dazzled by a display of the unity of meaning in society, he may conceive himself as included. But equally possible—therein lies the irony —he may get everything confused, take all that was presented him and proceed in a direction different from that intended. Impressed by the show of author-ity, persuaded of the gravity of his infraction, reminded of a unity of meaning, he may proceed inward. That is all he has to do to prepare himself to spread the deviant identity.

The way in which authority displays itself— authoritatively—provides matters to be considered by the subject. Once again in a position to reconsider the meaning of his behavior, still, the deviant subject is peculiarly placed. His own authority to bestow meaning has been temporarily reduced, dwarfed by an authority clearly more mighty. If not a child, he can be made to feel like one. Though possible to resist and discount the attitude of gravity conveyed by a display of authoritative being, it is difficult and unlikely. For a brief moment at least, the apprehended subject may join society in confirming the unity of meaning regarding the gravity of his behavior. What he did is in all likelihood quite important; why else the pro-duction?

But important to whom? To which unity of meaning will the subject now refer an attitude of gravity of which he has been made conscious? Though dwarfed, his authority has not been liquidated. On the one hand, thus, the subject maintains an option: The attitude of gravity may be referred to society *or* self. And on the other, authority itself may assist in expediting the wrong choice: Its agents may help in directing consciousness to the self. What you have done, they may say, is a matter of gravity both for yourself and society. And given the benefit of appro-priate on-the-job training, they may even say that, mainly, it is a matter of gravity for yourself. In either case—with the explicit assistance of organized authority or without—the subject may refer the consciousness of gravity to the self. Even *without* the explicit instructions of authority, implicitly he has already been turned in that direction: He has been made to feel self-conscious. He has been apprehended.

To direct a consciousness of gravity toward the self is to add meaning to already consummated behavior and to embark on a path leading to widespread deviant identity. To maintain that path, however, the subject must build the meaning of identity. To the logician, the way in which the meaning is built may seem faulty, unfortunate and even incomprehensible; for the subject, too, it may prove unfortunate, but it is not so incomprehensible. He builds the meaning of identity with the materials provided him. If twice he equivocates the meaning of key terms related to issues of identity, he is really not at fault. In truth, many terms related to issues of identity *remain* quite equivocal—even for specialists in the field. (. . .)

Notes

1 I do not wish to equate deviation with crime, though sometimes it does seem as if most jurisdictions in the United States desire just such an equation. Many activities are actionable and thus deviant even though well outside the jurisdiction of criminal law. Torts and many varieties of mental illness are only the most obvious examples. Despite the existence of non-criminal deviations, my discussion will stay close to the criminal on the grounds that they best reveal the part played by signification in the process of becoming deviant.

2 See Edwin Lemert, *Social Pathology: a Systematic Approach to Theory of Sociopathic Behavior* (New York, McGraw-Hill, 1951), ch. 2.

3 For a discussion of signifying among slum Negroes, see Roger Abrahams, *Deep Down in the Jungle: Negro Narrative Folklore from the Streets of South Philadelphia* (Hatboro, Pa., Folklore Associates, 1964), pp. 64, 267.

4 The internal relevance of terms of identity, as well as many other services provided by bureaux signifying deviant activity is a central thesis of the emerging neo-Chicagoan view. As such it provides a basis for a criticism of modern social institutions. Edwin Lemert has pointed to this aspect of a stress on secondary deviation as a possible reason for its new and perhaps spurious popularity among so many students of socio-logy. This perspective starts, Lemert has suggested, 'with a jaundiced eye on the collective efforts of societies to solve problems of deviance, particularly when this work of social control is propagandized as primarily on behalf of the deviants.' Moreover, Lemert observes with considerable justification that because of this feature, 'secondary deviance may be a convenient vehicle for civil libertarians or young men of sociology to voice angry critiques of social institutions.' What-ever its polemic uses or origin, there can be little doubt that the view that officials and professionals are mainly engaged in self-service is strong and entrenched among most sociologists sympathetic with the work of the neo Chicagoans. For example, see Erving Goffman, 'The medical model and mental hospitalization', in *Asylums* (New York, Doubleday, 1961; Penguin, 1968); Thomas Szasz, *The Myth of Mental Illness* (New York, Harper

& Row, 1961; Paladin, 1972); David Sudnow, 'Normal crimes', *Social Problems* (winter 1965), pp. 255–76; David Matza, *Delinquency and Drift* (New York, Wiley, 1964), ch. 4; Jerome Skonick, *Justice Without Trial* (New York, Wiley, 1966), ch. 8; Aaron Cicourel and John Kitsuse, *Educational Decision-Makers* (Indianapolis, Bobbs-Merrill, 1963); Aaron Cicourel, *The Social Organization of Juvenile Justice* (New York, Wiley, 1968). For the discussion of the polemical uses of the concept of secondary deviation and, more generally, an excellent reconsideration of the idea, see Edwin Lemert, 'The concept of secondary deviation', in *Human Deviance, Social Problems and Social Control* (Englewood Cliffs, N.J., Prentice-Hall, 1967).

5 For an especially well-designed study of exclusion see R. Schwartz and J. Skolnick, 'Two studies of legal stigma', in Howard Becker (ed.), *The Other Side* (New York, Free Press, 1964), pp. 103–17.

6 Erving Goffman, *Stigma* (Prentice-Hall, 1963; Penguin, 1970).

7 Howard Becker, *Outsiders* (New York, Free Press, 1963), pp. 32–3.

8 ibid., p. 34.

9 For an excellent literary treatment of the shock of discovery, see Anton Arrufat, 'The discovery', in J. M. Cohen (ed.), *Writers in the New Cuba* (Penguin, 1967).

10 Though the reader may recognize this process as quite similar to the appreciation of banality experienced under the influence of marihuana, it should be evident that using marihuana is unnecessary. Being taken by surprise, and several other readily available human events do just as well in preparing the subject for concrete discovery. Thus, there is no intention of limiting the relevance of these matters to the marihuana user. They apply equally to other apprehended forms of deviation.

4 Making a lesson happen: an ethnomethodological analysis

George C. F. Payne

Ethnomethodology is a rapidly developing field of study within sociology. However as yet, its influence on the sociological analysis of education has been minimal. In this paper it is my concern to show what an ethnomethodological analysis of some actual classroom events can look like. The materials I shall use to this purpose are a verbatim transcript of the utterances spoken by a teacher and a group of pupils during a particular school lesson.

Any sociological analysis is founded on certain assumptions concerning the nature of the social world and the possible ways it can best be investigated. In this respect ethnomethodology is no different from any other way of seeing the world sociologically. It is the differences in the specific assumptions about the nature of social life and about acceptable ways of studying it empirically which give the various sociological approaches or perspectives their distinctive characteristics.

A fundamental assumption of the ethnomethodological approach is that the social world is essentially an ongoingly achieved world.[1] The everyday world of social events, settings and relationships is all the time created and achieved by the members of society and these events, settings and relationships are assumed to have no existence independent of the occasions of their production. The ethnomethodologist assumes that the behaviour which occurs within some social situation or setting, or is part of some social relationship, is behaviour which continuously constitutes that setting, situation or relationship. The social world is seen to exist only in, by and through the behaviour which members produce. It is through the behaviour and the required work that goes into its production and recognition that members display to each other the nature of the social world. In their everyday activities, members are continuously displaying to one

another the relationships they consider relevant at the time, what they see as relevant identities for themselves and for the persons they are interacting with, what they consider the situation to be, and what they consider to be relevant activities etc. The orderliness of the social world is continuously demonstrated through everyday behaviour of members as they go around producing activities which indicate to others that they are recognising common factual states of affairs.

Because the social world is seen to have this nature, the method of its production becomes a central concern in ethnomethodological analysis. The ethnomethodologist assumes that the constant production of the social world is achieved through members' use of methodic practices and it is his concern to describe these practices. Members use these methodic practices or methods in making observations on, in making sense of, and in producing the social world. In a sense these methods are assumed to constitute the world. What amounts to an analysis for the ethnomethodologist is a description of the methods used by members to make the world happen.

For the ethnomethodologist, the concept 'member' has a particular meaning. It is not a political or legal concept, but rather a social and cultural notion. 'Members' are those with a shared stock of common-sense knowledge about the social world and a common competence in applying that knowledge. Membership involves a recognised competence in a natural language and observably adequate performance in identifiable speech communities. It involves having one's competence to make reasonable and sensible observations and to produce reasonable and sensible talk and activities taken for granted. Members, as social actors, assume that the social world is a factual reality which is there for 'anyone' to see and they regard it as a commonplace, generally taken for granted environment, which no competent member has problems recognising and acting upon. One's

Source: unpublished. George Payne is lecturer in sociology, Didsbury College of Education.

membership is something that is continuously demonstrated in everyday behaviour through the production of that behaviour in ways which indicate to others common recognition of the factual state of the world.

Further, membership involves the no problem ability to produce talk and conduct in ways which enable others to have no problems in making an adequate sense of what one is doing. In effect this requires the provision of materials in one's talk and activities which allow others to recognise without any difficulty what we are saying and doing. At the same time, it requires the ability to repair the essential indexicality of words and conduct.

Ethnomethodologists accept the premise that words and activities do not possess unequivocal meanings which are retained across different occasions of their use. They observe that the same words can have different meanings depending on the context of their use and recognise that members have to make adequate repairs of the essential indexicality of words and activities all the time. Members are continuously having to repair the contingent features of any social setting and in so doing they accomplish a hearing and seeing which constitutes the occasion for what it observably is.

To say that there is no social world independent of its production is to say that every aspect of its production is necessarily tied to that very production. In other words, any part of that production is in every way part of that production and at that moment nothing else in the world. This is not to say that the production will not be based on certain general principles of production because it obviously will be—in that it will be achieved through the use of members' methodic practices, and, as members' methodic practices, they will be general to the competent members of that society. Nevertheless, what these methodic practices produce in the way of action, or talk, will be essentially tied to the situation which is made, and only made by their production on that occasion.

In attempting to describe members' use of methodic practices, ethnomethodologists are seeking to uncover the structures of practical activity. These structures are assumed to have the combined features of being context free and yet being context sensitive.[2] That is to say although the ethnomethodologist recognises that talk and activities are 'situated' in that they always come out of, and are part of, some particular circumstances of their participants, he also notes that there is a very wide range of situations and interactions in which persons in varieties of identities can operate. The combination of these two observations suggests that there must be some formal apparatus or structures of practical activity which can be found across contexts, yet which can accommodate the situated character of any particular social occasion or event.

In a school, lessons do not 'just happen'. They, like all other social occasions, have to be achieved by the participants whose methodic procedures constitute any social event for what it is. Lessons, like any social event, have to be achieved on each and every occasion of their production and their achievement will be accomplished through members' occasioned use of culturally general methodic practices.

What follows is an attempt to uncover some of the methodic practices employed by a particular collection of members on the occasion of a particular lesson. It is an attempt to describe some methods by which members might routinely constitute a lesson as a social organisation in displaying its features in their talk. My concern is not with what makes a lesson a lesson, but how this particular lesson comes off as a member's accomplishment.

Let us consider the materials:

```
1   T: E:r . . . come o:n settle down . . . no one's
2       sitting down till we're all ready
            ((pause circa 7 seconds))
            ((general background noises))
3   T: Stand up straigh . . . bags do:wn.
            ((pause circa 8 seconds))
            ((general background noises getting
            quieter))
4   T: Down I sai.
            ((pause circa 5 seconds))
            ((general background noises getting
            quieter still))
5   T: Right quietly: sit down
            ((pause circa 9 seconds))
            ((general background noises))
6   T: *Right* now then what were we talking
7       about last time . . . yes/
8   P: Sir the Vikins how the . . . were going to
9       raid . . Wessex
10  T: How they were going to raid *Wessex yes*
        . . . and what had they raided *before*
        Wessex.
```

The above materials are the utterances spoken by a teacher and some pupils soon after they have entered a school classroom. For these utterances to constitute the beginning of a lesson they have to display features which constitute them as the beginning of a lesson and they have to be recognised as such by the participants who speak and hear them. Teachers can talk to pupils and pupils to teachers 'outside' lessons, before or after lessons, all, for example, in the same physical setting, but for the teacher-pupil, pupil-teacher talk to constitute a lesson, it has to display the features which constitute it as a lesson.

As members of a common culture, with a common knowledge of the social organisation of society, we all know that a lesson has identifiable features. We know, for example, that a lesson requires a complement of specific category-members to be observably present. A person recognisable as a teacher is required, and a person or persons recognisable as a pupil is required. But we also know that the co-presence of the two category-members does not make the lesson.

Both category members have to produce talk and actions which members can routinely recognise as a lesson. I suggest that these features can be regarded as oriented to features of a lesson, in that in the production of any lesson members orient to their existence and, in so doing, in effect achieve their existence.[3]

If the materials we have above were recorded from an actual lesson (and they were), we should be able to discover in them a machinery which could provide for them being heard as a possible lesson. The machinery would consist of the methods used by the members present to make the situation recognisable as a lesson and make the relationships operating between the members, lesson-relevant relationships.

Let us examine the materials in detail in an attempt to uncover some of the methods, cultural understandings and machinery which may have been employed in their production. To begin with, let us take the teacher's first utterance:

E:r . . . come o:n settle down . . . no one's
sitting down till we're all ready

and first let us concentrate on the second half of the utterance. I suggest that the speaker can be heard to be doing some membershipping work in his selection of 'no one'. To make a sense of this utterance, hearers have to make an adequate repair of these particular identifications, and in so doing can be membershipping themselves and the speaker into occasion-relevant categories. Hearers need a method for sensibly repairing 'no one'. Who can the 'no one' be describing?

As a membershipping device, 'no one' has interesting characteristics in that it can be heard as describing populations less than everybody in the world and more than nobody in the world. In this respect it has similar characteristics to the descriptor 'nothing'. It is not unusual to hear members say, 'I've done nothing all day', and yet understand that the speaker may have been doing things all day long—activities such as lying in bed or wandering about the streets, for example. If we were to hear a secretary say, 'I've done nothing all day—it's been one long day of interruptions', we would probably have no difficulty finding an adequate sense for 'nothing', although logically the utterance can be heard to be self contradictory. To find a sense we, as members of a common cultural community, would probably draw on our common-sense knowledge of a secretary's work and our cultural understanding of interruptions as events which upset or temporarily stop some other scheduled or procedurally organised activity. We would need to apply at least this sort of knowledge as part of the sense assembly procedures employed to make an adequate repair of the hypothetical utterance. We would at least probably draw on such cultural resources to hear this utterance as 'any man' can hear it as a sensible thing to say.

In the actual utterance under consideration, some methods, some sense-assembly procedures are re-quired to find a relevant population which 'no one' can be heard to be describing. One general method or procedure available to members is to hear words as collections or co-selections. That is to say, members can hear any one word as a co-selection with the words which precede it and follow it. The parts of an utterance can be heard as mutually constitutive in that how any part is heard can depend upon, among other things, how other parts are heard. It is the speaking and hearing of words as co-selections which helps to constitute situations to be observably what they are. How a 'no one' is heard, to whom it is heard to be referring, depends upon the co-selections that are made with it and which together constitute the situation of its production. I have suggested that 'no one' is an identification which can refer to a population more than 'nobody in the world'. Further, I suggest this implies that it can refer to specific collectivities and, to find the collectivity to which it refers, members hear it as an indexical particular that is constitutive of the situation of its utterance. We cannot find rules to tell us how always to hear 'no one', because it can be heard differently according to the occasion of its use. To find how any adequate sense for it may be achieved, it is necessary to analyse the specific occasion of its use.

In this case we notice that a particular co-selection of descriptors has been produced by the speaker. The 'no one' is a collectivity which on this occasion cannot sit down until it is given permission to sit down. Our common-sense understanding of our society tells us that sitting down is usually no sort of problem, because normally we do not have to ask permission before we can sit down. However, as members, we also know that there are places and situations when restraints on sitting down at will can and do operate. For example, at formal gatherings there can be set procedures for sitting down, and members can be seen to be rude by disregarding these formalities. There are also places, such as other people's houses, where seats can be offered to callers and where to wait to be offered a seat is the polite thing to do. But we all know there is a difference again between waiting to be told that one can sit down and being told that you cannot sit down. I suggest that the right to tell others not to sit down and the right to make conditions for sitting down are routinely associated by members with particular identities and relationships. That is to say, the activity of telling others they cannot sit down is recognised by members as being routinely bound to particular categories of membership, in that the activity is not one that normally any member can expect to execute without some repercussions.[4] Thus for a speaker to tell others they cannot sit down is to provide his hearers with a resource for recognising the speaker as one who is claiming the right to tell others they cannot sit down. The mere telling of others that they cannot sit down does not automatically mean that observers or hearers will recognise the speaker as having that right. An analysis of the speaker as an appropriate category to make such a claim is required to discover a possible legitimacy in the claim. For example, an analysis of the speaker as an inappropriate category to claim the right to tell others when they can sit down can provide for a hearing of such an utterance as a joke. It is possible, for example, for a pupil to be seen to be mimicking a teacher by telling the class they cannot sit down. But the finding of appropriate or inappropriate categories trades on the orientation of members to category-bound activities. Following the late Harvey Sacks, I suggest that the orientation to category-bound activities is a method that members can employ to make an adequate sense of what they hear and that, in this case, the speaker can be analysed by his hearers as an appropriate person to make such an utterance; in the making of the utterance, he can be observed to be displaying himself as that appropriate person. He can then be seen to be claiming for himself a particular identity or membership category. At the same time, he is providing for a possible membership category for his hearers. If they recognise him as an appropriate person to engage in that activity and recognise that it is they who are being spoken to and appropriately being spoken to in that manner, they have available to them resources for recognising themselves in this situation as being membershipped into categories who can be told they cannot sit down.

Through categorising the speaker and themselves they further provide for the recognition of a possible relationship that may exist between them and the speaker. In our culture, certain categories are routinely recognised as paired categories, and the pairing is recognised to incorporate standardised relationships of rights, obligations and expectations.[5] An orientation to the use of standardised relationship pairs is another method available to hearers in the analysis of utterances to discover and produce the features of a social situation or event. Thus a sense can be provided for an utterance through the membershipping of the speaker, through the membershipping of ourselves as hearers and through the recognition of the two membership categories as elements of a standardised relationship pair.

In a school, 'teacher' and 'pupil' are readily available categories for membershipping persons. Each category implies the other and together they involve a collection of rights, obligations and expectations for each other. Teachers and pupils can have themselves recognised as such by displaying the features of these rights, obligations and expectations through their talk. The right to tell members they cannot sit down is a right commonly associated with the relationship that can operate between a teacher and a pupil. In saying that 'no one's sitting down till we're all ready', the speaker can be heard to be claiming for himself a category to which the right to tell others they cannot sit down is associated, and the 'no one' can be heard as describing a population who in this situation can be told they cannot sit down.

A recognition of the activity the teacher can be heard to be providing for in this utterance can further help to substantiate the discovery and production of these identifications. I suggest that members would find it difficult to hear 'no one's sitting down till we're all ready' as a description of the world; in that, of the millions of persons around, the chances are that a good many of them were actually sitting down at the time the utterance was spoken. Alternatively, I can very easily, as a member, hear the utterance as some kind of order. Further, I can say, as a member, if it is not an order I do not know what it is, because that is what I hear it obviously to be. Some group of people are being told, not asked, that they cannot sit down. The hearing of it as an order can provide for the recognition of the speaker as a possible issuer of orders, and the recognition of the hearers as possible recipients of orders.

A characteristic of orders, verbal orders that is, is that they are normally given to persons who can hear them (unless they are specifically being passed on by some messenger). So the hearing of this utterance as an order can provide for an identification of 'no one' as a collectivity of persons co-present with the speaker.

This is not to say that the 'no one' can be heard to refer to everyone else who is present in the situation. For example, there may be inspectors or other teachers in the room. I myself was present there as an observer on this occasion. Hearers require some method to discover a relevant category that 'no one' can be describing and, in so doing, to find a relevant collectivity out of all the possible categories present. Here again I suggest that hearers' use of category pairings or standardised relationship pairs can be the method to discover such a collectivity and at the same time the method used to recognise the activity the speaker is providing for in his utterance as motivatedly relevant for them.

The finding of a co-present collectivity that can be identified as a legitimate recipient of orders can provide for the hearing of the utterance as an order. Thus the possible recognition of the category 'pupil' by some of the hearers present, as a relevant identification to this occasion, can provide for a possible identification of 'teacher' for the speaker, and can provide for a possible finding of the activity of issuing an order in the speaker's utterance.

The double aspects of the hearing of the utterance as performing some activity and as membershipping the speaker and the hearers are mutually constitutive productions; each analysis informs on the other analysed elements and together they provide for the constitution of the situation for what it is.

The utterance can further be heard as a particular sort of order in that it carries a condition for next action which individual hearers would find very difficult or impossible to recognise. How, for example, can any individual hearer know or recognise when everyone, presumably the speaker included, is ready.

The speaker has said that no one is to sit down till *we're all* ready. This can be heard to include the speaker, thus making it very difficult for any individual hearer to say when everyone is ready. Further, although the speaker has said that no one is to sit down till 'we're all ready', he has not said ready for what, and has not said what being ready will look like. In effect he has provided for himself the right to decide next action. He has issued an order and issued it in such a way that only he will be able to say when it has been carried out. In so doing he can be seen to be doing identification and relational work. Through his talk he is providing for his recognition as the member present with power over those co-present. He has provided for his recognition as the member in charge in this situation. He has formulated an order which includes a condition for next action, the fulfilment of which only he can determine.

Besides the identification and relational work produced and discoverable in this utterance, I suggest that the speaker can also be heard to be cueing those present into a collaborative project of some kind. He has told his listeners that they cannot sit down till 'we're all' ready. The 'we' can be heard to include the speaker himself, in the required state of readiness, which suggests that the readiness being referred to concerns some project involving both hearers and the speaker.

I also suggest that further materials which can provide for the hearing of this part of the utterance as a precursor to some collaborative project are available to hearers in the first part of the teacher's first utterance and in the utterances which immediately follow it.

A general method or procedure members use to make an adequate sense of what they hear is the 'wait and see principle'. That is to say, whatever members hear can be heard as part of some things that may 'come after' it. Members can expect that what may come after (and nothing may) will provide some warrant for a sense that has already been made 'for the present', or may provide for the making of a different sense. This also implies that what is heard at any one moment can be used to make some kind of retrospective analysis or re-analysis of what has already been heard. Thus the sense-assembly procedures used by members can include prospective and retrospective analysis, and in the making of an adequate sense of the utterances they hear, members may relate particular parts or whole utterances to what they have previously heard and what their current hearing orients them to expect to hear next. I suggest that the utterances in lines 1 to 7 in the materials we are discussing can be heard to constitute the setting up and initiating of a collaborative project, and that this hearing can be provided for by the prospective and retrospective analysis of the constitutive utterances.

I have said that the use of 'we' in the utterance,

'E:r . . . come o:n settle down . . . no one's sitting down till we're all ready', can be heard to orient hearers to the future production of some collaborative project. To this I add that the first part of this utterance, 'come on settle down', with the 'on' elongated can be heard by members as a call to order. That is a call to a state or condition of orderliness that some next activity requires. The 'come on' can be heard as an invitation to the hearers to recognise the relevance of this order in the present situation. Members commonly use the expression when invoking some generally recognised rules or standards which they expect hearers to recognise and, on this occasion, I, as a member, can hear the speaker saying, in not so many words, something like, 'come on settle down—you know you should be settling down, we all know that this is a situation which requires you to be settled down', etc.

However, for the hearers on this occasion to hear the utterance as a call to order, they have to analyse the speaker as an appropriate caller to order and the situation as one in which order is relevant. The same words wherever uttered do not necessarily constitute a call to order; where they are, they have to be produced and discovered as such through the sense-assembly procedures used by members. Members who can issue orders to others, and who can stop people from sitting down, can presumably be seen to be appropriate callers to order. In school, members recognise teachers as appropriate callers to order and included in the various occasions when they can be recognised as appropriate callers to order is the start of lessons. But for pupils to analyse this call to order as the precursor to a lesson they would probably require more material, which in this case they are soon provided with, and which I shall come to in a moment. An already mentioned methodic practice available to members in the analysis of appropriate callers to order is the orientation to category-bound activities. Certain activities are routinely recognised by members to be tied to certain categories. I suggest that in our culture the calling of pupils to order by teachers is an example and that these are likely to be readily available categories in schools.

The call to order that can achieve the co-orientation of members to the production of a state of order can be regarded as an initial step in the production of some collaborative project requiring order. In our materials, the speaker has immediately followed his call to order with the issuing of a condition of readiness. The juxtaposition of this work by the speaker, and the speaker's use of 'we', can be heard to provide for the recognition of the required readiness as the state of order which some collaborative project involving the speaker and hearer requires.

The possibility of this hearing can be provided for by a retrospective analysis of the utterance following possible hearings of subsequent utterances in the materials. In his next three utterances the speaker can be heard to be giving orders or instructions and, in so doing, can be heard to be providing his hearers with further resources for the recognition of the required state of order which can constitute the state of readiness which the collaborative project required. The hearing of the 'come and settle down' as a call to order can provide for the hearing of these subsequent instructions as amplifications on the description of the required state of order, and at the same time the hearing of these instructions and such amplificatory descriptions can provide for the hearing of the initial utterance as a call to order. It is in this way that the utterances can be discovered as mutually constitutive through the procedures of prospective and retrospective analysis.

In his next utterance, '*Right* now then what were we talking about last time . . . yes', the speaker can be heard to be providing for the beginning of a collaborative project of some nature. In the utterances before this one the speaker has not provided his hearers with recognisable turns to talk. He has observably been issuing orders, giving instructions, laying down conditions. He has been maintaining his right to speak by not providing for the transference of the talk to others. The silences or pauses can be heard as his pauses, in that the utterances which precede them do not provide for other speakers to speak, and in that no other speaker is observed to speak. In keeping the talk to himself, the speaker can also be observed to be doing further identification work by providing for his recognition as the member present who decides when others will be allowed to talk. However, with this utterance, he is observably transferring the talk to others by asking a question and thus making an answer the next relevant activity. In doing this he can be heard to be initiating some collaborative project and the possibility of this hearing can, through a retrospective analysis, provide for the hearing of the prior utterances as the calling for and establishing of an order recognisably required for the production of some collaborative project. At the same time, the hearing of this utterance as the beginning of a collaborative project also provides further warrant for the hearing of the previous use of 'we' as orienting hearers to the inclusion of the speaker in the required state of order or readiness.

It is possible that the speaker's concern to establish a state of order before providing for the beginning of the collaborative project results from his recognition of the fact that the collaborative project requires an order and will require it for the duration of its existence. Having the condition of order recognised as relevant to the beginning of the project, the speaker may then be able to refer back to it as a required condition of the project should its existence become in doubt during the period of the project. Thus the joint collaborative production can continue as long as the condition of order continues; when this state is broken in any way the teacher can refer to its breach as a moral issue. In this way the teacher's talk can be seen to be providing for a state of order as an oriented to feature of the particular collaborative project relevant to this occasion. Members speak of teachers being unable to teach when there is chaos in the classroom, when no one is listening to what the teacher is saying, when pupils cannot get on with their tasks. It is possible that this common cultural understanding of a lesson as a social situation requiring this form of order is what the teacher is trading off when he uses 'come on' earlier.

I have said that the hearing of the utterance, 'Right now then what were we talking about last time . . . yes' as the beginning of a collaborative project can provide for the hearing of the speaker's previous utterances as the calling for and the establishing of conditions that the project requires. Let us now examine this utterance in more detail to discover how it can be heard as the beginning of a collaborative project, and specifically as the beginning of a lesson.

To begin with, I suggest that the utterance can be heard to be doing some marking off or changing of activities. 'Right' can be heard as a marker in that what precedes it and what follows it are recognisably different activities. Before this utterance, we have seen that the teacher was doing all the talking. He was producing utterances which provided for his keeping the floor. He was issuing orders and laying down conditions of behaviour. His use of 'right' at the beginning of this utterance, and the possible hearing of the total utterance as a question, can be heard to be indicating to his hearers that the conditions he has been seeking have been established and that it is now appropriate to get on with the activity for which the conditions were required. Hearing the utterance as a question provides for the relevance of another person to speak by producing an answer. Providing a turn to talk to others is to provide for the collaboration of others in the joint production of the occasion. We notice that on this occasion the question is answered and observably answered adequately in that the teacher's next utterance indicates that he recognises the answer as an adequate reply. I suggest that these observed structural differences in the talk preceding and following the use of 'right' can provide for the hearing of 'right' as marking off or changing activities. Further resources for discovering the nature of the activity to which the speaker is orienting his listeners are available in the rest of this utterance.

In asking 'what were we talking about last time' without spelling out just what last time he is referring to, the speaker can be heard to be asking his hearers to discover an appropriate last time and in so doing to constitute this current talk as another instance of the talk that was produced in that identifiable last time. Through a retrospective analysis, the hearers have available to them, for the discovery of an appropriate last time, the identifications and relationships which have been provided for in the preceding utterances. To further provide for the use of these identifications the hearers also have the 'we' of this utterance. Thus a possible hearing of 'last time' is a time when we who are now present with our current identifications and relationships were last all together with similar identifications and relationships.

It is quite possible that since the last occasion when the speaker and some of his current hearers were together with their current identifications and relationships operative they may have met with different identifications or different relationships. For example, they could have met at some independent social function outside school. It is also possible that some of those present may have met the speaker even with their current identifications of 'teacher' and 'pupils' operative, but in this utterance the collective descriptor 'we' can be heard to be providing for an identification of the speaker and his hearers as an inclusive collectivity, and can thus be orienting those present to the occasion when the inclusive collectivity as an identification was operative. For this occasion to be recognised as a lesson, the pupils present have to recognise that they are membershipped not only as pupils, but also as a collectivity of pupils constituting a class. Through invoking this particular identity the speaker can be heard to provide for the recognition of this situation as another similar to the last time that that identification was operative.

This does not mean that every single person who was present before has to be seen to be present now, because particular individuals in the class may in fact be absent. What is relevant is that the categories of persons who were present before can be observed to be present on this occasion. The speaker, as teacher, is required to be present. His asking, 'what were we talking about last time', can be heard to be saying that he was present on the previous occasion. The other relevant category would be the collectivity, the class, with whom he was talking. The absence of one or more members of the collectivity does not prevent the identification of the remainder as the same collectivity. The remainder are still recognisable as the class. The hearers could also expect the speaker not to know exactly who was present and who was not, nor to know if there were persons present on this occasion who were not present last time the speaker was with this collectivity, nor if some who were present before are absent on this occasion. All this knowledge can be used by the hearers to provide for a hearing of 'we' which does not refer to the specific individuals present but to the occasion-relevant categories. It provides a warrant for the hearers membershipping themselves as a collectivity relevant to the occasion. The recognition of that identification by the hearers is a constitutive element in the production of this occasion as one relevant to the 'last time'. If the hearers present can recognise themselves as members of a class, and recognise the teacher's talk as possible lesson talk,

they have two resources for orienting to the situation as a lesson.

The hearers observably have no difficulty in understanding which 'last time' is being referred to because one of them answers the teacher's question immediately and, from the teacher's subsequent utterance, can be heard to have answered it adequately. The last time they were together, operating with the identifications they are currently operating with, was when they were talking about the Vikings raiding Wessex. In the last utterance of the teacher we can also notice that he asks another question and can thus be heard to be further orienting his hearers to their continued production of the collaborative project they have just begun. Thus we can observe that the lesson is under way.

Finally, I would like to suggest that the teacher's use of the descriptor 'we' in the utterance, 'Right now then what were we talking about last time . . . yes' can be heard to provide further for the hearing of the utterance as the commencement of the collaborative project. It is the same descriptor as was used to describe the collectivity which had to be ready for some unmentioned future activity in lines 1 and 2, in that it was used by the same speaker to the same hearers. Hearing it as the same descriptor, describing the same collectivity can provide for the hearing of this utterance as the beginning of the collaborative project for which those present had to make themselves ready. The 'we' who had to make themselves ready can now be observed to be ready in that those who have been precluded from talking are now being given the opportunity to talk and thus to collaborate in the joint production.

Thus in these few lines over the period of about half a minute, the members present at this place can be seen to have constituted the situation as the beginning of a lesson through their use of methodic practices and common cultural understandings.

In this article I have attempted to show what an ethnomethodological analysis of some classroom events can look like. Starting from the assumption that any lesson is an accomplishment produced and created by the members who are party to it, I have tried to uncover some of the practical reasoning and some of the methodic procedures used by members to bring off the event as a lesson. I have concentrated on the beginning of the lesson.

In seeking to uncover the practical reasoning, we can see how the members orient to the features of what they and 'everyone' knows to constitute a lesson and can see how in orienting to those features they make those features observable in their talk. It is only by observably orienting to those features in their talk that these very features are brought into existence as a social event.

Acknowledgments

I wish to thank the late Harvey Sacks for making available to the Didsbury Conversational Analysis Workshop his large body of unpublished materials. I also wish to thank John Lee of the University of Manchester for the help and advice he has given me in the preparation of this paper. Needless to say, I accept full responsibility for the formulation of the paper.

Notes

1 For a more detailed exposition of the methodology of ethnomethodology see H. Garfinkel, *Studies in Ethnomethodology* (Prentice-Hall, 1967).

2 See H. Sacks, G. Jefferson and E. Schegloff, 'A simplest systematics for the organisation of turn-taking for conversation', due to appear in *Language*, December 1974.

3 For a discussion of the nature of 'oriented to features', see H. Sacks, 'Aspects of the Sequential Organisation of Conversation', ch. 2 (unpublished; details available from G. C. F. Payne).

4 See H. Sacks, 'On the analysability of stories by children', in J. Gumperz and D. Hymes (eds), *Directions in Sociolinguistics: the ethnography of Communication* (Holt, Rinehart & Winston, 1972) for a discussion of 'category-bound activities'.

5 See H. Sacks, 'The search for help: no one to turn to', in E. S. Shneidman (ed.), *Essays in Self Destruction* (Science House, 1967) for a fuller explication of 'standardised relationship pairs'.

5 Subcultural conflict and working-class community

Phil Cohen

(. . .) Since the very beginning of the industrial revolution, the East End has provided a kind of unofficial 'reception centre' for a succession of immigrant communities, in flight from religious persecution or economic depression. First came the Huguenots, spinners and weavers, at the end of the 17th century, and still today their presence survives in surnames and place names in the area. Then throughout the 19th century there was a constant immigration of. Irish, mostly labourers, and small traders from Central Europe and, in the last two decades, Pakistanis, and, to a lesser extent, West Indians and Greek Cypriots. Today the East End is indeed like 'five parts of the world, put in one place'.

Each sub-community brought with it not just specific skills, but also its own traditions and cultural values. There was no question of assimilation into a dominant indigenous culture—either that of the 'native' dockland community, or of the English ruling class. What in fact happened, until recently, was that each new sub-community, in turn and over time, became an accepted, but differentiated, part of the 'East End' by allying itself with the longer established sections of the community against another, later sub-community. The outsiders become established, become insiders, by dissociating themselves from an even more conspicuous set of outsiders. Perhaps it is a natural human tendency to draw the line under one's own feet; at any rate, in the East End, integration has proceeded by means of conflict, rather than by dissolving it.

There are three main social factors underpinning this pattern of integration—the extended kinship structures which regulate socialization in each sub-community; second the ecology structure of the working-class neighbourhood; and finally the structure of the local economy. In reality these factors interact and reinforce each other—but it is important to understand them, because it is precisely the elimination of these factors, the transformation of these structures, which has caused the present state of tension in the area. So let us look at them briefly, one by one.

Extended kinship networks

This is a system by which the family of marriage remains linked by an intricate web of rights and obligations to the respective families of origin, and serves as a link between them. Based in the first instance on maintaining the close relationship between mother and daughter, so that when she gets married the daughter will continue to live as close as she can to 'mum', and extending in widening circles to include uncles and aunts, grandparents, nephews and nieces, and their relations, this system virtually turns the family into a micro-community, and in fact provides for many of the functions of mutual aid and support, that are elsewhere carried out by agencies in the community. Obviously such a system makes for cultural continuity and stability; it reduces generational conflict to a minimum—leaving home and getting married do not become life and death issues as they do in the nuclear family. First, because the extended family constitutes a much richer and more diversified human environment for the child; second, children tend to stay at home until they get married, or to put it another way, only leave in order to do so; third, getting married does not involve any divorce between the young couple and their families, but rather recruits new members into the kinship network. And although the extended family preserves historical traditions of the sub-community, handing them on from generation to generation, it does not serve to insulate it from the 'outside world'. On the contrary, it serves as the basis for eventual integration. For the

Source: University of Birmingham, Centre for Contemporary Cultural Studies, *Working Papers in Cultural Studies*, no. 2, 1972, pp. 9–27.

family both becomes firmly anchored in a given locality (matrilocal residence as it is technically called) and the network is continually expanding outwards; the net result is that over time the ties of neighbourhood are extended into ties of kinship and vice versa. If everybody knows everybody else in traditional neighbourhoods, it is not because they are related through interlocking kinship networks, but that schoolmates, workmates, pubmates, while they may or may not be related to relatives of one's own, will tend to be related to other mates, or mates to other relatives of one's own. But this cannot be explained simply in terms of the internal dynamic of kinship; the ecology of the neighbourhood also plays a part.

Ecology of the working-class neighbourhood

The close-packed back-to-backs facing each other across alleyways or narrow streets, corner shops and local pubs, the turning—all this helps to shape and support the close textures of traditional working-class life, its sense of solidarity, its local loyalties and traditions. And this in turn is underpinned by the extended kinship networks of the traditional working-class family, which have been so well observed in Bethnal Green.

But how does the ecology of the neighbourhood work in practice? Let us take the street as an example. In these neighbourhoods, the street forms a kind of 'communal space'—a mediation between the totally private space of the family, with its intimate involvements, and the totally public space; e.g. parks, thoroughfares, etc., where people relate to each other as strangers, and with indifference. The street, then, is a space where people can relate as neighbours, can express a degree of involvement with others, who are outside the family, but yet not as strangers, it maintains an intricate social balance between rights and obligations distance and relation in the community. It also serves to generate an informal system of social controls. For where the street is played in, talked in, sat out in, constantly spectated as a source of neighbourly interest, it is also policed, and by the people themselves. Nothing much can happen, however trivial (a child falling, a woman struggling with heavy parcels, etc.), without it becoming a focus of interest and intervention. The presence of corner shops and pubs in the turning also serves to generate social interaction at street level, as well as providing natural settings for 'gossip cliques' which, if they do nothing else, constantly reaffirm the reality of neighbourhood ties!

The net result is that neighbours as well as relatives are available to help cope with the day-to-day problems that arise in the constant struggle to survive under the conditions of the working-class community. And in many areas, including the East End, institutions such as loans clubs, holiday clubs and the like developed to supplement family mutual aid, and formalize the practices of 'neighbouring'.

The local economy

Perhaps the most striking feature of the traditional East End economy is its diversity; dockland, the many distributive and service trades linked to it, the craft industries, notably tailoring and furniture-making, the markets. This diversity meant that people lived and worked in the East End—there was no need for them to go outside in search of jobs. The extended family remains intrinsic to the recruitment of the labour force and even to the work process itself; son followed father into the same trade or industry, while many of the craft and service trades were organized into 'family concerns'. As a result of this, the situation of the workplace, its issues and interests, remained tied to the situation outside work—the issues and interests of the community.

There was a direct connection between the position of the producer and the consumer. The fierce pride of being an East-Ender was often linked to the equally fierce pride of craftmanship and skilled labour. And it was from this section of the working class—sometimes called the labour aristocracy—that the indigenous leadership was drawn; politically conscious and highly articulate in defence of local interest, both at the community level and at the point of production. This elite group was also the most socially mobile, tending to re-emigrate from the East End to the outer ring of the middle-class suburbs; as Jewish people used to put it: the distance from Bethnal Green to Golders Green was two generations. Yet their ranks were continuously replenished as new sub-communities established themselves as part of the respectable working class. There were also those less fortunate who, for a variety of reasons, fell by the wayside and remained permanent 'outsiders' vis-à-vis the 'established'. They were relegated to the ranks of the labouring poor caught in a vicious circle of poverty, ill-health, unemployment and lack of education. This residual group was doubly excluded—unskilled and lacking union organization, they had little or no bargaining power on the labour market; and stigmatized as 'pariahs' by the rest of the community, the scapegoat for its problems, and denied any effective voice in their solution.

At any given time, then, the social structure of the community as a whole, and of the sub-communities within it, tended to be polarizing into three distinct strata—the socially mobile elite who monopolize leadership, the respectables, who form the 'staple backbone' of the community, and the lumpen (so called) who are often driven to petty criminal activity to survive. And incidentally there is not a better example of the over-riding importance of the extended kinship structure on the pattern of East End life than the fact that when this lowest stratum began to evolve a kind of lumpen aristocracy based on criminal activity, it was the small family 'firm' that was taken as the model for its social organization!

The future perfect versus the historical present

The social structure I have described held until the early fifties; and then, slowly at first, but with gathering momentum, it began to change, and the pattern of social integration that had traditionally characterized the East End began, dramatically, to break down. Without going into a long argument about cause and effect, it is possible to say that this breakdown coincided with the wholesale redevelopment of the area, and the process of chain reactions which this triggered. The redevelopment was in two phases, the first spanning the decade of the fifties, the second from the early sixties to the present. Let us examine the impact of each in turn.

The fifties saw the development of new towns and large estates on the outskirts of East London—Dagenham, Greenleigh, etc.—and a large number of families from the worst slums of the East End were rehoused in this way. The East End, one of the highest density areas in London, underwent a gradual depopulation. But as it did so, certain areas underwent a re-population, as they were rapidly colonized by a large influx of West Indians and Pakistanis. One of the reasons why these communities were attracted (in the weak sense of the word) to such areas is often called 'planning blight'. This concept has been used to describe what happens in the take-off phase of comprehensive redevelopment in the inner residential zones of large urban centres. The typical pattern is that as redevelopment begins, land values inevitably rise and rental values fall; the most dynamic elements in local industry, who are usually the largest employers of labour, tend to move out alongside the migrating families, and are often offered economic incentives to do so; much of the existing dilapidated property in the area is bought up cheaply by property speculators and Rachman-type landlords, who are interested only in the maximum exploitation of their assets—the largest profits in the shortest time; as a result the property is often not maintained and becomes even further dilapidated. Immigrant families, with low incomes and excluded from council housing, naturally gravitate to these areas, and their own trades and service industries begin to penetrate the local economy. This in turn accelerates the migration of the indigenous community to the new towns and estates. The only apparent exception to planning blight, in fact, proves the rule. For those few areas which are linked to invisible assets—such as possessing houses of 'character', i.e. late Georgian or early Victorian, or amenities such as parks—are bought up and improved, renovated for the new middle class, students, young professionals, who require easy access to the commercial and cultural centre of the city. The end result on the local community is the same; whether the neighbourhood is upgraded or downgraded, long resident working-class families move out.

As the worst effects of the first phase, both on those who moved and on those who stayed behind, became apparent, the planning authorities decided to reverse their policy. Everything was now concentrated on building new estates on slum sites within the East End. But far from counteracting the social disorganization of the area, this merely accelerated the process. In analysing the impact of redevelopment on the community, these two phases can be treated as one. No one is denying that redevelopment brought an improvement in material conditions for those fortunate enough to be rehoused (there are still thousands on the housing list). But while this removed the tangible evidence of poverty, it did nothing to improve the real economic situation of many families, and those with low incomes may, despite rent rebate schemes, be worse off. But to this was added a new poverty—the impoverishment of working-class culture. Redevelopment meant the destruction of the neighbourhood, the breakdown of the extended kinship network, which, as we have seen, combined to exert a powerful force for social cohesion in the community.

The first effect of the high-density, high-rise schemes was to destroy the function of the street, the local pub, the corner shop, as articulations of communal space. Instead there was only the privatized space of the family unit, stacked one on top of each other, in total isolation, juxtaposed with the totally public space which surrounded it, and which lacked any of the informal social controls generated by the neighbourhood. The streets which serviced the new estates became thoroughfares, their users 'pedestrians' and, by analogy, so many bits of human traffic, and this irrespective of whether or not they were separated from motorized traffic. It is indicative of how far the planners failed to understand the human ecology of the working-class neighbourhood that they could actually talk about building 'vertical streets'! The people who had to live in them were not fooled. As one put it—they might have running hot water, and central heating, but to him they were still prisons in the sky. Inevitably the physical isolation, the lack of human scale and sheer impersonality of the new environment were felt worst by people living in the new tower blocks which have gradually come to dominate the East End landscape.

The second effect of redevelopment was to destroy what we have called 'matrilocal residence'. Not only was the new housing designed on the model of the nuclear family, with little provision for large low-income families (usually designated as problem families!) and none at all for groups of young single people, but the actual pattern of distribution of the new housing tended to disperse the kinship network; families of marriage were separated from their families of origin, especially during the first phase of the redevelopment. The isolated family unit could no longer call on the resources of wider kinship networks, or of the neighbourhood, and the family itself became the sole focus of solidarity. This meant that any problems were bottled up within the immediate interpersonal context which produced them; and at the same time family relationships were invested with a new intensity to compensate for the diversity of relationships previously generated through neighbours and wider kin. The trouble was that although the traditional kinship system which corresponded to it had broken down, the traditional patterns of socialization (of communication and control) continued to reproduce themselves in the interior of the family. The working-class family was thus not only isolated from the outside, but undermined from within. There is no better example of what we are talking about than the plight of the so-called 'housebound mother'. The street or turning was no longer available as a safe playspace, under neighbourly supervision. Mum, or Auntie, was no longer just round the corner to look after the kids for the odd morning. Instead, the task of keeping an eye on the kids fell exclusively to the young wife, and the only safe playspace was 'the safety of the home'. Feeling herself cooped up with the kids, and cut off from the outside world, it was not surprising if she occasionally took out her frustration on those nearest and dearest! Only market research and advertising executives imagine that the housebound mother sublimates everything in her G-plan furniture, her washing machine or non-stick frying pans.

Underlying all this, however, there was a more basic process of change going on in the community, a change in the whole economic infrastructure of the East End.

In the late fifties, the British economy began to recover from the effect of the war, and to apply the advanced technology developed during this period to the more backward sectors of the economy. Craft industries, and small-scale production in general, were the first to suffer: automated techniques replaced the traditional hand skills and their simple division of labour. Similarly the economies of scale provided for by the concentration of capital resources meant that the small-scale family business was no longer a viable unit. Despite a long rearguard action, many of the traditional industries—tailoring, furniture-making— many of the service and distributive trades linked to the docks rapidly declined or were bought out. Symbolic of this was the disappearance of the corner shops; where these were not demolished by redevelopment, they were replaced by the larger supermarkets often owned by large combines. Even where corner shops were offered places in the redevelopment area, often they could not afford the high rents. There was a gradual polarization in the structure of the labour force: on the one side the highly specialized, skilled and well-paid jobs associated with the new technology, and the high growth sectors that employed them; on the other the routine, dead-end, low-paid and un-skilled jobs associated with the labour-intensive sectors, especially the service industries. As might be expected, it was the young people just out of school who got the worst of the deal. Lacking openings in their fathers' trades, and lacking the qualifications for the new industries, they were relegated to jobs as vanboys, office boys, packers, warehousemen, etc., and long spells out of work. More and more people, young and old, had to travel out of the community to their jobs, and some eventually moved out to live elsewhere, where suitable work was to be found. The local economy as a whole contracted, became less diverse. The only section of the community which was unaffected by this was dockland, which retained its position in the labour market, and, with it, its traditions of militancy. It did not, though, remain un-affected by the breakdown of the pattern of integration in the East End as a whole, vis-à-vis its sub-community structure. Perhaps this goes some way to explain the paradoxical fact that within the space of twelve months, the dockers could march in support of Enoch Powell, and take direct action for community control in the Isle of Dogs!

If someone should ask why the plan to 'modernize' the pattern of East End life should have been such a disaster, perhaps the only honest answer is that, given the macro-social forces acting on it, given the political, ideological and economic framework within which it operated, the result was inevitable. For example many local people wonder why the new environment should be the way it is. The reasons are complex; they are political in so far as the system does not allow for any effective participation by the local working-class community in the decision-making process at any stage or level of planning. The clients of the planners are simply the local authority or commercial developer who employs them. They are ideological in so far as the plans are unconsciously modelled on the structure of the middle-class environment, which is based on the concept of *property*, and *private ownership*, on individual differences of status, wealth, etc.; whereas the structure of the working-class environment is based on the concept of community, or collective identity, common lack of ownership, wealth, etc. Similarly, needs were assessed on the norms of the middle-class nuclear family, rather than on the extended working-class family. But underpinning both these sets of reasons lie the basic economic factors involved in comprehensive redevelopment. Quite simply—faced with the task of financing a large housing programme, the local authorities were forced to borrow large amounts of capital, and also to design schemes which would attract capital investment to the area. This means that they had to borrow at the going interest rates (which in this country are very high) and that to subsidize housing, certain of the best sites had to be earmarked for commercial developers. A further and perhaps decisive factor is the cost of land, since very little of it is publicly owned and land values rise as the area develops.

All this means that planners have to reduce the cost of production to a minimum through the use of capital-intensive techniques—prefabricated and standardized components, which allow for semi-automated processes in construction. The attraction of high-rise developments (tower blocks outside the trade) is not only that they meet these requirements, but that they allow for certain economies of scale, such as the input costs of essential services, which can be grouped around a central core. As to 'non-essential' services, i.e. ones that don't pay, such as playspace, community centres, youth clubs and recreational facilities—these often have to be sacrificed to the needs of commercial developers, who of course have quite different priorities. Perhaps the best example of this happening is the notorious St Katharine's Dock scheme. This major contribution towards solving the East End's housing problem includes a yachting marina, a luxury hotel, luxury apartment blocks and various cultural amenities for their occupants, plus a small section of low-income accommodation, presumably to house the families of the low-paid staff who will service the luxury amenities. And lest anyone becomes too sentimental about the existing site, Telford's warehouses, etc., it should be mentioned that the original development by the East India Company in the early 19th century involved the destruction of the homes of thousands of poor families in the area, and met with such stiff opposition from them that it eventually required an Act of Parliament to get the scheme approved!

The situation facing East-Enders at present, then, is not new. When the first tenements went up in the 19th century they raised the same objections from local people, and for the same very good reasons, as their modern counterparts—the tower blocks. What *is* new is that in the 19th century the voice of the community was vigorous and articulate on these issues, whereas today, just when it needs it most, the community is faced with a crisis of indigenous leadership.

The reasons for this are already implicit in the analysis above. The labour aristocracy, traditional source of leadership, has virtually disappeared along with the artisan mode of production. At the same time there has been a split in consciousness between the spheres of production and consumption. More and more East-Enders are forced to work outside the area; young people especially are less likely to follow family traditions in this respect. As a result, the issues of the workplace are no longer experienced as directly linked to community issues. Of course there has always been a 'brain drain' of the most articulate, due to social mobility. But not only has this been intensified as a result of the introduction of comprehensive schools, but the recruitment of fresh talent from the stratum below—i.e. from the ranks of the respectable working class—has also dried up. For this stratum, traditionally the social cement of the community, is also in a state of crisis.

The economic changes which we have already described also affected their position and, as it were, *de-stabilized* it. The 'respectables' found themselves caught and pulled apart by two opposed pressures of social mobility—downwards, into the ranks of the new suburban working-class elite. And they, more than any other section of the working class, were caught in the middle of the two dominant but contradictory ideologies of the day: the ideology of spectacular consumption promoted by the mass media, and the traditional ideology of production, the so-called work ethic which centred on the idea that a man's dignity, his manhood even, was measured by the quantity or quality of his effort in production. If this stratum began to split apart, it was because their existing position had become untenable. Their bargaining power in the labour market was threatened by the introduction of new automated techniques, which eliminated many middle-range, semi-skilled jobs. Their economic position excluded them from entering the artificial paradise of the new consumer society; at the same time changes in the production process itself made the traditional work ethic, the pride in the job, impossible to uphold. They had the worst of all possible worlds.

Once again this predicament was registered most deeply in and on the young. But here an additional complicating factor intervenes. We have already described the peculiar strains imposed on the 'nucleated' working-class family. And their most critical impact was in the area of parent/child relationships. What had previously been a source of support and security for both now became something of a battleground, a major focus of all the anxieties created by the disintegration of community structures around them. One result of this was to produce an increase in early marriage. For one way of escaping the claustrophobic tensions of family life was to start a family of your own. And given the total lack of accommodation for young single people in the new developments, as well as the conversion of cheap rented accommodation into middle-class owner-occupied housing, the only practicable way to leave home was to get married. The second outcome of generational conflict (which may appear to go against the trend of early marriage, but in fact reinforced it) was the emergence of specific youth subcultures in opposition to the parent culture. And one effect of this was to weaken the links of historical and cultural continuity, mediated through the family, which had been such a strong force for solidarity in the working-class community. It is perhaps not surprising that the parent culture of the respectable working class, already in crisis, was the most 'productive' vis-à-vis subcultures; the internal conflicts of the parent culture came to be worked out in terms of generational conflict. What I think seems to happen is that one of the functions of generational conflict is to decant the kinds of tensions which appear face to face in the family and replace them by a generational specific symbolic system so that the tension is taken out of the interpersonal context and placed in a collective context, and mediated through various stereotypes which have the function of defusing the anxiety that interpersonal tension generates.

It seems to me that the latent function of subculture is this—to express and resolve, albeit 'magically', the contradictions which remain hidden or unresolved in the parent culture. The succession of subcultures which this parent culture generated can thus all be considered as so many variations on a central theme—the contradiction, at an ideological level, between traditional working-class puritanism, and the new hedonism of consumption; at an economic level between a future as part of the socially mobile elite, or as part of the new lumpen. Mods, Parkers, Skinheads, Crombies, all represent, in their different ways, an attempt to retrieve some of the socially cohesive elements destroyed in their parent culture, and to combine these with elements selected from other class fractions, symbolizing one or other of the options confronting it.

It is easy enough to see this working in practice if we remember that subcultures are symbolic structures, and must not be confused with the actual kids who are their bearers and supports.* Second, a given life style is made up of a number of symbolic subsystems, and it is the way these are articulated in the total lifestyle which constitutes its distinctiveness. There are basically four subsystems—and these can be divided into the relatively 'plastic' forms—dress and music, which are not directly produced by the subculture, but which are selected and invested with subcultural value in so far as they express its underlying thematic; and then the more 'infrastructural' forms—argot and ritual, which are more resistant to innovation but of course reflect changes in the more plastic forms. I suggest here that Mods, Parkers, Skinheads, Crombies are a succession of subcultures which all correspond to the same parent culture and which attempt to work out, through a system of transformations, the basic problematic or contradiction which is inserted in the subculture by the parent culture. So you can distinguish three levels in the analysis of subcultures; one is historical analysis which isolates the specific problematic of a particular class fraction, in this case the respectable working class; second, a structural or semiotic analysis of the subsystems and the way they are articulated and the transformations which those subsystems undergo from one subcultural moment to another; and third, the phenomenological analysis of the way the subculture is lived out by those who are the bearers and supports of the subculture. No real analysis of subculture is complete without all those levels being in place.

To go back to the diachronic string we are discussing, the original Mod lifestyle could be interpreted as an attempt to real-ize, *but in an imaginary relation*, the conditions of existence of the socially mobile white-collar worker. While their argot and ritual forms stressed many of the traditional values of their parent culture, their dress and music reflected the hedonistic image of the affluent consumer. The lifestyle crystallized in opposition to the Rockers (e.g. the famous riots in the early sixties) and it seems to be a law of subcultural evolution that its dynamic comes not only from the relations to its own parent culture, but from the relation to subcultures belonging to *other class fractions*, in this case the manual working class.

The next members of our string—the Parkers or Scooter boys—were in some senses a transitional form between the Mods and Skinheads. The alien elements introduced into music and dress by the Mods were progressively de-stressed and the indigenous components of argot and ritual reasserted as the matrix of subcultural identity. The Skinheads themselves carried the process to completion. Their lifestyle in fact represents a systematic inversion of the Mods—whereas the Mods explored the upwardly mobile option, the Skinheads explored the lumpen. Music and dress again became the central focus of the lifestyle; the introduction of reggae (the protest music of the West Indian poor) and the 'uniform' (of which more in a moment) signified a reaction against the contamination of the parent culture by middle-class values, and a reassertion of the integral values of working-class culture—through its most recessive traits—its puritanism and chauvinism. This double movement gave rise to a phenomenon sometimes called 'machismo'—the unconscious dynamics of the work ethic translated into the out-of-work situation; the most dramatic example of this was the epidemic of 'queer-bashing' around the country in 1969–70. The Skinhead uniform itself could be interpreted as a kind of caricature of the model worker—the self-image of the working class as distorted through middle-class perceptions; a metastatement about the whole process of social mobility. Finally the Skinhead lifestyle crystallized in opposition both to the Greasers (successors to the Rockers) and the hippies—both subcultures representing a species of hedonism which the Skinheads rejected.

Following the Skinheads there emerged another transitional form variously known as Crombies, Casuals, Suedes, etc. (the proliferation of names being a mark of transitional phases). They represent a movement back towards the original Mod position, although this time it is a question of incorporating certain elements drawn from a middle-class *subculture* —the hippies, which the Skinheads had previously ignored. But even though the Crombies etc. have adopted some of the external mannerism of the hippy lifestyle, such as dress and soft drug use, they still conserve many of the distinctive features of earlier versions of the subculture.

If the whole process as I have described it seems to be circular, forming a closed system, then this is because subculture, by definition, cannot break out of the contradiction derived from the parent culture; it merely transcribes its terms at a micro-social level, and inscribes them in an imaginary set of relations.

But there is another reason. Apart from its particular, thematic, contradiction, every subculture shares a general contradiction which is inherent in its very conditions of existence. Subculture invests the weak points in the chain of socialization, between the family/school nexus, and integration into the work process, which marks the resumption of the patterns of the parent culture for the next generation. But subculture is also a compromise solution between two contradictory needs: the need to create and express *autonomy and difference* from parents and, by extension, their culture; and the need to maintain the security of existing ego defences and the *parental identifications* which support them. For the initiate subculture provides a means of 'rebirth' without having to undergo the pain of symbolic death. The autonomy it offers is thus both real, but partial, and illusory, as a total 'way of liberation'. And far from constituting an improvized *rite de passage* into adult society, as some anthropologists have claimed, it is a collective and highly ritualized defence against just such a transition. And because defensive functions predominate, ego boundaries become cemented to subcultural boundaries. In a real sense subcultural conflict (i.e. Greasers versus Skinheads, Mods versus Rockers) serves as a displacement of generational conflict both at a cultural level, and at an interpersonal level within the family. One consequence of this is to foreclose artificially the natural trajectory of adolescent revolt. For the kids who are caught up in the internal contradictions of a subculture, what began as a break in the continuum of social control can easily become a permanent hiatus in their lives. Although there is a certain amount of subcultural mobility—i.e. kids evolving from Mods to Parkers, or even switching subcultural affiliations—Greasers 'becoming' Skinheads, there are no career prospects as such! There are two possible solutions; one leads out of subculture into early marriage, and, as we have seen, for working-class kids this is the normal solution. Alternatively, subcultural affiliation can provide a way in to membership of one of the deviant subgroups which exist in the margins of subculture and often adopt its protective coloration, but which nevertheless are not structurally dependent on it; such groups as pushers, petty criminals, junkies, even homosexuals.

This leads us into another contradiction inherent in subculture. Although as a symbolic structure it *does* provide a diffuse sense of affinity in terms of a common lifestyle, it does not in itself prescribe any crystallized group structure. I believe that it is through the function of *territoriality* that subculture becomes anchored in the collective reality of the kids who are its bearers, and who in this way become not just its passive support but its conscious agents. Territoriality is simply the process through which environmental boundaries (and foci) are used to signify group boundaries (and foci) and become invested with a subcultural value. This is the function of football teams for the Skinheads, for example. Territoriality is thus not only a way in which kids live subculture as a collective behaviour, but the way in which the subcultural group becomes rooted in the situation of its community. In the context of the East End it is a way of retrieving the solidarities of the traditional neighbourhood, which have been destroyed by redevelopment. The existence of communal space is reasserted as the common pledge of group unity—you belong to the Mile End mob in so far as the Mile End belongs to you. Territoriality appears as a magical way of expressing ownership; for the Mile End is owned not by the people but by the property developers. Territorial division therefore appears within the subculture, and in the East End mirrors many of the traditional divisions of sub-communities: Bethnal Green—Hoxton—Mile End—Whitechapel—Balls Pond Road, etc. Thus in addition to conflict between subcultures, there also exists conflict within them, on a territorial basis. Both these forms of conflict can be seen as displacing or weakening the dynamics of generational conflict, which is, in turn, a displaced form of the traditional parameters of class conflict. (. . .)

Note

* This paper was written in 1970, and this section was a provisional statement which somewhat underestimated material factors in the formation of subcultures, and therefore remains within an idealist problematic. For a revision of this position, see P. Cohen and D. Robins, *Aspects of the Youth Question*, Penguin (forthcoming).

6 The elasticity of evil: changes in the social definition of deviance

Albert K. Cohen

I

(. . .) Durkheim said that even in a society of saints there would still be crime.[1] By this he meant that, if all those acts we know as crime were extinguished, small differences in behaviour that have no moral significance would take on new and larger meaning. (. . .)

The issue can be broadened to include the definition of evil generally. Is there an inveterate tendency to redefine poverty, misery, injustice, oppression, and so on in such a way that, regardless of what we do about them, we will always have a plenitude of social problems and sociologists will never be out of work? We are all familiar with the notion that the sense of deprivation is always relative, that it depends not on objective circumstances alone but on the benchmarks or reference points from which we measure. Is there a tendency always to move those benchmarks in such a way that the sum of perceived evil will approximate a constant?

(. . .) The subject is not the constancy of evil, which is debatable, but its elasticity, which I take to be a fact, and the mechanisms that might account for its expansion and contraction. Furthermore, I am not, in this context, concerned with evil or social problems generally, but with that species of evil we call deviance —that is, the failure of human conduct to meet the standards or rules by which human beings themselves judge that conduct.

Durkheim's own explanation of what we might call 'Durkheim's paradox' was ingenious. Crime, he says, consists of acts that offend strong collective moral sentiments. Crime could disappear and the society of saints be ushered in only if the strength of those sentiments increased to the point at which they neutralised or outweighed the sentiments favouring the commission of those acts. But, he says, 'the very

cause which would thus dry up the sources of criminality would immediately open up new ones.' The reason is that

> these strong states of the collective consciousness cannot be thus reinforced without reinforcing at the same time the more feeble states, whose violation previously gave birth to mere infraction of convention—since the weaker ones are only the prolongation, the attenuated form, of the stronger. Thus robbery and simple bad taste injure the same single altruistic sentiment, the respect for that which is another's. . . . But, if this sentiment grows stronger, to the point of silencing in all consciousness(es) the inclination which disposes man to steal, he will become more sensitive to the offences which, until then, touched him but lightly.

It would be a short step from this to argue that, for any given society, the amount of crime would tend to approximate a constant. That is, if the collective sentiments were to grow weaker rather than stronger, more serious offences would then be considered less serious, the barriers to the commission of those offences should be reduced, and their frequency should be increased. However, at the same time, the less serious offences should cease to be regarded as criminal altogether. The increase of crime at one end of the spectrum should, then, be offset by the decrease at the other. Durkheim himself, however, did not push the argument this far. He was merely trying to establish that society is unthinkable without crime, and that a certain amount of crime, provided it does not exceed a certain level, is 'normal' rather than 'pathological'.

From time to time other scholars have been intrigued by the idea of the elasticity and the inevitability of deviance. To my knowledge, however, only Leslie Wilkins[2] has pursued this theme in a rigorous and systematic way, and his general theory of deviance

Source: Oxford University Penal Research Unit occasional paper no. 7, Blackwell, 1974, pp. 5–28.

is one of the major accomplishments of modern deviance theory. It is a fairly complex theory and I must warn you that my brief synopsis does some violence to it. The basic idea seems to be that the perceived deviance of some class of events is closely related to its rarity or unexpectedness, as these are perceived by human actors. Rarity or unexpectedness do not depend on the absolute and objective frequency of events but on their relative frequency within the total information set of the individual or society. This information set can be graphed as the area under a normal, bell-shaped curve. The relative frequency or probability of some class of events can be described in terms of its distance in terms of standard deviations (or sigmas) from the mean of the distribution. For any given individual or society, the distances, in sigma terms, that define deviance of various degrees are more or less fixed. Although the total amount of information may change greatly over time, and although the relative frequency of some kinds of events will increase and of others decrease, so that their sigma distances from the mean will change, there will always be some kinds of events that will fall one sigma from the mean, some that will fall two sigmas, some three, and so on. There will, therefore, always be events that are perceived or experienced as only mildly deviant, others as more seriously deviant, and so on. To be sure, not all events that are rare will be seen as deviant (in either the 'good' or the 'bad' direction)—only those that are relevant to the value system of the society. Still, those events that are relevant to the value system will occur, within the information set, with different frequencies, the distribution of these frequencies will approximate the bell-shaped curve, and the degrees of deviance that will be attributed to them will, therefore, range from the trivial to the heinous. On the basis of a mechanism, then, suggested by modern information theory, Wilkins has arrived at a position strikingly similar to our extrapolation of Durkheim's theory, a theory which relies on an entirely different mechanism.

II

I move on now to the chief business of this paper, which is to introduce you to another approach to the subject of the elasticity of deviance, the approach from the perspective of identity theory.

Identity theory begins with the notion that each of us has an interest in being or becoming somebody special, sufficiently different from his fellows to save him from anonymity, and different in ways that enable him to command some admiration, respect, or affection. Our cultures provide us with a repertoire of possible selves, of the kinds of things it is possible for people to be: physicians, criminologists, devoted parents, friendly neighbours, Dutch uncles, efficient administrators, expert chess players, and so on. From this repertoire each of us chooses or assembles a package, and he gives people to understand that this

is the sort of person he is. (Choosing is, of course, always more or less constrained, and sometimes it amounts to acquiescing in a self that is socially ascribed and to which there is no alternative.) Some of the choices are more or less permanent commitments; some of them we may exchange for others in time. In either case, they constitute, in effect, a set of claims we make about ourselves. Having made these claims, our public reputations and our private satisfaction with ourselves depend on our success in fulfilling these claims. It is this set of claims about the self that I am calling 'identity' (. . .)

The payoff or rewardingness of a particular identity depends on two things. First, in the world in which we move, how much importance is attributed to the kinds of things at which we claim to excel? (. . .) Second, in the world in which we move, how different from others must we be, or how much better, for the difference to be noticeable and worthy of remark? (. . .)

The first question refers to the *scales* along which identities are measured. The second question refers to the *sensitivity* or discriminating power of the scale, and this in turn determines whether a difference of a given magnitude will in fact distinguish me from others.

We may liken our identities to produce that we are trying to sell in a competitive market. Promoting the product means claiming for it some attribute that our competitors' products lack and persuading our customers that this attribute or quality is in fact desirable. For example, in order to create a market for deodorants it was first necessary to convince people that it is obnoxious for people to smell like people. This is like trying to increase the saliency of a particular scale. Or we may try to get our customers to attend to differences of degree that formerly made no difference to them. For example, if my product is toothpaste, I may seek to educate my customers to place value on subtle differences in flavour or consistency or germicidal potency. So it is with our identities.

In both of these respects, systems for evaluating identities are liable to change, and especially so when large numbers of people find it difficult, under the established system, to carve out for themselves satisfactory identities; either they are deficient in the attributes that are currently creditable, or they are not sufficiently different to stand out from the herd, or that portion of the herd from whom they want to stand out. We may then get pressure to re-order the saliency of different scales, or to recognise new scales, which amounts to the invention of new virtues. Or the pressures may be for changes in the way the scales are graduated. In either case, if the pressures are effective, we have new ways of defining and measuring merit, and different sets of pay-offs attached to the various identities.

A critical determinant of the rewardingness of any particular system of defining merit is the way in which the attributes for which merit is claimed are actually distributed in a population. (. . .) A corollary of this is that for some people to be more reputable, some must be less. (. . .)

There are, of course, many dimensions or scales along which merit may be measured: strength, wealth, intelligence, practical skills, ancestry, good looks, and so on, and claims along scales like these figure in all of our identities. But most of us make claims to merit along some moral dimensions as well: we are kind, or generous, or loyal, or brave, or pious, or obedient, or something. We compete then in a market for moral goods. If the GNMP (the gross national moral product) increases and is so distributed that we all become saints, one likely consequence is that we will come to attribute to behavioural differences, measurable only in terms of inches, moral significance hitherto attributed to differences measurable in terms of yards. We will still be assured of a constant supply of wickedness. The conclusion to which we come is the same as Durkheim's and Wilkins'; the mechanism, however, is a different one.

The fineness or coarseness of the discriminations that we make are not determined solely by the interests of those whose identities are at stake. Systems for differential evaluation serve also as screening mechanisms for allocating status positions and other rewards, and the supply of these rewards may vary in elasticity. The number of places for incoming students in universities, of public offices to be filled by appointment or election, of vacancies in organisations, of pulpits waiting to be occupied importantly affect the significance that will be attributed to differences along the relevant scales of intellectual, technical, and moral competence, and the cutting points separating the elect from the lost. (. . .)

Among the scales from which we may construct the moral aspects of our identities are the ways in which we respond to the moral blemishes of others. One way of being moral, and of being more moral than others, is by enlisting as a soldier in the war against evil—by exposing and punishing other people's wickedness. One way of being immoral, or less moral, is by failing to fight, or to fight with the proper élan. Some of us, like J. Edgar Hoover or, before him, Savonarola, so excel in this speciality that we become generals and field marshals. But other ways of responding to other people's deviance may also be the basis for reputable identities. Some of us, for example, may cultivate the virtues of tolerance and understanding, or promote a definition of deviance as sickness and of ourselves as dedicated physicians practising the merciful art of healing. For every scale along which goodness and deviance are measured, then, there are ancillary scales having to do with how one deals with other people's transgressions. Again, however, for identities constructed along these lines to be rewarding, there must be material for them to work on; there must be evil to combat, to forgive, or to heal. Those of us who develop stakes in such identities are likely to be among that class of people whom Howard Becker calls moral entrepreneurs: people who take

the initiative in ferreting out deviance and legislating new prohibitions, thus helping to maintain the supply of the deviance on which their own identities feed.

I am not yet prepared to defend this as a general model of the way things really happen. I offer it, nonetheless, in a serious and not a playful spirit. It may, for example, have some bearing upon the oft-noted tendency of the young to be morally outraged at what their elders see as relatively minor blemishes, or as evils, to be sure, but of limited and dwindling proportions. Take, for example, in the United States, racial prejudice and discrimination, police brutality, and political corruption. All three have, I think, declined materially over the past fifty years or so, if measured by the standards of 1920. The parental generation, measuring the present by the past it knew when it was young, takes some satisfaction and claims some merit for what it has accomplished. But this is cold comfort to the new generation, especially to those who claim to be moral men who cannot be at peace with themselves in an immoral society. If they are to validate these identities, they cannot rest on the moral plateaux their parents have reached. Rather they redefine these plateaux as sea level and find new peaks to scale. I am not cynically suggesting that they are making mountains out of molehills, any more than their parents are making molehills out of mountains. I am certainly not arguing that we should be less indignant about, for example, the exclusion of blacks from American trade unions and other institutionalised denials of equal opportunity than an earlier generation was about lynching. I am simply saying that each generation establishes its own benchmarks from which to measure wickedness, and that one determinant of where it places these benchmarks is its interest in finding unfinished moral work that might provide opportunities for earning moral credit. (. . .)

A different example of shifting benchmarks, and of the consequences of such shifts, is provided by 'extremism' in political and social movements. For some of us, a key portion of our identity is our claim to be among the vanguard of some movement. The claim implies the existence, among the adherents of the movement, of a scale, or several scales, for measuring merit: ideological purity, refusal to compromise with evil, militant activism, readiness to sacrifice oneself—and perhaps others—for the cause. There is something tricky about vanguardism, however; it tends to be a self-liquidating form of distinction. To the degree that the vanguard is successful in persuading others to join them, they may destroy their own uniqueness. To maintain their position they may find it useful, or even necessary, to move the front lines—the benchmarks from which devotion to the cause is measured—forward. What was previously radical may now become reaction or collaboration with the enemy. Interestingly, their strongest contempt and most bitter denunciations may be reserved for those closest to them on the scale. But this is to be expected. In the market in which they compete, the most dangerous competitors are those with the most similar products.

At the same time, from the perspective of those who stand outside the movement, the benchmarks have also shifted, with the difference that, to those inside the movement and those without they read, respectively, 'State of Grace' and 'Absolute Evil'. Those who continue to occupy what was formerly the extreme position come now to be perceived as relatively moderate and responsible and their demands as not altogether unreasonable. As L. M. Killian[3] has pointed out, the new extremists, even though they may be a small minority and may never achieve their revised objectives, may, by strengthening the bargaining power of those whose programme is less frightening to the establishment, make a useful or even critical contribution to the common cause.

Again, I hope that this is not taken to be a simplistic attempt at a comprehensive theory of social movements. The redefinition of revolutionary virtue—the escalation of rhetoric and tactics—can never be fully understood as the outcome of a struggle for identity alone. Disillusionment with the ineffectiveness of a less radical posture may play an important part and so may, paradoxically, the experience of *success*. Success, by altering one's conception of what is possible, may encourage a revision upwards of aspirations and therefore of greater 'extremism'. Anyway, not everybody who is in the movement is in it to validate a radical identity and has a need, therefore, to be 'more radical than thou'.

Identity theory extends, in important ways, to the behaviour of men as members of collectivities. Collectivities—nations, corporations, universities, families, ball teams—whatever their ontological status, are social objects. They are perceived as entities and actors in their own right. They have names and reputations, and they are feared, loved, hated, respected, and despised. They too have—or seek to establish—identities, and these identities too are compounded of claims that may lie along different scales: size, piety, justice, democracy, wealth, neighbourliness, invincibility, cultural attainments, and so on. Members of a collectivity have a stake in the collectivity identity, or corporate self, because it is one of the components of their own identities. They bear its name and, to some extent, whatever taint or aura attaches to that name. It is a source to them of pride or shame. We should expect, therefore, that the rules by which men in collectivities judge one another will demand behaviour that supports the collectivity's claims to distinction in the society of collectivities.

In like manner, social categories within a collectivity —for example, ruling élites of nations and organisations—may bear a common name and to some extent a common identity. This identity may, in fact, constitute the major grounds for their claims to rulership, deference, and privilege. It will, therefore, represent the category as exceptionally endowed with whatever attributes legitimise possession of disproportionate

shares of these values. It will incorporate claims that the members of the category govern themselves by more exacting rules than the common run of people. Thus ruling aristocracies, military officer corps, and communist party cadres cultivate an ideology of *noblesse oblige*. Each member has an interest in getting his fellow members to behave, especially in public settings, in ways consistent with the stereotype they seek to propagate. By the same token, members have an interest also in projecting an image of the lower classes or ranks as deficient in those same attributes and in finding, publicising, or inventing instances of deficiency to lend colour to the identity they are trying to fasten upon them.

It is difficult, however, to maintain the self-imposed discipline of *noblesse oblige*, and therefore, the credibility of the common identity. Being in possession of superior power and the instruments of social control, and reluctant to punish their fellows to whom they are often linked by informal bonds of solidarity, they are better able to avoid the consequences of their derelictions and over time are prone to relax the stringency of their codes. Eventually, however, this is likely to impair, in the eyes of their subject classes, the credibility of their claims, and to create an identity crisis of a sort. They are then likely to take corrective action which may take the form of a tightening up of the code, severe and public measures against some of their own to demonstrate to the world at large their intolerance of imperfection, and sometimes to a cleansing or purge of their ranks.

In more general terms, collectivity identity, like individual identities, may become blurred from time to time or may lose its credibility and the value of membership in the collectivity will consequently decline. To restore its original value, it will be necessary to take steps to re-validate it. For example, research in boys' gangs has shown that gangs that have established a reputation for toughness and have then gone soft, so to speak, and moved into a more pacific, club-like phase, begin to lose morale, cohesion and members. As this happens, the gang's leaders, or would-be leaders, begin to adopt a more bellicose posture and to lead the gang into more aggressive adventures calculated to restore its fading image to its pristine intensity. Gang solidarity then tends to pick up and vagrant members to return to the fold.[4] (. . .)

III

My emphasis thus far has been on the expansion of deviance in order to accommodate those whose identities would be enhanced by creating new scales of virtue, by changing the saliency of existing scales, or by enlarging the moral significance of differences along these scales. But the elasticity of deviance is a two-way stretch. By the same token we would expect those whose identities would be spoiled[5] by these changes to deny or subvert them. The counterculture, for example, is not only an attack on the existing institutions of property, authority, social stratification, and so on. It is an attempt to render worthless the currency in terms of which the identities of those who dwell comfortably within those institutions are currently valued. Were the counterculture to succeed, moral as well as material fortunes would be wiped out. What the conventional world finds most obnoxious about the counter-cultural world is not that the latter carries on so scandalously in terms of conventional values, but the message that those carryings-on convey: the utter contemptibility of the conventional morality as a system for evaluating identities. Not all deviant behaviour carries this meaning. Most behaviour that falls short of conventional morality and the criminal law is, in R. K. Merton's[6] terms, 'aberrant' rather than 'non-conformist'. That is, it violates the rules and tries to get away with it, but it does not necessarily denounce those rules or propose alternatives. (. . .)

Identity may also be defended by abandoning a moral rule when the application of that rule ceases to ennoble the self but serves rather to damn it. That is, identity may be defended by contracting the definition of deviance. An example is provided by the U-2 incident of 1 May 1960. On that date a United States plane crashed in the USSR. The Soviets' claim that the plane was engaged in military photographic reconnaissance was denied on the highest authority, by the President of the United States himself. The denial was welcomed by the American people. However naïve it may seem to us today, at the time most Americans believed that the United States did not do that sort of thing in time of peace. (. . .) It became progressively clearer, however, to the point where nobody could seriously deny them, that the facts were as the Soviets claimed them to be, and that we had been doing this sort of thing for at least three years. We were confronted by a sort of identity crisis, a severe dissonance between an image of the collective self from which we drew great pride and satisfaction, and acknowledged facts that were irreconcilable with that image. The dissonance was effectively reduced, for most Americans, by reconsidering the standards in terms of which we judged ourselves and invited others to judge us. Aerial reconnaissance and espionage of all sorts in the defence of liberty were no vice. At any rate, *no* great power could realistically be expected to deny itself the weapons and tactics used by its enemies against it. Any fool knew that! (. . .)

My main burden in this section will be to discuss a different set of mechanisms for reducing deviance. These mechanisms are set in motion by the accumulating costs incurred by the expansion of deviance; they are ways of reducing these costs by reversing the processes we have been describing—i.e., by defining deviance out of existence or to deviance of a lesser degree.

First and most obvious of the costs are the material costs of coping with, of 'doing something about',

deviance. Merely to present people with lists of rules carries little information. As Durkheim also remarked, people learn the meaning of deviance and the seriousness with which it is regarded by noting the pains to which people go to track down offenders and inflict, in the name of the collectivity, punishment (or, we may add, therapy) upon them.[7] But the machinery of social control—the establishment for doing something about deviance—is expensive to run. It may become one of society's main consumers of energies, resources, manpower. As the costs mount so do the pressures to economise, and one way of economising is to reduce the amount of deviance there is to control by deciding that some of it is really not all that bad or even not bad at all. These changes in the rules can be formally made in legislative or judicial forums, or informally through systematic non-enforcement, which amounts to the same thing: rules become dead letters, deviance has been repealed. (. . .)

The costs of coping with deviance may be aggravated by a process that Leslie Wilkins calls 'deviance amplification'. Efforts to control behaviour by stigmatising it as deviant may have the effect of stimulating the production of that very behaviour. This may happen precisely *because* people may come to accept the deviant identities that other people tag them with, *because* they are treated as enemies of society, *because* they are cut off from and isolated from contact with conventionally behaving people. (. . .)

It may also happen that (. . .) efforts to control behaviour by making it a heinous crime may not only fail to stamp it out, but may produce a large volume of ancillary crime and associated evil more distressing than the evil to which the rule was addressed. Specifically, if the interdicted product or service is one for which the demand is imperious and inelastic, then its price will rise to compensate for the risks of trafficking in an illegal market, and people will devote their energies increasingly to finding illicit ways of obtaining it. They may compromise or even jettison other commitments, responsibilities, and relationships. In short, we may now have to contend, not only with addiction, but with a black market, with vast numbers of property crimes, and with lives and families in shambles. If the population that supports this system of control sees the connection between what they are doing and what is happening in the world of drug use and addiction, they may decide that drug use and addiction are 'really' not crimes, that they are really 'medical problems' rather than 'police problems', and seek other, less draconian ways of dealing with them. (. . .)

There is still another kind of negative feedback that may be more important than any of the others. It results from another set of costs, what I will call *relational* costs. These refer to the damage to valued human relationships created by increasing social distance among people. I have made use, earlier in this lecture, of an image of society as a sort of arena in which people compete with one another for status and repute, usually at the expense of other people's identities. Society is that, but it is not only that. It is also, and even more profoundly, a co-operative enterprise, or a network of such enterprises, in which the welfare and survival of each depends on the help, support, and complementary performances of others. To serve these purposes, there must be a certain amount of solidarity, trust, and mutual respect, and all members of the functioning social unit must feel that they gain something from the common enterprise. As people are driven farther and farther apart by invidious contrast, communication among them tends to decline, resentment and dissatisfaction, particularly among the lower-ranking members, to increase, trust to erode, and solidarity to weaken. If the status and authority of the higher ranking members are purchased at too high a cost to the identities of the lower ranking members, the respect tends to turn to hostility and churlishness. At the extreme, those who are spurned or condemned as base, low, and deviant characters have little incentive to give loyalty, hard work, and cheerful co-operation in return. The common enterprise and the secure position of those whose privileges or power depend upon its prospering are jeopardised. At such times we often see a compensatory process set in motion. This entails a reduction in social distance, an emphasis upon likeness rather than difference. Leaders and élites begin to practise the common touch, to moderate their claims to moral superiority—to being 'holier than thou'— to seek out and then acclaim the virtues of the common man, to increase their accessibility and mingle with the crowd, to be 'one of the boys'.[8] (. . .)

Similar processes can be observed in 'natural' work groups and in schools. In both kinds of situations, achieving recognition by doing better than your peers is a risky business. You risk being defined, in the first case, as a 'rate-buster', in the second case—in American universities at least—as a DAR, a 'damned average-raiser'. (. . .)

The critical question seems to be: 'Does the high achiever (morally or otherwise) gain at the expense of the others or do they somehow share in the glory?' If the effect is simply to cheapen the value of their performances and to change the distribution of rewards in a zero-sum game, he will probably be resented and punished by his peers. There is a good chance however, that, before he goes this far he will decide to join the others in a tacit 'conspiracy in restraint of trade'. If, on the other hand, he performs *on behalf of* the collectivity and his goodness attaches to the collectivity name so that everybody gains from it, he may then find himself in the situation of the saint or athletic hero.

Something like this has also been observed in the attempts of families to cope with deviance on the part of their members and has been called 'normalisation'. In the early stages of alcoholism or mental illness, family members are characteristically reluctant to confront the aberrant member, to label him 'crazy' or 'alcoholic'. For one thing, they find it painful, as I think we all do, to accuse people with whom they sustain daily, intimate, solidary relationships of degrading flaws. They empathise and identify with him too intimately. For another, they seem to sense that, if they label the deviant this way, he will take it to mean—and quite correctly, too—that he is no longer to be regarded as a fully dependable member of the group, and no longer entitled to whatever authority or responsibility he may have had; that this will produce in him feelings of alienation and resentment; and that this in turn will make it harder to draw him back into fully responsible participation in the group. The members therefore strive to interpret his behaviour as a minor and transitory aberration, as a normal response to an abnormal situation, or as an expression of one of these inexplicable but passing moods that 'all of us' are subject to—in short, to 'normalise' the behaviour. In the meantime, they try to accommodate to it by adjusting their own behaviour to take up the slack or overcome the problems created by his behaviour.

Finally (. . .) we see similar processes at work on a broader societal level when major social groupings or categories—black versus white, young versus old, men versus women—face one another with growing anger over a widening gulf of moral differences. As one group advances, in the name of morality and justice, demands for the reconstruction of the social order, and accuses the other of oppression, exploitation, corruption, or phlegmatic indifference to suffering, the response of the accused commonly follows a pattern consisting initially of patronising amusement, followed by irritation and annoyance, followed by burning and honest indignation. They label the demands and conduct of the accusers as outrageous, immoral, absurd, and even criminal. Each party stands convicted of deviance in the other's eyes. They become increasingly polarised and bitter. The issue may be settled and the situation stabilised in different ways, including the threat and reality of violence. But other forces are also at work to reverse the process, perhaps not to the point where differences are obliterated, but at least to the point where communication is restored and the breach narrowed. What will happen, and when, depends on many things, among which are the degree to which the contending parties need one another, the capacity of one to make trouble for the other, the intensity of their affective involvement in one another's lives. When the breach becomes frightening, we often see an effort to 'normalise' behaviour analogous to what we have seen on the level of the family. Ralph Turner,[9] writing of reactions to such things as black militancy and student protest, has noted the tendency to redefine deviancy as legitimate or at least understandable 'social protest'— exaggerated, perhaps, but to some extent justifiable protest at 'real grievances'—and some of the conditions under which this redefinition is most likely to occur. An effort is made to find some legitimacy in the other party's demands and concessions are made. What this amounts to is no less than a compromising of differences, a redefinition of right and wrong, to bring people together and get on with the common enterprise.

I believe that such a process is discernible in the chronic skirmishing, sometimes approaching war, in the relationships between the young and not-so-young. I think that the old have a greater need for the affection, respect, and company of the young than the young do for their elders. The old are greatly pained by the growing estrangement, and as this estrangement reaches into their own families, they find it increasingly distressing to treat the novel ideas and ways of the young as bald and unadulterated deviance. There is something more precious to be preserved than their received notions of good and evil: their ties to their own children. I believe that the last twenty years or so have seen an extraordinary movement on the part of the older generation in the moral directions pointed by their children, so that many of them now accept, with a sense of fitness and necessity, what they would once have rejected as preposterous. Sometimes the resolution is more like that of the religious wars; neither party embraces the views of the other, but one,

the other, or both come to see the difference as one that is not irreconcilable with mutual respect and continued civil relations.[10]

The gap is not closed, because this seems to be an era in which the young continue to forge ahead with new demands, and they continue to see their parents as mired in the hang-ups of the past, standing pat or moving with glacial slowness. Moral movement, like observations from a train in a railway station, is relative to the position of the observer and what he can see from his window. I would describe the situation as a moving generation gap. Whether the elders are moving fast enough, or even whether the young are moving fast enough, is a question not proper to this paper. I would suggest, however, that there are few people of my generation reading this whose eternal verities of twenty or ten or even five years ago have not been displaced by a new set of eternal verities. Nor have we moved because—as we might like to think—we are solitary swimmers in a featureless sea, guided only by an inner moral compass; we have, rather, been swimming desperately in the wake of younger swimmers that we might not be cut off and left behind.

Notes

1 Émile Durkheim, *The Rules of Sociological Method*, University of Chicago Press, 1938, pp. 67–71. First published in French, 1895.
2 *Social Deviance: Social Policy, Action, and Research*, Englewood Cliffs, N.J., Prentice-Hall, 1965, pp. 45–104.
3 'The significance of extremism in the Black revolution', *Social Problems*, 20, summer 1972, pp. 42–9.
4 Leon R. Jansyn, 'Solidarity and delinquency in a street corner group', *American Sociological Review*, October 1966, pp. 600–4.
5 The expression is Erving Goffman's: *Stigma*, Prentice-Hall, 1963; Penguin, 1970.
6 In R. K. Merton and R. Nisbet, eds, *Contemporary Social Problems*, Harcourt Brace Jovanovich, 1971, pp. 829–32.
7 See George Simpson, *Emile Durkheim on the Division of Labor in Society*, New York, Macmillan, 1933, pp. 105–10. Durkheim was not speaking here of deterrence, which operates through fear. He had in mind the role of punishment in clarifying and strengthening the moral sentiments themselves. A similar point could be made about rewards for goodness. Such rewards may not only be goods and services that are bartered for right conduct. The conferral of rewards, especially publicly, officiously, and ceremonially—may perform the *didactic* function of helping to define, in a way that the mere reiteration of rules cannot, the precise meaning of goodness and its degrees.
8 The most convincing examples are those that come out of our own everyday experience. Is there anybody here who, having done the right thing in order to be true to his conscience, has never tried afterwards to 'explain it away' as something he 'had to do' for some starkly utilitarian reason ('In my business you can't *afford* to lie to your customers') or to avoid trouble ('I couldn't

take a chance on being caught cheating')? The sin of goodness is extenuated by denying its honourable intention. Or is there anybody who has not concealed his moral revulsion at somebody else's conduct, or who has criticised it on purely pragmatic grounds only, in order to avoid the presumption of moral superiority?
9 'The public perception of protest', *American Sociological Review*, 34, December 1969, pp. 815–31.
10 Jackson Toby had members of a sociology class interview students on interaction between parents and children over moral issues. '. . . the class members found that a dilemma is posed for parents who discover that their son or daughter has done something of which they disapprove: smoking pot, not attending church services, wearing shoulder-length hair, or resisting the draft. Parents either insist on conformity and run the risk of breaking off relations with a beloved child or they tolerate disapproved behavior because to them the solidarity of the family is more important than conformity. The students' interviews showed that most parents storm and threaten until they realise that their children will not back down; then they discuss; and finally they accept, sometimes with bitterness, often with grudging approval for a principled disagreement.' Later, he summarised these findings to a meeting of parents, and the comments of the parents modified the conclusions in one particular: 'our interviews with students frequently portrayed as a revision in parental attitudes what the parents claimed was only the fatalistic acceptance of an irreconcilable difference.' However, 'students and parents agreed fairly well as to what was going on between the generations.' Jackson Toby, 'Educational possibilities of consensual research', *American Sociologist*, 7, February 1972, pp. 11–13.

7 Problems of sociological fieldwork: a review of the methodology of 'Hightown Grammar'

Colin Lacey

(. . .) To write about one's own methodology and the problems of doing empirical research is inevitably to make gross assumptions about one's own theoretical orientations and even one's biography. While it is impossible in a short chapter to trace out the full implications of these two factors, I think it is important to outline some of the basic strands of my intellectual development. In this way I can provide the material for developing an internal as well as external critique of my methodology and view of sociology. This is the sort of exercise from which both reader and author can benefit. (. . .)

In contrast with the essentially narrow, competitive, crossword-puzzle, problem-solving world of the grammar school in which 'society' is static, or ignored, my interests developed through the political and union activities of my family and in reading Marx, Shaw and Russell. These writers, from very different vantage points, have a purposive, change-orientated view of society. All imply that it is possible to intervene into the dialectic relationship between personality and social structure, or, put in more recent terminology, into the intricacies of the social construction of reality. My concern was to promote those sorts of intervention that would lead towards an egalitarian society. It seemed to me self-evident that greater social and economic equality would lead to greater democracy and greater potential for the full development of individual personality, in turn leading to greater diversity and richness in social life.

This concern has remained a central underlying purpose. It predates my interest in sociology as such and it provides a support for my continuing interest. In fact, I feel sure that my interest in sociology depends on my seeing it as a tool, as a means for progressing towards a realisation of this purpose. If I felt that sociology was not 'useful' in this way, I

would probably turn to politics or journalism, or something.

If this perspective—sociology as a 'means' rather than an 'end'—implies that my involvement is peripheral, a dilettante interest, I must challenge the assumption. I see sociology as a vital analytical tool in the reconstruction of our society. As such, I am centrally interested in all aspects of its development, its theory, methodology and technology, its legitimation and status, not just in the eyes of an elite group of academics, but also the wider society. I see sociology developing to provide a basic ingredient in a generally available education in a self-understanding society.[1] In my view, the converse is also true; sociology as an end in itself, as an academic exercise among many others, is to run the risk of reducing its status to that of a hobby for secure academics. (. . .)

My own experience has led to a particular blend or synthesis of methodologies and approaches and, before embarking on the central core of the paper, it is perhaps important to know in outline what these were, up to the point at which I undertook my study of Hightown Grammar.

In 1960, after teaching for three years in Birmingham and London, I joined the Department of Social Anthropology at Manchester to read for an MA. Manchester at that time was diversifying. Max Gluckman had encouraged Tom Lupton to start micro-studies of shop-floor organisation. In particular, they were concerned to apply the careful fieldwork techniques of the social anthropologist to the attainable areas of industrial society. Participant observation is a much maligned word, but in Manchester at that time it involved the fullest possible transfer; that is, the transfer of the whole person into an imaginative and emotional experience in which the fieldworker learned to live in and understand the new world he had chosen. I have not used the term 'role-playing'. I think in retrospect I would use the term 'role-taking' (or role-making in the sense used by Turner)

Source: Marten Shipman, ed., *The Organisation and Impact of Social Research*, Routledge & Kegan Paul, 1976, pp. 63–81, 83–8.

because this implies involvement of the self in an exposed and vulnerable position. There could be no clinical distancing, the fieldworker was expected to enter in and take punishment until he or she had learned to survive.

The analyses of a wide range of fieldwork situations were united by Manchester's own peculiar blend of conflict theory and functionalism. The mix varied. The Marxists pushed criticisms of the structural reification, timelessness and ossification apparent in the earlier studies, and at one time a fruitful line in MAs developed in which classical anthropology was reanalysed using a conflict framework.[2] The idea of the study of Hightown Grammar grew out of this mix of social anthropological fieldwork techniques, a theoretical concern for social processes and social conflict and my own experiences within schools. (. . .)

General aims

It is easy to guess from what I have said already that a major concern of the study would be with the under-achievement of working-class children in grammar schools. Behind this lay an unworked-out set of assumptions that if schools changed sufficiently to allow radically different rates of upward mobility, there would be a chain reaction in which sets of unchallenged assumptions about the structure of our society would be examined and criticised; for example the public schools (privileged education) and eventually the inheritance of wealth (privileged social position). It seemed to me that the internal logic of a meritocratic society would bring about changes that were an essential precursor to the posing of problems relevant to an egalitarian society. Until those steps were taken most people would be unable even to understand this later stage. It would remain in the realms of utopian philosophy until the necessary experiences, gleaned from the 'meritocratic versus inherited social position' battle, had become a common occurrence. I was not unduly worried by some of the results of Dennis Marsden and Brian Jackson's work[3] which revealed the strains experienced by working-class families through the upward mobility of one of their daughters or sons. They were both walking contradictions of the 'defection' argument.

Problems of bias

Even before the study began a number of colleagues expressed opinions about the viability of the research. There were two strands of this opinion that foresaw as inevitable a broad irreducible streak of bias running through the study.

One group, made up mainly of the more traditional social anthropologists, argued that given my experience and closeness to schools, I could not obtain the necessary distance and therefore objectivity to make a study.

Another group expressed the view that it would be

important to 'open up' grammar schools to criticism and implied that a hefty dose of the 'right' bias would be a good thing.

I disagreed with both these views. I could not agree that the 'outsider' had to be totally outside the culture (for some social anthropologists an outsider also meant an outsider from the point of view of race and language in order to achieve 'distance' and make so called 'objective' judgments). Even at the planning stage of the study I felt disinclined to go along with the notion of 'objectivity'. Instead I saw it as my job to develop views of the system from a number of points of view—those of the parent, the teacher and the child. It was, I believed, through presenting these views and, more importantly, the intersection of these views that the researcher could illustrate the dynamics of the system. This task seemed to me to call for a specific approach to field-work requiring sympathy, naïvete, openness, a willingness to help where possible, and an ability to let people talk.

I had rather more sympathy with the second view. After all, every study is constrained by the limitations of the researcher and those limitations extend to the constraints imposed by the researcher's values. These may limit his insights and curb his imagination. This criticism made me determined to go beyond the usual social anthropological methodologies and construct models that could be tested at various points in the analysis. In this way my biases could perhaps lead to omission, but they could hardly lead me to constructing an account based simply on my prejudices. There are many instances of these tests within the book; the connection between 'performance' and 'behaviour' of pupils made by the teachers and the construction of sociometric indicators to test 'differentiation' and 'polarisation', for example. The chapter most affected by social anthropological criticism and which itself contains an implied criticism of much social anthropological writing, is chapter 7 where case studies are presented within an analytical framework to counteract the tendency to make 'apt illustration' from fieldwork notes. (. . .)

The field of study

The merging of one's own value orientations and the work already accomplished in the chosen field of study is a complex interaction to unravel. However, it bears directly on the development of my methodology and needs some explanation.

The major weakness of existing research in the field seemed to me to be its adherence to a simplistic theoretical model, around which elaboration had almost ceased to be useful. Bernstein has described this as an input–output model. I prefer the term a 'black-box' model of research because it describes more accurately the nature of its limitations. The model assumes that in order to demonstrate an effect it was necessary only to show correlations between inputs and outputs. The contents of the black box, the social mechanisms and process, are neglected and not without cost. At whatever level of generality the model is used, societal or institutional, the element of social determinism is extremely strong. There is nothing to counteract it. Nor is there anything inherent in the methodology associated with the model to challenge the notion that the factors considered by the researchers are necessarily the salient ones as far as the social actors are concerned. The framework of variables to be considered is imposed; there is little chance of developing an alternative perspective from these research reports. There is one further drawback to this type of research. It produces descriptions of the school system that document, for example, the under-achievement of working-class children but give very little indication of how the school system or individual teachers can change in order to alter or modify this effect. In fact, because of the 'social determinism' element and the imposition of an analytical framework which rarely contains variables relating to the school or the classroom, the implication for many teachers is that it cannot be changed. The idea that the causes of under-achievement are to be found solely in low material standards or attitudes held by working-class families, I found totally unacceptable. Elaborations of this model can only take place in three directions:

1 Superimposition of different scales of black-box model.[4]
2 Elaboration of input and output variables.
3 A moving black box, a follow-through cohort study.

In the period leading up to the study the major effort of researchers in this field had undoubtedly been in the direction of the elaboration of variables. Asher Tropp had attempted to put almost all the variables anyone had ever heard of in a complex model of causation. Stephen Wiseman had attempted a similar exercise with ecological units and in the USA number crunching proceeded on a grand scale.

It seemed useful, therefore, to work within the framework of established black-box findings and to use if necessary the first alternative of different scales of application of the model, but to work in the opposite direction, that is, from within the black-box out towards the community and wider society. The implication of this direction was that I would need to immerse myself within the system in order to be able to feel, recognise and describe the constraints of the various roles within the school and be able to put together a descriptive model or series of models of the processes that I recognised. The idea was to describe the system from a number of perspectives. Only in this way did I feel that I could include an analysis of how these intersected to produce a social process.[5]

The research strategy

(. . .) The broad strategy which we worked out for Hightown was as follows:

1 To choose the school carefully with advice from HMIs and the local authority and present definite reasons for our choice.
2 To enter the system above the school in the authority system and move down through the authority system to the school.
3 To teach (participate) and observe, but to move slowly out of the teacher role towards a research role with much greater flexibility and access to pupils.

The decision to teach was reached through a number of lines of reasoning:

1 Entry to the school would be facilitated if the headmaster felt he was getting additional, worthwhile teaching assistance.
2 Long-term participation (a three-year period of association was initially proposed) in a school would require the researcher to build up in the first period a fund of goodwill on which to draw to support his later roles. These would be incomprehensible to the staff of the school unless they were developed out of an established relationship. Within the last year of the study it was expected that the contact would be attenuated and a monitoring relationship set up. This attenuation could, it was felt, put some strain on the relationship with the school. If a considerable fund of goodwill had been created, this would not be so marked.
3 Most importantly, to gain a teacher perspective as one of the essential elements in putting together a pattern of interacting perspectives.

My operational strategy was designed to examine the 'process' of grammar school education as it developed from the lower school, through the middle school to 'O' level and the sixth form. I therefore selected three points in the school from which I could eventually cover the whole school during a three-year period, albeit at different intensities of participation and observation (see Table 7.1).

Table 7.1

Start with	(3 years later)	→finish with	methods
1 1st year (120 boys)		→3rd year	teach and observe
2 4th year (120 boys)		→6th formers or leavers	observe
3 Lower 6th form (50 boys)		→leavers	teach and observe

The intention was to teach for the first year and then give up most of my teaching to move towards a freer research role in the second and third years. In the third year in particular I planned to move outside the school into the community and the home.

The plan was far too ambitious. In my desire to include everything I saddled myself with a killing workload and a far too attenuated contact with any one form at any time. It required a tremendous effort to keep going on all fronts and learn in some detail the personal data for 300 boys. By the second term I had given up the detailed study of the sixth form. Looking back, it is easy to see this mistake in the context of a common participant observer syndrome. The feeling develops very vividly at times that the real action, the real social drama is going on somewhere else. While you are in the staffroom there are important discussions in the headmaster's study; while you observe 3A, a really critical series of lessons is being taught in the room next door. The root of this feeling is in the nature of one's task. The participant observer records as accurately as possible selected aspects of the everyday life of people in everyday situations. There is rarely anything dramatic, there is rarely anything of outstanding interest taking place.[6] Classrooms can be incredibly boring places. The interest in the situation emerges as the observer puts together the pieces of an amorphous and intricate puzzle in which even the pieces are not defined. Until this is done the tensions and strains on the researcher are considerable and the 'it is all happening somewhere else' syndrome flourishes. (. . .)

Change of research role

The movement from a teacher role to a freer, research role was accomplished smoothly without too much strain on my relationships with the staff. Several incidents did, however, illustrate the potential dangers of living within the informal worlds of both staff and pupils. Before relating these incidents, it is necessary to describe the actual changes that took place in my research role.

Even during my first year at the school my role differed considerably from a normal teacher role:

1 I was not employed by the local authority and had a special negotiated relationship with the headmaster, which staff and pupils knew about.
2 I observed classes on a regular basis, something other teachers never did.
3 I was more available to staff and pupils, who found me interested in matters not usually discussed by other teachers.

This interest gradually established a flow of information from both staff and pupils about things they thought would interest me, from formal events like public speaking competitions to informal events like fights in the park. My change in role was accomplished by building on these existing differences and moving out of my classroom teaching role (I retained some sixth-form teaching). I held informal discussion groups, which were established during school hours (boys could be excused Religious Education) but continued during lunch-time on an informal basis. I visited the homes of boys to talk over problems with them or their parents. I entered informally into conversations with boys in and around the school and invited boys to my home, which was only a few hundred yards from the school. I entered into informal activities after school and eventually ran a school cricket team (second-year). The final stage of this change of role was never achieved. I had planned to move out of the school and meet boys in clubs, coffee bars and informal out-of-school groups like regular street football games. (. . .)

The change in role brought an increase, gradual at first and then steep, in the amount of information received about pupils. The discussion group ranged over topics from marriage and sex through general questions about the school and its relation to jobs and earning a living, to individual masters and the boys' relationships with them. One of the groups had been 'set up' to include most of the anti-group boys from one fifth-year class and this group of between six and eight boys provided without doubt the most stimulating and entertaining discussions I enjoyed in the school. The discussions had a life of their own.

It was this group that proposed and carried out an experiment within the classroom to 'prove' that Mr Bradley 'had his knife into' Morris, one of the boys in the group. Morris was programmed to keep quiet and work diligently for the first part of the lesson. Then when the classwork had been set and the customary buzz of conversation had established itself, he was to start talking like the rest of the class. According to the boys in the group, Mr Bradley noticed him immediately and told him off. They were delighted with their experiment and its result.

The completely informal, relaxed relationship with this group of boys contrasted with the classroom role of the teacher and the formal relationship generated through the teaching persona. The group was noisy, frank, sometimes lewd, but always (in marked contrast to the classroom) interested and sincere. I was constantly surprised by the degree to which they appreciated their own position in the school, and the way in which they were prepared to examine and discuss it. (. . .)

My participation and involvement in these situations demonstrated more clearly than any other method the way some aspects of the pupil/adolescent world are cut off from the teacher and the school. They also demonstrated the way the teacher role is shaped and constrained by pressures outside the classroom emanating from the community, mediated by the headmaster and to some extent enshrined in the behaviour codes and punishment system.

Classroom observation perspective versus teaching perspective

I hope it is still clear at this stage that although there were numerous supporting reasons for the decision to teach, the main purpose was to explicitly take on a teacher perspective. This linked into the theoretical orientation of examining the system in action and describing the dynamic interaction of perspectives.

The classroom observation perspective

The question of how much I as an observer altered the teachers' or children's behaviour in the classrooms I observed seemed secondary to the question of how I interpreted what went on. After I had observed all the masters teach it was quite clear that I could fairly easily observe in most of the classes within the school. However, there were some masters who were going to be constantly worried by my presence. One began by asking me 'What are you doing?', asked three or four times 'What shall I tell the boys?', and finished after the lesson by asking pointedly, 'What can you possibly get out of it?'. He conveyed such a strong sense of discomfort that I felt I could not possibly impose myself. Afterwards, a group of masters asked me about what went on in his lesson. Hardly waiting for an answer, they told me that he once made a boy stand in the corner for a whole lesson holding a sand bucket in one hand and a water bucket in the other. He tried to teach ecology by linking it with the Queen's progress round Australia. 'What do these boys care about the Queen's visit? He's a nut.' It was quite clear that the man was under pressure from both his fellow teachers and his pupils and I decided I could not increase the pressures he already felt.

The contrast between my observer position, feeling free from the responsibilities of classroom control, and his tense irritability, worried by problems of the classroom and lack of support from his colleagues, highlights the problem of the observer versus the teacher perspective. Remarks from boys that I interpreted as lacking menace or threat obviously stung him into reprisals of sarcasm or anger.

During my first weeks in the school a whole series of incidents made it apparent that the observer role would enable me to achieve a pupil perspective far more easily than a teacher perspective. An example from my field notes illustrates this:

Mr P. was shouting at a pupil, already in tears, as I went into the staffroom.

Mr P. (bursting into the staffroom with great energy and in great anger): Hill, been at it again—truanting!

Mr J: What again—not for a whole day!

Mr P: No, he's been in the toilets for my lesson. He'd lost his exercise book and was frightened to face up to it. I asked him whether he thought he'd get away with it—he said 'No'.

Mr J: He was caned about a fortnight ago for truanting.

Later, I left the staffroom and passed the boy in the corridor. Mr P. was ranting at him in a loud voice:

Mr P: What sort of trick do you think this is—deceitful, low, sly—shows you've no backbone.

Hill was crying—tears streaming down his face.

Mr J. (later): The only way to cure it is to cane him and cane him every time he does it.

(Later) Mr P. laughed about his 'go' at Hill and said it was all a big act.

The teaching perspective

An important finding from teaching at Hightown was that even with a strong desire to break out of an authoritarian mould—as I had—my teaching represented only a modified version, a more permissive version, of this style. And I had not been subjected to pressures from the bottom streams of the third and fourth years.

This experience led me to observe the socialisation of young teachers. I noted their timetables, the gossip about them, the sort of advice they were given and finally, when they were judged to be ready, their induction into the 'hard core', that is the group of teachers who were central to the running of the school.

All these investigations showed that their induction was also structured by the processes of differentiation and polarisation. Young teachers had to deliver their message, define and do battle with the enemy. The enemy had to be the right enemy. Young teachers were sanctioned (as I was) for helping the wrong types. Interestingly enough, they were also sanctioned for being too emotionally involved and too zealous in their punishment of wrong-doers. The contrasting examples of Mr P. and Mr L. illustrate this last point.

As I described previously, Mr P. pointed out that his outburst had been 'all an act'. In doing this he was distancing himself from the person we had all seen ranting in the corridor. That person had been an aspect of the 'mask', the 'teaching persona', and the act had been a necessary unpleasant act that did not, however, reflect on the personal qualities of Mr P. In this Mr P. had been successful. Other masters had made it clear that they were on his side by suggesting the cane and also by allowing the remark to go unchallenged. Mr L., describing a similar incident, told how he had caught a boy called Chegwin in some wrong-doing by standing in a doorway and grabbing him as he passed. Mr L. spoilt the whole story as far as the rest of the staff were concerned by ending with an emotional outburst: 'I despise him, detest him and loathe him.'

This lack of 'professional distance' led a senior member of staff to interrupt Mr L. with a long discourse on how to handle Chegwin. 'He is a decent boy at heart, despite a poor home background, and a limited ability—we will have to ride him with a light rein.' He carried on in this way until Mr L. left the room. His departure was marked by the raising of eyebrows, the puffing of cheeks and the shaking of heads.

I still remember vividly incidents like those described by Mr P. and Mr L. As an observer of these incidents, I felt little affinity with the teachers—all sympathy for the pupils. Yet, as is clear in the description above, many of these teachers were sincere in their desire to help and encourage their pupils to learn. I had to teach in order to appreciate the strains that on occasion turned reasonable, kindly men into bellowing, spiteful adversaries. They left the staffroom in good order; it was in the classroom that things went wrong.

The section in Hightown on the teaching persona was the outcome of that experience. It was only through the creation of a second 'me' that I could survive. Every event within the classroom had to be judged on two criteria: first, its own merit; second, its effect on the classroom order. It is the second criterion that is difficult to understand as an observer.

Why did Mr A. suddenly pounce on Jimmy Green? Answer—because Jimmy Green was venturing, perhaps unwittingly, across a threshold that Mr A. judged was essential for his control in the classroom. Practically all the teachers at Hightown were domino theorists and most had learned their lesson through hard experience.

Mr L. failed to develop this second self. He was progressively sanctioned by other teachers not so much for the intensity of his outbursts or the punishments he inflicted, but for the fact that they were 'real'. They were spiteful and vindictive. Finally, he was humiliated by his exclusion from the staff cricket XI which was to play the school First XI. He had failed to develop a 'teaching persona' acceptable to staff and pupils. My participation as a teacher enabled me to watch with a certain amount of apprehension but with fascination the way in which small group pressures were manipulated by prominent members of staff. The manner of his exclusion illustrated the working of these informal pressures.

The staff team[7] had been put up in the staffroom. Mr L. came into the room and all went quiet. He went over to the notice board and looked at this list. He turned angrily to the staff who were there and complained that there were some people in the team who were not really 'staff' (I was not in the room), and with a 'flourish' took out his pen and crossed off his name as twelfth man. As he left the room there were guffaws of laughter and a number of choice comments.[8] Mr L. left the school for a job 'nearer home' that did not involve a promotion. I felt it important not to underestimate the pressures on the new staff to conform to staff mores.

Participant observation and other methods

The core methodology of the study was without question participant observation and observation. Yet in a sense the most important breakthrough for me was the combining of methods, and the integration of these in the analysis.

The observation and description of classrooms led quickly to a need for more exact information about individuals within the class. I used school documents to produce a ledger of information on each boy, for example, address, father's occupation, previous school, academic record, and so on. I built on this record as more information became available from questionnaires. This information enabled me to check immediately any change taking place in seating arrangements or patterns of association outside the classroom and, most importantly, to interpret the significance of the development within the established structure of the classroom.

During the early period of observation a high proportion of the incidents and interaction I observed were simply not interpretable. I could see one boy punch another, or two boys joking; I could record the interaction between a master and a boy; but very little added up to produce a structure, or even more important, the sorts of processes I was attempting to unravel.

The key series of observations for me was in the music teacher's class as described in Hightown. He simplified the pattern of interaction by imposing his mental picture of the class on to the physical layout of the classroom. This idea of the teacher having a crude conceptual picture of the class began to fit into my own developing ideas of the classes I taught. I had vivid impressions of the 'clever boys', the 'good boys', the ones that 'rarely understood', the 'bad boys' and the 'characters', but the others, probably between a half and a third of the class fell into the undifferentiated middle. Even after teaching them for some months, it was difficult to recall their names.

The idea of the master imposing his view of the class on to the pupils in the class followed quickly from this and soon I was looking for a way to check how far this imposition[9] actually affected the way children thought of each other, interacted with each other, maybe even made friends with each other. The idea of using sociometric indicators for this purpose, therefore, evolved from the problem and my relationship with it.

The analysis of the sociometric data was a completely new experience. I can still remember the excitement as one after the other of my ideas about the patterns of relationships held up during the analysis. The conceptualisation of the processes of differentiation and polarisation grew out of this interplay between observation and analysis of sociometric data. Looking back, I now feel that I under-utilised these findings in my subsequent fieldwork (by this time I was also teaching at Manchester University). I collected no direct *interview* evidence on the complexities of the structure. I watched for changes and knew about quarrels, fights and emerging friendships, but I omitted to ask questions about how other boys viewed boys outside their own group. I did this in a formal questionnaire (can't get on with choices and diaries etc.) in a systematic way, but should have done much more in following up particular insights from the analysis in informal but patterned interviews. The next strategy would have been to explain my analysis

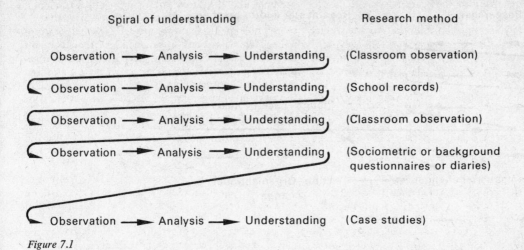

Figure 7.1

to some of the boys who were closest to me so that they would also act as observers of the process. I began this with two boys, one who was having difficulty within the sixth form and for whom the analysis provided an explanation of his difficulties, a form of therapy, and one who did in fact start to provide me with a self-generated analysis of his own classroom.

What I did was to 'escalate insights' through moving backwards and forwards between observation and analysis and understanding (see Figure 7.1). This diagram could obviously be complicated by adding a large number of cycles in this process,[10] as I built upon certain methods and insights to achieve a deeper understanding. An important point to notice is the way certain insights or levels of understanding are associated with certain methods of data collection. In other words, just as methods such as classroom observation or participation as a teacher have impor-

tant theoretical repercussions, so other methods such as the use of sociometric data and their analysis using sociomatrices can have important effects on the shaping of concepts and the deepening of one's understanding (which is perhaps another way of saying the same thing). I feel very strongly that the world under investigation seen through one method of collecting data becomes enormously distorted by the limitations of that data and the available methods of analysis.

The extension of this process that I began at Hightown and would certainly advocate in any similar study can be portrayed schematically as shown in Figure 7.2.

The effect of this strategy is twofold:

1 the pupil or teacher is brought into the analysis as a positive contributor—almost as a research assistant;
2 the system itself is changed in that within it there are new perspectives that might alter it.

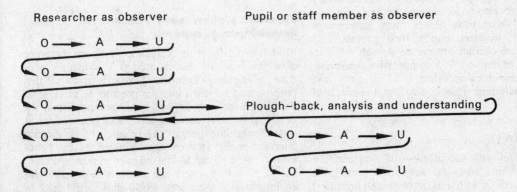

N.B.
Plough–back can occur at the stage when the researcher has developed models.

Figure 7.2

62   *Colin Lacey*

Researcher   Headmaster and/or teachers

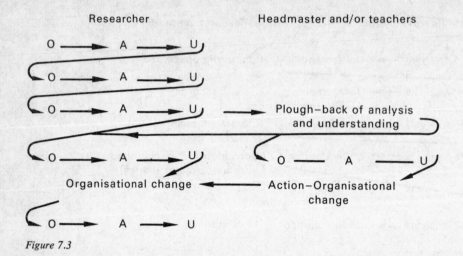

Figure 7.3

This second possibility occurred at Hightown but not in any planned way. It was coincident that while I was studying the school there was a change of headmaster. After a year in which the new head allowed the school to run itself in the established pattern, he introduced fairly radical changes. He de-streamed the third year (which I was studying) and did not stream any of the new intakes. In the span of two years the innovation worked its way through the school which was then completely de-streamed.[11] There is no way for me to assess how far these changes were the result of ideas and intentions that the new headmaster brought to the school and how far what had happened was influenced by the results of my analysis of differentiation and polarisation, of which he was aware. In any event, it does provide us with a paradigm for the study of innovation and an interventionist research strategy (see Figure 7.3).

In other words, episodes of innovation and change can occur through research and augment that research. These innovations need not occur by chance—they can be planned episodes in research designs.

It will be some time before local government administrators, teachers, pupils, their parents, and researchers have enough confidence in each other to plan this sort of research in a co-operative enterprise. Yet this degree of co-operation is a necessary first step in understanding, if not controlling, the effects of innovation.

Levels of analysis

I dealt early on with the problem of bias and my desire to combine so-called subjective participant observation methods with tests of the models produced using so-called objective indicators. There is also a second dimension on which it is possible to obtain a critical appraisal of the explanations produced by the research. The research was planned to integrate a

number of levels of analysis from the macro to the micro levels. It is therefore possible to test this research by examining the compatibility of the models produced at these different levels. In the book 'Hightown' I begin by describing the community and the school within the community, and taking an historical view before moving into the school. Within the school I investigate one cohort, then a single class within the cohort, and finally I move on to individual case studies. In the final chapter on staff-pupil relations I link back again to more macro levels when I consider the career and professional aspects of the teacher role. A useful critical exercise is to read the book from this point of view to establish how far the six to eight models used in the description of Hightown Grammar contain mutually contradicting or reinforcing elements. In order to use the book as a sociological tool (as opposed to using it to learn about schools), and it was certainly intended as such, it seems essential to approach the book critically in this way. (. . .)

The models produced: some substantive and methodological consequences

Models are a form of explanation and are therefore closely related to understanding. The models produced in Hightown Grammar have an interventionalist purpose and are therefore designed to be as close as possible to the everyday world of the teacher and the pupil, while still retaining analytical penetration. It was not the intention of the research to be directly interventionalist (the changes initiated by the head-master ran counter to the planned research design) but to provide teachers and students in general with an insight into their own world that would lead to further debate, the redefinition of problems and the development of new solutions. There was also an attempt to diagnose the points at which intervention is possible.

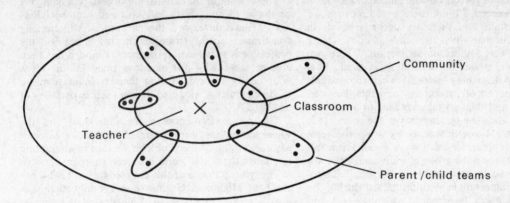

Figure 7.4

The model of the classroom as a competitive arena, presented in Hightown Grammar, is a good example of this aspect of the study. The analysis shows how the teacher perspective transforms competition between individuals with markedly different resources relevant to the competitive process into a competition of equals. In other words, the dynamics of the classroom situation make demands that cause the teacher (often despite his private feelings) to ignore the fact that the unequal resources of his pupils are relevant to the classroom.

Figure 7.4 shows the classrooms within the community. The pupil-parent teams are included in shaded areas that represent the size of each team's resources. The teacher frequently conducts the competitive aspects of the classroom process as though the differences made explicit in the diagram do not exist. My interest in the classroom situation has developed out of this early insight. It has involved me in two lines of inquiry and in developing new models of co-operation between sociologists and educationalists.

One line of enquiry has been into the training and professional socialisation of teachers. The question that intrigues me is how far the teacher and the school can modify the classroom role of the teacher in the face of community, professional and situational pressures. The possibilities of change seem to exist at three different levels:

1 A modification of the competitive process, to produce less differentiation and polarisation. This would involve a modification of the teacher's role within the classroom and perhaps some organisational change.
2 A reversal of the usual allocation of resources—that is, a compensatory strategy—in the face of pupil and community pressures.
3 A redefinition of the teacher role and the part played by education within the community.

Most innovation and change within our schools aims at levels 1 or 2 above,[12] yet each year a large number of student-teachers leave universities and colleges ideologically committed to level 3 change. This process of change and the way in which the ideological commitment of young teachers merges with the gradually changing practice within our schools have become some of my central sociological concerns. Future research of this problem seems to me to require co-operative work including social scientists, curriculum analysts, pupils and teachers. The practical forms of co-operation have still to be worked out but the theoretical notion behind this co-operation has been suggested earlier in this section.

The second set of ideas that emerged from the Hightown study and have continued to involve me have been the concepts of differentiation and polarisation. These processes resulted from a particular and perhaps peculiar set of pressures on a group of individuals, held together in an organisation over a considerable period of time and for long periods of each work day. They therefore emerged clearly within an observational study and were capable of documentation using sociometric techniques, despite the inaccuracies of the technique and 'noise' created by other processes at work within the classroom. Viewed at a higher level of abstraction these processes are, however, a universal characteristic of human relationships. Actors within social settings pursue social strategies that derive from the actors' experiences and expertise, are relevant to the social situation and are an attempt to achieve the often complex and unworked-out aims of the actor. The peculiar nature of Hightown Grammar rests in the similarity of the pupils' previous experience and expertise, the uniformity and pervasiveness of the academic and behaviour norms imposed by the school and the persistence of the social situation (the classroom) over a period of years.[13] In these conditions the strategies chosen by individual pupils have a regularity and persistence and sometimes a generality that persuades the teacher (or the observer) that what he is observing is the individual and not simply strategies adopted by that individual; that is, strategies that are sometimes chosen, sometimes forced on him in the situation in which he is observed. I think there were times when I made this mistake and there are perhaps points in Hightown Grammar when the analysis comes close to obscuring this important distinction. There are times, however, when the distinction is clear. It is made clear by describing incidents where individuals manipulate one set of subcultural understandings in one situation and then partake actively in another— for example, when the teacher leaves the room. It is made clear at a theoretical level by using the term subculture to represent a set of ways of behaving and understanding, and not a group of individuals who are indelibly marked by experiences or personal characteristics. (An important realisation gained during the Hightown study was the extent to which the selection and adoption of a social strategy was part of a competitive process. Another competitive element in the classroom is the battle to define the situation so that strategies over which one has established a claim are seen to be most relevant to the situation.) Changes in the social setting could markedly upset even well-established structures made up of stable patterns of adopted strategies. This was obviously the case within the discussion group I describe in this chapter. I also have records of a case study where I experimented with the usual situational constraints affecting the selection and running of a cricket team. My team of 'playground'[14] cricketers brought forth a new set of relationships and behaviours on a Saturday morning that again had little relationship to the usual school-day patterns.

These insights have had important repercussions on the way I now view adolescent and adult socialisation. I have developed the concept of situationally constrained social strategies in my study of the professional socialisation of teachers, and it has been able to show why, for example, many of the ideas adopted by students during their training year are relatively quickly modified during their early years of teaching.

The connection between the individual and the social setting has been illustrated by these researches. My conception of the problems we face in attempting to change the social world has been sharpened.

The main purpose of this chapter was to review my study of Hightown Grammar in broadly methodological terms. In doing so, I illustrated the way in which my own values and preoccupations fed into the research and were developed and refined during and through the process of the research.

Finally I described how these developments directed me into new channels of enquiry.[15]

If a student can obtain a feeling for the movement from ideas to research—a realisation that his deepest concerns about society can become the basis for his research—then he need see no dichotomy between these two. If he can come to see, in time, that the research, grounded in these deep concerns, is his principle means of refining and developing them, then he will hardly settle for their separation.

Notes

1 See R. J. Frankenberg, 'The Sociologically-Minded Person and the Self-Understanding Society', University of Keele Inaugural Lecture, 1970.

2 See Peter Worsley's MA thesis and Curl Bequest Essay. My own MA thesis would have been an application of Weber's paradigm of authority types to a Nilotic tribe in which institutionalised leadership failed to develop.

3 B. Jackson and D. Marsden, *Education and the Working Class*, Routledge & Kegan Paul, 1962. See also M. Young and P. Willmott, *Family and Kinship in East London*, Routledge & Kegan Paul, 1957, for the effects of upward mobility on the relationships within working-class families.

4 The model can be applied to the education system as a whole (Coleman's 'Equality of Opportunity' Report), grammar schools (Early Leaving Report—probably the purest 'black box' design), or individual schools (Julienne Ford's *Social Class and the Comprehensive School*, Routledge & Kegan Paul, 1970).

5 I was anxious to present more than a simple 'underdog' perspective. The discussion between Alvin Gouldner and Howard Becker on this issue is illuminating with respect to many facets of the problem but overlooks the central issue. If sociologists are involved (for whatever reasons) in 'understanding' social behaviour then it is important to understand the full complexity of the problem. The intersection of perspectives seems

essential to this end. See J. D. Douglas, ed., *The Relevance of Sociology*.

6 Bill Watson summed up this aspect of fieldwork in a remark made in a seminar. He was describing how he arrived in an African village full of romantic notions of what he would find. 'What did I find? A load of unemployed bums!'

7 The staff team had a regular fixture list and Mr L. had played on a number of occasions. He had bought all the correct kit and had taken lessons, in his own time. He was very keen and had let it be known. The staff/school match was a special fixture. The whole school turned out to watch and there was competition for places in the team.

8 The incident was described to me later by teachers who were obviously satisfied by the way things had gone.

9 In *Hightown Grammar* I made a clear distinction between 'differentiation'—imposed by the teacher—and 'polarisation'—a product of pupil interaction. I have modified my position slightly and now see differentiation to be in part produced by intra-group competitive pressures. In other words, the children themselves bring into the classroom some of the criteria which will be used in judging them. They use these criteria to judge each other.

10 The process is portrayed here as inevitably progressive. My filing system shows otherwise. On more than one

occasion I worked hard and enthusiastically on a 'new' idea, only to find an almost identical analysis planned or even worked out in my filing system.

11 C. Lacey, 'Destreaming in a "pressured" academic environment', in S. J. Eggleston, ed., *Contemporary Research in the Sociology of Education*, Methuen, 1975, pp. 148–66.

12 It has been a characteristic of sociologists studying education that they have underestimated the difficulties of bringing about even minor changes. They have not, therefore, made studies of innovation and change in educational institutions. This is an important gap in the literature.

13 Only the family presented the actor with a more consistent set of pressures over a longer period of time.

14 A term sometimes used to describe those boys who played cricket with a soft ball and an asphalt wicket. They specialised in fast bowling and big hitting and were regarded by some teachers (e.g. First XI coach) as poor cricketers in the proper sense. They were not normally chosen as school team members. I chose my second-year school team mainly from 'playground' cricketers. It was outstandingly successful.

15 J. S. Coleman, 'A research chronology', in P. E. Hammond, ed., *Sociologists at Work*, Basic Books, 1964.

Section II The organization of teaching

8 The teacher in the authority system of the public school*

Howard S. Becker

Institutions can be thought of as forms of collective action which are somewhat firmly established.[1] These forms consist of the organized and related activities of several socially defined categories of people. In service institutions (like the school) the major categories of people so defined are those who do the work of the institution, its functionaries, and those for whom the work is done, its clients. These categories are often subdivided, so that there may be several categories of functionaries and several varieties of client.

One aspect of the institutional organization of activity is a division of authority, a set of shared understandings specifying the amount and kind of control each kind of person involved in the institution is to have over others: who is allowed to do what, and who may give orders to whom. This authority is subject to stresses and possible change to the degree that participants ignore the shared understandings and refuse to operate in terms of them. A chronic feature of service institutions is the indifference or ignorance of the client with regard to the authority system set up by institutional functionaries; this stems from the fact that he looks at the institution's operation from other perspectives and with other interests.[2] In addition to the problems of authority which arise in the internal life of any organization, the service institution's functionaries must deal with such problems in the client relationship as well. One of their preoccupations tends to be the maintenance of their authority definitions over those of clients, in order to assure a stable and congenial work setting.

This paper deals with the authority problems of the metropolitan public school teacher. I have elsewhere described the problems of the teacher in her relations with her pupils,[3] and will here continue that discussion to include the teacher's relations with parents,

principals, and other teachers. The following points will be considered in connection with each of these relationships: the teacher's conception of her rights and prerogatives, her problems in getting and maintaining acceptance of this conception on the part of others, and the methods used to handle such problems. The picture one should get is that of the teacher striving to maintain what she regards as her legitimate sphere of authority in the face of possible challenge by others. This analysis of the working authority system of the public school is followed by a discussion which attempts to point up its more general relevance. The description presented here is based on sixty long and detailed interviews with teachers in the Chicago public schools.[4]

Teacher and parent

The teacher conceives of herself as a professional with specialized training and knowledge in the field of her school activity: teaching and taking care of children. To her, the parent is a person who lacks such background and is therefore unable to understand her problems properly. Such a person, as the following quotation shows, is considered to have no legitimate right to interfere with the work of the school in any way:

> One thing, I don't think a parent should try and tell you what to do in your classroom, or interfere in any way with your teaching. I don't think that's right and I would never permit it. After all, I've a special education to fit me to do what I'm doing, and a great many of them have never had any education at all, to speak of, and even if they did, they certainly haven't had my experience. So I would never let a parent interfere with my teaching.

Hers is the legitimate authority in the classroom and the parent should not interfere with it.

Source: *Journal of Educational Sociology*, 27, November 1953, pp. 128–41; also appeared in H. S. Becker, ed., *Sociological Work*, Aldine.

Problems of authority appear whenever parents challenge this conception, and are potentially present whenever parents become involved in the school's operation. They become so involved because the teacher attempts to make use of them to bolster her authority over the child, or because they become aware of some event about which they wish to complain. In either case the teacher fears a possible challenge of her basic assumption that the parent has no legitimate voice with regard to what is done to her child in school.

In the first instance, the teacher may send for the parent to secure her help in dealing with a 'problem child.' But this is always done with an eye to possible consequences for her authority. Thus, this expedient is avoided with parents of higher social-class position, who may not only fail to help solve the problem but may actually accuse the teacher of being the source of the problem and defend the child, thus materially weakening the teacher's power over her children:

You've got these parents who, you know, they don't think that their child could do anything wrong, can't conceive of it. If a teacher has to reprimand their child for something they're up in arms right away, it couldn't be that the child did anything wrong, it must be the teacher. So it's a lot of bother. And the children come from those kind of homes, so you can imagine that they're the same way.

The teacher feels more secure with lower-class parents, whom she considers less likely challengers. But they fail to help solve the problem, either ignoring the teacher's requests or responding in a way that increases the problem or is personally distasteful to the teacher.

[They] have a problem child, but you can't get them to school for love or money. You can send notes home, you can write letters, you can call up, but they just won't come.

If you send for [the child's] parents, they're liable to beat the child or something. I've seen a mother bring an ironing cord to school and beat her child with it, right in front of me. And, of course, that's not what you want at all.

This tactic, then, is ordinarily dangerous in the sense that the teacher's authority may be undermined by its consequences. Where it is not dangerous, it tends to be useless for strengthening authority over the child. This reinforces the notion that the parent has no place in the school.

Parents may also become involved in the school's operation on their own initiative, when they come to complain about some action of the school's functionaries. Teachers recognize that there are kinds of activity about which parents have a legitimate right to complain, for which they may legitimately be held responsible, although the consequences of the exercise of this right are greatly feared. They recognize,

that is, that the community, in giving them a mandate to teach, reserves the right to interfere when that mandate is not acted on in the 'proper' manner. As Cooley put it:[5]

The rule of public opinion, then, means for the most part a latent authority which the public will exercise when sufficiently dissatisfied with the specialist who is in charge of a particular function.

Teachers fear that the exercise of this latent authority by parents will be dangerous to them.

One form of this fear is a fear that one will be held responsible for any physical harm that befalls the child:

As far as the worst thing that could happen to me here in school, I'd say it would be if something awful happened someplace where I was supposed to be and wasn't. That would be terrible.

This, it is obvious, is more than a concern for the child's welfare. It is also a concern that the teacher not be held responsible for that welfare in such a way as to give the parents cause for complaint, as the following incident makes clear:

I've never had any trouble like that when the children were in my care. Of course, if it happens on the playground or someplace where I'm not there to watch, then it's not my responsibility, you see. . . . My children have had accidents. Last year, two of the little boys got into a fight. They were out on the playground and Ronald gave Nick a little push, you know, and one thing led to another and pretty soon Nick threw a big stone at Ronald and cut the back of his head open. It was terrible to happen, but it wasn't my fault, I wasn't out there when it happened and wasn't supposed to be. . . . Now if it had happened in my room when I was in there or should have been in there, that's different, then I would be responsible and I'd have had something to worry about. That's why I'm always careful when there's something like that might happen. For instance, when we have work with scissors I always am on my toes and keep looking over the whole room in case anything should happen like that.

Another area in which a similar fear that the parents will exercise their legitimate latent authority arises is that of teaching competence; the following incident is the kind that provokes such fears:

There was a French teacher – well, there's no question about it, the old man was senile. He was getting near retirement. I think he was sixty-four and had one year to go to retire. The parents began to complain that he couldn't teach. That was true, of course, he couldn't teach any more. He'd just get up in front of his classes and sort of mumble along. Well, the parents came to school and put so much pressure on that they had to get rid of him.

The teachers' fear in these and similar situations is that intrusion by the parents, even on legitimate grounds, will damage their authority position and make them subject to forms of control that are, for them, illegitimate—control by outsiders. This fear is greatest with higher class groups, who are considered quick to complain and challenge the school's authority. Such parents are regarded as organized and militant and, consequently, dangerous. In the lower-class school, on the other hand:

> We don't have any PTA at all. You see, most of the parents work; in most families it's both parents who work. So that there can't be much of a PTA.

These parents are not likely to interfere.

To illustrate this point, one teacher told a story of one of her pupils stabbing another with scissors, and contrasted the reaction of the lower-class mother with that to be expected from the parents of higher status whose children she now taught:

> I sure expected the Momma to show up, but she never showed. I guess the Negroes are so used to being squelched that they just take it as a matter of course, you know, and never complain about anything. Momma never showed up at all. You take a neighborhood like the one I'm teaching in now, why, my God, they'd be sueing the Board of Education and me, and there'd be a court trial and everything.

It is because of dangers like this that movement to a school in such a neighborhood, desirable as it might be for other reasons, is feared.[6]

The school is for the teacher, then, a place in which the entrance of the parent on the scene is always potentially dangerous. People faced with chronic potential danger ordinarily develop some means of handling it should it become 'real' rather than 'potential,' some kind of defense. The more elaborate defenses will be considered below. Here I want to point to the existence of devices which teachers develop or grow into which allow them some means of defense in face-to-face interaction with the parent.

These devices operate by building up in the parent's mind an image of herself and of her relation to the teacher which leads her to respect the teacher's authority and subordinate herself to it:

> Quite often the offense is a matter of sassiness or back-talk. . . . So I'll explain to the parent, and tell him that the child has been sassy and disrespectful. And I ask them if they would like to be treated like that if they came to a group of children. . . . I say, 'Now I can tell just by looking at you, though I've never met you before, that you're not the kind of a person who wants this child to grow up to be disrespectful like that.

> You want that child to grow up mannerly and polite.' Well, when I put it to them that way, there's never any argument about it. . . . Of course, I don't mean that I'm not sincere when I say those things, because I most certainly am. But still, they have that effect on those people.

The danger may also be reduced when the teacher, over a period of years, grows into a kind of relationship with the parents of the community which minimizes the possibilities of conflict and challenge:

> If you have a teacher who's been in a school twenty years, say, why she's known in that community. Like as not she's had some of the parents as pupils. They know her and they are more willing to help her in handling the children than if they didn't know who she was.

If the teacher works in the same neighborhood that she lives in she may acquire a similar advantage, although there is some evidence that the degree of advantage is a function of the teacher's age. Where she is a middle-aged woman whose neighborhood social life is carried on among those women of similar age who are the parents of her pupils, the relationship gives her a distinct advantage in dealing with those same women in the school situation. If, however, she is a younger woman, parents are likely to regard her as 'a kid from the neighborhood' and treat her accordingly, and the danger of her authority being successfully challenged is that much greater.

In short, the teacher wishes to avoid any dispute over her authority with parents and feels that this can be accomplished best when the parent does not get involved in the school's operation any more than absolutely necessary. The devices described are used to handle the 'parent problem' when it arises, but none of them are foolproof and every teacher is aware of the ever-present possibility of a parent intruding and endangering her authority. This constant danger creates a need for defenses and the relations of teacher and principal and of teacher to one another are shaped by this need. The internal organization of the school may be seen as a system of defenses against parental intrusion.

Teacher and principal

The principal is accepted as the supreme authority in the school:

> After all, he's the principal, he is the boss, what he says should go, you know what I mean. . . . He's the principal and he's the authority, and you have to follow his orders. That's all there is to it.

This is true no matter how poorly he fills the position. The office contains the authority, which is legitimated in terms of the same principles of professional education and experience which the teacher uses to legitimate her authority over parents.

But this acceptance of superiority has limits. Teachers have a well-developed conception of just how and toward what ends the principal's authority should be used, and conflict arises when it is used without regard for the teachers' expectations. These expectations are especially clear with regard to the teacher's relationships with parents and pupils, where the principal is expected to act to uphold the teacher's authority regardless of circumstances. Failure to do this produces dissatisfaction and conflict, for such action by the principal is considered one of the most efficient defenses against attack on authority, whether from parents or pupils.

The principal is expected to 'back the teacher up'— support her authority—in all cases of parental 'interference.' This is, for teachers, one of the major criteria of a 'good' principal. In this next quotation the teacher reacts to the failure of a principal to provide this:

That's another thing the teachers have against her. She really can't be counted on to back you up against a child or a parent. She got one of our teachers most irate with her, and I can't say I blame her. The child was being very difficult and it ended up with a conference with the parent, principal, and teacher. And the principal had the nerve to say to the parent that she couldn't understand the difficulty, none of the other teachers who had the child had ever had any trouble. Well, that was nothing but a damn lie, if you'll excuse me. . . . And everybody knew it was a lie. . . . And the principal knew it too, she must have. And yet she had the nerve to stand there and say that in front of the teacher and the parent. She should never have done that at all, even if it was true she shouldn't have said it. [Interviewer: What was the right thing to do?] Well, naturally, what she should have done is to stand behind the teacher all the way. Otherwise, the teacher loses face with the kids and with the parents and that makes it harder for her to keep order or anything from then on.

This necessity for support is independent of the legitimacy of the teacher's action; she can be punished later, but without parents knowing about it. And the principal should use any means necessary to preserve authority, lying himself or supporting the teacher's lies:

You could always count on him to back you up. If a parent came to school hollering that a teacher had struck her child, Mr. D—— would handle it. He'd say, 'Why, Mrs. So-an-So, I'm sure you must be mistaken. I can't believe that any of our teachers would do a thing like that. Of course, I'll look into the matter and do what's necessary but I'm sure you've made a mistake. You know how children are.' And he'd go on like that until he had talked them out of the whole thing.

Of course the teacher would certainly catch it later. He'd call them down to the office and really give them a tongue lashing that they wouldn't forget. But he never failed them when it came to parents.

Not all principals live up to this expectation. Their failure to support the teacher is attributed to cowardice, 'liberalism,' or an unfortunate ability to see both sides of a question. The withholding of support may also, however, be a deliberate gesture of disapproval and punishment. This undermining of the teacher's authority is one of the most extreme and effective sanctions at the principal's command:

[The teacher had started a class project in which the class, boys and girls, made towels to be given to the parents as Christmas presents.] We were quite well along in our project when in walked this principal one day. And did she give it to me! Boy! She wanted to know what the idea was. I told her it was our Christmas project and that I didn't see anything the matter with it. Well, she fussed and fumed. Finally, she said, 'Alright, you may continue. But I warn you if there are any complaints by fathers to the Board downtown about one of our teachers making sissies out of their boys you will have to take the full responsibility for it. I'm not going to take any responsibility for this kind of thing.' And out she marched.

Teachers expect the same kind of support and defense in their dealings with pupils, again without regard for the justice of any particular student complaint. If the students find the principal a friendly court of appeal, it is much harder for the teacher to maintain control over them.[7]

The amount of threat to authority, in the form of challenges to classroom control, appears to teachers to be directly related to the principal's strictness. Where he fails to act impressively 'tough' the school has a restless atmosphere and control over pupils is difficult to attain. The opposite is true where the children know that the principal will support any action of a teacher.

The children are scared to death of her [the principal]. All she has to do is walk down the hall and let the children hear her footsteps and right away the children would perk up and get very attentive. They're really afraid of her. But it's better that way than the other.

Such a principal can materially minimize the discipline problem, and is especially prized in the lower-class school, where this problem is greatest.

The principal provides this solid underpinning for the teachers' authority over pupils by daily acts of 'toughness,' daily reaffirmations of his intention to keep the children 'in line.' The following quotation contrasts successful and unsuccessful principal activity in this area:

For instance, let's take a case where a teacher sends a pupil down to the office. . . . When you send a child down to this new principal, he goes down there and he sits on the bench there. . . . Pretty soon, the clerk needs a messenger and she sees this boy sitting there. Well, she sends him running all over the school. That's no punishment as far as he's concerned. Not at all.

The old principal didn't do things that way. If a child was sent down to the office he knew he was in for a rough time and he didn't like it much. Mr. G.—— would walk out of his office and look over the children sitting on the bench and I mean he'd look right through them, each one of them. You could just see them shiver when he looked at them. Then he'd walk back in the office and they could see him going over papers, writing. Then, he'd send for them, one at a time. And he'd give them a lecture, a real lecture. Then he'd give them some punishment, like writing an essay on good manners and memorizing it so they could come and recite it to him the next day by heart. Well, that was effective. They didn't like being sent to Mr. G——. When you sent someone there that was the end of it. They didn't relish the idea of going there another time. That's the kind of backing up a teacher likes to feel she can count on.

The principal is expected to support all teachers in this way, even the chronic complainers who do not deserve it:

If the principal's any good he knows that the complaints of a woman like that don't mean anything but he's got to back her just the same. But he knows that when a teacher is down complaining about students twice a week that there's nothing the matter with the students, there's something the matter with her. And he knows that if a teacher comes down once a semester with a student that the kid has probably committed a real crime, really done something bad. And his punishments will vary accordingly.

The teacher's authority, then, is subject to attack by pupils and may be strengthened or weakened depending on which way the principal throws the weight of his authority. Teachers expect the principal to throw it their way, and provide them with a needed defense.

The need for recognition of their independent professional authority informs teachers' conceptions of the principal's supervisory role. It is legitimate for him to give professional criticism, but only in a way that preserves this professional authority. He should give 'constructive' rather than 'arbitrary' orders, 'ask' rather than 'snoop.' It is the infringement of authority that is the real distinction in these pairs of terms. For example:

You see, a principal ought to give you good supervision. He ought to go around and visit his teachers and see how they're doing—come and sit in the room awhile and then if he has any constructive criticism to make, speak to the teacher about it privately later. Not this nagging bitching that some of them go in for, you know what I mean, but real constructive criticism.

But I've seen some of those bastards that would go so far as to really bawl someone out in public. Now that's a terrible thing to do. They don't care who it's in front of, either. It might be a parent, or it might be other teachers, or it might even be the kids. That's terrible, but they actually do it.

Conflict arises when the principal ignores his teachers' need for professional independence and defense against attacks on authority. Both principal and teachers command sanctions which may be used to win such a conflict and establish their definition of the situation: i.e., they have available means for controlling each other's behavior. The principal has, as noted above, the powerful weapon of refusing to support the teacher in crucial situations; but this has the drawback of antagonizing other teachers and, also, is not available to a principal whose trouble with teachers stems from his initial failure to do this.

The principal's administrative functions provide him with his most commonly used sanctions. As administrator he allocates extra work of various kinds, equipment, rooms, and (in the elementary school) pupils to his teachers. In each category, some things are desired by teachers while others are disliked—some rooms are better than others, some equipment newer, etc. By distributing the desired things to a given teacher's disadvantage, the principal can effectively discipline her. A subtle use of such sanctions is seen in this statement:

Teacher: That woman really used to run the school, too. You had to do just what she said.
Interviewer: What did she do if you 'disobeyed'?
Teacher: There were lots of things she could do. She had charge of assigning children to their new rooms when they passed. If she didn't like you she could really make it tough for you. You'd get all the slow children and all the behavior problems the dregs of the school. After six months of that you'd really know what work meant. She had methods like that.

Such sanctions are ineffective against those few teachers who are either eccentric or determined enough to ignore them. They may also fail in lower-class schools where the teacher does not intend to stay.[8]

The sanctions teachers can apply to a principal who does not respect or protect their authority are somewhat less direct. They may just ignore him: 'After all if the principal gets to be too big a bother, all you have to do is walk in your room and shut the door, and he can't bother you.' Another weapon is hardly a weapon at all—making use of the power to request transfer to another school in the system. It achieves its force when many teachers use it, presumably causing higher authorities to question the principal's ability:

> I know of one instance, a principal of that type, practically every teacher in her school asked to leave. Well, you might think that was because of a group that just didn't get along with the new principal. But when three or four sets of teachers go through a school like that, then you know something's wrong.

Finally, the teachers may collectively agree on a line of passive resistance, and just do things their way, without any reference to the principal's desires.

In some cases of extreme conflict, the teachers (some of whom may have been located in the school for a longer period than the principal) may use their connections in the community to create sentiment against the principal. Cooperative action of parents and teachers directed toward the principal's superiors is the teachers' ultimate sanction.

The principal, then, is expected to provide a defense against parental interference and student revolt, by supporting and protecting the teacher whenever her authority is challenged. He is expected, in his supervisory role, to respect the teacher's independence. When he does not do these things a conflict may arise. Both parties to the conflict have at their disposal effective means of controlling the other's behavior, so that the ordinary situation is one of compromise (if there is a dispute at all), with sanctions being used only when the agreed-on boundaries are overstepped.

Colleague relations

It is considered that teachers ought to cooperate to defend themselves against authority attacks and to refrain from directly endangering the authority of another teacher. Teachers, like other work groups, develop a sense that they share a similar position and common dangers, and this provides them with a feeling of colleagueship that makes them amenable to influence in these directions by fellow teachers.

Challenging of another teacher so as to diminish her authority is the basic crime:

> For one thing, you must never question another teacher's grade, no matter if you know it's unjustified. That just wouldn't do. There are some teachers that mark unfairly. A girl, or say a boy, will have a four 'S' report book and this woman will mark it a 'G'. . . . Well, I hate to see them get a deal like that, but there's nothing you can do.

Another teacher put it more generally: 'For one thing, no teacher should ever disagree with another teacher or contradict her, in front of a pupil.' The result in terms of authority vis-à-vis students is

feared: 'Just let another teacher raise her eyebrow funny, just so they [the children] know, and they don't miss a thing, and their respect for you goes down right away.' With regard to authority threats by parents it is felt that teachers should not try to cast responsibility for actions which may provoke parental interference on another teacher.

Since teachers work in separate rooms and deal with their own groups of parents and pupils, it is hard for another teacher to get the opportunity to break these rules, even if she were so inclined. This difficulty is increased by an informal rule against entering another teacher's room while she is teaching. Breaches of these rules are rare and, when they do occur, are usually a kind of punishment aimed at a colleague disliked for exceeding the group work quotas or for more personal reasons. However, the danger inherent in such an action—that it may affect your own authority in some way or be employed against you—is so feared that it is seldom used.

In short, teachers can depend on each other to 'act right' in authority situations, because of colleague feeling, lack of opportunity to act 'wrong,' and fear of the consequences of such action.

Discussion

I have presented the teacher as a person who is concerned (among other things) with maintaining what she considers to be her legitimate authority over pupils and parents, with avoiding and defending against challenges from these sources. In her view, the principal and other teachers should help her in building a system of defenses against such challenges. Through feelings of colleagueship and the use of various kinds of sanctions, a system of defenses and secrecy (oriented toward preventing the intrusion of parents and children into the authority system) is organized.

This picture discloses certain points of general relevance for the study of institutional authority systems. In the first place, an institution like the school can be seen as a small, self-contained system of social control. Its functionaries (principal and teachers) are able to control one another; each has some power to influence the others' conduct. This creates a stable and predictable work setting, in which the limits of behavior for every individual are known, and in which one can build a satisfactory authority position of which he can be sure, knowing that he has certain methods of controlling those who ignore his authority.

In contrast the activities of those who are outside the professional group are not involved in such a network of mutual understanding and control. Parents do not necessarily share the values by which the teacher legitimates her authority. And while parents can apply sanctions to the teacher, the teacher has no means of control which she can use in return, in direct retaliation.

To the teacher, then, the parent appears as an unpredictable and uncontrollable element, as a force which endangers and may even destroy the existing authority system over which she has some measure of control. For this reason, teachers (and principals who abide by their expectations) carry on an essentially secretive relationship vis-à-vis parents and the community, trying to prevent any event which will give these groups a permanent place of authority in the school situation. The emphasis on never admitting mistakes of school personnel to parents is an attempt to prevent these outsiders (who would not be subject to teacher control) from getting any excuse which might justify their intrusion into and possible destruction of the existing authority system.

This suggests the general proposition that the relations of institutional functionaries to one another are relations of mutual influence and control, and that outsiders are systematically prevented from exerting any authority over the institution's operations because they are not involved in this web of control and would literally be uncontrollable, and destructive of the institutional organization, as the functionaries desire it to be preserved, if they were allowed such authority.[9]

Notes

* This paper is based on research done under a grant from the Committee on Education, Training, and Research in Race Relations of the University of Chicago.
1 Cf. E. C. Hughes, 'The study of institutions', *Social Forces*, 20, March 1942, 307–10.
2 See my earlier statement in 'The professional dance musician and his audience', *American Journal of Sociology*, 57, Sept. 1951, 136–44.
3 Howard S. Becker, 'Social-class variations in the teacher-pupil relationship', *Journal of Educational Sociology*, 25, April 1952, 451–65.
4 Details of method are reported in Howard S. Becker, 'Role and career problems of the Chicago public school teacher' (unpublished Ph.D. dissertation, University of Chicago, 1951).
5 Charles Horton Cooley, *Social Organization*, New York, Charles Scribner's Sons, 1927, p. 131.
6 See Howard S. Becker, 'The career of the Chicago public schoolteacher', *American Journal of Sociology*, 57, March 1952, 475; ch. 9 of this Reader.
7 Cf. *The Sociology of Georg Simmel*, trans. Kurt Wolff, Chicago, Free Press, 1950, p. 235: 'The position of the subordinate in regard to his superordinate is favorable if the latter, in his turn, is subordinate to a still higher authority in which the former finds support.'
8 See Becker, 'The career of the Chicago public schoolteacher', 472–3.
9 Cf. Max Weber: 'Bureaucratic administration always tends to be an administration of "secret sessions": in so far as it can, it hides its knowledge and action from criticism. . . . The tendency toward secrecy in certain administrative fields follows their material nature: everywhere that the power interests of the domination structure toward *the outside* are at stake . . . we find secrecy.' In H. H. Gerth and C. Wright Mills (eds), *From Max Weber: Essays in Sociology*, Routledge & Kegan Paul, 1948, p. 233.

9 The career of the Chicago public schoolteacher[1]

Howard S. Becker

The concept of *career* has proved of great use in understanding and analyzing the dynamics of work organizations and the movement and fate of individuals within them. The term refers, to paraphrase Hall, to the patterned series of adjustments made by the individual to the 'network of institutions, formal organizations, and informal relationships'[2] in which the work of the occupation is performed. This series of adjustments is typically considered in terms of movement up or down between positions differentiated by their rank in some formal or informal hierarchy of prestige, influence, and income. The literature in the field has devoted itself primarily to an analysis of the types, stages, and contingencies of careers, so conceived, in various occupations.[3] We may refer to such mobility through a hierarchy of ranked positions, if a spatial metaphor be allowed, as the *vertical* aspect of the career.

By focusing our attention on this aspect of career movement, we may tend to overlook what might, in contrast, be called the *horizontal* aspect of the career: movement among the positions available at one level of such a hierarchy. It need not be assumed that occupational positions which share some characteristics because of their similar rank in a formal structure are identical in all respects. They may, in fact, differ widely in the configuration of the occupation's basic problems which they present. That is, all positions at one level of a work hierarchy, while theoretically identical, may not be equally easy or rewarding places in which to work. Given this fact, people tend to move in patterned ways among the possible positions, seeking that situation which affords the most desirable setting in which to meet and grapple with the basic problems of their work. In some occupations more than others, and for some

individuals more than others, this kind of career movement assumes greater importance than the vertical variety, sometimes to such an extent that the entire career line consists of movement entirely at one level of a work hierarchy.

The teachers of the Chicago public schools are a group whose careers typically tend toward this latter extreme. Although it is possible for any educationally qualified teacher to take the examination for the position of principal and attempt ascent through the school system's administrative hierarchy, few make the effort. Most see their careers purely in teaching, in terms of movement among the various schools in the Chicago system.[4] Even those attempting this kind of vertical mobility anticipate a stay of some years in the teacher category and, during that time, see that segment of their career in much the same way. This paper will analyze the nature of this area of career movement among teachers and will describe the types of careers found in this group. These, of course, are not the only patterns which we may expect to find in this horizontal plane of career movement. It remains for further research in other occupations to discern other career varieties and the conditions under which each type occurs.

The analysis is based on interviews with sixty teachers in the Chicago system. The interviewing was unstructured to a large extent and varied somewhat with each interviewee, according to the difficulty encountered in overcoming teachers' distrust and fear of speaking to outsiders. Despite this resistance, based on anxiety regarding the consequences of being interviewed, material of sufficient validity for the analysis undertaken here was secured through insisting that all general statements of attitude be backed up with concrete descriptions of actual experience. This procedure, it is felt, forced the interviewees to disclose more than they otherwise might have by requiring them to give enough factual material to make their general statements plausible and coherent.

Source: *American Journal of Sociology*, 57, March 1952, pp. 470–7; also appeared in H. S. Becker, ed., *Sociological Work*, Aldine.

I

The positions open to a particular teacher in the system at a given time appear, in general, quite similar, all having about the same prestige, income, and power attached to them. This is not to deny the existence of variations in income created by the operation of seniority rules or of differences in informal power and prestige based on length of service and length of stay in a given school. The fact remains that, for an individual with a given amount of seniority who is about to begin in a school new to her, all teaching positions in the Chicago system are the same with regard to prestige, influence, and income.

Though the available teaching positions in the city schools are similar in formal characteristics, they differ widely in terms of the configuration of the occupation's basic work problems which they present. The teacher's career consists of movement among these various schools in search of the most satisfactory position in which to work, that being the position in which these problems are least aggravated and most susceptible of solution. Work problems arise in the teacher's relations with the important categories of people in the structure of the school: children, parents, principal, and other teachers. Her most difficult problems arise in her interaction with her pupils. Teachers feel that the form and degree of the latter problems vary considerably with the social-class background of the students.

Without going into any detailed analysis of these problems,[5] I will simply summarize the teacher's view of them and of their relation to the various social-class groups which might furnish her with students. The interviewees typically distinguished three class groups: (1) a bottom stratum, probably equivalent to the lower-lower and parts of the upper-lower class,[6] and including, for the teacher, all Negroes; (2) an upper stratum, probably equivalent to the upper-middle class; and (3) a middle stratum, probably equivalent to the lower-middle and parts of the upper-lower class. Three major kinds of problems were described as arising in dealings with pupils: (1) the problem of *teaching*, producing some change in the child's skills and knowledge which can be attributed to one's own efforts; (2) the problem of *discipline*, maintaining order and control over the children's activity; and (3) the problem of what may be termed *moral acceptability*, bringing one's self to bear some traits of the children which one considers immoral and revolting. The teacher feels that the lowest group, 'slum' children, is difficult to teach, uncontrollable and violent in the sphere of discipline, and morally unacceptable on all scores, from physical cleanliness to the spheres of sex and 'ambition to get ahead.' Children of the upper group, from the 'better neighborhoods,' were felt to be quick learners and easy to teach but somewhat 'spoiled' and difficult to control and lacking in the important moral traits of politeness

and respect for elders. The middle group was considered to be hard-working but slow to learn, extremely easy to control, and most acceptable on the moral level.

Other important problems arise in interaction with parents, principal, and colleagues and revolve primarily around the issue of authority. Parents of the highest status groups and certain kinds of principals are extremely threatening to the authority the teacher feels is basic to the maintenance of her role; in certain situations colleagues, too, may act in such a way as to diminish her authority.

Thus, positions at the teaching level may be very satisfactory or highly undesirable, depending on the presence or absence of the 'right' kind of pupils, parents, principal, and colleagues. Where any of these positions are filled by the 'wrong' kind of person, the teacher feels that she is in an unfavorable situation in which to deal with the important problems of her work. Teachers in schools of this kind are dissatisfied and wish to move to schools where 'working conditions' will be more satisfactory.

Career movement for the Chicago teacher is, in essence, movement from one school to another, some schools being more and others less satisfactory places in which to work. Such movement is accomplished under the Board of Education's rules governing transfer, which allow a teacher, after serving in a position for more than a year, to request transfer to one of as many as ten other positions. Movement to one of these positions is possible when an opening occurs for which there is no applicant whose request is of longer standing, and transfer takes place upon approval by the principal of the new school.

The career patterns which are to be found in this social matrix are not expected to be typical of all career movements of this horizontal type. It is likely that their presence will be limited to occupational organizations which, like the Chicago school system, are impersonal and bureaucratic and in which mobility is accomplished primarily through the manipulation of formal procedures.

II

The greatest problems of work are found in lower-class schools and, consequently, most movement in the system is a result of dissatisfaction with the social-class composition of these school populations. Movement in the system, then, tends to be out from the 'slums' to the 'better' neighborhoods, primarily in terms of the characteristics of the pupils. Since there are few or no requests for transfer to 'slum' schools, the need for teachers is filled by the assignment to such schools of teachers beginning careers in the Chicago system. Thus, the new teacher typically begins her career in the least desirable kind of school.[7] From this beginning two major types of careers were found to develop.

The first variety of career is characterized by an immediate attempt to move to a 'better' school in a 'better' neighborhood. The majority of interviewees reporting first assignment to a 'slum' school had already made or were in the process of making such a transfer. The attitude is well put in this quotation:

When you first get assigned you almost naturally get assigned to one of those poorer schools, because those naturally are among the first to have openings because people are always transferring out of them to other schools. Then you go and request to be transferred to other schools nearer your home or in some nicer neighborhood. Naturally the vacancies don't come as quickly in those schools because people want to stay there once they get there. I think that every teacher strives to get into a nicer neighborhood.

Making a successful move of this kind is contingent on several factors. First, one must have fairly precise knowledge as to which schools are 'good' and which are not, so that one may make requests wisely. Without such knowledge, which is acquired through access to the 'grapevine,' what appears to be a desirable move may prove to be nothing more than a jump from the frying pan into the fire, as the following teacher's experience indicates:

When I put my name down for the ten schools I put my name down for one school out around —— ['nice' neighborhood]. I didn't know anything about it, what the principal was like or anything, but it had a short list. Well, I heard later from several people that I had really made a mistake. They had a principal there that was really a terror. She just made it miserable for everyone. . . .
But I was telling you about what happened to me. Or almost did. After I had heard about this principal, I heard that she was down one day to observe me. Well, I was really frightened. If she had taken me I would have been out of luck, I would have had to stay there a year. But she never showed up in my room. . . . But, whatever it was, I was certainly happy that I didn't have to go there. It just shows that you have to be careful about what school you pick.

Second, one must not be of an ethnic type or have a personal reputation which will cause the principal to use his power of informal rejection. Though a transferee may be rejected through formal bureaucratic procedure, the principal finds it easier and less embarrassing to get the same result through this method, described by a Negro teacher:

All he's got to do is say, 'I don't think you'll be very happy at our school.' You take the hint. Because if the principal decides you're going to be unhappy, you will be, don't worry. No question about that. He can fix it so that you have every

discipline problem in the grade you're teaching right in your room. That's enough to do it right there. So it really doesn't pay to go if you're not wanted. You can fight it if you want, but I'm too old for that kind of thing now.

This has the effect of destroying the attractive qualities of the school to which transfer was desired and of turning choice in a new direction.

Finally, one must be patient enough to wait for the transfer to the 'right' school to be consummated, not succumbing to the temptation to transfer to a less desirable but more accessible school:

When I got assigned to —— [Negro school], for instance, I went right downtown and signed on ten lists in this vicinity. I've lived out here for twenty-five years and I expect to stay here, so I signed for those schools and decided I'd wait ten years if necessary, till I found a vacancy in the vicinity.

The majority of teachers have careers of this type, in which an initial stay in an undesirable 'slum' school is followed by manipulation of the transfer system in such a way as to achieve assignment to a more desirable kind of school.

Thirteen of the interviewees, however, had careers of a different type, characterized by a permanent adjustment to the 'slum' school situation. These careers were the product of a process of adjustment to the particular work situation, which, while operating in all schools, is seen most clearly where it has such a radical effect on the further development of the career, tying the teacher to a school which would otherwise be considered undesirable. The process begins when the teacher, for any of a number of possible reasons, remains in the undesirable school for a number of years. During this stay changes take place in the teacher and in the character of her relations with other members of the school's social structure which make this unsatisfactory school an easier place in which to work and which change the teacher's view of the benefits to be gained by transferring elsewhere. Under the appropriate circumstances, a person's entire career may be spent in one such school.

During this initial stay changes take place in the teacher's skills and attitudes which ease the discomfort of teaching at the 'slum' school. First, she learns new teaching and disciplinary techniques which enable her to deal adequately with 'slum' children, although they are not suited for use with other social-class groups:

Technically, you're not supposed to lay a hand on a kid. Well, they don't, technically. But there are a lot of ways of handling a kid so that it doesn't show—and then it's the teacher's word against the kid's, so the kid hasn't got a chance. Like dear Mrs. G——. She gets mad at a kid, she takes him out in the hall. She gets him stood up against the wall. Then she's got a way of chucking the kid under the chin, only hard, so that it knocks his head back against the wall. It doesn't leave a mark on him. But when he comes back in that room he can hardly see straight, he's so knocked out.

Further, the teacher learns to revise her expectations with regard to the amount of material she can teach and learns to be satisfied with a smaller accomplishment; a principal of a 'slum' school described such an adjustment on the part of her teachers:

Our teachers are pretty well satisfied if the children can read and do simple number work when they leave here. . . . They're just trying to get these basic things over. So that if the children go to high school they'll be able to make some kind of showing and keep their heads above water.

She thus acquires a routine of work which is customary, congenial, and predictable to the point that any change would require a drastic change in deep-seated habits.

Finally, she finds for herself explanations for actions of the children which she has previously found revolting and immoral, and these explanations allow her to 'understand' the behavior of the children as human, rather than as the activity of lunatics or animals:

I finally received my permanent assignment at E——. That's that big colored school. Frankly, I wasn't ready for anything like that. I thought I'd go crazy those first few months I was there. I wasn't used to that kind of restlessness and noise. The room was never really quiet at all. There was always a low undertone, a humming, of conversation, whispering, and shoving. . . . I didn't think I would ever be able to stand it. But as I came to understand them, then it seemed different. When I could understand the conditions they were brought up in, the kind of family life and home background that they had, it seemed more natural that they should act that way. And I really kind of got used to it after awhile.

At the same time that these changes are taking place in the teacher's perspectives, she is also gradually being integrated into the network of social relations that make up the school in such a way as to ease the problems associated with the 'slum' school. In the first place, the teacher, during a long stay in a school, comes to be accepted by the other teachers as a trustworthy equal and acquires positions of influence and prestige in the informal colleague structure. These changes make it easier for her to maintain her position of authority vis-à-vis children and principal. Any move from the school would mean a loss of such position and its advantages and the need to win colleague acceptance elsewhere.

Second, the problem of discipline is eased when the teacher's reputation for firmness begins to do the work of maintaining order for her: 'I have no trouble with the children. Once you establish a reputation and they know what to expect, they respect you and you have no trouble. Of course, that's different for a new teacher, but when you're established that's no problem at all.'

Finally, problems of maintaining one's authority in relation to parents lessen as one comes to be a 'fixture' in the community and builds up stable and enduring relationships with its families: 'But, as I say, when you've been in that neighborhood as long as I have everyone knows you, and you've been into half their homes, and there's never any trouble at all.'

The 'slum' school is thus, if not ideal, at least bearable and predictable for the teacher who has adjusted to it. She has taken the worst the situation has to offer and has learned to get along with it. She is tied to the school by the routine she has developed to suit its requirements and by the relationships she has built up with others in the school organization. These very adjustments cause her, at the same time, to fear a move to any new school, which would necessitate a rebuilding of these relationships and a complete reorganization of her work techniques and routine. The move to a school in a 'better' neighborhood is particularly feared, desirable as it seems in the abstract, because the teacher used to the relative freedom of the 'slum' school is not sure whether the advantages to be gained in such a move would not be outweighed by the constraint imposed by 'interfering' parents and 'spoiled' children and by the difficulties to be encountered in integrating into a new school structure. This complete adjustment to a particular work situation thus acts as a brake on further mobility through the system.

III

Either of these career patterns results, finally, in the teacher's achieving a position in which she is more or less settled in a work environment which she regards as predictable and satisfactory. Once this occurs, her position and career are subject to dangers occasioned by ecological and administrative events which cause radical changes in the incumbents of important positions in the school structure.

Ecological invasion of a neighborhood produces changes in the social-class group from which pupils and parents of a given school are recruited. This, in turn, changes the nature and intensity of the teacher's work problems and upsets the teacher who has been accustomed to working with a higher status group than the one to which she thus falls heir. The total effect is the destruction of what was once a satisfying place in which to work, a position from which no move was intended:

I've been at this school for about twenty years. It was a lovely school when I first went there. . . .

Of course, the neighborhood has changed quite a bit since I've been there. It's not what it used to be.

The neighborhood used to be ninety, ninety-five per cent Jewish. Now I don't think there are over forty per cent Jews. The rest are Greek, Italian, a few Irish, it's pretty mixed now. And the children aren't as nice as they used to be.

Ecological and demographic processes may likewise create a change in the age structure of a population which causes a decrease in the number of teachers needed in a particular school and a consequent loss of the position in that school for the person last added to the staff. The effect of neighborhood invasion may be to turn the career in the direction of adjustment to the new group, while the change in local age structure may turn the career back to the earlier phase, in which transfer to a 'nicer' school was sought.

A satisfactory position may also be changed for the worse by a change in principal through transfer or retirement. The departure of a principal may produce changes of such dimension in the school atmosphere as to force teachers to transfer elsewhere. Where the principal has been a major force upholding the teacher's authority in the face of attack by children and parents, a change can produce a disastrous increase in the problems of discipline and parental interference:

I'm tempted to blame most of it on our new principal. . . . [The old principal] kept excellent order. Now the children don't seem to have the same feeling about this man. They're not afraid of him, they don't respect him. And the discipline in the school has suffered tremendously. The whole school is less orderly now.

This problem is considered most serious when the change takes place in a 'slum' school in which the discipline problem has been kept under control primarily through the efforts of a strict principal. Reactions to such an event, and consequent career development, vary in schools in different social-class areas. Such a change in a 'slum' school usually produces an immediate and tremendous increase in teacher turnover. A teacher who had been through such an experience estimated that faculty turnover through transfer rose from almost nothing to 60 per cent or more during the year following the change. Where the change takes place in a 'nicer,' upper-middle-class school, teachers are reluctant to move and give up their hard-won positions, preferring to take a chance on the qualities of the new incumbent. Only if he is particularly unsatisfying are they likely to transfer.

Another fear is that a change in principals will destroy the existing allocation of privilege and influence among the teachers, the new principal failing to act in terms of the informal understandings of the teachers with regard to these matters. The following quotations describe two new principals who acted in this fashion:

He knows what he wants and he does it. Several of the older teachers have tried to explain a few things to him, but he won't have any part of it. Not that they did it in a domineering way or anything, but he just doesn't like that.

He's a goodhearted man, he really means well, but he simply doesn't know anything about running a school. He gets things all mixed up, listens to people he shouldn't pay any attention to. . . . Some people assert themselves and tell him what to do, and he listens to them when he shouldn't.

These statements are the reaction of more strongly intrenched, 'older' teachers who depend greatly for their power on their influence with the principal. Their dissatisfaction with a new principal seldom affects their careers to the point of causing them to move to another school. On the other hand, the coming of a new principal may be to the great advantage of and ardently desired by younger, less influential teachers. The effect of such an event on the career of a younger teacher is illustrated in this quotation:

I was ready to transfer because of the old principal. I just couldn't stand it. But when this new man came in and turned out to be so good, I went downtown and took my name off the transfer list. I want to stay there now. . . . Some of those teachers have been there as long as thirty years, you see, and they feel like they really own the place. They want everything done their way. They always had things their way and they were pretty mad when this new principal didn't take to all their ideas.

Any of these events may affect the career, then, in any of several ways, depending on the state of the career development at the time the event occurs. The effect of any event must be seen in the context of the type of adjustment made by the individual to the institutional organization in which she works.

IV

This paper has demonstrated the existence, among Chicago schoolteachers, of what has been called a 'horizontal' plane of career strivings and movements and has traced the kind of career patterns which occur, at this level, in a public bureaucracy where movement is achieved through manipulation of formal procedures. It suggests that studies of other occupations, in which greater emphasis on vertical movement may obscure the presence and effects of such horizontal mobility, might well direct their attention to such phenomena.

Further research might also explore in detail the relations between the horizontal mobility discussed here and the vertical mobility more prominent in many occupations. Studies in a number of occupations might give us answers to questions like this:

To what extent, and under what circumstances, will a person forgo actions which might provide him with a better working situation at one level of an occupational hierarchy in the hope of receiving greater rewards through vertical mobility? Hall notes that those doctors who become members of the influential 'inner fraternity' undergo a 'rigorous system of selection, and a system of prolonged apprenticeship. The participants in the system must be prepared to expect long delays before being rewarded for their loyalty to such a system.'[8] We see that the rewards of eventual acceptance into this important group are attractive enough to keep the fledgling doctor who is apprenticed to it from attempting other ways of bettering his position. Turning the problem around, we may ask to what extent a person will give up possible vertical mobility which might interfere with the successful adjustment he has made in terms of horizontal career movement. A suggestion as to the kinds of relationships and processes to be found here comes from the following statement made by a high-school teacher with regard to mobility within the school system:

That's one reason why a lot of people aren't interested in taking principal's exams. Supposing they pass and their first assignment is to some school like M—— or T——. And it's likely to

be at some low-class colored school like that, because people are always dying to get out of schools like that. . . . Those schools are nearly always vacant, so that you have a very good chance of being assigned there when you start in. A lot of people I know will say, 'Why should I leave a nice neighborhood like Morgan Park or South Shore or Hyde Park to go down to a school like that?' . . . These guys figure, 'I should get mixed up with something like that? I like it better where I am.'

Finally, we have explored the phenomenon of adjustment to a particular work situation in terms of changes in the individual's perspectives and social relationships and have noted the way in which such adjustment acted to tie the individual to the particular situation and to make it difficult for him to consider movement to another. We may speculate as to the importance and effects of such a process in the vertical mobility prominent in many occupations. One further research problem might be suggested: What are the social mechanisms which function, in occupations where such adjustment is not allowed to remain undisturbed, to bridge the transition between work situations, to break the ties binding the individual to one situation, and to effect a new adjustment elsewhere?

Notes

1 Paper read at the Institute of the Society for Social Research held in Chicago, 8–9 June 1951. The material presented here is part of a larger study reported in 'Role and career problems of the Chicago public school teacher' (unpublished Ph.D. dissertation, University of Chicago, 1951).
2 Oswald Hall, 'The stages of a medical career', *American Journal of Sociology*, 53, March 1948, 327.
3 See Everett C. Hughes, 'Institutional office and the person', *American Journal of Sociology*, 43, November 1937, 404–13; Oswald Hall, op. cit., and 'Types of medical careers', *American Journal of Sociology*, 55, November 1949, 243–53; and Melville Dalton, 'Informal factors in career achievement', *American Journal of Sociology*, 56, March 1951, 407–15.
4 The Chicago system has a high enough salary schedule and sufficient security safeguards to be safe as a system

in which a person can make his entire career, thus differing from smaller school systems in which the teacher does not expect to spend her whole working life.
5 Later papers will provide detailed analysis and documentation of the statements made in this and the following paragraph.
6 The class categories used in this estimate are those used by W. Lloyd Warner and Paul Lunt in *The Social Life of a Modern Community* (Yale University Press, 1941).
7 Further documentation of this point may be found in Miriam Wagenschein, 'Reality Shock' (unpublished MA thesis, University of Chicago), 1951, and in John Winget's Ph.D. thesis, 'Ecological and Socio-cultural Factors in Teacher Inter-school Mobility'.
8 Hall, 'The stages of a medical career', p. 334.

10 The craftsman teachers

H. Gracey

(...) Becky Yager is the most sophisticated and knowledgeable in the craftsman ideology of teaching. She earned her Master of Education degree at the progressive John Dewey College of Education in Metropolitan City, and did her early teaching in progressive private schools. When asked about her goals in teaching, Becky replied that she 'could write books about that.' In an attempt to briefly summarize her approach she said, 'Practically, I try to provide experiences which will help children learn about the world around them,' expressing the basic craftsman methodology, and, 'More grandiosely, there are things like imparting one's democratic, humanitarian cultural heritage to the children,' alluding to the basic goals of the craftsman teachers. Becky does not feel that teaching involves taking a group of children through a preset curriculum at a prescribed pace. Rather, she thinks teaching should involve creating a curriculum around the abilities and interests of individual children, so that learning is part of their lives, not something separate from their spontaneous interests. Becky described what she would do in her ideal classroom:

> In an ideal situation, I would *really* start with the child. I would ask, What does he need to know, and what does he want to know? What is he prepared to know? What will help further his growth? What stage of what period of growth is he ready for? Is it important that he watch a caterpillar crawl along a branch? Mostly, my job has to do with knowledge, with the acquisition of knowledge. I think this should be my primary responsibility as a teacher: to provide them with knowledge they need. Supposing, for example, a child comes in, in a first grade, who is really very much interested in space and atomic

Source: *Curriculum or Craftsmanship: Elementary School Teachers in a Bureaucratic System*, University of Chicago Press, 1972, pp. 43–5, 51–8.

development. Well, this kid's probably ready for it, and so he goes on with it. On the other hand, there are other kids, like one youngster this year, who said, 'What's a carrot?' Obviously he needs a lot of learning about vegetables, soil, seeds, and experiences with those things. In an ideal situation, for me, I would gauge the kinds of knowledge the children are ready for, determine this for each child, and work with him on this basis.

The 'books' which Becky says she could write describing her educational goals and teaching methods have, to some extent at any rate, already been written by the past and present faculty of the John Dewey College. In these publications they present the conception of education developed at the college, which is a combination of progressive education and modern ego psychology referred to as modern education, and their conceptions of the teaching process and the role of the teacher in this kind of education. A very brief summary of some of their ideas is contained in one recent publication directed toward teachers.

> The teacher's task is to present the curriculum in such a way that knowledge not only shall be acquired but that it shall become part of the individual's general power to cope with intellectual problems and personal difficulties; that children not only master the techniques for understanding but that they continue to be eager for learning; that they not only be capable of disciplined learning from others but that they gain strength in being able to learn independently through their own activity and initiative; that they not only become aware of a wider and wider world but that they feel deeply and vitally connected with it.

The foundation of the teacher's role in modern education, another publication states, is 'establishing basic mutuality of thinking and feeling between herself and the children while maintaining her position as an adult, individually and as an agent of adult society'. The modern teacher, it can be said, is a person who has one foot in the child's world of thought and feeling and the other in the adult world, and her task is helping the child cross over gradually from one to the other.

Four basic components of the role of the modern teacher are listed in a recent publication of the college. First, she learns to perceive and relate to pupils as individuals rather than as members of the classroom group. This individual relationship is conceived of as the necessary precondition to genuine interaction, which in turn is the foundation of modern education. Second, the teacher gives the children emotional support in the conflicts they inevitably experience in the process of growing up, in this way helping them acquire 'a positive self-feeling.' Third, the teacher learns to understand and empathize with the child's thought processes so she can guide his learning toward 'the building of the integrative and adaptive functions of the ego . . . she takes responsibility for leading children toward reference systems of reality and objectivity.' Finally, she develops a social control system in the classroom which is based on the functional requirements of the children's learning, one that is 'rational rather than arbitrary.' She gains acceptance for this system through encouraging children's identification with her and the class program rather than through fear and punishment: 'The teacher, alongside the parents, becomes a potential identification figure for ego-ideal realization.' Thus, on the basis of a foundation in individual relationships with each child, the college people feel, the modern teacher establishes emotional, cognitive, and authoritative ties which enable her to help the child move part of the way from his world of childhood to her world of adulthood. This is the task of the educational process in the elementary school, and the kind of teacher role in which Becky has been trained and which she has tried to carry out in her work. (. . .)

[The following description of Becky's classroom reflects the compromises she has developed between her educational goals and the structure of the educational organization. The kinds and degrees of satisfaction and frustration with her work that arise from this compromise are also considered.]

Becky Yager's first grade: April

Becky Yager opens the outside door of her first-grade classroom at 8:35 and admits the waiting children, greeting each by name. After hanging up their coats the children go to their desks, look around, talk to one another, watch the guinea pigs in their cage, and look at books. More children come in; many gather around Becky to tell her things, and two clean the guinea-pig cage, turning the animals loose on the floor. At 8:40 the first school bell rings and a boy turns off the lights in the room. All the children go to their desks. Becky says, 'Clear your desks.' The children become quiet and Becky says, 'Calendar helper, tell us what day it is.' A child goes to the large calendar hanging on the wall at the front of the room, points to the number, and says, 'Today is Monday, April 14,' and returns to her seat. Becky says, 'Kenny, turn on the lights.' The same boy who had turned them off without a command rushes from his seat at the back of the room near the windows to the light switch on the opposite wall, flicks the lights on and dashes back to his seat. Becky now leads the children in a discussion of making butter. The class has recently visited a dairy farm and is going to make butter as a result of what they learned. The children contribute statements about the various stages of butter-making. After this Becky goes to a large lettering paper hung on the blackboard and asks the children for words they will need to write their story about the trip to the farm. As children offer words, Becky asks them to use them in sentences. Most of the children are raising their hands to offer words and sentences. Becky writes six of these sentences on the paper, underlining the special words in each of them. She says to the class, 'For our writing lesson today, you can write this story or be grown-up. . . .' The children finish her sentence for her, saying, 'and write your own story.'

Here the first two activities of the day, the discussion of butter-making and the writing lesson, are introduced in direct relation to the recent trip to the dairy farm. These lessons are an attempt to make classroom activities a continuation of this trip so they will have inherent meaning. An important part of the classroom social control system has been seen in operation, the turning off of the lights. This is a signal for children to go to their desks and become quiet. Kenny, one of the most active and potentially disruptive children in the class, is in charge of the lights, and by this time of the year he knows his job well enough to carry it out at least partly without commands from Becky. He gets a feeling of importance, and a great deal of physical exercise, during the day as he races back and forth across the rear of the room between his desk and the light switch. Becky now has to interrupt this work to carry out required school procedures, the 'opening exercises' and an arithmetic lesson from the required text.

A little after 9:00 o'clock, Becky calls two children to the front of the room and they recite the Twenty-third Psalm and lead the Lord's Prayer and the Pledge of Allegiance. Becky plays the piano and the class sing 'America.' When this is finished Becky comes to the front of the room and says, 'Paper helpers, please get out paper and buttons. Children, please take out your arithmetic books.' Two girls go to the cabinet and the rest of the class begins talking as materials are distributed. The room becomes quite noisy. Becky says, 'Kenny, put the lights out.' The children become quieter when the lights go off. After the paper and buttons have been distributed, Becky has Kenny turn the lights back on and says to the class, 'Let's have some stories about nine.' Children raise their hands, and when called on offer various combinations of numbers which add up to nine. Some of the class arrange the buttons on their desks into these 'groups' as they are suggested. Becky holds up cards with various combinations of nine on them, asks children to read them, and has the class make groups of buttons corresponding to them on their desks. Most children are now busy making groups of buttons and Becky looks around the room, asking a few children what groups they have on their desks. After this Becky says, 'Open your books to the pages on nines.' Various groups which make nine are illustrated on these pages with different objects, such as sailboats and dolls. In response to Becky's instruction, the children circle various groups in their books, such as six boats and three boats. Becky asks some children what groups they have circled. She apparently knows which children will be having trouble with this work.

The required routines and lessons of the school which cannot be made part of a meaningful class project have here been introduced as actual interruptions of the class program, and when Becky finishes with the arithmetic lesson she returns to the class projects and the classroom work associated with them.

At about 9:20 Becky says, 'Put your books away. Paper helpers collect the buttons. Put your desks in our science circle, I have something to share with you.' The children push their desks toward the edge of the room and put their chairs in a large circle in the center of the room. When they are seated Becky picks up the topic of milk and the making of butter which the class discussed earlier. Then she reads an article from a Metropolitan City newspaper concerning two new lion cubs born at the zoo. She shows a picture of the cubs around the circle. The children begin to get restless, and begin to talk and poke one another. Becky says, 'Put your hands in your laps and think of a question you would want to ask if you went to the zoo.' A few questions are suggested, but the children become more restless and begin to poke and wrestle with one another again. Becky says, 'Quietly put your desk and chairs back.' The children jump up, shove, and whoop. Becky says, 'Kenny, put out the light.' The noise gradually subsides and Becky says, 'Let's get ready for our writing lesson.' Children take pencils and lined paper from their desks as Becky continues, 'Turn on the lights. All fold your hands on your desk for a minute.' She then reviews the instructions for the writing lesson—'either write your own story or copy the one we wrote'—and most of the children begin writing with intense concentration. As they work Becky goes around the room helping them spell words they want to use and admiring their work. A child who wants to use a word he cannot spell raises his hand. Becky goes to him and asks him to use the word in a sentence. If he is using it correctly, Becky writes the word on the blackboard for the child to copy into his story. Children show each other their stories, and some begin to draw pictures to illustrate their stories.

In this sequence, Becky has brought the children back to the project in which they are currently engaged, evolving out of their trip to the dairy farm, and introduced the topic of their next trip, which will be to the Metropolitan City Zoo. The abstract idea of this new project, however, holds the attention of the children for only a few moments. Becky is not surprised, since this is the first introduction of the idea. More discussions will be held, and more work done in preparation before the actual trip is undertaken. The trip will be followed by a series of related activities such as those being carried on now in conjunction with the past farm trip. Becky returns the class to work stemming from the farm trip—the writing lesson for the day—when their tolerance for the abstract idea of the zoo trip has been passed and they become disruptive. The writing lesson, it should be noted, is totally effective in restoring order to the class, as the children get down to work on something which seems to be interesting to most of them. If they elect to write their own stories, the only limitation on the words they are allowed to use is their *need* for the word to express what they want to say. (. . .) Children are acquiring a vocabulary of words which are meaningful because they *need* them to express a part of their experience. Language skills are being taught in [this class] as intrinsic parts of children's experience, not as abstract technical exercises.

It is 9:50 when Becky calls the first reading group to the 'reading circle,' a group of chairs under the windows, separated from the classroom by a long, low bookshelf and walled off from the block-playing area by the piano, which extends lengthwise into the room. About a third of the class gathers in this area, and Becky conducts a reading lesson with them while the remainder of the class writes, draws, or plays with blocks or with the guinea pigs. Fifteen minutes later Becky sends the reading group back with the instructions to 'get out your workbooks,' and a new group immediately assembles in the circle. As she instructs them, Becky occasionally asks a noisy child in the room to 'be more quiet, because it's awfully hard for us to hear our words.' All four guinea pigs are out on desks, children are building with the blocks on the other side of the piano, others are cutting illustrations from magazines, and some are coloring or playing with clay at their desks. Becky has the reading group do some writing; they sit on the floor and write with the paper on their chairs. When they are busy she leaves them and asks two children to 'take the mural out into the hall.' A boy and girl get a long sheet of brown paper and jars of paint and brushes from the shelves at the back of the room and carry them into the hall. The painting is a partially completed class mural depicting the dairy farm they recently visited. Becky goes into the hall with the children, closing the classroom door behind her. The children in the room continue with their activities. When Becky returns she asks the reading group to return to their desks, and another group assembles in the circle. Becky plays a word game with this group, which has only four members. She occasionally reprimands children who are not working at their desks. Most are at their desks, conversing occasionally with their neighbors. Some children wander into the reading area to get books. Three or four others watch the lesson. One comes and sits in the circle. Becky asks him if he want to visit. She asks one of the group to give him a book and tell him what page they are on, and carries on with the lesson. The remainder of the class is still involved in various activities. Some talk to each other and walk about the room. Becky starts the reading group on their workbooks and says, 'Kenny, turn out the lights.' When they are off she asks individual children what they are working on, and if they give an acceptable activity in reply, Becky asks them if they will please do it at their own desks. Then she has the lights turned back on and goes to the cabinet over the sink to get out cookies for milk-and-cookie time.

Becky has succeeded in spending most of the morning working with children in small groups, and after milk-and-cookie time she will spend fifteen minutes with yet another reading group before it is time to get the children ready to go home for lunch. During the snack time Becky reads the class a story about some animals at the Metropolitan City Zoo, as another step in preparation for their forthcoming trip. Each possible moment of the day is put to use in the service of the project-organized instructional program and the goal of individualized instruction in a classroom of twenty-five six-year-old children.

Becky is not, however, satisfied with her work. She is unable to achieve her teaching goals, she says, 'with these particular children in this particular time and place.' Becky feels very strongly the discrepancy between her goal of individualized instruction using material which is meaningful to the children and the organizational necessities of group instruction and the required curriculum. In the public schools, Becky says, 'I cannot come close to my ideal situation of teaching each child according to what he needs to know and is ready to know.' There is too great an emphasis on the acquisition of 'empty skills' in the first grade, Becky feels, from the school, the parents, and the children themselves. She described the problem in this way:

First, the curriculum we are given is not centered on child interests and needs. Then the children themselves have certain expectations of school, because of the community in which they live, their parents' attitudes, and reports from their older brothers and sisters, which don't go with the kind of teaching I think is right. Then, the parents have certain expectations of what the curriculum ought to be, which I feel is a rather rigid approach; for example, that in first grade you study one and one are two, you study one hundred words or three books, and this makes up education.

The school system which defines her task—the teaching of the curriculum—and the people with whom she must carry it out, the children and their parents, all tend to define early childhood education as a formalized set of routine activities, whereas Becky tries to make it an intrinsically meaningful part of the children's lives.

A second and equally serious source of frustration for the craftsman teachers is the social structure of the organization within which they are trying to realize their goals. They, along with the other teachers, are required to conform to the school's requirements for cleanliness, order, and quiet in the classroom, and they must maintain sufficient order among the majority of the children to enable them to spend some of the day working with the small reading groups. Becky, it will be remembered, required each child not 'in group' with her to be at work on some project which kept him at his desk. She had instituted a highly structured system of social control in the class which enabled her to spend much of the day working with the children in groups, but which at the same time severely limited the freedom of expression and activity of most of the children in the class for much of the day. Once this structure is established, Becky controls individual children by calling them to account for their activities in terms of the classroom rules and routines. When necessary, she has the lights turned out and reminds the class as a whole of the rules under which they are supposed to be operating.

The craftsman teachers feel most keenly the contradiction between the desire to relate personally to individual children, which is the first goal of their teaching orientation, and the necessity of organizing their classes into smoothly functioning groups to maintain order. This order, as all teachers discover in their first year, is essential as a prerequisite to teaching and learning in the classroom. Its creation, however, precludes personal relationships with individual children, because the class must first be related to as a group, and then the children are related to as members of this group—that is, in their role as pupils rather than in their individuality. In sociological terms, Becky has learned what every teacher must learn, regardless of her philosophy or orientation; that twenty to thirty children in a classroom must first be organized into a functioning group before they can be taught the curriculum, and that this ultimately means that the teacher relates to the class as a group and to its members in their roles as pupils. The organizational structure of the school negates the key craftsman goal of individualized instruction.

[Other] primary-grade craftsman teachers [in this school] have responded differently to this fundamental conflict between their teaching goals and the organizational requirements. Hannah Gilbert has created a more formal and structured classroom organization than Becky has, whereas Alice Davis is trying to work within a much less formal, and consequently much more chaotic, classroom organization. (. . .)

11 Teaching and learning in English primary schools

Ann C. Berlak, Harold Berlak, Naida Tushnet Bagenstos and Edward R. Mikel

The English primary school has become the symbol for many school reformers of the 1970s—the standard by which to measure and judge the deficiencies of elementary schooling in America.[1] This paper, based on a six-month participant-observation study of several English informal primary schools, raises questions about the common images of these schools found in much of the popular and professional literature.[2] In particular, the focus will be on three related issues which are central to a discussion of the English informal schools: (1) what role does the child play in making educational decisions? (2) to what extent does the impetus to learn originate in the child and to what extent is it extrinsic? (3) who sets and maintains educational performance standards? The analysis of these issues is set within a framework we developed from the observation and interview data we collected and from a systematic effort to use our personal experience in American schools. The framework consists of fifteen basic tensions or dilemmas which we believe confront teachers daily in the classroom.[3] The issues raised are analyzed in terms of three of the dilemmas:

1 teacher making learning decisions for children versus children making learning decisions,
2 intrinsic versus extrinsic motivation,
3 teacher setting and maintaining standards for children's learning and development versus children setting their own standards.

This paper clarifies some of the reasons for casting these issues in terms of dilemmas, refines these three dilemmas further, and analyzes and interprets a portion of the data collected in terms of the dilemmas.

Why another study of the English primary schools?

There were several reasons why we joined the multitude of American educators visiting English schools.

Source: *School Review*, 83 (2), 1975, pp. 215–43.

First, the literature, although compelling because it implies that there is a form of mass schooling virtually free of conflict and coercion, raised many questions. The popular, predominantly glowing descriptive accounts rely heavily on anecdotes or 'vignettes' which portray only selected classroom events. For example, Silberman's influential *Crisis in the Classroom* presents a picture of English primary schools largely in terms of 'items,' most of which exemplify how children are 'intrinsically' motivated, make their own choices about what they should learn, set their own standards, move about in the classroom without apparent external controls, and, within this free atmosphere, achieve a high standard of academic and artistic performance. 'Items' dealing with problems that plague American teachers, such as deviant children and reluctant learners, are noticeably absent. The following are not atypical of the many vignettes and brief descriptions included in Silberman and other writings on the English primary school:

Item: A junior school in Leicestershire County, serving a working-class and lower-middle-class neighborhood. A class of eight- and nine-year olds, a happy, buzzing group, are returning to their room from physical education. A visitor engages the teacher in conversation as the children are putting their shoes and socks and clothes back on. . . . The conversation continues for a while. Suddenly the visitor becomes aware that all thirty-eight children are busily at work: some are reading, some are writing essays and poems, some are filling in answers in workbooks; one cluster of youngsters are measuring one another's height and constructing graphs of the results; several others are in the science corner, performing an experiment.[4]

. . . Here most of the classrooms open onto a wide central corridor which was used quite as much as the classrooms themselves. Along the whole length of the corridor were easels, work-benches, nature tables, displays of paintings and collages. There was a 'store' where two children sold cardboard cereal boxes, cookie tins, and candy bar wrappers for play money which had to be carefully counted and the correct change returned. *Children moved in and out of the rooms and up and down the corridor freely and calmly.* As I walked by, one little boy painting at an easel stopped to inspect a boat his friend was building at a nearby workbench, then went back to work.[5]

Such descriptions were puzzling because schools are obviously complex social institutions. We knew that there was more to the schools than the pictures presented in such accounts; although selected descriptions need not be misleading, these were surely incomplete. Just as many spectators fail to notice or appreciate interior line blocking in a football game, it appeared to us that these reports failed to describe the less apparent school events. As plays diagrammed in a playbook are unknown to the stadium spectator, so apparently were the structures beneath the observed behaviors.

Much of the literature that theorized about open or informal education also left us perplexed. Several writers were interested in identifying 'beliefs' or commitments which motivate teachers' classroom behavior. However, the ways in which these writers identified the beliefs raised questions about whether they had captured accurately the operational philosophy which in fact governs or influences teachers' classroom behavior. Rathbone, for example, attempting to identify teachers' 'implicit' or 'fundamental' rationales, suggests that 'open education sees teaching more as a lateral interchange . . . between two persons of nearly equal status. . . . It is the student who is most often the initiator. . . . A teacher is in a sense a travel agent. He helps a child go where the child wants to go.'[6] Such generalizations were derived from 'observing open education teachers in action and reading the books and articles they refer to most often.'[7] Rathbone gives no indication of the extent of his observations or the data from which he makes the inferences about teachers' beliefs, nor does he present evidence that the books he surveyed were read by teachers or, if read, that they influenced the teachers' behavior.

Barth, describing 'the philosophical, personal and professional roots from which these [open education] practices have sprung and upon which they [open educators] depend so completely for their success,'[8] argues that most open educators 'strongly agree' with statements such as the following: 'If a child is fully involved and having fun with an activity he is learning,' 'Children have the competence and right to make significant decisions concerning their own learning,' 'Children are innately curious and will explore their environment without adult interven-

tion.'[9] Barth provides no data to support these assertions about teachers' beliefs beyond the statement that 'since these assumptions were assembled I have "tested" them with several British primary teachers, headmasters and inspectors and with an equal number of American proponents of open education. To date . . . there has not been a case where an individual has said of one of the assumptions, "No, that is contrary to what I believe about children, learning or knowledge".'[10] Despite the questionable derivation of his conclusions, their validity appears to have been accepted by other writers and researchers.[11] While exceptions to the views about English teachers' beliefs reviewed above can easily be found in the literature, as R. S. Peters says of the Plowden Report, most of these 'read very much like attempts to deal with awkward objections while retaining the main emphasis.'[12]

The study by Chittenden and his colleagues,[13] one of the few research efforts to develop a 'conceptualization' of open education based on the systematic collection of data, argues, quoting David Hawkins, that '"where the best practice excels the best theory in quite essential ways," . . . educational research should look to the practitioner more seriously, rather than the other way around.'[14] Yet, in their interim report most of the assertions about open education and statements of guiding principles and characteristics of the philosophy of the Educational Development Corporation (EDC) appear to be drawn from the literature on open education and interviews with advisers and EDC project staff, not classroom teachers, and it is the latter who in this situation are the practitioners. In our view, the advisers' statements, taken by Chittenden to indicate 'essential directions of growth . . . which . . . educators are attempting to promote,'[15] are either a reflection of the adviser's creeds or what the advisers believe should be teachers' creeds. There are no grounds for accepting such assertions as indicative of teachers' operational philosophies or even of their creeds.

The theoretical analyses of the schools also contain numbers of apparent contradictions among writers on crucial issues. Featherstone states, for example, 'There is no abdication of [teacher] authority and no belief that this would be desirable.'[16] Lillian Weber, discussing the role of children's choices, claims, 'The teachers' role in informal education could be summed up as implementing and opening up a child's purposes. Where she [the teacher] thought her role was to direct the children's learning, then informal education in the school was incompletely conceived and certainly incompletely realized.'[17]

Perhaps such contradictions may be attributed to the ambiguities of language in attempts to communicate about complex phenomena, rather than to differing perceptions of the schools. Nevertheless, such apparent contradictions suggest a great deal of uncertainty about how the actors in a school situation meet the conditions of school life, in this instance

uncertainty about who controls what in the classroom and about who believes what concerning the
exercise of control.

There was still another reason to suspect something was amiss in the writing on open education.
We knew intelligent and sensitive teachers in Saint
Louis area schools who were trying 'open education'
in their classrooms, and many reported feeling frus-
trated because they could not approximate the English
model as they understood it. An alarming number of
children were not, in their judgment, making wise
decisions about their own learning, staying with a
task long enough to complete it satisfactorily, or
exhibiting the joy of self-motivated study. Popular
explanations for the difficulties were that English
children are different and 'it can't be transplanted' or
that American teachers and/or administrators are
unable to free themselves of their own preconceptions
or bureaucratic tangles. We wanted to find out
whether an important source of the difficulty might
be that the literature on which the teachers' ideas
depended provided them with inadequate or misleading ideas.

The concerns outlined above represent our fore-
shadowed problems as we left for England to engage
in a participant-observation or field study in the
manner of Philip Jackson's *Life in Classrooms*, Louis
Smith's *Complexities of an Urban Classroom*, and
William Whyte's *Street Corner Society*. We hoped
that the participant-observer methodology, which had
not to our knowledge been employed to study the
primary schools, would facilitate the clarification of
the questions we had posed.

The development of a framework and language

During our first weeks in the English schools we
gradually began to understand that the images of the
schools conveyed in the literature were to some extent
distorted. The way in which this understanding
developed is exemplified by our experience during the
first weeks of our study of Mr Thomas's classroom.
In his classroom, in a school in an affluent suburban
area, we observed thirty children on a Wednesday
morning who, after a brief discussion with the teacher,
went about their work individually: some began to
work on 'maths,' others to study spelling or to write
original stories in much the way Silberman described
in the 'item' quoted above. We observed no teacher
behavior on that morning which appeared to direct
the children to what they were to do. It appeared that
the children were choosing to learn, did their work
carefully, and were pursuing their own interests.
However, during the following days, we observed
events and patterns which appeared to account for
the behavior observed on that Wednesday morning.
On the following Monday morning we observed Mr
Thomas set work minimums in each subject of the
week—a different pattern, but a familiar decision-
making locus nevertheless. On the following Friday

morning we saw him collect the children's work
'diaries' where each child had recorded in detail the
work he had completed during the week. Over the
weekend, Mr Thomas and, as we were to later
discover, sometimes the head checked each record
book and wrote comments in the diaries such as
'good,' 'more maths,' or the ominous 'see me.' Such
'items,' which explained some of the apparently
spontaneous classroom behavior, had not appeared
in the literature. As we talked to Mr Thomas about
the work minimums and record books, he indicated
that he thought that 'checking up on the child' was
not only proper but necessary.

Our four- to six-week stays in each of three schools
and shorter visits to thirteen other schools confirmed
that the events that Silberman *et al.* describe did
occur, but they were only part of the story; we
recorded many other episodes or 'vignettes' which
others had apparently not observed or had not considered sufficiently important to report. As we began
to analyze the data, we saw that the classrooms could
be characterized by phrases such as 'student choice,'
'intrinsic motivation,' and 'setting of standards by
children,' but such characterizations were only
partly true, and differentially true for different classrooms. We also realized that the existing conceptualiz-
ations of the complex patterns of thought and
organization which lay beneath the observable events
were inadequate. Put simply, we came to doubt the
claims, implicit or explicit, that English informal
teachers subscribe to a particular set of educational
commitments or that belief in a particular set of
abstract propositions accounts for their behavior. We
became increasingly certain that whatever accounted
for their behavior, it was not the beliefs attributed to
them by the Plowden Report or by such researchers as
Barth, Rathbone, and Chittenden.

Searching for a way to conceptualize our data, we
found no difficulty in accepting an assumption shared
by Barth, Chittenden, Rathbone, *et al.* that something
in the minds of the actors (teachers in this instance)
affects in some way the behavior they manifest in
school. Conceptualizing the complex relationship
between thought and action is difficult, particularly
when the arena of human action is a complex social
institution like the school, which is the product of
and subject to many external political and social
influences. We were guided in our effort by the ideas of
George Herbert Mead and Herbert Blumer and the
social research position known as 'symbolic interactionism.'

Crucial to the perspective of symbolic interactionism is the relationship of mind and action as expressed
in the idea of meaning. Thus, an individual's action is
construed as arising out of the meanings the individual
takes from what he perceives and interprets in a
situation, including the action of others in the immediate situation, the meaning he has made of his
own action, and the action of others in present and in
past situations. Institutions and social processes can

be best understood by focusing on the actors and how they construct their actions. Individuals, in this case children, teachers, and administrators, no matter how oppressive the situation may be, are not viewed merely as reactors to forces playing on them from without or within. In Blumer's words, the actor makes 'indications' to himself about his action and the actions of others in the immediate and in similar past situations, and about potential future actions by himself and others.[18] There is no presumption that this process is always carefully deliberated or that at any given moment a teacher is fully aware of the meaning of an act, only that there is a process internal to teachers which affects their schooling behavior.

Our problem, restated in the language of symbolic interactionism, became, What are the teachers' 'meanings' that are implicit in their behavior? Our analyses are based on: (1) extended and thorough observations of the settings; (2) knowledge of how settings are perceived by teachers, which was gained by the researchers participating (necessarily to a limited degree) in the teachers' role; (3) knowledge of how teachers construe their own teaching behavior, which was gained by asking teachers to talk about specific instances of their own behavior, which, because the instances were observed by the participant observer, were first-hand experiences shared by both. This latter point needs to be understood; our conversations and interviews explored reasons for their behavior and ideas of teachers associated with observed events, rather than the teachers' abstract beliefs.

In the process of trying to identify fundamental aspects of the teachers' meanings, we found ourselves noting what appeared to be 'inconsistencies' or contradictions, for example, Mr Thomas letting one student decide how much maths to do while telling another exactly what was required. We found ourselves saying, 'On the one hand A is true (Mr Thomas construes schooling in terms of children's decisions, and children do make decisions), but on the other hand so is B (children are frequently told what to do, and Mr Thomas appears to construe schooling in terms of teachers making decisions).'

The search for a framework to deal with these apparent 'contradictions' resulted in the postulation of fourteen dilemmas which appear to conceptualize the complexity of teachers' meanings of schooling situations and the complex behavioral manifestations of these meanings.[19] Apparent inconsistencies in a teacher's behavior and language could be explained if we hypothesized that the teacher is drawn to some degree toward both poles of a dilemma. Because our interest was in clarifying the relationships of thought and action, we focused on specific patterns of resolution in behavior of these tensions or conflicts.

As we continued to work the data, we found the concept of dilemma or polarity an extremely powerful construct for ordering and interpreting our data. We are persuaded, at least tentatively, that while particular dilemmas may manifest themselves in distinctive ways in 'open' classrooms, they are not unique to the classrooms we observed and appear in many other schooling situations.

The general conflict-tension orientation is consistent with the position that, in a society where institutions at least in part reflect the diversity of beliefs of the adult population, it is unlikely that those in authority in the institutions will conduct schooling according to a single philosophical or psychological orientation. This is so not only because teachers in their institutional roles mirror society but because they are actors in the society and within each of them and among them there are contrary notions about the proper way children should be reared, what is success and how it is pursued in the society, what traditions are precious and need to be sustained, what is a just allocation of the resources of the society, and so on.

Three methodological issues require some clarification, particularly because we have criticized much of the writing on English informal schools as anecdotal and distorting. The reliance primarily on data from three schools raises the issue of whether the schools studied in depth are representative. We make no claims that these schools are representative by any of the criteria normally used in survey research. Our claim is that these schools are not atypical of primary schools in the Leicester-Leicestershire area. Our confidence in this claim is based on the following: (1) we made the selection of the three schools with the advice of officials in the relevant educational authorities, and we explicitly stated our criterion of non-atypicality; (2) we interrupted our extended stays in the three schools with short-term visits to thirteen other schools in the area in order to obtain personal knowledge about whether the schools we were studying were unusual in terms of organization, size, quality of staff, and resources; (3) we specifically posed the question, and received confirmation from our informants regularly, of how unusual the schools we visited were.

The second issue is whether the data we collected within each school represent the full diversity and complexity of that setting. Stated differently, what grounds if any does the reader have for trusting our accounts of what goes on in informal classrooms over accounts of others in the writings we have cited? We have no prima facie case for being keener observers than others who have observed and interpreted the English primary schools. We can merely point out what steps we took to satisfy ourselves that we had obtained data which fairly represented the complexity of the situation. First, we remained in each of the three settings for an extended period. In these schools our presence was taken for granted, we could go unescorted to virtually any location in the setting, and we had available for consultation reliable informants who were participants or were otherwise familiar with the setting.[20] Second, following

Malinowski's injunction, we made a deliberate effort to decrease as much as possible the influence of preconceived ideas on our perceptions. In practical terms, this led us to segment systematically the school-day by time and location and to make general observations of each segment in order to 'turn up' as many events and patterns as possible. In addition, we solicited from children, teachers, and frequently the head and other informants their views about each segment; we also asked them to comment on our perceptions and on the way we had segmented the settings. Those events which were significant to the actors, or to us in terms of the questions we brought to the study, were given additional attention. For example, the decision to segment turned up the 'checking up by the head' pattern which occurred between 9:00 and 10:00 a.m. on Fridays and, in any given location, only once in three or four weeks. The existence of this regular event and its significance might easily have been missed if we had not remained in the setting for an extended period of time and if we had not systematically segmented the setting and then attempted to discover the meanings of such events to the head, the teachers, and the children.

A third issue is whether the data, which we report in the form of quotations drawn from observations and interviews of two teachers only, are a fair representation of the data collected, even assuming the data themselves are a fair reflection of informal schooling in Leicester and Leicestershire. A full response to this problem would require a detailed description of our process of data analysis, an impossible task in an article this length. In general, the analysis was characterized by a search for both instances and counterinstances of the generalizations and interpretations and a search for examples which would confound the emerging polar concepts we were developing. Obviously, the reader has no independent means of validating our final selection of illustrations of the concepts without a complete reading of the data.

In order to provide a basis for understanding the framework in this paper, we report the findings using data drawn from interviews with and observations of only two of the twenty-two teachers studied in depth. The two teachers were selected because they manifest patterns common to many of the teachers studied. We present a general picture of these two teachers and their classrooms before turning to an analysis of the data.

Mrs Lawton   In a primary school in one of the poorer sections of Leicester, Mrs Lawton teaches twenty-five 7-year-olds. The morning is devoted primarily to work in the 'basics'—reading, maths, and writing—with a brief interruption for assembly. Mrs Lawton sets daily minimum work expectations: everyone will write a story, all but the strongest readers will read individually to the teacher or the head, and each will do a given maths task. Moreover,

each child works with a small group at his maths and his story at a specified time. During a work period, Mrs Lawton may tell one child to write a longer story, more often than not ignoring a child's apparent reluctance, but may be satisfied with a shorter story from another child. When a child has finished the required work, or if no work is required at a given time, generally in the afternoons, he may 'choose' from activities such as reading corner, painting, Wendy house, or blocks. At such times, one might see three children in 'dress-ups' wheeling a carriage across the playground unbeknown to the teacher, who might be 'hearing' the last of her students read.

Mr Thomas   On Mondays, Mr Thomas makes explicit the minimum each child should accomplish for the week in a variety of academic areas. Students can choose to go beyond the minimum or to do other activities, including observing pets and discussing football. They can, in general, allocate their own time during the mornings of the entire week. Thus, the observer might, at any given time on any morning, see children working on various academic tasks while others are chatting quietly, painting, or working with a cooking group. On Fridays, Mr Thomas and perhaps the head check to make sure students have completed their assigned tasks to the adult's satisfaction; those few who have not will either confer with the teacher or be sanctioned. In the afternoons the students engage in one of a number of schoolwide 'commitments' or 'minicourses.' At 1:00 p.m. they deploy themselves to various locations in the school to join in dance, music, science, 'topic,' art, or other activity groups.

Patterns of resolutions to the three dilemmas

Teacher making learning decisions for children versus children making learning decisions

Our effort to conceptualize the complexities and apparent inconsistencies in what the teacher and what the child control[21] in the learning situation and under what circumstances differing patterns of control are exercised led us to posit that there was a dilemma facing the teachers we observed. There appeared to coexist a simultaneous pull in two directions—toward the teacher making learning decisions and toward the children making the decisions.

In this section we present a framework which may be used to order the complex ways the dilemma is manifested and resolved. Decisions—not necessarily deliberated—are made about: (1) *whether or not* a child will study in a given area, (2) *what* specifically is to be learned within that area, (3) *when* the task is to begin and when it is to be completed, and (4) *how* the learner is to proceed with the task. In a given learning situation, the child, or the teacher, or both jointly exercise one or more of these decisions. Joint decisions appear to have one of two emphases:

Type of decision	Who decides			
	Teacher decides	Child and teacher decide jointly		Child decides
		Choose from options	Negotiate	
Whether or not to learn				
What should be learned				
When it should be learned				
How it should be learned				

Figure 11.1

either the child chooses from among a set of options or he engages with the teacher in a process that resembles negotiating. The large number of possible patterns of resolution to the dilemma is now evident; a teacher can follow different patterns of resolution for different children, and at different times of the year, or for different subjects or learning experiences. Figure 11.1 represents the array of possibilities.

'I think they need freedom but also guidance,' Mrs Lawton claims, indicating that she is drawn to both sides of the dilemma. In fact, she resolves the dilemma by making almost all of the decisions on *whether or not* and most of the decisions about *what*, *when*, and *how* in the 'basics'—reading, writing, and maths—while leaving most decisions in the nonbasics to the children. 'I direct them, but I give them choice as well. Especially with 'activities' and creative work, I allow them to choose more than with written work. I give them suggestions about what to write about, but . . . if they have an idea then they write about what they would like to.'

The class is divided into four groups, and Mrs Lawton sets the time for each group to work on the 'basics.' There are variations; for example, children who want to write first thing in the morning are allowed to do so even if this entails departing from the teacher's schedule. Those few children who do not finish the required work during the specified period will usually be called away from a chosen activity and directed to finish.

Minimal student influence is evident regarding *what* specifically will be learned in academic subjects: children often decide what to write about, and at times they may choose from a very limited number of maths tasks. They have no choice of basal readers, however, as these are selected by the teacher from a sequence of readers prescribed for the entire school. Generally, Mrs Lawton decides *how* a task will be

learned; for example, all students will practice 'money' by taking a turn in the 'shop' and by doing a work sheet, though a child may decide when he will 'play' in the shop.

Most decisions beyond the minimum in the academic area and in the creative and nonacademic realm are the child's as long as he has completed the 'basic' work. It is the child who decides whether or not to do the daily art project, read in the reading corner, dabble or work seriously at the workbench (limited only by care of tools and safety considerations), play at the Wendy house, or at learning a game. Choices are, of course, generally limited by the materials placed in the environment. Lego plastic blocks were removed as an option from the room because, as Mrs Lawton said, 'the children were no longer learning anything from their use.'

We observed frequent examples of negotiated decisions, particularly in the nonbasics: the teacher and child discussed a writing topic, what he might construct at the workbench, what he might do in his 'choice' time, or how to best proceed at a given task. Thus, we see that Mrs Lawton many times a day resolves the dilemma of decision making according to a pattern which in her case appears to depend particularly on whether she considers the subject 'basic.'

Mr Thomas explicitly expressed that he feels pulled toward each side of the dilemma:

I have yet to come to terms with myself about what a child should do in, for instance, mathematics. Certainly I feel that children should as far as possible follow their own interests and not be dictated to all the time, but then again . . . I feel pressure from . . . I don't really know how to explain it, but there's something inside you that you've developed over the years which says the children should do this. . . . I as yet can't accept, for instance, that since I've been here I've been annoyed that some children in the fourth year haven't progressed as much as, say, some less able children in the second year in their maths, because they've obviously been encouraged to get on with their own interests. But I still feel that I've somehow got to press them on with their mathematics.

His resolution to the dilemma is to make most of the decisions about whether or not a child will learn in a given area. In academic areas the child has virtually no control over *whether or not*: 'I insist on what I call the bread and butter.' In fact, Mr Thomas requires work each week in nearly all curriculum areas: art, maths, reading, writing, handwriting, spelling, 'topic' (similar to a research report). This behavior reflects his expressed desire 'that children take part in practically everything there is to offer.' Students are granted only slightly more control over whether they will work in nonbasic areas. Mr Thomas argued, in opposition to a number of other teachers in the school, that all children be required to participate in Sports Day, and his position on the issue prevailed. Every afternoon all children in the school leave their home teacher to attend 'commitment groups,' courses usually lasting a week in areas such as physical education, dance, science, creative writing, music, or library. Teachers limit students' choice of commitment group by either negotiating with students or requiring them to choose a different group every week or two. Mr Thomas (along with the majority of the teachers) expressed the view that this control over *whether or not* is rightfully in the teacher's domain.

Mr Thomas sets weekly work minimums in each subject area—a specific number of assignment cards or pages to complete. Work minimums are, however, negotiable, and Mr Thomas or the student will not infrequently initiate negotiation in order to adjust minimums to the abilities or interests of the child. In those areas (maths, reading, spelling) where minimums are defined in terms of sets of sequenced cards, children are given almost no choice about *what* or *how* to learn. In handwriting, creative writing, and topic research, Mr Thomas provides sets of non-sequential assignment cards which suggest optional activities from which students may choose if they do not have an idea of their own.[22] In these subjects, although the general area is assigned, the choice of what to work on within an area or how to proceed is up to the children. They choose how they will express what they have learned in the topic area they select, perhaps making a display or giving a play.

The children have almost complete freedom to decide *when* during the week to do their required work, and minimums are set so that perhaps only 60–75 per cent of a child's time each morning is controlled by the teacher. Thus, Mr Thomas argues that it's quite

appropriate during a work period for a child 'to tell another what he's done last night or how he got on at football during playtime.'

The foregoing indicates the complexity of the decision-making procedures in English informal classrooms (or indeed in any classroom). Barth and Rathbone suggest that the more willing a teacher is to allow children to make independent decisions, the closer that teacher is to the open-education idea and, by implication, the English model. If our data are at all representative of what goes on in English primary schools, then Barth and Rathbone are wrong. In virtually all classrooms, the teachers' resolutions to the dilemma are a combination of opposites—a resolution that takes into account, according to explicit or implicit principles, the claims of both poles of the dilemma. Although we found important variations in the patterns of resolution, the generalization that children in informal classrooms control their schooling—even when qualifications are added—is, we are convinced, a gross distortion of the complexity that obtains in the classrooms we observed.

Intrinsic versus extrinsic motivation

The pull of this dilemma is that, on the one hand, teachers are drawn to the idea that the impetus for learning comes—and should come—primarily from within the learner and, on the other hand, to the idea that some kind of action by the teacher or others is required for learning to be initiated and sustained by a child.[23] Action may include urging, threatening, rewarding with praise, candy or tokens, or punishing failure to perform. We present data to demonstrate that both intrinsic and extrinsic motivation are part of the meanings manifest in complex patterns of behavior of the teachers who were studied.

Our analysis suggests three categories of ideas associated with this dilemma. First, teachers have differing ideas about the capacity of a particular subject area or activity to interest, and hence motivate, a child. For example, a teacher will say something to the effect that experimenting with chemicals is 'intrinsically' more interesting to children than learning to diagram a sentence or that children are more likely to be 'intrinsically' motivated to learn measurement than the multiplication tables.

Second, teachers also have different ideas about an individual child's capacity to be motivated. For example, a teacher may say that 'Jane is intrinsically motivated to read, but Joe needs to be pushed.' Thus, teachers have differing views about the capacity of a given child to initiate and sustain involvement in learning without a teacher's push (or other form of action) and differing views about the intrinsic motivating capacity of a subject or activity. The mix of the two we call the 'flash point,' which is the teachers' subjective estimate of how much extrinsic motivation is required to get a child to want to learn in a given area. (Little extrinsic motivation required in a given area for a particular child indicates a low flash point.) Teachers, of course, have differing estimates of the 'flash point' for any group of children in a given area or learning activity. This estimate is only the teacher's best guess as to what is empirically correct, and, as with any empirical judgment, the teacher may be mistaken.

Third, teachers have different valuations of the importance of a child's intrinsic motivation in a given domain of learning. For example, a teacher may feel that it is relatively important for children to be intrinsically motivated to read. This same teacher may believe that the flash point for reading for any given child is high, that is, that the child is not easily motivated to read. Thus, the teacher makes a value judgment (it is important that children be intrinsically motivated to read) and an empirical judgment about where the flash point is for a given child in a given subject (Jack is not easily motivated to read).

These two sets of judgments—one empirical and the other valuational—may be represented on a two-dimensional space. We are suggesting that those views of a teacher that can be plotted in this space partly account for his pattern of behavior in motivating children. Figure 11.2 is an effort to account for these

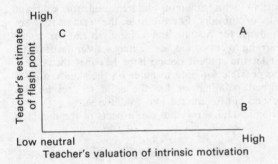

Figure 11.2

patterns; the X axis represents the teacher's valuation of intrinsic motivation in a given area, and the Y axis represents the teacher's estimate of the flash point in that area for a given child. Point A in the space would be grounded in a behavioral pattern of richly 'provisioning' the environment, that is, the teacher arranging the environment with stimulating materials and doing a number of other things to spark interest. Point B represents the pattern where there is no use of extrinsic motivation (e.g., candy, threats) and few provisions for stimulating a child's interests, since these are seen as unnecessary. Point C represents the pattern of the popular image of the traditional teacher where there is, as in pattern B, little effort expended by the teacher to spark interest although, in contrast to B, there is much use of extrinsic motivation. Since teachers may see intrinsic motivation as important in one activity but not in another, and estimate that

one child is intrinsically motivated but another is not for a given activity, a teacher could be charted with respect to motivation for each child in each subject. However, it seems likely that further analysis will disclose that there are characteristic patterns of teachers in different schooling situations.

Mr Thomas feels pulled toward both intrinsic and extrinsic motivation in the classroom: 'If they are not interested in what they are doing, if I can't interest them in what they are doing then it becomes a case of having to do it.'

On what basis does Mr Thomas decide when to rely on intrinsic motivation? For learning the 'basics' he does not depend on intrinsic motivation: the children are in fact told what they must do, and there are sanctions for those few who fail to do so. He argued: 'If a child doesn't do what I think he should do in a week, then instead of joining his commitment group in the afternoon he'll probably spend time in the library.' This statement suggests what the use of sanctions means to him: that some children are intrinsically motivated in 'commitments' though not in the basics and that the use of extrinsic motivation is not unjustified in such cases.

However, Mr Thomas values 'natural' interest, expects it to appear in some children, and uses it when it appears. 'Richard . . . is a very creative boy . . . he's got to be left alone before he produces his really best work.' Mr Thomas's behavior reflects the value he places on internal motivation: a child who, for example, brought him animals in various conditions of health or who demonstrated interest in pursuing virtually any subject was generally excused from some part of the work minimums.

Mr Thomas frequently spends time evoking student interest. For example, when he requires the children to write a story or read a book, he devotes time to helping them alight upon a book or topic of interest, providing suggestions, pictures, or articles with no manifest pressure to pursue the interest in a particular direction. 'I try to show an interest in their reading. We discuss what they read quite often—we used to do book reviews but this . . . didn't work out very well. I like to call them together, and perhaps it's something somebody's done and I like to get really enthusiastic about it.' At no time did we see Mr Thomas initiate any new activity without attempting to 'motivate' the children; this is consistent with his apparent assumption that the flash point is high in most subjects or activities for at least some children but that intrinsic motivation is valued.

Mrs Lawton does not rely very heavily on intrinsic motivation in the 'basics.' Both observational and interview data suggest that she believes the flash points are high for virtually everyone—'With these children, most of their interests come from what I've put into them'—and that intrinsic motivation is not highly valued in the basics. She forces—gently, but forces nevertheless—children to read, write, and do maths, and forbids them—kindly, but forbids them nevertheless—to 'choose' before they finish assigned tasks. 'I would say, "Finish your maths cards before you build," because Robert is a bit like that. I don't think he finds writing very easy. . . . He does try to dodge written work. If he doesn't do his work in the morning it's there for him to do in the afternoon.' She often 'motivates' with praise, perhaps sending a child to show a particularly good story to the head.

Mrs Lawton seems to value intrinsic motivation more in creative work than in the basics. 'I think in creative work if they do something they want to do, you get better results.' This value, coupled with an assumption of a high flash point in the nonbasics, results in her playing an extremely active role in 'sparking' interest in the nonbasics: 'When I come in at the beginning of the term I don't have ideas on everything I'm going to do, but I've got something to start off with. If I find something that interests them, then I carry on with that.' 'If' suggests that she feels at least uncertain about whether children will display intrinsic motivation. Thus, when she introduced a unit on 'shapes,' she arranged an elaborate display, but she was unwilling to rely on the display alone to spark interest. She conducted frequent short discussions and provided daily optional art projects to encourage interest. She claimed that feeling intrinsic motivation is important in all curriculum areas. 'If I've got a child that's genuinely interested in something I'd never say, "You can't do that,"' but the observational data suggests that she sees intrinsic motivation in some areas as less important than extrinsically motivated work in the basics. Observations indicate that the obligation to write almost always takes precedence over a child's manifest interest in building with blocks, or self-initiated projects in art or at the workbench.

However, Mrs Lawton resolves the dilemma under consideration differently for different children. For example, at one point the students were working with blocks of different shapes at the maths table. Our notes read: 'One boy says of another, "He's playing with the blocks" (implying he should be working). The teacher allows the boy who is playing to continue. She directs two others to sort the blocks into several groups and to write about what they've done.' Here is an example of simultaneously resolving the dilemma for some in terms of intrinsic motivation and for others in terms of extrinsic motivation.

In summary, our data suggest that English teachers resolve the dilemma of intrinsic versus extrinsic motivation by recognizing the claims of both poles and motivating differently for different tasks and students. Within this range of resolutions, we found many patterns. However, virtually all English teachers, at those times when they did not extrinsically motivate, brought into the classroom stimulating materials and provided options in order to spark interest. We saw few instances of teachers who depended heavily on intrinsic motivation with no provisioning. Classrooms of those few teachers who failed to provision

were barren and dull, and these teachers were considered by their heads to be inferior teachers.[24]

Teacher setting and maintaining standards for children's learning and development versus children setting their own standards

What are the patterns of teachers' meanings in the area of setting standards? By now it must be clear that the complexity of this issue is masked by statements such as, open educators believe that 'the preferred source of verification for a child's solution to a problem comes through the materials he is working with'[25] (rather than the imposition of teacher standards).

Analysis of the data suggests that the dilemma as it is manifested in the schooling situation can be better understood if a distinction is made between who sets standards and who decides whether standards have been met by the child. As with the 'decision' dilemma, these responsibilities can be with the teacher (or other school authorities—and the school authorities may be acting only as proxies for standards set by others outside the school), or with the child, or the teacher and child can jointly carry out these tasks in any given activity. The complexity of the issue is increased when one considers that a teacher can follow different patterns with different children and for different tasks or subjects. For example, the teacher may set standards for reading and writing but not for art or 'learning to cooperate,' or he may set standards in art but let the student decide if he has met them. It is also possible for both to agree on the standard of 'a finished painting' or for the child to feel he has finished but for the teacher to disagree.[26]

Figure 11.3 shows the two aspects of the meaning

Figure 11.3

related to this dilemma: who sets the standards and who decides whether a child has met them.

Mrs Lawton's pattern of setting standards is most evident in her response to written work. The absence of data on teacher standard setting in such areas as block building, carpentry, and most art projects suggests that she is concerned primarily with standards in the basics. With respect to daily writing, it is clear that she sets standards such as length of a story or accuracy of spelling, in most cases unilaterally, and decides whether students meet these standards. She called back a boy who put his writing away without finishing and told another boy, 'You've only done one line.' Our field notes report: 'John D. says, "I couldn't do any better on that story." Teacher: "Of course you can."'

Mrs Lawton allows a few children to set standards and to evaluate their work against them while others are made to conform. The data clearly suggest a response to differences among children. She says: 'Usually because Mary works well I let her do what she wants to do . . . but I know her standards are quite good and she works hard when she is working. . . . Some children who do bad work I know I could tear the page out and say I'm not accepting that and they would do better. Some children would be absolutely devastated. . . . It depends on the child. There is no set rule.'

Most children measure themselves against Mrs Lawton's standards in maths, but she seems to allow fewer to do so in writing. She is likely to check a child's story before dismissing him from writing, though students rarely check with her before handing in maths work.

Mr Thomas sets clear standards in most areas of work: 'I insist on presentable work. . . . I expect [him] . . . to do what he's capable of doing and I become annoyed if I feel he hasn't accomplished this.' One child said to the interviewer, 'Mr Thomas told me I could do better, and I do now.'

Many children seem to measure their work against their presumption of what the teacher's standards are. Relatively few regularly asked the teacher whether a story was long enough or neat enough. Relatively few were punished or pushed to go beyond what they were content with; a few received criticism when the record books were checked, on Fridays. The exceptional student was told that he wasn't measuring up: 'You are getting careless' written on a paper. 'I'll chat with them about a story they've done which I've enjoyed, or I'll chat to the children I'm not so pleased with.' Our field notes suggest a number of instances of positive evaluation: 'So far so good.'

In summary, a preliminary analysis of the data again suggests a variety of patterns of resolution to the dilemma of setting standards. Although in general teachers set standards in academic areas, these standards seem to be set for individuals rather than for groups. The data suggest that teachers distinguish between children who can evaluate themselves against the teacher's standards and those who cannot and teachers intervene primarily with the latter group.

Some speculations and implications

Open education, a popular and ambiguous phrase, is associated by many of its more ardent proponents with freedom, child centeredness, priority on creative expression, and rejection of traditional distinctions among school subjects. Detractors, increasingly vocal, associate the term with the near absence of standards

in basic subjects, priority on psychological well-being over intellectual development, focus on the immediate experience over the labor of learning, and respect for and mastery of tradition. There are a number of sober and considered qualifications made by writers about both of these overdrawn images, but if the past is any indication of the future, these will go unheeded much as the sober voices were unheeded in other school reform efforts in the recent past.

Is the cause worth advancing? If the schools we studied in any way represent what is possible in informal schooling, we think the answer is yes. Although the schools we observed, in our opinion, reflect the injustices of the British political system, they were, in general, better places for children to spend their days than are American schools. The measure of 'better' is simply that, if we had the choice, we would send our own children to any one of thirteen of the sixteen schools we studied rather than to any of the American elementary schools, private or public, we presently know of or have known.

We make no effort to predict whether practices of English informal schools will be successfully transplanted. What we have attempted to document is that the efforts to describe or to theorize about the English schools have distorted their reality. This distortion, we believe, has occurred because the images of neither the ardent advocates nor the detractors are grounded in a study of the day-by-day occurrences in such schools.[27] The language of freedom, self-motivation, and child-set standards commonly used to characterize these schools does not, even with added qualifications, we argue, capture the complexity of the actual schooling; indeed, such language distorts and, we think, leads others to misunderstand the English experience. It is not an overgeneralization to say that in no school we studied did a child have a choice not to learn to read or do maths, and there are virtually no instances of children being allowed to do nothing. This is no surprise, except perhaps to those who have come to believe that open or informal education is synonymous with permissiveness. Adult standards and sanctions were at all times operative in all the schools and all the classrooms we observed. On the other hand, as we have argued, children did make significant decisions and did follow their interests in the schools we observed.

How can informal education be characterized in terms that more accurately reflect the reality? To answer this, we return to our conception of schooling. We have suggested that a useful way to conceptualize schooling is in terms of a set of persisting dilemmas and that it is the teacher acting as self and agent who makes the de facto resolutions to the dilemmas. We have tentatively identified fourteen basic tensions or conflicts and have dealt with three of them in this essay. We suspect, though we are by no means certain, that informal schooling in England can be described in terms of characteristic patterns of resolving a set of dilemmas, although not in terms of how any one or two dilemmas are resolved. In other words, it is possible to make some generalizations about the grounded rationales of the English teachers we observed and to make comparisons to schooling in other settings.

This view of schooling as personal and complex resolutions to basic dilemmas merely acknowledges that schools, like other institutions, are subject to the complex and diverse influences of the social and political order. As a consequence, it is unlikely that we can have public schools where the immediate desires of children come first in all or even most circumstances (whether this is desirable is a separate question), because window washers, corporation executives, university professors, and teachers who directly or indirectly influence what the schools do want their own children to master and comprehend

the intellectual and social traditions they see as instrumental to conventional success. At the same time, these persons, at least to some extent, value personal growth and fulfilment, which, again directly or indirectly, influences what transpires in classrooms. Questions such as whether a teacher is child centered or not are, we believe, better conceptualized in terms of how teachers deal with the conflicting claims implicit in the dilemmas we have identified. In general, we believe that teachers' behavior in the classrooms we observed was responsive to the complex and conflicting claims of the dilemmas. In our view, the English informal teachers' concrete resolutions to these dilemmas may be useful guideposts to American school reformers interested in transplanting English informal methods to American elementary schools.

Notes

1 There are three types of schools for young children in England, each of which is administered by a separate head or principal: the infant school, for children age $4\frac{1}{2}$ to 7; the junior school, for children age 8 to 11; and the primary school, for infants and juniors. In this paper, unless specified otherwise, the term 'primary school' refers to all three types of schools.

2 The data for this study were gathered from January to July 1972 by two of the writers, Ann and Harold Berlak, in schools administered by the Leicester and Leicestershire Education Authorities. Three schools were studied in depth during stays of four to six weeks each. Supplementary data from thirteen other schools were collected during visits of from one to four days each. The schools studied in depth were a middle/lower-middle-class primary school located in a suburb characterized by modest tract houses; an infant school in one of the poorer areas of Leicester; and a junior school in an affluent middle-class suburb. The data—consisting of field notes; tape-recorded interviews with all the teachers and heads and at least ten students in each of the three schools studied in depth; interviews and informal discussions with heads and teachers in other schools and with other education officials; documents distributed by school officials, including curriculum guides, memoranda of operational procedures, etc.—represent a combined expenditure of 912 observational hours.

3 The theoretical orientation of schooling viewed as a series of basic tensions or dilemmas is discussed subsequently.

4 C. Silberman, *Crisis in the Classroom* (New York, Random House, 1970), pp. 234–5.

5 J. Schlesinger, *Leicestershire Report: The Classroom Environment* (Cambridge, Mass., Center for Research and Development on Educational Differences, 1969), p. 1; italics added. For additional, essentially similar vignettes, see Liza Murrow and Casey Murrow, *Children Come First* (New York, McGraw-Hill, 1971); Bill Hull, *Leicestershire Revisited*, Occasional Paper no. 1 (Newton, Mass., Educational Development Corp., June 1970), pp. 5–6; J. Featherstone, 'Schools for children: what's happening in British classrooms', *New Republic*, 19 August 1967, p. 17.

6 C. Rathbone, 'The implicit rationale of the open education classroom', in *Open Education*, ed. C. Rathbone (New York, Citation Press, 1971), pp. 106–7.

7 ibid., p. 99.

8 R. Barth, 'So you want to change to an open classroom', *Phi Delta Kappan*, October 1971, pp. 97–99.

9 ibid., p. 98.

10 ibid., p. 99. A similar statement appears in R. Barth, 'Open education: assumptions about children's learning', in *Open Education*.

11 See R. E. Traub et al., 'Closure and openness: describing and quantifying open education', *Interchange* 3, nos 2–3, 1972, 69–84.

12 R. S. Peters, 'A recognizable philosophy of education: a constructive critique', in *Perspectives on Plowden*, ed. R. S. Peters (Routledge & Kegan Paul, 1969); Silberman; and B. Gross and R. Gross, 'A little bit of chaos', in *Open Education*, ed. E. Nyquist and B. R. Hawes (New York, Bantam Books, 1971), are examples of writers who, whatever their intent, throw the weight of their analyses on the 'open' or child-centered aspects of teachers' beliefs and behavior. Featherstone's later work, *Informal Schools Today* (New York, Citation Press, 1971), and several of the interviews with heads published by the Educational Development Corporation raise questions more directly with such assumptions; see, for example, 'Infant School' (Newton, Mass., EDC, 1969): 'Battling Brook Primary' (Newton, Mass., EDC, undated); and E. Biggs, *Mathematics Concepts for Younger Children* (New York, Citation Press, 1971).

13 M. Amarel, A. Bussis, E. Chittenden and M. Tanaka, 'Analysis of an approach to open education', interim report, mimeographed (Newton, Mass., EDC, August 1970).

14 ibid., p. 14.

15 ibid., p. 43.

16 J. Featherstone, *Schools Where Children Learn* (New York, Liveright, 1971), p. 39.

17 Lillian Weber, *The English Infant School and Informal Education* (Englewood Cliffs, N.J., Prentice-Hall, 1971), p. 109.

18 H. Blumer, *Symbolic Interactionism* (Englewood Cliffs, N. J., Prentice-Hall, 1969), ch. 2. Our notion is that meanings

which guide behavior are 'forged by the actor out of what he perceives, interprets, judges' (ibid., p. 73), who has sorted out of his individual experiences the requirements of his role and the social codes, norms, values, and constraints perceived in situations, institutional arrangements, and the like. For a more complete discussion of the methodology, see ch. 1 in ibid., 'The methodological position of symbolic interactionism'; and S. Bruyn, *The Human Perspective in Sociology: The Methodology of Participant Observation* (Englewood Cliffs, N.J., Prentice-Hall, 1966).

19 The fourteen dilemmas are as follows: childhood unique vs. childhood continuous; developing in children shared norms and values vs. developing subgroup consciousness; whole child vs. child as student; each child unique vs. children having shared characteristics; equal allocation of resources vs. differential allocation; expecting self-reliance of the disadvantaged vs. giving them special consideration; uniform application of sanctions vs. selective application; civil liberties vs. school *in loco parentis*; learning as social vs. learning as individual; knowledge as public vs. knowledge as personal development and/or discovery; teacher making learning decisions for children vs. child making learning decisions; intrinsic motivation vs. extrinsic motivation; learning as molecular vs. learning as holistic; and teacher setting standards for growth and development vs. children setting own standards. A more complete description of the framework and an analysis of the other dilemmas appear in an unpublished manuscript available from the authors.

20 B. Malinowski, *The Argonauts of the Western Pacific* (Routledge, 1922).

21 We will here avoid the difficult question of whether the term 'control' is appropriate. There is little question that in English or in American schools, by law and tradition, it is the teacher who has the power to grant decision-making privileges. In the English schools we observed that the power is real and is used, as evidenced by the many instances in the data where the teacher unilaterally altered the decision-making pattern.

22 Sets of assignment cards from which children may choose are present in almost every classroom. These provide students with options of two sorts: they may provide many alternative forms of the same activity, such as a group of many SRA cards all similar in procedure but differing in the content of the story; or a set of cards may provide many different sorts of activities designed to accomplish a similar goal, such as multiple activities designed to give handwriting practice. The latter sort provides a choice of *how*, the former a very limited choice of *what*.

23 The extent to which teachers believe they can rely on intrinsic motivation has, of course, its counterpart in learning theory, Piaget and Berlyne, e.g. assume natural curiosity, and Skinner and reinforcement theorists assume motivation as the result of a history of reinforcement.

24 A memorable example was a young teacher who was not to be rehired the following year. The head gave precisely this reason: that the teacher failed to provision for the students and spark interest because he believed students would be intrinsically interested and needed no external 'push'.

25 Barth, op. cit., p. 131.

26 While two questions—who sets the standards, and who determines whether for a given area the standards have been met—are logically distinct, in practice the questions are easily confounded. A teacher may intend that a child set his own standards for art; yet, when the child is doing art, the teacher intervenes continually with evaluative statements. From a psychological point of view, the child probably feels that the teacher both sets the standards and determines whether the criteria are being met. It is possible, though unlikely, that the teacher can, as a practical matter, keep these two questions distinct at all times in all areas. The problem of what the standards shall be in a given area, another important source of variation among teachers, will not be examined at this time. Salient concepts here would be whether the standards are qualitative (i.e., is the product 'creative' or 'clear'), quantitative (i.e., how many maths problems should be assigned), temporal (i.e., how long should one work on maths), and absolute vs. relative (i.e., the paper should be neater than the previous paper, or it should approach a given standard of neatness).

27 This includes English writers as well, the Plowden Report no less than the Black Papers (C. B. Cox and A. E. Dyson, eds, *The Black Papers on Education*, London, Davis-Poynter, 1971).

12 The child as conversationalist: some culture contact features of conversational interactions between adults and children

Matthew Speier

In sociology and anthropology alike, studies of children have come under the heading of socialization. It is necessary to introduce my report about adult–child conversations with a brief discussion of this specialization, if only for the simple reason that sociological problems formulated within its conventional framework have tended to exclude the problems raised in this paper. The notable absence of treatments of the child as a conversationalist are primarily due to two reasons: a general underdevelopment of conversational analysis as part of the study of human interactions and a deeply embedded ideological position about children held by adult professionals. This ideological position[1] will be summarized before presenting some findings in the study of children's conversational interactions with adults. I will not take up any space here to discuss the general topic of conversational analysis in interactional sociology, since I have done so elsewhere.[2]

A review of the literature in the field of socialization, particularly its standard references,[3] will amply document that a set of working suppositions is deeply engrained in the choice of research problems and findings that result. I would like to refer to this set of suppositions as *the classical formulation of socialization*. I treat it as classical because it is a formulation that is rooted in adult folklore or commonsense understanding about children. Adult professionals doing sociological studies of children have oriented their work around a set of implicit conventions. Taken together, these conventions form an adult ideology about children that differs from lay ideology only in so far as it is systematically working out professional problems and solutions that are responsive to the ideology; i.e. how scientifically correct the ideology is, how defective it might be, how it could be remedied. In other words, the lay adult and the professional are equally oriented to child behaviour as regards their implicit ideological positions about the nature of that behaviour, save that the two do different things with their knowledge, have different organizational responsibilities, with different objectives and social constraints.

I can delineate *five main ideological conventions* that inform the sociologist who operates under the classical formulation of socialization when he makes an investigation of children's behaviour:
1 Children are adults in the making.
2 Children get socialized or 'made' into adults mainly by adults who teach culture, i.e. 'norms', 'values', 'roles', 'behaviour systems', etc.
3 Children progressively develop into competent social members.
4 Children's development can be either successful as they grow up through stages of life or it can be deviant anywhere along the way.
5 Children are defective social participants by virtue of precompetence or incompetence at behaving appropriately.

What this position amounts to very simply is that a child is treated as a special kind of social actor who is continually in need of learning how to participate in society. The problem of social participation is generic to the ideological position. It says: children are continually working out that problem by learning how to shape and fit their behaviour to an adult normative order which calls upon them to orient and conform to it. The over-riding interest the position therefore promotes is how well (or poorly) children go about working out that problem.

What the sociologist has overlooked, however, is that his attribution of this problem to the child is part and parcel of his own adult ideology as to what is socially important about children's behaviour. In actuality the child's problem is an adult's problem to the extent that an adult is committed to recognizing and obligated to helping the child work through that

Source: unpublished. The author is assistant professor, Department of Anthropology, University of British Columbia.

problem. Adult recognition and help take interactional form and involve on-going adult supervision and regulation of children's lives. The sociologist, then, has tended to adopt the position of an adult in his society when he has formulated research questions about child development and child rearing. It would seem that sociologists like other adults can look at children *only* from within the moral, normative order to which they subscribe. Curiously enough the only notable departure from this position within the profession has been the development of a counter-ideology along the lines suggested some time ago by Dennis Wrong[4] in his paper on the oversocialized man. More recently there has been a developing counter-ideology that attacks adult social arrangements as unsuitable for children's development and proposes the recognition of children's rights and the integrity of their own social contribution (e.g. the works of Paul Goodman and John Holt).

I am not advocating a counter-ideology in this paper, but offer instead a non-ideological or non-critical stance to the analysis of children's behaviour, one that falls within the mode of ethnomethodological or formal interactional analysis. In this mode I propose the following modification in our sociological reasoning about childhood studies. Adult ideological conventions (what sociologists might also think of as theoretical suppositions) must be re-allocated from being a purely natural resource for analysis to the position of being a basic topic for the analysis itself. That is, the classical formulation of socialization theory is not the special provenance of the sociologist but originates from the latter's position as an adult in his society. In actuality lay socialization theories are an ideological basis for adult interaction with children. One finds these theories at work in the everyday world of adult–child relationships and activities. In case it be supposed that I am suggesting we adults stop using an adult ideology where children are involved, I am not (although there may be good reason for so doing). In case it be supposed also that I am recommending that sociologists drop the ideology, *I am asking instead that they examine it as a vital part of the phenomena they are studying, and that they refrain from adopting this ideological position when they make research formulations in their studies.* To carry the modification further, I propose the term 'socialization' be dropped from our technical vocabulary and used only as a member's term (a lay concept).

In sum, then, I have argued that the five ideological conventions exhibited in the standard works of the field constitute a classical formulation of the problem of socialization, and that this formulation is an interpretive imposition of adult lay conceptions onto the data of childhood behaviours, taking, as it were, only one half of the interactional picture into consideration. The children's half, that part of the interactional picture not represented by the ideology, has been left unformulated in the analysis. To use a very crude metaphor, which will serve to introduce my next point, sociologists have been going about their study of children mainly like colonial administrators who might be expected to write scientifically objective reports of the local populace in order to increase their understanding of native culture, and who do so by ideologically formulating only those research problems that pertain to native behaviours coming under the regulation of colonial authority. Such a 'science' would be designed to serve the successful management of the native culture; it would be a practical 'science' of human management. Commitment to such a practical 'science' would originate out of an ideological interest in controlling the native culture and not out of a 'passionate disinterest' in the culture for its own sake.

The metaphor of colonial administration, though not intended to be taken as more than a metaphor, is useful in two ways. It refers to a social situation in which two cultures are put into routine contact. It also refers to a situation in which one culture is in a position to manage the affairs of the other culture. To leave the metaphor aside (saying additionally only that sociologists have tended to fit the metaphor because they do their research on children like good adults), I want to propose that these two points be taken seriously in the context of this report. A modification of outlook in our research should point innovatively to the recognizable existence of *children's culture* (or cultures). It is a culture which is separate from, but intimately related to its counterpart, adult culture. The *two cultures* are in routine contact with each other. Thus we borrow from classical anthropology the notion of *culture contact*.

If there is any scepticism about the existence of children's culture, it is a reflection of our own adult ideological commitment which has all but obscured the fact of its existence. The work of parenthood consists mainly of the practical 'science' of child management in the family household. Likewise the work of a teacher is devoted largely to the practical 'science' of child management in the classroom and around the school establishment. Yet the Opies, for example, have documented the existence of children's culture among schoolchildren in Great Britain by accumulating a vast amount of data on children's traditional lore and games which do not originate out of the practical activity of child management. Likewise my own research on children's play activity at home, and my filming of children's interactions associated with school activity outside the classroom, indicates the existence of children's culture.[5] It would appear to essentially be neither a miniaturized nor a half-baked adult culture, nor an imitated version of it—but a culture in its own right.

This paper will focus on culture contact. *It will seek to elucidate the structural characteristics of that contact in terms of the methods children and adults use to converse or talk to one another.* If the adult ideological position is an important feature of contact behaviour, an analysis of conversational interaction between members of both cultures should exhibit this contact feature as a major constitutive element of adult–child conversations. Our task is two-fold, then, because our interest is in the characteristics of adult–child relationships across the two cultures and it is to be explored through the more technical medium of conversational analysis.

The general features of conversation to which we shall make reference—those that interactants methodically orient to and achieve—are in themselves not unique to adult–child conversations, but may occur in any conversation whatsoever. However, the contact features involve distinctive methodical practices adults and children use for generally handling their conversational interactions. That is, *the contact features might be thought of as parameters of adult–child conversations* (although I suspect that some of these features may also be discovered in conversations between persons who stand in super- and subordinate relationships to each other). As this focus indicates, we will not examine conversations strictly between children (when they are out of the presence of adults) but concentrate instead on the methodical basis for making and sustaining contacts between the two cultures.

The intention of my opening remarks has been to re-orient the student of conventional socialization studies in the direction of a hitherto neglected domain called conversational analysis, itself a major subdivision of interactional analysis (i.e. all interaction is not spoken). Conventional socialization research has not developed this domain, but has instead formulated research questions out of an ideological commitment to adult ways of conceptualizing children's behaviours. These questions for the most part have not been worked out in terms of relevantly defined interactional events routinely occurring in the everyday contacts between adults and children. Finally, the ideological position has tended to relegate children to a class deficient of social participants, thus rendering them as 'poor relatives' of adult society, culturally speaking. Thus, in some very important and ironic way conventional research has confirmed the existence of adult culture by the very way it has ignored the activity of children's culture.

I would now like to turn to a summary of some of the more significant general findings I have made pertaining to culture contact features of adult–child conversational interactions. I will introduce each contact feature by briefly noting the general conversational feature to which it is related as a distinctive analytic unit of conversation. In analysing each contact feature we will find that a child has a very special status as a conversationalist. This status is accorded him when adult members of his culture decide to speak to him and when they decide to engage him in on-going conversation. This status is also achieved when the child attempts to speak to adults in his everyday environments and likewise attempts to engage in or carry on conversation with them. The child's special conversational status is an invariant condition of conversational contacts between the cultures.

Restricted conversational rights

It is a generally recognized observation that conversationalists simply don't speak whenever they please, but instead 'place' their speech at some appropriate point in the course of a conversation. Watching out for appropriate moments to fit into the flow of a conversation involves a speaker in methodically taking a turn at talking, and this may be achieved in numerous ways. This problem turns on how a speaker may exercise *his right to speak in the first place*. The existence of 'rights to speak' as an oriented to feature of conversations is a phenomenon that enters into the internal management of a conversation. Conversationalists can be observant about *who* is placing his speech in whatever places he so chooses. Some party to a conversation may be more privileged or specially entitled to speak wherever he so decides within the conversation. He may be accorded special rights as a conversationalist to speak very freely, where conversational freedom might mean a liberty to breach normal rules of turn-taking, distribution of speech, answering questions, etc.

How are such rights achieved or accorded a speaker? It would seem to be a phenomenon governed in part by the relative social positioning that social actors take in given situations and environments. This positioning may be organized into a set of relevant social membership categories[6] for routine environments. The enactment of social positions involves interlocking sets of obligatory actions for doing the routine activities of an environment. For example, in courtroom settings, rights to speak are intimately tied to the membership categories of the court: the presiding judge or magistrate has preferential rights of communication in the setting. He may over-rule out of turn, speak at length, silence any member of the court if he deems it appropriate and necessary, etc. Courtrooms are very specialized conversational settings, but preferential rights may be accorded to speakers taking social positions in a whole variety of ordinary social circumstances. I presume one of the main criteria conventional sociologists have used in designating so-called 'leadership roles' among social groupings has been: he who speaks most often must be taking or asking for the position of leader from those to whom he speaks. This is of course a naive assumption because the mere frequency of speech in itself is not necessarily right-proferring upon the speaker, even if he should go unchallenged in a single conversation. It would seem that a speaker who is in a privileged position to talk has a right to 'monopolize' a conversation without being over-ruled or accused of illegitimately doing so. To accuse another of monopolizing is to say he is not entitled to talk as much as he has. Sacks has suggested the notion of 'owning a conversation',[7] which might involve a speaker who rightfully possesses the entire occasion of a single conversation; i.e. perhaps having rights to convene, topically control, and terminate a conversation.

While there may exist special categories in our culture for those who dominate a conversation, there are other categories that reserve a right of preferential communication for their occupants, vis-à-vis others who have standardized relationships to them. Two such relationship pairs are 'adult–child' and 'parent–child'. These pairs have considerable bearing on the issue of conversational rights for children.

I wish to point out, following Sacks's lead,[8] that children have restricted conversational rights. The manner in which they can participate in conversations with adults is internally controlled by an asymmetrical distribution of speakers' rights, wherein adults claim rights of local control over conversation with children, and children are obliged to allow them that control. Children's failure to do so can be met with the sanctioning power of adult speakers.

What are some distinctive contact features of adult–child interactions that show differential and restricted conversational rights in operation? One feature involves the unit of conversation called 'silence'. Adults can exercise their right *to enforce silence upon a child speaker or a group of children*. In cases where children are talking and acting among themselves in the proximity of a disapproving adult or parent, the latter can reproach them with a demand for silence. This type of routine contact between the two cultures involves the adult as *an interactant at a distance*; e.g. the children are playing in another part of the house. Adults use their right to enforce silence as an appropriate acoustic condition of households; e.g. 'If you must make all that noise, you'll have to go outside and play'. In such contacts nothing more than a brief exchange of this sort may occur; often it does not develop into a conversational engagement with a mutually sustained involvement among the participants.

Much parental work is of a sort that calls for monitoring of children's activity from a distance, and that work is specially entitled with the *right to intervene* if deemed necessary. Such interventional behaviour does not rely on the normal politeness rules shown to other adults. The overseeing function of adults and parents allows for categorical use of asymmetrical rights of intervention. Children, conversely, must not intervene without some care to display politeness rituals as acceptable *pre-intervention behaviour*. Although children may refrain from displaying it, they always leave themselves open to criticism by so doing. Getting a child to display politeness, especially in front of others, is a socialization technique from a parent's point of view. However, it can be more than that if the intervention is done for the benefit of onlooking adults. In such circumstances adult contacts with children are culturally enforced by

the presence of other adults, who can jointly make and confirm criticism made initially by one adult, i.e. in the case of enforcing silence, all adults can collaborate in the enforcement. It should be pointed out, however, that the meaning of 'silence' can vary from an injunction against talk to diminished volumes of speech and noise, the latter being called 'quiet'.

(1 A teacher in second-grade classroom giving geography lesson. B and F are second-graders.)

1	*Teacher*:	What is that province? Brian?
2	*B*:	B.C.
3	*T*:	What is that one?
4	*F*:	Alaska.
5	*T*:	That's close but it's a state.
6	*T*:	Simon I'm going to ask you to leave if you don't keep your mouth closed. You talk *too much out of turn*. (emphasis mine)[9]

(2 The following children are playing with an electric train in the front of a house: Guy, $7\frac{1}{2}$; Steve, $8\frac{1}{2}$; Brooke, $6\frac{1}{2}$; Leanne, 7.)

1	*G*:	Will you girls get out of here, who, we never said you could, you could come in, we wanted to play alone. Now you guys have to come butt in, don't turn it on, don't turn it on until the girls go.
2	*S*:	How do you put this on reverse?
3	*G*:	You can't put this one in reverse.
4	*Mother*:	Listen Guy they don't have to get out.
5	*G*:	Well they're in the way too much, you guys just watch/
6	*Mother*:	Let them play too, let them play/
7	*G*:	You guys just watch, just go up there and watch for awhile/
8	*B*:	Guy.
9	*Mother*:	Listen, that's not fair/
10	*G*:	I said I would give them their turn to control it.
11	*Mother*:	Well you don't have to act like such a boss. Let everybody enjoy it Guy.[10]

(3 Two mothers having coffee at mother A's home. She tells her children, Dougie, 3 yrs, and Brenda, 4 yrs, to go into the playroom.)

1	*MoA*:	Will you kids please get into the playroom. Dougie, I told you not to bring that in here. You have to be quiet. Daddy's sleeping you know.
2	*Sg5*:	Crayons at home.
3	*MoB*:	That means you too Susie.
4	*Sg5*:	I wanta donut first, huh.
5	*MoB*:	Not until you ask politely. And don't yell you two.[11]

Turning to silence of the kind that calls for no speech whatever, consider a conversational engagement among adults and children where talk is sustained over the course of some mutual activity such as dinner or just talking in a room together; e.g. at home or in the classroom. One adult method for the enforcement of silence is to terminate the child's right to continue on a topic of talk that has developed into a disagreement or argument. This termination can be accomplished because the adult reserves the right to enforce absolute silence. A standard practice in circumstances of this nature is to use a terminating device that in effect characterizes anything else a child may say as '*back-talk*'. In some very literal sense all talk is talking back to a previous speaker. I-talk-to you-and-you-talk-back-to-me is a fundamental unit of interchange in conversation, a pair of utterances. This is not what is meant, of course, by the common-sense term 'back-talk'. At some point an adult decides he is not going to allow a child to say any more in a conversation, where it is clear the child will want to. Remarks such as 'I don't want to hear another word about it', or 'That's final', or 'Any more back-talk and you'll be in trouble', display the power of termination belonging to an adult speaker.

(4 This is a gathering in the television room in the home of a family. Members of another family are also present in the room. The participants include the father (A) of the house and his 8-year-old girl, S. Their guests include a father (B) and his two children, T., a 7-year-old boy, and R., a 5-year-old-boy. The mothers of these three children are in another part of the house. The three children are sitting watching television while Fa(A) and Fa(B) are just entering the room.)

1	*S*:	Oh, oh. Here comes Dad.
2	*T*:	Yeah. Mine always watches hockey and we never/
3	*Fa(A)*:	O.K., kids.
4	*T*:	Yeah. See?
5	*R*:	Aw, gee.
6	*Fa(B)*:	See what, T?
7	*S*:	Aw, it's just like always, Mr. B. Why can't/
8	*Fa(A)*:	Come on kids. 'It's hockey night in Canada'.
9	*Fa(B)*:	Heh, heh.
10	*R*:	Aw, Dad. This is *our* show!
11	*Fa(B)*:	R., why don't you go and see what mommy's doing?
12	*Fa(A)*:	Yeah, S. Go ask mother for some ginger ale. Would you like some pop, R?
13	*Fa(B)*:	Sure you would. Wouldn't you/ Tiger?
14	*R*:	Gee, and we got here *first too!*
15	*Fa(B)*:	That's enough.
16	*R*:	Aw, gee.[12]

Closely tied to this termination phenomenon is another feature of culture contact that exhibits the restricted rights of the child, namely, an adult also reserves the right to dismiss a child from his presence. *Dismissal rights* can be used to methodically achieve silence, especially when a child is trying to intervene upon adult cultural activity. Another term for the same methodical application might be *removal rights*, which has even broader application to situations in which adults can remove a child from a place or from the presence of others, but this is not relevant here.

The enforcement of silence need not occur only when children and adults have argumentative speech or when children engage in challenging behaviour. (Challenging is a characterization of speech that derives from the existence and recognition of adult authority over children; adults can be treated as *speaking from authority* where children are concerned.) It can also be done when adults wish to pursue the course of a conversation among themselves and find that children are running interference by talking to them while they are already talking to someone else, or similarly, when children address someone to whom they are already talking. This is usually characterized as *interruptional behaviour* by adult conversationalists. We wish to point out that such behaviours can bring injunctions of silence if only to afford conversational continuity to adult talk in the occasion. A notion that can be useful in understanding this aspect of enforced silence is '*protecting a conversation*'. It may be necessary for adult conversationalists to engage in protective methods for conversational development against children's interferences. Why these are treated as interferences is another question. In any case, enforced silence may be a method of ensuring the life of a conversation.

Finally, an adult may enforce silence indirectly by refraining from talking to a child. This is done perhaps because the adult doesn't feel like undergoing sociability, and the restricted rights of the child permit him the opportunity to relax constraints on social interaction normally operating among adults. Thus, in adult terms, an adult can afford to get away with impolite behaviour by simply refusing to be conversational. This may be the case especially when the adult is preoccupied with some solitary activity of his own; e.g., reading the evening newspaper or a book, watching a television programme, etc., and does not want to alter the allocation of his involvement, to use Erving Goffman's term.[13]

Notes

1 Throughout my discussion of this ideological position in conventional socialization research I am indebted to the late Harvey Sacks. Many of the ideas I present are borrowed in some form from Sacks's lecture on the subject delivered and tape-recorded in Berkeley, in the summer of 1968 at the conference on 'Language, Society, and the Child', sponsored by the Anthropology Department at Berkeley.

2 See Speier, 'Some conversational problems for interactional analysis', in D. Sudnow, ed., *Studies in Interaction*, N.Y., Free Press, 1971; also 'The everyday world of the child', in J. D. Douglas, *Understanding Everyday Life*, Routledge & Kegan Paul, 1971; 'The Organization of Talk and Socialization Practices in Family Household Interaction', unpublished doctoral dissertation, Department of Sociology, University of California, Berkeley, 1969.

3 See Speier, 'The Organization of Talk . . .', pp. 1–45, and 'The everyday world of the child', pp. 188–9. The most recent addition to the standard reference works in the field is J. Clausen, *Socialization and Society*, Boston, Little, Brown, 1968.

4 'The oversocialized conception of man in modern sociology', *American Sociological Review*, 26, 1961, 184.

5 See Speier, 'The Organization of Talk . . .', ch. 5, on playing house. I have recently begun to film children's activities in connection with school routines; i.e. leaving for school, walking to school, recess behaviour in the school yard, returning home at lunch and after-school behaviour around the school grounds. A myriad of interactions and a whole range of activities transpire in these periods when children are on their own, although the behaviour is entirely organized as part of school routines that occur *outside* the classroom. I hope to get a project going in which children will film their own activities in and around the school to get at their own conceptions of relevant events in that environment and how they see it as a culturally organized environment of children.

6 See Sacks, 'The search for help', in D. Sudnow, op. cit.; for a summary of Sacks's concept of a membership category device, see Speier, 'The everyday world of the child', pp. 204–9.

7 Sacks suggested this to a small seminar at Berkeley, where he delivered a lecture on his work, in 1966, to a group of persons connected with the cross-cultural language socialization project.

8 Sacks, UCLA Lectures, no. 2, spring 1966.

9 Robert MacKay, 'The Acquisition of Membership in First Grade Classrooms', unpublished Master's thesis, Department of Anthropology and Sociology, UBC, 1967.

10 Transcript 15, Seminar Data, M. Speier, 1969–70, collected and transcribed by Gary Parkinson.

11 Transcript data from S. Persky and L. Salutin, 'Some Strategies and Findings of a Conversational Analysis of a Household Routine', presented to Summer Workshop at the conference, 'Language, Society, and the Child'.

12 Author's fieldnotes, Raw Data, vol. I, SFN 9.

13 *Behavior in Public Places*, Collier-Macmillan, 1963, pp. 43–63.

13 The mobilisation of pupil attention*

M. Hammersley

The purpose of this paper is to describe the order that the teachers in one school seek to impose on classroom interaction and the means by which they impose it. However, I shall be concerned primarily with 'instruction', the teacher talking at length to the whole class, with interspersed question and answer sessions. This seems to be the basic teaching technology in the 'traditional' teaching prevalent in this school. It appears to be a fairly common teaching technology, and, to the extent that this is true, the description in this paper will have a rather broader relevance than simply to the classrooms observed in this school. I regard teaching technologies as collectively produced and sustained rather than as idiosyncratic. Furthermore, they are also adapted, in one way or another, and to one degree or another, to the constraints operating on schools and teachers.[1] The nature of 'classroom order' is a crucial area of investigation if we are to understand selection and socialisation processes in school, since the classroom is one of the major settings in which they occur. I also see the description of versions of teaching operating in different types of locale as logically prior to attempts to explain their nature and distribution.

The teachers' concern with classroom control in instructional phases of lessons can be divided into two partially conflicting subconcerns. On the one hand, the teacher sets out to engage and maintain the attention and effort of pupils and to motivate their participation. On the other, he seeks to control the extent, nature and timing of pupils' participation so that he can control lesson-topic.[2] This paper will deal with the generation and maintenance of attention and participation. I have dealt with the control of participation elsewhere.[3]

Not only are pupils to arrive at and leave the school at certain times, their school day is carefully sliced up and allocated and their presence required at different times in different parts of the building. The teacher's first concern in lessons is the establishment and defence of an official classroom gathering. The building of separate classrooms obviously makes the task of protecting the lesson from external intrusion a little easier than it otherwise would be. It does not solve the problem, however, since, to be effective as communication barriers, walls need to be recognised as such.[4] 'Conventional situational closure' is a status which must be claimed and enforced for a setting. While other schools and other lessons will have ensured that pupils know 'how to behave in classrooms', pupils have many motives for not complying with such rules or not obeying teacher's orders.[5] As a result, the teachers have continually to establish the sanctity of the lesson at the beginning of and throughout each lesson.

The classroom encounter is constituted by the teacher via the enforcement of certain rules defining pupil activity (regarding space, time, noise, etc.), knowledge and membership boundaries. Classes sometimes had to line up outside the classroom and wait for the teacher to give them permission to enter 'his' room. In other cases pupils could go in, though there were noise and activity limits. Late arrivals were expected to address the teacher and offer some account to him for their lateness:[6]

(1) ((Pupil comes in late and sits down))
   T: Did you just appear from nowhere?
   ((Teacher signals pupil to come out, pupil goes to the front))
   T: Don't you think you should apologise for being late?
   ((Pupil doesn't answer, looks at his feet))
   T: Where've you been?
   ((Pupil tells him))
   T: Where's the apology?
   ((Pupil apologises))[7]

Source: unpublished. Martyn Hammersley is lecturer in educational studies, The Open University.

(2) ((Some pupils enter late))

    T: I shall cancel a PE lesson and you can do some work.

    P: Sir it was Mr Scott.

    T: I'll see Mr Scott but it's your duty to come to your next lesson on time.

In these two examples, class members are being required to recognise the boundaries of the lesson. It has a beginning, defined by the teacher, at which they should be present.[8] If, on the other hand, the teacher is delayed and comes to the classroom after the pupils have already arrived, pupils are not entitled to demand remedy from him for his lateness. If they do, it will be seen either as 'cheek' or as a joke, though he may, as he arrives, apologise without waiting to see if his apology is accepted. Pupils cannot be involved in activities which are more important than coming to lessons, or at least such activities are extremely rare. Furthermore, the decision as to whether any particular activity or contingency constitutes a warrant for lateness or absence lies with the teacher, though he is of course subject to certain bureaucratic rules regarding this. The teachers are allowed greater leeway than pupils in delaying their arrival for, or absenting themselves from, lessons and are certainly not accountable to pupils.

Class members are not free to leave the classroom before the end of the lesson without permission from the teacher, and permission is given only on the basis of a few warrants, and even then not automatically. The most common warrants are official errands, going to the toilet and sickness. Sometimes reasons are clearly signalled by the teacher as inadequate.

(3) ((Harris goes out to the front in a written-work phase of a lesson))

    P: Sir can I have a drink?

    T: A drink? Give over

    ((Harris walks back to his seat))

    T: Let me know in time next Thursday and I'll 'av' a pot of tea sent for you.

The teacher's reply indicates not only that the warrant is not adequate but that the pupil ought to know that it is inadequate, thereby implying an absence of commonsense on the part of the pupil. When permission is given, it is often accompanied by injunctions to return quickly or within a specified time. Even when the bell goes at the end of the lesson it is for the teacher officially to dismiss the class:

(4) ((Bell rings))

    T: Don't get up. It's a message to me that, it sez let 'em go if you're ready, an' I'm not yet.

Pupil and teacher visitors were expected to approach the class teacher first, even if their business was with a pupil. Both were expected to have an acceptable warrant for the intrusion, and, in the case of pupils, could be held publicly accountable for that warrant.[9]

The teachers were similarly concerned with illegitimate knocking, and with curtailing inlooking and 'unjustifiable' outside activity that might cause interference or encourage outlooking:

(5) *T*: (   ) Can you give me any suggestions as to what

    P: Sir

    T: a tall story is?

    (Greaves, another teacher, enters the classroom)

    G: Can I interrupt a second?

    T: Yes.

    G: Right Mr Philipson's class in maths, stand up ((Some pupils stand))

    G: Mr Philipson's class is this all that goes to Mr Philipson?

    P: Sir

    T: Stand up (you) who go to Mr Philipson for maths.

    G: I think that's about all actually. Right, somebody yanked the handle of my door just now as you came in from Mr Philipson (   ) Did anyone (play around with) my door. Did you *see* anybody yank the handle of my door (I can say that several boys have seen someone.) Nobody knows anything about it. Well I'd better say what I was saying to the other half of you. I shall expect the boy to come to me either later this afternoon or tomorrow morning. ('Av you got that) If he hasn't done that I shall take great pleasure in keeping this class—Mr Philipson's class— in one playtime. Right, now I think I know who that was, I expect him to own up. Right, thank you Mr Walker.

(6) ((The teacher interrupts his talk in a lesson to ask Harris, a pupil sitting towards the back of the room: Was that Arnold?

    The teacher seems to have noticed by some break in Harris's attention that someone had been looking into the classroom from the corridor. All but one of the windows with the corridor are covered with pictures, and, later in the lesson, when he has set the class some written work, the teacher pins up a poster over the remaining one.))

Those of the teachers who had classrooms on the ground floor looking out on to the yard had inlooking and outlooking problems caused by pupils arriving late, going on errands, playing games in the yard, being let out early for break or lunch, etc.

Far more problematic than protecting the boundaries of the classroom from external attack, however, is the task of defending the lesson from disintegration via internal defection. It is not sheer physical presence that is required of pupils. They must form one encounter and pay attention to the 'official' environment. The teacher works to organise the gathering so that he is the hub, the focal point of attention and interaction, as though classroom interaction were to be constituted by the addition of twenty or so separate dyads. He spends the bulk of his time facing pupils, talking to all of them simultaneously, and the desks are arranged so that ideally they all sit facing him. Desks are sometimes separated, seats are sometimes assigned. Pupils require permission to move about the classroom unless general permission has been given and, as with exit from the room, only a limited number of warrants will be accepted, and even those not necessarily. When movement is allowed, it is to be within certain parameters of single-mindedness, noise-restriction, speed, etc., enforced by the teacher.

Pupils are to watch and listen to the teacher, to follow what he is saying and to try to answer his questions. When written work is set they are to get on with it carefully, and at 'reasonable' speed, eschewing any breaks or alternative activities. Any spare time after the work has been finished should be taken up with 'productive' activities, 'going over' work done, doing extra work or perhaps reading, though the teacher may *allow* those who have finished to read comics or engage in some other enjoyable task in order to motivate those still working.

When he has set written work, the teacher still monitors pupil behaviour and at different points he will look up from what he is doing to check that pupils are 'working'. In talking to the whole class, as a subsidiary activity to his discourse, the teacher is constantly scanning the stream of behaviour for signs of inattention. Even when he selects an answerer for a question and focuses on the face of the chosen pupil, he is simultaneously keeping a check on what's going on in the rest of the room. He organises his speed of delivery, his persistence with a point or topic as opposed to the insertion of a question or the setting of written work, as well as his decision to continue seeking an answer to a particular question, to reformulate it, or provide the answer himself, according to his assessment of the state of attention.

For their part, pupils present normal appearances of 'attending' or 'working'. When they engage in what they know to be 'illicit' activity, they usually disguise it, gambling on the fact that since the teacher has only one pair of eyes, only minimal and appropriately timed appearances will be required to satisfy him.[10] They continually glance at the teacher in order to time their disguises correctly, and this is particularly obvious where they are engaged in mock or real fights in the classroom: blows are timed more according to judgments of the teacher's scanning programme than to the defences of the opponent.

The teacher starts official classroom proceedings by setting the stage for the lesson rather than by launching straight into it. At some point after the entrance of pupils into the classroom he initiates the following kinds of preliminaries: publicly checking that all pupils have access to the necessary materials so that they will have no excuse for future inattention on the grounds that they are searching for them; telling pupils to leave pencils, pens, rulers, etc. on the desk and to close books—thereby removing some of the potential resources for pupil distraction; and demanding that pupils stop talking, sit up straight facing the front, etc.

(7) ((Noise of class entering, talking))
P: Sir can we read those short stories?
((Movement noise and talking continues apparently no answer from the teacher))
T: Right, a'right, close your books look this way. Now, you boys at the back, no reason why you shouldn't have books, are there any left?
P: No sir.
T: Right, right oh will you share with him please, (   ) you share with him. All you need to do is . . . ((much shuffling of chairs)) All you need to do is to sit . . . ((noise continues)) Oh dear me can we have the noise stopped as soon as possible. Now look this way. Anybody tell me, keep your feet still, and everything else, anybody tell me what a legend is?

(8) *T*: Cook, sit yerself please behind Johns, Harper move forward one.
Pn: (   )
P: Give cats a chance.
T: You not the desk.
P: Sir can I sit there sir?
T: I've told you where to sit.
Pn: (   )
T: Right sit still let's have a bit of attention, You now have *some idea* how knights were trained.

(9) ((The teacher gives out exercise books, paper and maps; general noise and activity))
T: Right pencils down. I'm waiting to get started now shut up, shut up, shut up. You can notice the difference can't you. Now before we have pencils falling off desks let's have them in the groove.
Arms folded. I can still see a lot of arms not folded. Fool of the week award to you. Are we ready to start now? Have we come down from the clouds of insanity, down to the ground. Do we know which way up we are. Do we know when our tongues are wagging eh Bannister, it is Bannister isn't it.
P: Yes.
T: I wonder why I've remembered your name, is it because of all that brilliant work you've done. Well if not today's your chance.

The teachers seem to insist on more rigorous 'full attention' at these starting-points than further into the lesson, though stage-setting often forms the first move in a cycle of demands that recur throughout the lesson. The teacher does not, of course, list all the acts he proscribes but uses general injunctions such as 'settle down', and reference to some proscribed activities to stand for all the relevant others; he expects pupils to know what is prohibited.

Something which, as can be seen from (8) above, sometimes forms an integral part of stage-setting is seat reassignment or the threat of it. However, this can occur at any stage of the lesson, being designed to prevent the fragmentation of the encounter into a number of smaller gatherings. The teacher seeks to organise the interaction so that to the extent that pupils interact with one another they do so through him. Inattention on the part of one pupil constitutes a potential source of escalating misattention involving others. When the teacher detects 'day-dreaming' or pupil to pupil interaction he often acts directly to curtail them. Attention demands can range in structure from minor expressions such as pauses in talk, staring or pointing at the relevant pupil(s), raising voice volume and repetition of phrases, to verbal insertions into topic-centred discourse.

(10) *T*: Leach, even for our cat a look is enough, I don't have to say anything.

(11) *T*: Now it's the same with moulding *anything*, you must have a tapered mould and this is why the metal producers fell on this particular shape for metal. Will you stop talking please ((Name)) unless you've got something important to say. Now let's move on.

(12) *T*: What's the difference between a civil war and an ordinary war?
P: Sir
P: Sir
P: Sir
P: Sir a civil war eh both (   ) . . .
T: Morton
P: Sir
T: Will you come an' sit by yerself.

(13) *T*: Sometimes it swings round an' the hawk goes up in the sky, *hangs* over what it's after.
P: Sir (   )
P: Sir (   )
T: an' it suddenly goes sh : : ; picks it up, an' it's trained, it's well trained, it comes back.
P: Sir they (   )
        (
P: Sometimes it eats it.
T: Occasionally yes—I'll paralyse you Short I'm sick to death.

(14) *T*: Did you ever see the series on the invisible man Arnold?
P: Yes.
T: Well sitting behind a little book like that you are not invisible, put it down and keep still.

The more extreme attention demands often involve physical assault, off-the-cuff or caning, as well as more subtle techniques:

(15) ((The teacher brings out a pupil for 'talking' and tells him to stand with his nose against the blackboard: 'This is a trick a schoolmaster taught me'. The rest of the class watch. The teacher draws a circle round where the pupil's nose touches the board and tells him to keep his nose in that circle until he is told to sit down, a period of about fifteen minutes.))

Attention demands addressed to specific pupils must also be seen as implicit warnings to all pupils, but some demands are directed at the class as a whole or large segments of it.

(16) *T*: Before we go on, I've got a message for you which I hope you'll be able to understand. Don't talk when someone else or I am talking. Have the seven or eight constant interrupters heard that? Secondly, keep still. Listen to what the other lads and I have to say, see if you can pick something up. If you're in doubt about how to do it look around at the five lads who've been doing it perfectly. I notice the five lads didn't need to turn round; they knew who I was talking about, the restless ones had to look round to see who they were supposed to be copying.

Attention demands, general and specific, are sometimes recurrent throughout a whole lesson, cyclical moves in negotiation.

The teacher provides frequent slots for the participation of pupils by asking questions integral to the topic he is expounding, thus using pupils' motivation to take part to generate attention. But his questions do more than this; they enable him to go beyond the visual appearances presented by pupils and function as checks that official proceedings are being 'taken in'. Indeed, some questions seem to be pure attention checks:

(17) *T*: And these, all these plants are?
P: (   )
P: Small
P: Small
T: Small, so therefore man being?
P: Big
P: Big
Pn: (   )
T: Big will have a good?
P: View
T: View around him couldn't he

(18) *P*: near a plain sort o'
T: It was on a plain right ((writes on blackboard)) plain, on, a, flat, piece, of, land and

that is called a what?
P: Plain
P: Plain
T: Plain. A plain right

(19) T: I wouldn't advise ⌐ ost of you to try
swimming it ((the English Channel)) but of
course it can be swum is that true or false?
P: True
P: True sir
T: True, right.

Such questions are unselective as regards answerer,
and usually involve the following features alone or in
combination: the requirement of an answer which
has been provided, sometimes even in answer form
in the last few utterances, which requires the provision of a missing word; and/or which involves a
yes/no, true/false answer. When not calling on information already given, these questions usually draw
on 'general knowledge'—what 'a pupil of this age
ought to know'. Hence it is attention and not understanding that they are designed to test. Furthermore
they keep up the number of questions asked, thus
providing for pupil participation, and promote
competition to answer teacher questions, while
minimising digression from topic since the answer is
'easy' and anyone who knows can shout it out.

Topical questions can also be used to have a
preventive effect: the fact that there may at any time
be a question, possibly even directed at a particular
pupil, or alternatively that there may later be writing
to be done based on what is being said now, may
counter pupil inattention. Topic-centred questions are
sometimes actually used to *demand* and restore
attention. Instead of interrupting his presentation of
lesson topic to insert the kind of direct attention
demand mentioned earlier, a teacher may merely
direct a question at suspicious quarters.

(20) T: What's the difference between a civil war
and an ordinary war?
P: Sir
P: Sir
P: Sir
P: Sir a civil war eh both (   )
T: Morton
P: Sir
T: Will you come an' sit by yerself. Massie
can you finish what Fraser was going to tell
us?
P: No sir
T: I didn't think you'd be able to
P: Sir the . . .
T: Put yer hands on the desk let me see
what yer doin' with 'em. Forget about
Massie Morgan concentrate on what I'm
saying
P: Sir Sir
T: or what some of the others are saying.
Finish it yerself then since Massie can't.

(21) T: if you don't plough up underneath the
top soil that you do plough up. What do we
call the blade of a plough, the blade of a
plough Bannister, any ideas Roger
Bannister? What's the question? No idea
have you? No idea. What's the blade of a
plough called the part that does the cutting
of the soil of turning it over? Ploughshare.
ploughshare.

In this use of questions, the teacher asks a question
specifically not to get an answer but as a summons,
and also to imply to the pupils that he knows when
they are not attending even though he may not always
show it. In general the question asked is 'easy',
ensuring that it is a pupil's attention, not his 'intelligence' or 'knowledge', that is being tested. Example
(21) indicates that failure to answer any question may
be taken by the teacher to suggest lack of attention, a
hypothesis that can be tested by the asking of an
'easier' question. Attention demands which operate
by means of topical questions highlight the continuous
importance of pupil attention to the teachers. Teacher
concern with the establishment and maintenance of
pupil attention underlies and interpenetrates even
those classroom activities that are apparently concerned with the transmission of knowledge.

An important feature of the teachers' insistence on
the attention of pupils should be noted. The teachers'
demands, which are attempts to enforce informal
rules, that is, the pupils are expected to *know*, cover
not just pupil actions which might prevent other
pupils hearing or seeing official events, or merely
those which might seduce them from attending, or
simply those which display that a pupil is not attending, but rather any which imply lack of 'proper
respect' for the official environment, and thereby the
teacher and the school. What is required of pupils
is a 'proper attitude'. What the teachers demand
when they demand attention is not simply the direction of the eyes in the right direction, but 'full'
attention; in other words, the suppression of anything
but very minor subsidiary activities like head-
scratching or nose-blowing. They even attempt to
prescribe physical posture, frequently issuing injunctions to 'sit up straight', 'stop leaning back on your
chair', 'get your head off your hands', etc. One
teacher justified his demand that pupils 'sit up' in the
following manner:

(22) T: A considerable number of you people are
going to have the biggest spinal deficiencies
later. ((He draws a diagram on the board of
how one should sit on a chair)). I'm not
laughing about this, I'm serious.

I am arguing here that this is pure rhetoric, as the
teachers, including this teacher, showed no sign of
following their own physiotherapeutic advice in
either the classroom or the staffroom.

Exhibiting a 'proper attitude' also involves taking
what the teacher says and does in the sense that he

'obviously' means it; in other words, perceiving and treating him as the teacher and taking what he says 'for real'. The official environment must be treated as serious not funny, important not trivial, gospel not moonshine, powerful not puny, interest-consuming not as a casual background, and thus as grounds for enthusiastic participation, not yawns, argument, etc.

The warrants that class members must use to request permission to leave the room are excuses,[11] and thus are deferential towards classroom proceedings: they propose the future absence be expunged as no reflection on the justification or importance of classroom events, they do not make the grounds for teacher control topical. That excuses are used, and that they are used in request form, makes such pupil absences doubly deferential, as well as opening pupils up to refusal and negative character definition:

(23) ((Pupil asks to go to the toilet))
> *T*: You're a scrounger, you're always scrounging
> *P*: I'm not, is wanting to go to the toilet scrounging?
> *T*: Don't shout at me. Stand up straight when you're being talked to. Ten minutes, if you're any longer I'll keep you in playtime or dinner-time.

This example also illustrates the authority maintenance device Goffman calls 'looping'.[12] Instead of following on from the topic raised by the pupil and offering justifications for his character definition of the pupil, the teacher treats the demand for an account as itself an accountable matter and as further grounds for character definition.

In the same way, 'setting the stage' must be seen as a demand that pupils put on a 'proper attitude' for the coming lesson; in other words, that they recognise the importance of what is to be said and done. The demand for attention then is also a demand for respect, for authority-recognition; attention is *paid*.

This 'respect' is simultaneously part of the cultural competence which the teachers are seeking to inculcate, *and* an essential requirement for their exercise of control over pupils. By inculcating and enforcing what they consider to be a proper attitude to 'authority', the teachers are also engaged in the crucial task of establishing and maintaining the basis for their own control of pupils. Control by pure coercion is difficult to achieve, unstable and certainly very time consuming, and, though the teachers undoubtedly occupy a very powerful position in relation to pupils, their coercive and exchange resources are not, in themselves, sufficient to guarantee pupil conformity. Teachers in a state school are not simply given a licence to teach pupils irrespective of the latter's wishes; they are simultaneously charged with the duty to teach the pupils allocated to them. Compulsory schooling, therefore, while avoiding the need for schools to attract a clientele, makes control of pupils more difficult by preventing pre-selection and reducing the possibilities of expulsion as a threat and as a method of getting rid of 'trouble-makers'.[13]

Different power resources take different amounts of time to operate and are more or less certain in their effects, always relying on a background of support or at least non-intervention by others. Though the teacher has the power of the state behind him, that support is neither immediate nor automatic. The backing of the state is not guaranteed for *whatever* he does to pupils, and, though he is partially insulated from authoritative witnesses, since he has more chance of having his as opposed to pupils' accounts believed and because the classroom shields him, he must nevertheless be careful not to leave evidence such as marks on pupils or do anything he cannot easily deny. Furthermore, requests for support from head or colleagues or for the transfer of a pupil may themselves endanger a teacher's reputation, since he is expected, as a competent practitioner, to be able to control classes by his own means.

Power depends on what people value at a particular time and compared to what. The teacher in this school has control over certain things that the pupils value: break and dinner-time in the yard, PE and games lessons; interesting or uninteresting, oral or written work in lessons; immediate release or detention at four-o'clock; as well as the use of physical punishments. However, he does not have the power of selection since there is no streaming; nor are pupils generally dependent on him for effective preparation for external examinations. Most of the pupils were not on courses leading to external examinations. Given the rather limited power resources teachers in this school have to rely on, it is always a matter of judgment what will dissuade who from what and when. These resources have to work more by threat and bluff than by their full-scale exercise. They are all devalued by frequent use because the deprivation of valued goods they involve or the pain they cause become commonplace or demythologised and therefore not something necessarily to discourage action. The teacher has to be very careful therefore not to devalue his currency. It seemed that the teachers recognised that with a small number of the pupils they had already run out of punishments and all that could be done was avoidance of confrontation, humouring, etc.[14] Some of the available power resources also have the unfortunate characteristic of causing the teacher as much inconvenience as pupils, for instance having to supervise a class in break-time or after school, instead of having coffee in the staff-room or getting home.

Powerful positions do not operate without the exercise of effort and skill on the part of the occupier, and this is especially so when the latter is in continuous face-to-face contact with those over whom he is to exercise power. Given this and the contingencies of the power resources available to these teachers, authority, or rather the manipulation of an authoritative image, becomes a crucial weapon in the classroom power-game.

Authority is not something which is simply delegated. While the teachers are regarded by head, local and central government officials, and important publics, as having certain legitimate functions and methods, and consequently are provided with certain power resources, their exercise of control depends largely on their getting their authority recognised by the pupils.

The groundwork for teacher control is laid outside the classroom, and even outside the school. The value of schooling is widely promulgated and widely accepted as obvious, though its value may be seen differently by different groups. Also, the compulsory nature of schooling makes it a fact to be recognised, and tends to result in its value being taken for granted to a considerable extent. Hence, because siblings and parents of children now at school have usually themselves attended schools, schooling appears a 'natural' stage in 'growing up'.[15] The activities of the other teachers and the head in classrooms, corridors and hall also of course provide the foundation on which a teacher builds in his own classroom.

However, this groundwork does not remove the necessity for the teacher to establish and defend his authority: pupils and teachers do not necessarily agree on what shape education should take or on what the roles of teacher and pupil involve. In particular, the extent of legitimate teacher control has to be settled and is never settled once and for all. While other schools and other lessons to some extent serve as preparation for later secondary school lessons, pupils have many motives for not complying with teachers' rules, some of these motives even being a direct product of the way in which the teachers organise classroom interaction.

In their attempts to generate and maintain authority in the classroom, the teachers in this school seemed to use three basic strategies. First, they presented authoritative appearances, they presented their claimed status and the consequent obligations on pupils as facts, as something normal, natural, and unchangeable which must be taken account of not questioned. It is for this reason that the pupil's demand for an account in (23) above is itself treated as accountable.

In ordinary conversation participants are expected to display involvement and even prove it by the production of 'appropriate' responses. However, the teacher in the classroom doesn't just expect but actively demands *full* attention and participation as a natural right, without offering accounts of any kind. The teacher takes for granted, and by taking for granted, aims to establish 'beyond question' rights to deference and control. He seeks to establish an asymmetrical structure of interaction; he insists not just on different rules being applicable to pupils and teacher, but also on the exclusive right of teachers to decide publicly when a rule has been broken, to challenge the offender, and to decide on punishment.

Infractions of classroom rules are publicly treated as moral deviance, and hence as potentially a basis for inferences about the character of offenders, rather than as counter-claims and a basis for negotiation.

One of the things the teachers were concerned with in the enforcement of classroom rules was the attitude to those rules which underlay the pupil's action and the likely public appearance of attitude.[16] A teacher's response seemed to turn on whether he saw the action as merely a lapse, or as a specific challenge. One criterion for differentiation is the timing of the action. Pupil actions which are possibly produced as part of an escalating sequence of disturbance or as replies to a teacher demand or which could be seen as such by other pupils will be dealt with and dealt with more drastically than those not seen as potentially forming part of such a context. Similarly, the teachers' frequent insistence on an offender providing an account is a way of negating the possibility of an action being seen, either by the offender himself or by other pupils, as a challenge which went unmet, since excuses, which are all that will be accepted, are restorative in function. In the same way, undisguised 'illegitimate' classroom activities would usually be treated as more serious offences than disguised deviance, since the disguise *can* be taken as paying deference to the official environment.

This concern with the attitude to classroom rules implied by pupil actions is particularly clear in the following example:

(24) *T*: On Friday we'll be talking about the
things they left, how things looked in those
days . . .
((A pupil has been clearing up his equipment
and then while the teacher is still talking he
brings it out to the front to put away))
T: I'm only the teacher here, if you lot feel
like getting up and going you might as well
go. ((The pupil goes back to his seat. The
teacher tells him to stand up and asks him:
'Aren't you ashamed?,' asks for an apology,
asks for it again louder, and then says
'Say you won't do it again'.))

The teacher rules out any expressions or actions at odds with his authority as the product of bad manners or social incompetence. This is often done by means of age-comparisons:

(25) *T*: Given the fact that you came in like a lot
of five-year-olds we'll treat you like five-year-
olds. Right we'll do it my way. I don't care if
we do it till break.

The implication here is that people of different ages or at least of five and thirteen can normally be expected to behave differently; in other words, those of thirteen should be able to 'behave properly'. Moreover, the behaviour of five-year-olds can be explained as the product of their five-year-oldness. The description of thirteen-year-olds' behaviour as what could be expected from five-year-olds cancels the need for any consideration of possible rationales for this behaviour, or any questioning of its 'improper' nature. It is described as the product of 'childishness' or 'immaturity', something which the pupils *ought*, and, if they are going to be treated as adult, *will have to*, grow out of.

The same implications can be made in terms of 'sex' and 'intelligence':

(26) *T*: Now—WILL YOU STOP BEING SO SILLY *the next boy who laughs in that stupid manner like a little girl I shall drop on quickly*

(27) *T*: I'd like you to line up like intelligent boys.

In (26) silliness, stupidity, childishness and girlishness are all used to characterise the same piece of behaviour. They seem to be used as synonyms, reinforcing the imputed character of anyone who engages in that behaviour. In (27) 'intelligence' is attributed to 'proper' behaviour, the implication being that non-conformity will be seen as merely further evidence of stupidity. In other examples such labels are not so clearly used, but the import seems to be the same:

(28) *T*: Can you two control yourselves now you're out of arm's reach?

The teacher is legislating a definition of what male adult competence is, characterising the implications of 'properly managing one's own affairs' for action in this setting. This status is highly valued by pupils but is something which it is difficult for them to sustain, given typical treatment by others, not least by the school itself. It is, of course, only by the maintenance of such dependence that schools are able to maintain control over pupils on the basis of authority. The teacher uses the behaviour of a pupil or of the pupils as a whole to show the kind of thing such competence would proscribe and to establish that this pupil is not yet, or all the pupils are not yet, capable of acting properly and therefore cannot be treated as adults.

(29) *T*: You're paying a lot of attention looking at a magazine aren't you. Manners maketh man, that's why you must be a boy then, you haven't any. How many questions have you answered? One in a month.

The teacher usually doesn't actually degrade the offending pupil permanently. That would give the latter little to lose and everything to gain from full-scale rebellion. He demands that the pupil remedy the infraction by showing regret and sometimes by providing an account, even if that only amounts to a 'don't know'. In other words, the pupil is invited to join the moral community which his action offends by dissociating himself from and denouncing the self which committed the offence, thus reinforcing the moral validity of the rules. The teacher also seeks to gain the support of the remainder of the pupils in making the character inferences, thus reinforcing the moral community to which the scapegoat, the offending self which will be attributable to the pupil if he does not dissociate himself from the action, is contrasted. However, when other pupils laugh at a victim of teacher degradation, thus asserting their own superiority to him, the teacher sometimes subsequently generalises his characterisation of the offender to others or all of them. He thus maintains the legitimate basis for control and hopefully motivates each one to attempt to prove that the indictment is not true of him, even if it is true of the others.

Even physical punishments gain much of their power from the identity they impose rather than through their sheer impact.[17] Useful for the teacher in this respect is that the pupils' 'a fool for being caught' coincides with his 'stupid boy'. The acceptance of such punishment by pupils is particularly effective in publicly authorising the teacher's control, since it recognises his right to infringe severely the normal self-territories of pupils.[18]

The second major strategy adopted by these teachers to establish their authority is to 'demonstrate' their superiority. They do this first by asking questions to which *they* know the answers but which pupils are unable to answer, although the fact that it is they who set the questions obviously potentially detracts from the impact of this. Second, they challenge pupils and take them on in confrontations, although again the fact that there are rules proscribing 'cheeky' pupil behaviour potentially detracts from the effectiveness of the demonstration.

Little further needs to be said about teacher questions. The manner of knowledge presentation itself tends to 'display superiority', and the teachers frequently pronounced definitively on topics and problems to which there is no one right answer, or in relation to which there is no general consensus in the society. They unilaterally defined what were the *relevant* and correct inferences to be drawn from a particular piece of information. They did not indicate that this was a relevance and correctness for *present purposes*; in other words, for *their* present purposes.[19]

To the extent that the teacher successfully imposes an asymmetrical 'order' on classroom interaction, he turns his claimed authority into a fact to be reckoned with. By successfully demanding attention and disciplined participation, the teachers actually 'demonstrate' their competence as teachers, that they *are* teachers, and therefore their 'superiority' to pupils. Similarly, the acceptance of physical punishment by pupils doesn't just involve recognition of teacher authority but displays the impotence of the punished. Moreover, pupils know what 'good discipline' is, and seem to judge a teacher at least partially in terms of how well he is able to achieve what is presumed to be his goal. Any 'failure' to maintain 'discipline', whatever the motive, is in danger of being seen as weakness, and thus lack of 'authority' and of being exploited by pupils.[20] In equal-to-equal interaction[21] demands for attention or 'disciplined' interaction, pronouncements on the other's immaturity, stupidity, etc. would be treated as challenges requiring response in kind unless face is to be lost.[22] Failure to respond to such challenges with a counter-insult not merely signifies recognition of teacher authority but reinforces it by implying failure of nerve or lack of creativity in inventing an effective response; i.e. inferiority in interpersonal skill. The teachers try to use success in interactional terms to legitimise their claims to superior status, to establish their authority.

As I have said, the fact that teachers insist on classroom rules, under which most effective counter-challenges would be illicit, detracts from the effectiveness of these exchanges. But it is important to note that if a teacher insults a pupil, and the latter offers no response, the teacher's authority is reinforced; but if a counter-challenge is returned and the teacher is forced to resort to denying the legitimacy of the reply rather than 'topping' it, his 'superiority' is not demonstrated and his authority is thereby weakened.

Besides issuing what are in effect challenges in the form of attention and participation demands, teachers also sometimes, in the way in which they make these demands, elaborately 'take on' pupils: for instance by inviting or demanding reply. Question-form attention demands are an example, and the 'easier' the question the more effective is the put-down if the pupil fails to answer. However, the easier the question, the more likely it is that the pupil can provide an adequate answer, which opens up the possibility of the teacher himself losing face. Where an answer is produced, face-saving on the part of the teacher may sometimes be achieved if he treats the answer as though the question had not been an attention demand at all. Alternatively, the answer may be accepted grudgingly with the implication: 'You did well to get that one didn't you'. The following excerpt includes an elaborate 'take on' which eventually backfires on the teacher:

(30) *T*: Look don't be looking at them you
     ((Arnold)) turn round here. You're being
     extremely stupid this morning aren't you.
     Those simple questions that I've asked you,
     you've either not known or you've 'ad a wild
     guess. It's even written on the board.
     Pn: ((Laughs))
     P: Sir
     T: What's that say there?
     P: Ingot
     P: Ingot
     P: Ingot
     T: So what's this

P: (   )
       (
T: shape of metal called?
P ((Arnold)): Ingot
T: Now d'you think it's possible for you to
remember that for the next
          (
P: No
T: ten minutes?
Pn: (   )
T: Right, stand there facing this way, ((The
teacher has already made Arnold stand up; at
this point he moves him further forward))
there don't touch the bench an' we'll ask you
again in a few minutes. It is amazing how
quick you boys can remove things from yer
memory. We've *been* through it this morning
we've been through it at least twice before.
:   :   :
T: I wonder who can remember, I wonder
who can remember, the melting point or the
maximum temperature in a blast furnace.
P: Sir
T: Arnold?
P((Arnold)): Ingot sir
Pn: ((Laughter))
T: 'S'going to be very difficult for C—
((Arnold's new school next year)) *All right*.
Now just stop a minute. Stop. We shouldn't
laugh at this boy, we should pity 'im. He's
just either being very silly or he is very silly
Pn: ((Laughter and talk))
T: Arnold 'ow can ingot be the answer to a
temperature. Listen to the question. What's
the maximum *temperature*, or the
minimum or maximum in a blast furnace?
Sh : :
P: Sir, Sir.
P((Arnold)): About two thousand
T: *Good*. See that was a case of just simply
'aving a sleep an' thinkin' all I've got to do is
remember the next question he's going to ask
me. You see how silly you make yourself
look by doing that. Two thousand degrees.
Short is certainly enjoying that so he can
answer the next question, perhaps he'll do as
well out of it eh?

Ordinary attention demands may also sometimes be designed to 'take on' the pupil:

(31) *T*: Dunn, why are you there?
     P: Eh?
     T: Why are you there?
     P: To sit down
     T: I assume it's to chat up Harris.

A vague question which requires more than a yes/no answer makes reply difficult. The question is so opaque that the pupil cannot answer it without further information regarding its intent, but when he asks for clarification all he gets is a repeat. His feeble reply is capped by a smart, prepared, retort which is especially smart since the question was about the pupil's own behaviour.

By demonstrating interactional skill-witticisms, sarcasm, challenges, etc., the teachers hope to show that they deserve their superior position, that they deserve respect. In this they rely on lack of solidarity among pupils, that pupils will appreciate the skill with which the teacher causes one of their number to lose face and will therefore judge him superior and justified in his claims to control classroom interaction. He is naturally aided in this by the fact that loss of face by one pupil allows others to feel superiority to that pupil.

The third form of strategic action the teachers use to maintain control is what might be called strategic easing of the pains of pupilhood: lack of autonomy in organising one's work, boredom, low status, etc.[23] Strategic easing can take at least three different forms. In the first place it may involve the offer of an exchange, though it is an exchange which generally cannot be bargained over. The teacher sets the terms of the exchange, since explicit bargaining would undermine the presentation of teacher authority as beyond question, and indeed even the offer of exchanges may do this. The relaxation of a certain rule or rules, for instance against pupil-to-pupil conversation, is offered in exchange for conformity to other requirements, for instance 'getting on with the work'. Alternatively, conformity in one phase of the lesson, or in one lesson, is required in return for a relaxation of rules, for instance against playing cards or reading magazines in another. Or again the offer may be of one of the, to pupils, more pleasurable lessons or lesson activities: films, games in the yard or gym, quizzes, plays, etc., in return for work in this lesson or lesson phase.

(32) ((Group activity lesson))
   T: Now remember at the end of the lesson when I say sit down do as I say, I haven't interfered much with what you were doing during the lesson so do as I say at the end.

Yet another kind of resource the teachers may claim to offer relates to pupils' reputations and the consequences which are seen as tending to flow from bad reputations.[24]

(33) *T*: Who were you in trouble with?
   P: Mr Greaves
   T: Well I'll tell Mr Greaves that you behave well in my lessons. Whenever I hear some things about Abbis and Wilson, for instance, I occasionally hear things, I tell them that you behave all right in my lessons. I hope I'm able to do that in the future.

(34) *T*:((to a particular pupil)): We started the lesson off on the wrong foot, let's try and put it right shall we.

In (33) the teacher is trying to use claimed influence over other teachers' opinions of pupils in order to buy 'good behaviour'. In (34) the teacher seems to be offering to wipe a pupil's slate clean in return for compliance 'from now on'.

The second kind of strategic easing is accomplished via threats, either threats to institute formal or informal punishments—the latter including full enforcement of rules or institution of disliked lesson activities such as exercises, grammar, maths, etc.—or threats to curtail what is formulated in the threat and probably, though not necessarily, has been previously formulated as easing activities.

(35) *T*: I'm going to stop some of your PE and you can do some writing.

Here a formal part of the curriculum, PE, is defined as an easing activity, and is portrayed as something which does not necessarily occur but is conditional on 'good behaviour' in other lessons. What is easing and what isn't must depend on the valuations of the pupils. Teachers' strategic easing is tailored to what they know about pupils' preferences; in this case that in general they like PE and dislike writing. The formulation of things as better than they could be made as a device for trying to elicit 'good' behaviour seems to be a common technique used by these teachers.

(36) *T*: Let's have you all sitting up straight; if you're going to behave like infants you'll be taught like infants.
   :   :   :
   ((Teacher hits Leach))
   T: You should know me by now I won't tolerate constant chattering. If I have to come from this desk again I shan't be just straightening flies out of your hair.
   :   :   :
   T: I realise these days that you're allowed to do a lot of very lax things these days like wobbling on your chairs but unless we're very careful we'll be having a session of playing soldiers standing up straight. Now come on sit up straight, hands off desks.

Threats that easing activities presently being engaged in will be curtailed if 'behaviour' does not improve are also common.

(37) ((Lesson in yard))
   T: Now if you make too much noise we'll have to go back into the classroom.

(38) *T*: Come on behave yourselves or we'll go back to grammar.

The final kind of strategic easing I have in mind is that process which, while no doubt pervasive, is very difficult to produce direct evidence for: where, without any signal to pupils, the teacher modifies his normal requirements and responses on the basis of the anticipated consequences of his actions, particularly in relation to likely 'trouble' in the senses of time consumption, loss of face, and physical danger.[25]

(39) ((Teacher talking in the staffroom to other teachers and R))
   T: You've got to try and avoid confrontations, although they sometimes force confrontations on you, you could spend all your time trying to persuade or force the reluctant to work, if there's some who are willing to work it's better to concentrate on them.

(40) ((T to R in the staffroom))
   T: Discipline's gone since the immigrants came, clout one of the West Indians and you're in trouble.

(41) ((Teacher-to-teacher conversation in the staffroom))
   T1: Has the younger Harris been up to anything recently? He used to be fine but he's become all sulky recently.
   T2: Just ignore him, he gets on with his work okay.
   T1: Oh yes I know.

(42) ((Double period mostly taken up with teacher talking, towards the end the pupils become restless. Afterwards T comes over to talk to R))
   T((to R)): You can see the problem there, I talked too long. I've a tendency to do that, I overshot, when the first bell went I promised myself that I'd stop in five minutes, I got a shock when I looked at my watch.

This 'realism' is probably so pervasive that to talk of the suspension of 'normal' expectations and reactions is inaccurate. Rather, what are suspended are ideal expectations and reactions. The teachers seem to ignore much deviance that occurs in the classroom, and select instead what to deal with as well as how to deal with it on the basis of various grounds, of which the most important are probably perceived underlying 'attitudes' and 'seriousness' of the offence.[26] But, as I'm suggesting here, also important is the teacher's assessment of the likely reactions of pupils, and this involves taking into account pupil notions of fairness, and pupil and class characters, and deriving from these how pupils are likely to respond to various different possible measures, what are the chances of each of these measures succeeding, and at what cost in time, effort and face. Such assessments and decisions, of course, often have to be made 'on the spur of the moment'.

The fact that the teachers must establish their authority with pupils by these forms of strategic interaction may be taken to indicate something about the nature of power—that its exercise is never un-

problematic. Alternatively it may be taken to indicate something about the relative weakness of the position of these teachers vis-à-vis pupils. However, the two points are not mutually exclusive. To argue for the importance of strategic interaction and negotiation processes does not mean denying the importance of differences in the weight of the power resources available to different actors and organisations. The area which is open to negotiation or gains by strategic action will vary according to the weight of power resources controlled by the different sides. Nevertheless, it is important to recognise the costs that can be involved in using particular power resources, and the contingencies involved in the *exercise* of any power resources. In the case of these teachers, while they have ultimate power resources which pupils cannot match, these resources are such that they cannot be used all the time with all the pupils, other power resources must be fashioned to maintain routine control, and I have tried to show that this problem is solved by the teachers through the use of strategic action.[27]

The description and explanation of the kind of 'order' that emerges in classrooms is a crucial component of any investigation of what 'good behaviour' and 'good pupil' mean, of the conditions underlying the display of intelligence in school,[28] and of the perspectives and lines of action developed by pupils.

Acknowledgments
I would like to thank the pupils, teachers, and head of the school in which the fieldwork was carried out for their friendly co-operation. There are many others who have contributed over the last few years in one way or another, but most of all I want to thank Isabel Emmet for many careful readings of this work in various drafts, and my wife for discussion and suggestions.

Key to transcripts

R:	Researcher
T:	Teacher speaks.
P:	Pupil speaks.
Pn:	Two or more pupils speaking at once.
(( ))	Observer descriptions.
((name))	Pupil's name stated but untranscribable.
(55)	Transcript-quotation reference number.
( )	Uncertain/guessed materials or indecipherable words.
Clark	Speech overlap
(	
Anyway forget	
the next	Raised voice.
WILL YOU STOP	Extra loud voice.
: : :	Stretch of interaction omitted.
Sh : : :	Sound prolonged.
All you . . .	Speech tails off.

Notes

* This report uses data derived from fieldwork in an inner city boys' secondary modern school. The fieldwork involved observation in classrooms, aided by a tape recorder, with background material supplied by informal observation and participation in the staffroom.

1 On the constraints operating on teachers see, for example, R. Sharp and A. Green, *Education and Social Control*, Routledge & Kegan Paul, 1975.

2 Obviously all the teachers did not teach in exactly the same way, but they did seem to work on the basis of the same presuppositions about goals and methods. This would not be sheer accident, of course. Even though their work is largely carried out in isolated settings, there is considerable staffroom discussion of pupils and their actions, into which assumptions about aims and methods are built. There is *some* access to colleagues' treatment of pupils in the more public areas of the school and to a lesser extent in the classroom, and a sense of common fate prevails in the staffroom. I observed eleven of the fourteen full-time staff teaching at one time or another but my observations were focused on, and my recordings restricted to, four of the teachers. The reader is inevitably reliant on my judgment that what I have described is common to all the teachers I observed.

3 See M. Hammersley, 'The organisation of pupil participation', *Sociological Review*, August 1974.

4 See E. Goffman, *Behavior in Public Places*, Collier-Macmillan, 1963, p. 152.

5 On the use of rules in reputation-building, see C. Werthman, 'The function of social definitions in the development of delinquent careers', in the President's Commission on Law Enforcement and the Administration of Justice, *Task Force Report: Juvenile Delinquency and Youth Crime*, Washington, US Government Printing Office, 1967.

6 I shall discuss the nature of pupils' accounts to teachers a little later.

7 Extracts from fieldnotes and tape transcripts are not intended as evidence in the sense of my description being simply derived from them. Rather, they are an indication of the kind of evidence I have used and the way I have used it and provide some opportunity for readers to construct alternative interpretations.

8 While the teacher has to work to a timetable, the actual beginning of each lesson is decided and signified by him.

9 One exception occurred during the course of the fieldwork: on one occasion a pupil visitor asked to talk to a member of the class in private. The teacher granted the request even after being refused information on what it was about, and the two pupils went outside the classroom to confer for a few seconds. Though it's very close to explaining away contrary evidence, I suggest that the explanation for the teacher's surprising decision lies in the particular pupil who made the request; he was generally regarded as 'trouble' by the teachers. I shall elaborate on this explanation later.

10 On timed glances and appearances, see D. Sudnow, *Studies in Social Interaction*, New York, Free Press, 1972.

11 On accounts, see S. Lyman and M. B. Scott, *A Sociology of the Absurd*, Appleton-Century-Crofts, 1970.

12 *Asylums*, Penguin, 1968, p. 41.

13 Of course pre-selection and expulsion are really practicable measures for a voluntary school only in a sellers' market. Where there are selective and unselective schools in a compulsory education system, pre-selection and expulsion are exercised by the former at the expense of the latter. In a comprehensive system, the positioning of catchment area boundaries often becomes a major concern of schools.

14 On avoidance of provocation, see R. A. Stebbins, *Teachers and Meaning*, Leiden, Brill, 1975; D. H. Hargreaves, S. K. Hester and F. Mellor, *Deviance in Classrooms*, Routledge & Kegan Paul, 1975.

15 On schooling as a mass superstition, see P. Goodman, *Compulsory Miseducation*, Penguin, 1971; E. Reimer, *School is Dead*, Penguin, 1971; I. Illich, *Deschooling Society*, Penguin, 1973.

16 Teachers usually suspect, often rightly, that offenders are playing to the pupil audience.

17 Obviously punishments vary in their degradatory intent and effect: compare canings in front of the whole class and outside the classroom; detentions involving standing on a white line in the hall and those involving a whole class missing a PE lesson.

18 See E. Goffman, *Relations in Public*, Penguin, 1972.

19 On this see my article: 'School learning: the cultural resources required to answer a teacher's question', in P. E. Woods and M. Hammersley, eds, *School Experience*, Croom Helm (forthcoming).

20 See E. Rosser and R. Harré, 'The Meaning of Trouble', in this volume, and V. Furlong, 'Anancy goes to school', in P. E. Woods and M. Hammersley, op. cit.

21 By equal-to-equal interaction I mean interaction where each participant accords the others equal interactional rights.

22 Some subcultures have elevated such exchanges to an art, see, for instance, C. Mitchell-Kernan, 'Signifying and marking: two Afro-American speech acts', in J. J. Gumperz and D. Hymes, eds, *Directions in Sociolinguistics*, New York, Holt, Rinehart & Winston, 1972.

23 On easing, see M. Cain, 'On the beat', in S. Cohen, ed., *Images of Deviance*, Penguin, 1971; see G. Sykes, *The Society of Captives*, Princeton, 1958, on the pains of imprisonment; on the particular pains of pupilhood, see P. Woods, 'Having a Laugh', in this volume.

24 As I shall suggest, if a pupil has a bad reputation with teachers, instead of 'picking on' him, teachers may allow him greater autonomy, in order to avoid trouble.

25 There is also some indication from staffroom talk that concern is not just with trouble for oneself but also with causing trouble for colleagues, what colleagues did was seen as having consequences for one's own dealings with pupils.

26 On reactions to deviance, see Hargreaves, Hestor and Mellor, op. cit., ch. 8.

27 How successful these strategies are depends on the power of the teachers vis-à-vis pupils and on the negotiation strategies of pupils.

28 See Hammersley, op. cit.

14 Ad hocing in the schools: a study of placement practices in the kindergartens of two schools

K. C. W. Leiter

Overview

In this paper I am concerned with the placement of students in particular classes. I will examine the practices teachers use to assign students to classes having particular characteristics, to place them in ability groups within classes, and to promote them to the next grade. I investigated these practices in two kindergarten classes in two southern California school districts. (. . .) The examination of these practices leads me to deal with the adult models used by the teacher to accomplish and sustain the factual properties of the students as social objects.

(. . .) Although the study by Cicourel and Kitsuse (1963) comes (. . .) [close] to the approach taken here because they attempted to study the evaluation process itself, they did not have access to the counseling sessions between the high school counselors and their students. In this study I not only obtained accounts by the teachers evaluating their students, I also recorded screening interviews between kindergarten teachers and incoming kindergarten students which formed the basis for placing students into one of two homogeneous kindergarten classes at one of the schools studied. (. . .)

The students at School A are differentiated into two homogeneous kindergarten classes: a 'mature' class and an 'immature' class. The basis of this differentiation is the students' performance in an interview with one of the teachers. This interview is essentially the administering of a developmental test designed by Ilg and Ames (1964) of the Gesell Institute. The students are screened in this manner either during the Spring or in the Fall when the parents bring their children to the school to register, and the interview is part of other tests which include a speech and hearing examination, a health examination

Source: A. V. Cicourel *et al.*, eds, *Language Use and School Performance*, Academic Press, 1974, pp. 17, 19, 21–49, 52–6, 58, 73.

and verification of the child's birthdate (in California a child must have turned 5 by December 2nd in order to enter kindergarten). At the end of the year a kindergarten student was either 'retained' in kindergarten for another year or he was placed in one of three first grades. One of these first grades served as an unofficial 'junior' first grade. All of the 'weak' students were placed there. The decision to 'retain' a student or send him on to first grade was made by the kindergarten teachers who then discussed their decisions with the principal so that he could deal with the student's parents regarding any question about the placement.

(. . .) At School B, I found a tracking system which was structurally different from that at School A. The two kindergarten classes were 'team taught' by two kindergarten teachers. The free teacher would come into her colleague's class to teach two of the four ability-groups during 'activity time.' The kindergartens were heterogeneous, but within each class there were four homogeneous ability-groups: reading, high readiness, average, and low readiness. Each group had its own curriculum and the tracking system was used both in forming the ability-groups and then perpetuating them through first grade placements. Students were not 'retained' in kindergarten at School B. At the end of the year a kindergarten student was either placed in one of the two 'regular' first grades or in the 'junior' first grade.

Placement settings in the two kindergartens

In this section specific settings are examined in which kindergarten teachers in both schools are either actively engaged in placing students or gathering information for that purpose. Kindergarten 'settings' is intended as an analytic notion, because, in actual practice, all of the activities within the classroom inform placement decisions.

School A

(. . .) The screening interview itself consisted of three parts: an initial interview, complete-a-man, and copy forms. The initial interview consisted of the teacher asking questions of the child about her age, her family, and what she did during her last birthday party. In the 'complete-a-man' part of the interview, the teacher presented the student with a pencil and a dittoed drawing of a half-completed man—the student was supposed to fill in the missing parts and talk about the drawing. In the 'copy forms' part of the test, the teacher presented the student with drawings of a square, triangle, circle, and a divided rectangle and asked the student to copy each one as it was presented to him. For the first two parts of the screening interview, the teacher works from a dittoed face sheet. This sheet served as a script for the teacher with lines and spaces for her to write in the student's replies. This dramaturgical terminology is used so that the transcripts of the interview can be examined vis-à-vis the script to locate and demonstrate the situated character of the screening test.

The sheet as a script does not tell the teacher how she is to get the information from the child. It only provides her with questions which do not specify what it is they call for. For example, the first line of the Initial Interview reads as follows:

How old are you?——Shows fingers;——Counts them——. For every interview one of the teachers said the following:

Teacher:	How old are you La?
Student:	Four.
Teacher:	Four?
Student:	Four now.
Teacher:	You're four now?
Student:	I already had my birthday.
Teacher:	I see. Can you show me on your fingers how much is four? How many fingers are four? (Student holds up hand showing four fingers by tucking her thumb towards her palm.) That's right. Can you count them?
Student:	Yeah.
Teacher:	Let me hear you.
Student:	One, two, three, four.

Her colleague handled the same part of the initial interview in the following manner:

Teacher:	Okay Pe, how old are you?
Student:	Five years old.
Teacher:	Five, good. Do you know when your birthday is?
Student:	No.

At this point Teacher 2 moved on to the next question on the script, 'Did you have a birthday party,' which she rewords as, 'Do you remember ever having a birthday party?'

The comparison between the two teachers' treatment of the same section of the script suggests that the two differ in their reading of the script and its requirements. The first teacher interprets each entry of the script as instructing her to ask the child in order: (1) how old he is, (2) if he can show his age on his fingers, and (3) to count the fingers (or ask the child to count them). The second teacher on the other hand reads the same part of the script as saying: Ask the child how old he is, if he shows his fingers mark 'yes' in the slot, and if he counts them as well mark 'yes' in the slot. This comparison points to the 'open structure' of the script. The 'open structure' of the interview script results in the teacher's use of elicitation practices to manage the interview situation. These elicitation practices are not contained in the script but are used by the teacher to sustain the interview and to get information from the child.

Expanding students' talk   Both teachers expanded the remarks of the students they interviewed. Following are two examples from different teacher–student interviews as well as different sections of the screening interview. The first example comes from that part of the interview where the teacher asks about the occupation of the student's father. The second example is from the complete-a-man section of the interview.

(a) *Teacher*: Do you know what kind of work he does?
Student: I'm not there.
Teacher: No you're not there so it's hard to tell sometimes isn't it humm?

(b) *Teacher*: How do you think he feels inside?
Student: Sad.
Teacher: Do you think he's sad inside? Do you . . . How can you tell?
Student: Cuz he mouth's sad.
Teacher: Oh you made him a sad mouth did you. Oh I thought you were going to make him a happy mouth. You made him a sad mouth, that's how you can tell e's sad inside humm?
Student: Umm humm.

In both of these examples the teacher is expanding the child's answer to her questions by filling in what she presumes to be the intent or meaning behind it. The specific examples of this practice are:

Teacher: No you're not there so it's hard to tell sometimes isn't it humm?

and

Teacher: Oh you made him a sad mouth did you. Oh I thought you were going to make him a happy mouth. You made him a sad mouth, that's how you can tell he's sad inside humm?

Not only does the teacher go beyond the surface form of the student's answers, there is also an upward inflection and rise in intonation of the teacher's voice at the end of both of the expansions, which suggests that the teacher is using the expansions as a communications check. She seems to be saying in effect, 'Is this what you mean?' The teacher's use of expansions in this manner parallels their use by parents as reported by Bellugi and Brown (1964) in their study of the child's acquisition of syntax.

Providing a context   One of the teachers provided the students with a gestalt-like context in order to keep the interview going.

  (a) *Teacher 1*: What does that look like to you Ha?
  (b) *Teacher 2*: Pe, I have here a picture of a man and the poor man doesn't have all of his parts. Look at him. . . . Now with this pencil, will you move your chair closer, and make the parts that the man needs?

In the first example (a) the teacher not only leaves it up to the child to figure out what it is that's being presented to him, she asks him for his definition of it. In the second example, however, the other teacher provides the child with a context against which to compare the drawing when she says, 'I have here a picture of a man and the poor man doesn't have all of his parts.' With such a context the teacher is helping the student locate the missing parts and is also informing the student about the nature of the task. (. . .) The manner in which the teacher presents objects to the child affects how the child sees those objects.

Leading questions   A third practice which was used by both teachers was providing cues to the students through the use of leading questions. This practice was used mostly during the complete-a-man section of the interview and was an effort on the part of the teacher to help the student 'see more' in the picture. The reader is invited to note not only the leading questions but also the feed-back that the teacher provides the student when he completes a part of the 'man' in the example below.

  Teacher: What does this look like to you Ha?
  Student: It looks like a one-legged monkey.
  Teacher: A one-legged monkey?
  Student: Yeh an' one ear.
  Teacher: A one-legged monkey with one ear huhh?
  Student: And one arm and no eyes.
  Teacher: No eyes. Why don't you give him what he needs then, okay? Take that pencil and . . . all the things he needs.

(. . .) I want to point out several features of this exchange. Because of the student's 'strange' answer to her initial question, during the first seven lines the teacher has to decide whether or not the student has recognized the task by being able to name the parts that are missing from the drawing.

The teacher has to evaluate the student's answer on the spot and has to decide whether or not the student really knows what is going on. That decision process involves the 'expansion' elicitation practice. The expansion 'Teacher: A one-legged monkey with one ear huhh?' is formed by combining two previous utterances by the student, 'It looks like a one-legged monkey' and 'Yeh an' one ear.' In addition, the teacher temporarily suspends the fact that the student is supplying missing parts to a 'monkey.' At a later point in the interview she tried to get the student to see the drawing as a 'man':

  Teacher: Does a monkey wear clothes?
  Student: Yeah.
  Teacher: Okay does he still look like a monkey?
  Student: Umm humm . . . I like different kinds of monkeys.
  Teacher: What kinds of monkeys do you like?
  Student: The ones with clothes on.
  Teacher: Okay . . .

The series of leading questions which the teacher uses not only enable the student to 'see more' in the drawing but also provide feedback for his actions and statements because the teacher monitors and connects them across the interview. Examples both of the use of leading questions and the teacher's monitoring of the student's replies are found in the following section:

  Student: Put a leg there and put a nose on here (*he draws*).
  Teacher: Is that all he needs now look closely and see if he's missing anything.
  Student: No.
  Teacher: Now did you tell me he had one ear?
  Student: Yeah right there.
  Teacher: All right should he have one ear?
  Student: No, no he needs another one.
  Teacher: Oh he does (*student draws*) umm humm.

Here the teacher first provides the student with a leading question, 'Is that all he needs . . . ,' and a command, 'now look closely and see if he's missing anything,' in an effort to get the student to see additional missing parts. When the student indicates that the drawing is not 'missing anything,' the teacher then retrieves a statement made by the student at the beginning of the exchange and confronts him with it— 'Now did you tell me he had one ear?' The teacher is linking the student's utterances across the interview and connecting them with a leading question, 'All right should he have one ear?,' which in turn relies on the assumption that the student possesses common knowledge or 'what everyone knows' (Cicourel, 1973; Garfinkel, 1967).

The screening interviews as a situated accomplishment
The situated accomplishment of the interviews consists of the teachers' use of these and other elicitation practices. That some of these practices cut across all of the interviews while others are teacher-specific and child-specific underscores rather than detracts

from the accomplished nature of the screening interviews. They are necessarily accomplishments because there exists no set of instructions for telling teachers how they are to obtain information. To view these practices as being faulted versions of how the teachers should have proceeded if they had conducted the interviews 'scientifically,' is to ignore the fact that the ideals of science, like the script used by the teacher, do not provide either the teacher or the child with instructions for carrying them out. (. . .) Therefore, the elicitation practices are not to be regarded as faulted versions of how the teachers should have proceeded; they couldn't have proceeded in any other manner and still sustain the interview as social interaction. Without their use, the interviews would have degenerated into silence occasionally broken by talk.

Reflexive features It is important to note that the teacher is involved in both deciding what is happening in the interview and simultaneously making it happen. The 'essential reflexivity' of the teacher's use of elicitation practices lies in the fact that she evaluates the information she receives from the student while at the same time she produces that information through her decision to 'probe' the student or by continuing on with the next part of the interview. The teacher's use of leading questions to help the student 'see more' in the complete-a-man section of the interview (see p. 118) is an excellent example of the interview's essential reflexivity: it is through the teacher's use of leading questions that the student comes to 'see' that there are more parts to be added and which parts are needed; while at the same time the teacher views the parts added as the 'results' of the test. Hence through her use of the elicitation practices, she decides what is happening as she makes it happen. In this manner, the elicitation practices provide 'continuous (reflexive) feedback' thus enabling her to sustain the sense of 'what's happening' (Cicourel, 1973). In conclusion, then, the elicitation practices are essential for the accomplishment of the screening interviews. They are essential in the sense that through their 'seen but unnoticed' use the teacher is able to sustain the sense of the interview as an ongoing interaction while at the same time producing its ongoing character.

Indexical features The second aspect of the accomplished nature of the screening decisions which is illustrated by the teacher's discussion of Ka is the indexical nature of the screening results. A context must be created or in this case remembered to decide the specific sense of the results. An example of this property is found at the beginning of the section:

> *Teacher*: . . . And why she put that in there (*a square inside of which is a circle with lines radiating out from it*) I don't know if it's to represent a flag or something.

> *Int.*: No. I think that was the (*draws on a piece of paper*) thing. A couple of the kids did that. . . .'
> *Teacher*: Oh that's right this was one of the . . .

The comments of the teacher and the interviewer suggest that the recognition of the screening results depends on supplying a context. The teacher does not recognize the object drawn by the student even though it can be easily described. She recognizes it after the interviewer supplies her with a context consisting of his drawing the object and pointing out that several students represented it in the manner depicted by the student being discussed. The reader may say at this point, 'Well, the student did such a bad job that it was unrecognizable.' This is not the case for the teacher's comment: 'I don't know if it's to represent a flag or something,' suggests that the object is recognizable as a something. The object drawn by the student can be taken to be any number of things—it is potentially equivocal even though it can be described easily. Because of its potential equivocality, labeling the object or deciding its specific sense is not an easy matter. Deciding the specific sense of the object requires that the member (teacher, researcher or anyone else reading the screening results) supply a context consisting of the setting, the occasion of the drawing, the person who drew the object, the intent of the person, etc. In fact the teacher's remark, 'I don't know if it's to represent a flag or something,' suggests that she is attempting to assemble such a context to make the object sensible.

Scenic features (. . .) Another placement practice that was observed during the screening decisions meeting was the use of the student's age as an interpretive scheme for evaluating the student's performance. This practice is illustrated when the teacher makes the following comment about Ka:

> *Teacher*: . . . But for a child who will be that old it seemed to me that she should have been a little more outgoing . . .

Here the student's age becomes in effect a scheme of interpretation for evaluating behavior and assigning the student a score on the screening test. This use of age is dramatically illustrated by the following comments made by the teacher about another student to her colleague:

> *Teacher 1*: I put the child down as a five-minus.
> *Teacher 2*: Five minus, umm humm.
> *Teacher 1*: And I think that's about right.
> *Teacher 2*: Umm humm (*Office secretary calls Teacher 2 out of the room*).
> *Teacher 1*: Maybe I ought to put her five plus because she does have a May birthday and she can do all this. I think I will: a five plus. She would be one of the more mature ones.

Note that the decision is made on the spot and that

the basis for the change is largely the child's age and what age stands for in the teacher's scheme.

Promoting students   Another placement setting at School A was the promotion of students into the first grade and assigning them to specific first grade teachers. The ground rules for how the kindergarten students were to be placed into the first grade became apparent to me in a meeting with the new principal and the two kindergarten teachers. The meeting was scheduled to familiarize the principal with the techniques used to screen the incoming kindergarten students and to make the arrangements for the screening.

Once these arrangements had been made, the principal asked the teachers if they would like to help organize the first grade classes for the next year. He then placed on the table three large pieces of cardboard with strips of tape across each one and the name of a teacher at the top. He also placed on the table two envelopes from which he took pictures of the present kindergarten students. The teachers were to write on the back of each student's photograph two or three 'descriptors' of the student and then place the picture on one of the pieces of cardboard. The instructions for placing the students with the teachers were as follows:

Principal: Here are these pictures of (*Teacher 1's*). Now—
Teacher 1:   No, mine were here first my friend. These are (*Teacher 2's*)—Wait a minute those are mine.
Principal: Now what I want you to do is take each one of these and on the back with a felt pen or something write two or three descriptors. (*Picks up a picture.*) What's outstanding about this child, Pa (——): sunny, cheerful, aggressive, retiring?
Teacher 2:   Would you please write a long list that we could choose from, those are great (*laughs*).
Teacher 1:   No she's outgoing, an' strong academically.
Principal: Okay then that goes on the back here. Now recognizing that (*jet overhead masks out talk*). (*First Grade Teacher A*) is a different kind of person, what would be good for this child? Now does this child need somebody strongly oriented academically? Does she need that kind of strong hand? Here's a warm mother (*tapping First Grade Teacher B's card*): I came into the auditorium and she had Li on her lap. Li had gotten money at lunch time but she didn't bring it quite by accident because the student teacher thought she'd brought money for her lunch and she had to take it back which just crushed her. And First Grade Teacher B instead of saying 'It's all right now you just get in line and go,' there she was sitting there with this child—you know it was beautiful.

Now we're going to have some kids in here who are going to need a Momma-type. All right here's your Momma (*tapping First Grade Teacher B's card*). Here's a gal we want to protect (pointing to First Grade Teacher C's card which is actually going to be the new teacher's class). We don't want to give her really tough ones. I will not have her picking up all the kids that are difficult.
Teacher 1:   Hummm.
Principal: People who have the experience, people who have the know-how pick up the tough ones because they know more and can protect against that kind of child. So these are the two that we give the really difficult kids to and—Now you know how First Grade Teacher A teaches: it's very open and noisy and undisciplined (*now holding Su's picture*).
Teacher 1:   Couldn't stand it—
Principal: Well this is right. What kids will benefit by being—
Teacher 1:   Su should go right there (*puts picture on First Grade Teacher B's card*).
Principal: All right you'd have Su over there, see. Now when you get these——you slip them in like this . . .

The cards were put in the teacher's lounge by the principal for the teachers to consider the arrangement of students. If any of them did not want a particular student in their class or questioned the placement of a particular child, they were to signify this by turning the child's photograph on its side:

Principal: If during the time that this is up there somebody says 'I'm not so certain I want this child,' or 'this child with this teacher.' This is the signal (*turns the picture on its side*). Now that says, 'Hey, let's think about that. We may want to do it but we may want to move.'

In this manner the tracking system at School A was initiated: Its foundations rested on the instructions, typifications, and rationales given by the principal. There were three first-grade teachers at the school; only two were to continue the next year, and the third was to be replaced. Each of the three teachers is typified by the principal. One is typed as being 'strongly oriented academically'; the other teacher is typed as 'a warm Mother'; and the third is 'a new teacher.' The placement practices constitutive of this form of tracking (the Personality Track) will be examined in the third section of this chapter. I will confine my discussion to where the students were placed.

The two kindergarten teachers set about the task outlined by the principal in the following way. First, both teachers divided their classes into three groups of students: strong, average, and weak. The 'strong' students were those who, in the words of one of the teachers, '. . . have the ability of being accurate and able to go rapid an' be able to respond to the concepts that are presented very quickly . . .' The 'average' students were those who demonstrated to the teacher that they knew the material presented in class but whose performance was flawed by slowness or messiness. The 'weak' students were those who interacted poorly with their peers and who did not verbalize in class. Then the students were placed in the following manner. All the 'strong' students were placed with the teacher who was typified as being 'strongly oriented academically'; the 'average' students were placed with the new teacher although some of them were placed with the 'strong' students while others were placed with the 'weak' students; and the 'weak' students were placed with the teacher who was typified as a 'warm Mother.'

School B

The kindergartens at School B were organized into two heterogeneous classes and within each class there were four homogeneous ability-groups. Two methods were used in forming the ability groups: interviewing the students and using routine classroom activities to provide information about the students' abilities. (. . .)

Classroom activities During activity time, the teachers would walk around the room and interact with the students as they played with games and other available objects. The classification of these routine activities and the manner in which the teachers interacted with the students provided them with information about the students' abilities. For example, one of the teachers was observed helping a student put the blocks away after activity time. She asked the student to put the larger of two blocks on one shelf and the smaller on the other shelf. The student put the wrong block on the top shelf. The teacher then asked him to put a square block on the first shelf and a round one on the second. The student couldn't tell the difference between the two blocks. At the end of the day I overheard the teacher relate this interchange to her colleague, but in her account she had generalized the child's performance to difficulties with shape perception and eye-hand coordination. (. . .)

During activity-time the students were watched to see which activities they chose and how long they stayed at any one activity before going on to another one. If a student consistently went to the play-house (a chest full of 'grown-up' clothes and a wooden 'stove') the teachers regarded that student as being insecure and needing the role-playing activity which they connected with this activity. The teachers also noted which role the student took while playing in the play-house. (. . .) If a student went from one activity to another in rapid succession without finishing one before beginning another, such a student was labeled 'immature.' (. . .)

For the casual observer, and maybe for the students who are engaged in them, these activities are just games to occupy one's time or to keep the students busy or out of trouble. To the teacher these activities represent something altogether different. The routine activities of the classroom are devices for assessing the levels of performance (and establishing levels of performance) of the different students. The activities tacitly embody for the teachers developmental requirements and signify to her different levels of the students' abilities.

The teacher's practical interest and task are the location and identification of the students' abilities to form ability groups of homogeneous students. From her perspective as determined by these practical circumstances and practical interests, the child is not just playing but is behaving in ways that provide evidence of his abilities. The teacher's use of routine classroom activities in this manner is characteristic of her competence and characterizes her as a member of this particular setting as opposed to a casual observer.

Promotion Another placement setting within the kindergartens at School B is the promotion of the students to either first or junior-first grade. At this school, no student is retained in kindergarten at the end of the year. He is promoted to either one of two first grades or to the junior-first grade. From junior-first a student is promoted either to a first grade or to second grade. The student's position within one of the four ability groups at the end of the year is the largest factor in this decision. (. . .) Students who were in the first two ability groups were placed in one of the two first grades while the students in the low ability group were placed in the junior-first-grade.

Ad hocing in the schools: placement practices

I will now discuss the practicing used by the teachers within the placement settings for placing their students into specific classes, ability groups within those classes, and for promoting them into the next grade. Two kinds of placement practices were observed at the two schools participating in the study: Personality Tracking at School A and Ability-Group Tracking at School B. Both placement practices are characterized by the teachers' use of social knowledge in the form of social types and the teachers' use of tacit knowledge of human behavior and practical circumstances to assign meaning and find meaning in the students' behavior.

Social types used in the schools

Before detailing the placement practices which constitute the tracking system at each school, I will review some of the social types used by the teachers at both schools to interpret and identify the student's behavior. By social type I mean an idealization used by members of a group to identify and interpret objects (including people), and events in their environment (Klapp, 1962; Strong, 1943). The importance of these social types comes from a conception of the tracking systems as products of the socially organized routine activities of the teachers. Some of those activities within the placement settings were described in the previous section (the elicitation practices and the use of routine classroom activities as devices for locating students' abilities) and additional activities will be described in this section. But before we begin such a discussion our first task is the description of the common-sense constructs (social types) used by the teachers to interpret their students' behavior. Four social types regularly used by the teachers at both schools were 'immature child,' 'bright child,' 'behavior problem,' and 'independent worker.' I will give brief definitions of each of these types *from the perspective of the teacher*,[1] as an introduction to my analysis of the placement practices which form the basis of the tracking systems.

Immature child   The 'immature child' is one who has a very short attention span as indicated by the fact that he cannot sit still during a lesson and is easily distracted by, and himself distracts, other students. The 'immature child' typically is called by the teachers a 'young 5-year-old.' Sex and size are also grounds for labeling a student 'immature.' More often than not an immature child turns out to be a small boy rather than a small girl. When a girl is termed 'immature' it indicates that she is not acting in accordance with her chronological age which is used by the teachers as a tacit developmental model of the child. In the following example, taken from an interview with one of the kindergarten teachers at School B, we can see all of the above grounds for labeling a child 'immature.' The teacher in this section is describing one of two cases in answer to a question about what kind of behavior would require the teacher to send a student out of the room.

> *Teacher*: Then we have had one other little boy who is very very immature and he was a November birthday. Just a little, little boy and he was either practically sitting on my lap half of the time or running around the room and just making it—if they're so bad that you can't keep the rest of the class involved, if they're disturbing the rest of the class, that's when I feel it's necessary to get them out of the room, refer them for counseling.

Bright student   The 'bright student' is defined by the speed with which he learns the material presented in class. He is a student who learns quickly and without the teacher having to dispense much time or effort as the following examples taken from interviews with different teachers indicate:

> *Teacher*: . . . but he's a bright child, he learns very quickly and umm at the first of the year he didn't know much about letters or anything but

he learned them just like that (*snaps her fingers*) when they were presented.

> *Teacher*: He's performed very well amm he's confident, he grasps ahh concepts very readily and without any repetition.

Another basis for labeling a student 'bright' is the student's high performance level despite what the teacher perceives to be poor social behavior in the class during the presentation of the material, as the following example suggests:

> *Teacher*: Now this is Pa, he's a very interesting child because he's one of the ones who's extremely bright but is a behavior problem in school. And umm one of the reasons he's probably a behavior problem is because he—well I guess I really shouldn't say he's a behavior problem but he's immature because he's young and we probably expect too much of him. He's an October birthday which would make him one of the youngest in the class . . .
>
> *Int*:   What are some of the things that give you the impression that he was bright?
>
> *Teacher*: Ohh he has a fantastic memory: In the group I can read a story and he can be looking out the window or talking to his neighbor and I can ask him the question and he knows the answer like that you know. At first I would, he would be talking so after I read something or if we'd been discussing something I would say 'Pa, what have we been talking about?' And I was doing it because I figured he wouldn't know—and he did.
>
> *Int*:   Umm humm.
>
> *Teacher*: And so it was in the total group that he's catching a lot of what they're hearing and if he's a child who can talk to his neighbor and still know the answer you know you've got a bright child on your hands . . .

This account also reveals the grounds for labeling a student 'immature.' In fact this is exactly what the teacher does when she proposes:

> *Teacher*: well I guess I really shouldn't say he's a behavior problem but he's immature because he's young and we probably expect too much of him. He's an October birthday which would make him one of the youngest in the class . . .

Finally, the bright child is 'very verbal.' He not only talks a lot, but his talk is heard by the teacher as reflecting mastery of the materials presented in class, not just as idle chatter. For example during a reading lesson I was observing at School A, one of the students interrupted one of her classmates with the phrase 'that's fascinating,' and the teacher turned to me and said 'great vocabulary.' In short, what would normally be sanctioned (interrupting another student) in this case was taken as a sign of the student's brightness: the action was not seen as an interruption by the teacher but as a display of knowledge.

Behavior problem The 'behavior problem' is typified by a big boy who repeatedly engages in fights with other children for what the teacher perceives as ['no reasons at all.'] The following example illustrates:

Int.: What was the counselor's evaluation or haven't you received that yet?
Teacher: Well he . . . Well I have and he was very worried about this child and called the mother right away. He came in and observed in the room about 15 minutes during our activity time and he said that in 15 minutes he found about 25 times that he got into a disagreement with a child. Just in that period of time. He'd walk past a child and go like that (*teacher swings her arm with closed fists in hitting motion*) for absolutely no reason at all or trip them or push them or try to get something going. You know. And we felt he should be removed from school if he continues to disrupt. So we've really been isolating him now and when he starts and send him over to the office. This kind of thing because he really does disrupt and get everybody else keyed up—as I said Thursday and Friday he wasn't here. It was just beautiful, it was great. It just takes this to get everybody going.

The important points to note in this account are the repeated hitting of the child's peers and the teacher's inability to find a reason for this behavior. These two features of the child's behavior are what define him as a 'behavior problem.'

Independent worker The student who is an 'independent worker' is defined by the teachers as one who can work with little or no supervision and who finishes the task begun before going on to another. The following example illustrates not only the grounds for labeling a student an 'independent worker' but also suggests the practical reasons for the teachers' use of this social type.

Int.: We are interested in knowing the kinds of abilities and achievements that you think a child going into the first grade from kindergarten should be able to have and do? Could you start by giving a few?
Teacher: All right, well umm. Well I think they should be able to listen for a reasonable amount of time 15 to 20 minutes with a total group situation. Umm they're—how shall I put this— they're ready for, they could be ready for first grade and still be at different listening levels. Some will be able to listen for an hour and some won't. But they still would be ready for that kind of thing if they could listen for 15 to 20 minutes. I think they should be able to work independently for a reasonable length of time without having

any direction from the teacher or having an adult right there with them. Umm they really should know how to work independently by the time they leave kindergarten because during activity time they're all choosing independent activities and some of them are out on the patio working with blocks without direct supervision and Mrs (——) and I will take groups off to the side so they will be completely on their own. So in this way we're hoping they will be independent.

The teachers' use of these social types to interpret and identify the behavior of the students constitutes a placement practice which is common to both schools. This placement practice forms the basis for two other practices which are specific to each school: the ability track and the personality track. The use of social types as a placement practice will be examined within the context of these school-specific placement practices.[2]

School B: the ability group track

These social types drawn from the teachers' accounts form one of several practices which underlie the ability-group tracking at School B. I will examine the teachers' use of these social types to identify a student within a particular ability group level in the tracking system. (. . .)

In the [following] interview segment a teacher is asked to justify her placement of a particular student in the junior-first grade class.

Int.: What were your reasons for putting him into junior-first as opposed to first.
Teacher: Well it takes him longer to learn things.
Int.: Umm humm, I see.
Teacher: It takes him longer to learn letters and sounds and this kind of thing. But it could be just because he's the youngest, you know. It's just another year for him to acquire—I don't believe in junior-first but since we have it there I have to put somebody in it.
Int.: What do you mean by 'it takes him longer to learn letters'? Do you have a schedule?
Teacher: No. It's just that we have to work more with him to learn. And not just with him but say with the whole lower group than we do with the others.

Note the teacher's comment ['it takes him longer to learn letters and sounds and this kind of thing. But it could be just because he's the youngest, you know.'] Placement in junior-first as a result of the student's performance is linked to the student's 'immaturity,' defined above as a social type. The teacher uses the social type 'immature' to 'explain' the student's performance without explicating the relation between them. The social type, then, becomes an interpretive aid for both placing a student within a particular ability group as well as the next grade. (. . .)

In this account [a teacher] was asked to go down her list of students and tell the interviewer where she had placed them for the following year and her reasons for the placement.

Teacher: Ti is, will not be in our school next year. He's moving on the Mesa right now. I'm not sure if the school he's going to has a junior-first but he'd be a question mark. He'd be one that you'd almost have to wait until September to really know how much mature he ahh. He's very verbal umm does well in anything verbal, well he knows all of his letters and he knows all of his beginning sounds and he hears things well. His eye-hand-coordination is very poor and he is a very poor listener and very silly and immature.

Int.: Would you—Had he remained here, where would you have put him?

Teacher: I think I would have put him in a first grade. Regular first would be amm the high-low group. And alerted the kindergarten err first grade teacher that perhaps if he didn't work out he'd be considered—Or it could work the other way. But the problem with putting Ti in a junior-first is he's a follower—

Int.: Umm humm—

Teacher: And he would tend to mimic the behavior of the other children. And he could grow a lot over those three months. He's a young boy so he'd be a really big question mark. But as it turns out I really don't think the school he's going to ... I don't know if any of the schools on the Mesa have a junior-first. He may be in a regular first anyway.

These (...) accounts suggest that social types are used in the placement of students and as justification for placement decisions. Furthermore, tacit knowledge is used as an unexplicated link between the social type and the student's behavior. (...) The link between the social type and the student's behavior is the conception of behavior as 'contagious': certain people are more susceptible to the behavior around them than others. It is just such a theory of behavior which forms the tacit resource for the teacher's statements:

Teacher: So ahh he's the one that is the follower and I would rather like to see him in a room where he'd have good models to follow than in a room where he'd have poor models to follow.

and

Teacher: ... but the problem with putting Ti in a junior-first is he's a follower—

Int.: Umm humm—

Teacher: ... and he would tend to mimic the behavior of the other children.

Another feature of the teachers' use of social types as constitutive of ability group tracking is that they are grounded in the practical circumstances encountered by the teachers in teaching kindergarten. (...) In her description of why this particular student was placed in junior-first, the teacher reveals (...) practical circumstances which underlie her decision.

Int.: What are your reasons for putting him into junior-first as opposed to first?

Teacher: Well it takes him longer to learn things.

Int.: Umm humm I see.

Teacher: It takes him longer to learn letters and sounds and this kind of thing. ...

Int.: What do you mean 'it takes him longer to learn letters'? Do you have a schedule?

Teacher: No. It's just that we have to work more with him to learn. And not just with him but say with the whole lower group.

When asked ['*Interviewer*: What do you mean "It takes him longer to learn letters"? Do you have a schedule?'] the teacher does not say that the student has no idea of what the materials mean. Instead she invokes the practical circumstances of having to spend too much time with this student (and the lower group):

Teacher: No it's just that we have to work more with him to learn. And not just with him but say with the whole lower group.

This example suggests that it is *in and through* these practical circumstances that the teacher identifies the student as having difficulty in learning and as a 'slow' student. The practical circumstances and practical interests of the teacher determines which social type she will use to interpret the student's behavior and place him at one level of the tracking system rather than another. Thus social types are not just theoretical abstractions; they are grounded in the practical circumstances and interests of the user.

This feature of social types and their use as constitutive of ability group tracking is revealed by re-examining the social types discussed at the beginning of this section. Underlying the teachers' use of the social type 'immature' is a very practical teaching concern—keeping the attention of 28 students while one of the students is misbehaving and diverting the attention of the others. This practical concern is revealed in the following excerpt (...):

Teacher: ... if they're so bad that you can't keep the rest of the class involved, if they're disturbing the rest of the class, that's when I feel it's necessary to get them out of the room, refer them for counseling.

This practical consideration also underlies the teacher's use of the social type 'bright child.' The time the teacher can spend in individual work with her students is limited; therefore, students who require less time free the teacher to work more with those students who need more individual help. This is reflected in the following example of a teacher talking about a 'bright child.'

> *Teacher*: He's performed very well amm he's confident he grasps ahh concepts very readily and without any repetition.

The teacher's phrase ['and without any repetition'] suggests that such a student frees the teacher from working with this student.

The teacher's practical interest in having some free time during the day contributes to the use of the social type 'independent worker.' (. . .) This means that the social types and their definitions are not criteria which transcend the social setting in which they are used. Instead, the teacher's accounts demonstrate that the social types are embedded within the setting. They take on their specific sense from the setting and at the same time organize the setting through their use by the teacher to recognize and interpret the students' behavior in particular ways. The social types, then, are not just a mere overlay on the setting by the teacher, rather they are an inseparable part of the setting which they organize

through their situated usage. (. . .)

Finally, a word needs to be mentioned concerning the ontological status of the practices described in this article. The above list of practices is not a finite list – there are other practices which space does not permit mentioning and which await discovery. Further research is needed to determine which of these practices are situated and which are invariant to the situation. The practices described in this article are everyday activities which form 'seen but unnoticed' sense-making methods for locating and describing students as possessing factual properties in order to place them into special classes, ability groups and into the next grade. Finally it would be a mistake for the reader to view these practices as 'faulty' or the result of poor teaching. These practices however faulty they may seem are part and parcel of the accomplishment of social interaction. Furthermore they are not to be conceived of as being capable of remedy through more formalized testing procedures . . . Similar (but situated) practices are essential to the process of more 'standardized' tests as well.

Notes

1 These definitions may well differ from those found in educational texts. My intent is to capture in these definitions, however, the teacher's use of these terms.

2 [Only the section relating to the ability track is reproduced here.]

References

Bellugi, U. and Brown, R. eds (1964), *The Acquisition of Language* (Monographs of the Society for Research in Child Development, no. 92), Lafayette, Ind., Child Development Publications.

Cicourel, A. V. (1973), *Cognitive Sociology*, Penguin.

Cicourel, A. V. and Kitsuse, J. (1963), *The Educational Decision-Makers*, Indianapolis, Bobbs-Merrill.

Garfinkel, H. (1967), *Studies in Ethnomethodology*, Englewood Cliffs, Prentice-Hall.

Ilg, F. and Ames, L. B. (1964), *School Readiness: Behavioral Tests Used at the Gesell Institute*, N.Y., Harper & Row.

Klapp, O. E. (1962), *Heroes, Villains and Fools*, Englewood Cliffs, Prentice-Hall.

Strong, S. M. (1943), 'Social types in a minority group: formulation as a method', *American Journal of Sociology*, 48, 563–73.

15 Assessing children's school performance
Hugh Mehan

Contrastive performance assessment

As part of a larger sociolinguistics study,[1] I investigated the school performance of elementary school children in contrasting educational environments by videotaping and analyzing adult–child interaction in the classroom, in testing encounters, and the home (Mehan, 1971).

One of the Southern California schools studied used a series of psycholinguistic tests to evaluate the child's language skills. Children's results on these tests contributed to decisions made to place children in one of the three first grade classrooms (see Leiter, no. 14 in this Reader). The children who scored lowest on the diagnostic tests were all placed in one classroom. Their poor test performance, coupled with their low SES (and often Chicano origin) seemed to make these children prime examples of the 'culturally deprived child'[2] placed in a special classroom designed to accelerate their academic progress.

One of these children's sources of trouble on the school's diagnostic tests was an inability to respond correctly to questions asking for discriminations about sentences with prepositional phrases which express locational reference. Because the children had had difficulty with prepositions and other grammatical forms, the teacher presented them with 'language development' lessons to teach them the requisite grammatical forms. My informal comparison of the children's responses on the Fall diagnostic test with their work in early language development lessons showed that some children gave correct responses in one situation but not the other. The children's differential performances on tests and lessons prompted me to examine those situations to see whether the socially organized features of the interrogation

procedure itself contributed to the children's performance and the school official's evaluations of it.

Examining the assumptions of the formal test

The educational test is constructed with the following assumptions about (1) the nature of cognitive abilities, (2) the meaning of test items, (3) the basis of the respondent's performance, and (4) the testing situation.

(1) The educational test, though not always an IQ test, incorporates the assumptions about the nature of mental abilities which originated in intelligence testing theory. Spearman (1923) proposed that each individual possesses a general intelligence factor (g). Intelligence is viewed as a fixed mental capacity 'of the individual to act purposefully, to think rationally, to deal effectively with his environment' (Wechsler, 1944:3). The implication is that intelligence is an underlying mental ability. Underlying mental abilities are composed of previously learned experiences, accumulated knowledge, and skills. Simply stated, if learning opportunities and all other factors are equal, those persons who learn the most and perform the best probably have greater innate mental capacity than those who learn and perform most poorly (Mercer, 1971:322–3). Tests measure these experiences learned in the past.

(2) The tester assumes that the meaning of instructions, questions, and answers is obvious to the test taker and is shared among the test constructor, test taker, and test administrator. The test items serve as unambiguous stimuli which tap the respondent's underlying attitudes about or knowledge of certain factors.

Each test item is considered to be clear and unambiguous because the test constructor assumes that persons taking the test have had experience with the test items, whether they be words, pictures, or objects, and that the test experience will be the same as the

Source: H. P. Dreitzel, ed., *Childhood and Socialization* (Recent Sociology, no. 5), Collier-Macmillan, 1973, pp. 243–56; adapted from Armer and Grimshaw, eds, *Comparative Social Research*, New York, Wiley, 1973.

prior experiences he has had with these items. Because of this assumed similarity of experience test takers will interpret the items in the same way the test constructor did when he compiled the items. Because each test item will be interpreted only in the way intended by the test constructor, the test taker's reasons or purposes for making certain choices, or for giving certain explanations are assumed to match the purposes of the tester.

Each question asked has a correct answer which consists of a connecting link between stimulus instruction and test item. The respondent who answers questions properly is assumed to have searched for and found the intended connection between questions and materials. While correct answers to questions are seen as products of correct search procedures, incorrect answers are seen as the products of faulty reasoning, or the lack of underlying ability, knowledge or understanding.

(3) The educational tester makes the same assumptions about the measurement of behavior that the experimental psychologist makes: 'A psychological experiment, then, can be symbolized by S–O–R, which means that E (understood) applies a certain stimulus (or situation) to O's receptors and observes O's response' (Woodworth and Schlosberg, 1954:2). The test taker, like the experimental subject, responds to the stimulus, and his response is a direct and sole result of the 'stimulus acting at that moment and the factors present in the organism at that moment' (ibid.: 3).

(4) The respondent's behavior is considered to be the sole result of his underlying abilities and stimulus application because other factors and variables which might be influential are able to be standardized and controlled.

> Standardization implies uniformity of procedure in administering and scoring the test. . . . Such standardization extends to the exact materials employed, time limits, oral instructions to subjects, preliminary demonstrations, ways of handling queries from subjects, and every other detail of the testing situation (Anastasi, 1968:23).

The tester (or experimenter) is supposed to present the stimulus while holding other factors in the situation constant. The test is supposed to be standardized in its presentation of stimuli so that all respondents face the same conditions which make comparisons of performances and replications possible.

The assumptions made by the formal test include: (1) the abilities being tested are the products of past experience, (2) cultural meanings are shared in common by tester and respondent, (3) the respondent's performance is an exclusive function of underlying abilities and stimulus presentation, (4) stimuli are presented to respondents in standardized ways, extraneous variables in the testing situation are controlled, and (5) the tester passively records the respondent's performance.

The structure of the testing encounter was examined in two ways. First, six of the first grade children who took the Spring test were videotaped. After the test was over, I informally interrogated the children about their perceptions and understandings of the testing materials. Second, versions of the formal test which systematically altered its features were presented to the first grade children.

The language development tests employed by the school are picture identification tasks in which children are asked to identify the grammatical forms represented by a series of pictures by pointing to the one that correctly characterizes it. Instead of using only one kind of stimulus, I used three alternative versions of the picture identification task. I had children demonstrate their knowledge of orientational prepositions by manipulating their hands, manipulating small objects, and by drawing pictures in response to the instructions I gave. I contrasted the formal testing characteristic of a strange and unfamiliar environment by presenting the 'orientations tasks' to children in the less formal surroundings of the classroom, and (to a few) in the familiar settings of their homes. To examine the 'common culture' assumption, the general research design required that one test be presented in Spanish to those children familiar with that language, and that all children's definitions and conceptions of testing materials be analyzed. Six classroom and six home testing encounters were videotaped.[3]

Results of children's performances

The results of the children's performances on the two sessions of school administered tests and the 'orientations tasks' appear in Table 15.1. A table of scores like this one, or a more general comment like: 'Adam has command of prepositions,' or 'Sarah does not comprehend the negative or the orientational preposition' is characteristically provided to teachers after a testing session and is entered into the child's school record. I will now examine this table of scores to see what it reports about the child's abilities and the manner in which results are reported. Such a table of scores or a general descriptive statement (1) obscures the child's understanding of the materials and task, (2) does not capture the child's reasoning abilities and (3) does not show the negotiated, contextually bound measurement decisions which the tester makes while scoring the child's behavior as 'correct' or 'incorrect.'

The child's conception of the task

One question on the school language test (the Basic Concept Inventory, Englemann, 1967, henceforth BCI) asks the respondent to decide which child in a group is the tallest. Because the heads of the children are obscured, the child taking the test is supposed to reply that he can't make that judgment. However, many children examined selected one of the children in the picture as the tallest. When I interviewed the children after they took the Spring test, and I asked them why they chose that boy, they replied that he was the tallest boy because 'his feet are bigger.' Investigating the thread of reasoning used by the children, then, showed that they understood the *intent*

Table 15.1 Results of language testing in three first grades

A   Individual results

child	school tests fall	spring	variations class	home
1 (Jean)	73	69	93	100
2 (Clarc)	10	50	86	86
3 (Lesli)	46	76	44	65*
4 (Lora)	10	25	33	60*
5	50	61	86	
6	52	54	77	
7	75	85	75	
8	65	70	80	
9	60	75	75	
10	40	50	50	
11	15	25	37	
12	60	75	55	
13	35	70	75	
14	55	85	87	
15	35	65	67	
16	63	77	80	
17	50	54	60	85*
18	85	95	93	
19	56	86	55	75*
20	10	35	33	
21	85	95	95	
22	35	50	45	
23	75	85	85	
	1140	1512	1566	

B   Results by classroom

classroom	school tests fall	spring	classroom variations
#1	49.5	65.7	68.0
#2	73.0	87.0	
#3	77.0	82.0	

*Tested in Spanish at home.

of the question—to discriminate and compare—but they were not using the same criteria as the tester. Because they were not using the criteria *intended* (but never explicated), answers which indicated that one child was taller than another were marked wrong. However, in this case, a wrong answer does not index a lack of ability, but rather the use of an alternative scheme of interpretation.

Another question on the BCI asks the child to decide which of two boxes a ball is in after the tester has told him which box the ball is *not* in. The child is expected to point to the box which the tester hasn't touched. The question following that on the BCI asks the child to decide which of *three* boxes a ball is in after the tester has told the child which box does not contain the ball. The child is expected to say the problem can't be solved. Many children failed to answer this question correctly; they chose one, or sometimes both, of the remaining two boxes. In a follow-up interview, when I asked the children why they chose one of the other boxes (instead of saying the problem could not be solved) they replied: 'You said it's not in that one.' I think children find it untenable to doubt an adult's word. An adult has told the child that a state of affairs actually exists: 'There is a ball in one of these three boxes.' He has been told that the ball isn't in one, so, he reasons: 'It must be in one of the other two because the adult said so.' That is, these children's answers may have been wrong, but not necessarily because they didn't have the proper reasoning ability; rather, they lacked the sophistication necessary to doubt an adult's word.

A question from another language development test instructs the child to choose the 'animal that can fly' from a bird, an elephant, and a dog. The correct answer (obviously) is the bird. Many first grade children, though, chose the elephant along with the bird as a response to that question. When I later asked them why they chose that answer they replied: 'That's Dumbo.' Dumbo (of course) is Walt Disney's flying elephant, well known to children who watch television and read children's books as an animal that flies.

On another BCI question the child is asked to 'find the ones that talk' when presented pictures of a man, a boy, a dog, and a table. Children frequently include the dog along with the man and the boy as an answer to this question. For those children who have learned to say their pets 'speak' or 'talk' that is not an unlikely choice. Deciding that the child doesn't know how to use the verb 'talk' correctly would, in this case, be erroneous, for that decision would have resulted from an unexamined assumption that both adult and child attribute the same characteristics to objects or are attending to them in the same way.

For a question from another language development test, children are presented a picture of a medieval fortress—complete with moat, drawbridge, and parapets—and three initial consonants: D, C, and G. The child is supposed to circle the correct initial consonant. C for 'castle' is correct, but many children choose D. After the test, when I asked those children what the name of the building was, they responded 'Disneyland.' These children used the same line of reasoning intended by the tester, but they arrived at the wrong substantive answer. The score sheet showing a wrong answer does not document a child's lack of reasoning ability; it only documents that the child indicated an answer different from the one the tester expected.

These descriptions demonstrate that the child can exist simultaneously in a number of different 'realities' or worlds (Schutz, 1962:207–59), i.e., the 'factual' world of everyday life and the world of fantasy. The child who says that animals can fly and talk is (from the adult point of view) mixing and blending the characteristics of fantasy and everyday worlds. The test, however, assumes the child is attending to stimulus items only from the viewpoint of the everyday world where dogs do not talk and elephants do not fly. The test assumes further that the child keeps the world of play, fantasy, and television out of the testing situation. Yet, as these anecdotes demonstrate, the child of age 4–6 does not always keep his realities sequentially arranged. Because the child may be operating simultaneously in multiple realities, valid interrogations must examine why a child answers questions as he does and must determine what children 'see' in educational materials; they must not use test results exclusively.

In sum, a document of the children's correct and incorrect responses, such as Table 15.1, does not show the variation in the children's answers across materials, tests, and languages of interrogation. Conventional testing techniques cannot determine if a child's wrong answers are due to his lack of ability or are due to his equally valid alternative interpretations. Differences in tester and child meaning of educational materials does not lend support for the 'common culture' assumption of the educational test.

The test assembly process

A table of correct answers (e.g., Table 15.1) is a static display which does not capture the contextually bound, fluid and dynamic activities which constitute its production.[4] When I reexamined the videotape of the testing sessions which produced Table 15.1, I found that these results were not as unequivocal as they appeared in tabular form.

Testers deviated from the requirements of a mechanical, uniform presentation of instructions and stimuli to respondents. The school test required a series of pictures to be presented to respondents, each with the instruction 'look at the picture.' The following variations on that introductory comment are just some of those recorded during the school-administered testing session which I videotaped. (Similar deviations occurred in the informal tests that I presented and may be observed in any interrogation; cf., Friedman, 1968, who documents the same phenomenon in social–psychological experiments.)

FT[5]	1:7	Look at that picture and show a find . . .
	4:17	Y'see all the things in that picture
	8:1	Let's look at that one
	11:1	Now you look at those pictures

3:3	I want you to look at that picture and tell me what you see by looking at the picture
1:8	Look at this picture now
5:9	See all those pictures?
5:10	What those?
5:11	Okay, now I want you to find the right ones.

Under the criteria of the formal test, test takers are supposed to respond only to stimulus materials presented to them, but these respondents are not receiving the same stimulus instructions. Some are being told to look and find the correct pictures; others are being told just to look. No child, however, is told what constitutes a correct answer. The child is expected to operate without this information.

When I reexamined the testing videotapes, I found that when children were asked a question, they presented many displays. If I looked at one of the other displays the children presented, rather than those originally scored, a substantially different evaluation of each child's performance would have been obtained. In cases where a child had been marked wrong, an instance of the correct display was apparent in his actions, and vice versa. If that display, rather than the one noted by the tester had been recorded, the child's overall score would have changed.

When answering questions, the child is supposed to touch that picture or part of it that best answers the question asked. Often the children either did not touch any part of the objects represented in the picture, or covered more of the picture than was required by the question. Because the child's response was ambiguous, the tester had to determine the boundaries of the answering gesture to the stimulus picture. Depending on which picture the space between the pictures was assigned to, the tester either marked the child right or marked him wrong.

When the children touched two or more pictures in succession, the tester had to decide which of the movements was intended by the child as his answer. On a number of occasions, the children began to answer before the complete question was asked. Regardless of whether or not the correct picture was touched, the tester did not count the action as an answer. It seemed that the responses had to be given *after* questions had been completely asked in order to be considered answers-to-questions.

Some children touched the page of pictures with both of their hands simultaneously, and also laid their palms flat on the page while answering a question. In these cases, one hand touched an 'incorrect' part of the page while the other hand touched the 'correct' part. To count the child's answer as correct in these cases, the tester had to assign the status of 'hand indicating an answer' to one hand and not the other.

The following example is representative of the way in which the tester assigned the status of 'answer' during the orientations tasks. In the hand manipulation phase of the orientations task, after I finished my instruction: 'Put your hand below the table,' Clarc placed his hand in the air:

(1) hand raised

I repeated the substance of the instruction: 'Below the table,' and Clarc modified his initial response. He lowered his hand slowly until it was parallel with and off the side of the table top:

(2) hand off to the side

He paused there, and I said nothing. His hand continued in the arc he had been circumscribing until it was as far down below the table as it would go:

(3) hand underneath, but not touching the underside of the table.

At that point, realizing that I had, in fact, influenced his behavior and thereby modified his answer, I attempted to neutralize this influence by saying, 'Put it anywhere you want.' Clarc left his hand in the last position (3), and I scored that 'final' placement 'correct.' But note, there are at least three separate displays given in response to the question asked. The production of multiple responses was obviously influenced by the challenges I made of the child's responses. With each challenge, the child modified his behavior until his arm could literally go no further under the table. Had I recorded either of his first two displays as his 'answer' rather than challenging those displays, the child would have been considered wrong for this question.

The protocol conditions of the formal testing procedures are violated in other ways. In the school tests, the child is supposed to touch the correct picture as soon as the question is read. Often more than one picture is to be touched in response to a question. Ideally, the child is supposed to touch all pictures as soon as the question is read. Often the child only touches one. When this occurs, a tester employs various practices to elicit further answers from the child. A tester may prompt the child with verbal cues like 'that one,' or 'is that the only one?' These cues tell the child to continue searching for more answers in the series. A similar cue is provided non-verbally when the tester pauses after a response and does not immediately go on to the next question. The pause serves as a cue to the child to keep looking for a correct answer. When the tester provides a commendatory comment like 'good,' 'fine,' or goes immediately on to the next question, the child is prohibited from providing any more responses or changing answers he has already given.

Not only do testers contribute to respondents' productions, but respondents interrupt and thereby contribute to their interrogation. During a test, the tester is supposed to ask questions and the respondent is supposed to answer them. But if a respondent asks the tester a question instead of just answering the tester's question, the adult is forced to respond to the demand made of him by the respondent, i.e., the adult/tester has to respond to the demand made of him by the child/respondent *before* the child answers the original test question.[6] The tester can ignore the child's request and repeat the original question, he can pause and say nothing, or he can provide a 'neutral' comment like 'do whatever you think is best.' Regardless of the tester's reaction to the child's request, though, the child gains further information that influences his interpretation of the original request made of him.

The following interchange exemplifies the manner in which the child gains supplemental information from a tester's responses to his questions. A child was asked to draw a circle above the line. She placed her pencil on the paper at a point slightly above the diagonal line she had drawn and asked: 'Above?' 'Right here?'

I interpreted the child's action as a request for information about the suitability of an answer which she was considering giving. She had not yet committed herself to producing a particular answer, but was asking for confirmation of a possible answer in advance of its production.

That request for information required me to respond in some way. Regardless of my action, the child would learn something about the suitability of the answer she was proposing. I chose to repeat the question as a way out of the dilemma posed by her question. The child then reviewed the entire paper. Her pencil wandered all around the area of the line—both above and below it. She finally settled on this point:

While performing this act, she asked: 'Right here?' Perhaps exasperated, perhaps convinced that she now 'knew' the answer, perhaps unable to restrain myself, I said 'Okay.' The child drew a circle at the second point and got the question right.

Summary

This examination of testing interactions shows test assumptions are not met in practice. Stimulus items are not presented in standardized ways. Test materials do not always have the same meaning for tester and child. The child's performance is not just the result of his ability and the stimulus presented but is also influenced by contextually provided information. The respondent's answers are not the product of the tester's passive record keeping; they emerge from the tester's interpretive assessment of the child's actions.

The tester is not just examining and recording the child's response. He is actively engaged in assigning the status of 'answer' to certain portions of the child's behavioral presentation. The tester is according differential status to similar behavioral displays produced by the child as answers-to-questions because

the tester is not seeing the child's display in isolation from other aspects of the testing situation. The fingers used to point and the hand laid on the page are included in a perceptual field and are seen against a constantly changing background of features which includes the questions asked, the child's restlessness, his performances on previous questions, teachers' reports about him, and the tester's expectations for the child's performance on any particular question. Therefore, the 'same' behavioral display, seen against different backgrounds, is interpreted differently; it obtains a different reading. In short, test taking and test scoring are interpretive interactional processes which should be approached and studied as such. (. . .)

Notes

1 The overall contrastive study of language acquisition, language use, and school performance utilized data gathered in 1969–70 from two elementary schools in Southern California. Cicourel is studying the demands that multiple sources of information make on teachers' and children's information processing. Jennings and Jennings are studying the interactional aspects of the psycholinguistic assessment of the child's acquisition of syntactic structures. Leiter is analyzing the decision-making processes school officials use to place children in elementary school classrooms. MacKay is contrasting teachers' and children's conceptions of classroom and testing materials. Roth is examining the conception of the child's abilities which intelligence tests provide educators (see Cicourel, et al., in preparation). In related studies, Boese (1971) described the deaf child's acquisition and use of natural sign language, and Shumsky (1972) describes the structure of interpretations of an encounter group session.

2 Lower class American Indian, Black, Chicano, Puerto Rican, and other 'minority' children perform poorly in school by comparison with their middle class school mates. This poor performance has been said to be the result of a cultural or hereditary deficiency by some educators and researchers (see Jensen, 1969; Herrnstein, 1971; Bereiter and Englemann, 1966; Hunt, 1961; Deutsch, 1964). The *hereditary* deprivation argument, defended primarily by Jensen and Herrnstein, is explained and critically examined by Roth in Cicourel *et al.* (in preparation). The *culturally* deprived child is said to be the product of an impoverished environment. It is argued that overcrowded facilities, infrequent social contact, inconsistent discipline, absence of cultural artifacts provide limited opportunities for the lower class child to be verbally expressive, develop cooperative, perceptual, and attitudinal skills. As a result, the child is said to possess an impoverished language and has few of the skills and experiences required by the middle class oriented school.

The two forms of the cultural deprivation explanation of the lower class child's school failure have been attacked by linguists, sociologists, and anthropologists (see, for example, Labov, 1969; Gumperz, 1972; and a collection of essays in Williams, 1970), who argue that the lower class child does not come from a *deprived* environment or speak a *degraded* language, but rather possesses a *different* culture and speaks a language which has some different grammatical rules and rules

for social usage. These cultural and linguistic differences produce anomalies for the lower class child in the classroom as he is expected to perform in ways he has not been taught.

Care must be taken in saying the Black, Chicano, or other minority child possesses a different culture. Although many proponents of the 'difference' thesis recognize the existence of alternate cultures, it is possible that the child's behavior which is called culturally different may be treated in the same way that behavior which is called culturally deficient: as behavioral attributes to be eradicated. A third proposal, called 'bi-cultural' by Valentine (1971) and others recognizes and seeks to preserve the ethnic child's unique cultural identity while allowing him to develop skills which allow him to operate in the white middle class culture if he so chooses.

Although the 'deficit' rather than the 'difference' or 'bi-cultural' thesis has been the dominant view among educators during the last two decades, the 'deprived' child's 'impoverished' cultural or linguistic system has not been shown to inhibit actual classroom interaction. Indeed the academic and behavioral difficulties of the 'deprived' child have been documented by the use of data gathered from formal tests conducted outside the classroom. This report, then, is in part an examination of the 'deficiency' thesis which advertises its findings without a critical examination of the methods used to assess the child's abilities.

3 This is obviously not the first critical examination of educational tests. Educators, psychologists, and sociologists have long been concerned with the accuracy and fairness of educational tests. Previous criticisms of testing, however, have dealt only with the *product* and *results* of testing, i.e., the test scores of different groups of children have been compared. When differences in test scores (read: ability) have been found, attempts have been made to make tests 'culture free' (e.g., Goodenough draw-a-man, David-Eel's games, the Raven Progressive Matrices), or to develop culture-sensitive tests (e.g., by translating tests into the respondent's native language—e.g., the Peabody Picture Vocabulary Test, the Stanford-Binet, and the WISC). (Mercer, 1971, presents a concise summary of his literature.) The examination of tests reported here differs from previous ones in that testing is treated as an interactional accomplishment. The meaning of the testing situation, the source of the respondent's answer, and

the tester's scoring are examined from within ongoing testing situations.

4 The way in which production procedures and practices are said to constitute socially organized settings is explained by Garfinkel (1967), Garfinkel and Sacks (1970), Cicourel (1968, 1969, 1970, and forthcoming), and Zimmerman and Pollner (1970).

5 Numbers refer to the full transcript of the school-administered testing session; transcripts which are part of this study may be examined upon request.

6 Sacks (1967–70) and Schegloff (1968, 1971) have proposed that when one question follows another in conversation, the question asked second is answered before the one asked first. Schegloff (1971) calls this an 'embedded question' sequence:

Turn	Speaker	Response
1	Tester	question
2	Child	question
3	Tester	answer
4	Child	answer

References

Anastasi, Anne, 1968, *Psychological Testing*, New York, Macmillan.

Bereiter, Carl and Siegfried Englemann, 1966, *Teaching Disadvantaged Children in the Preschool*, Englewood Cliffs, N.J., Prentice-Hall.

Boese, Robert, 1971, 'Natural Sign Language and the Acquisition of Social Structure', unpublished PhD dissertation, University of California, Santa Barbara.

Cicourel, Aaron V., 1968, 'Verso una sociologia evoltiva del linguaggio e del significato', *Rassegna Italiana di Sociologia*, 9, 211–58; reprinted, 1970, as 'The acquisition of social structure: towards a developmental sociology of language and meaning', in Jack Douglas, ed., *Understanding Everyday Life*, Chicago, Aldine; Routledge & Kegan Paul, 1971.

Cicourel, Aaron V., 1969, 'Generative semantics and the structure of social interaction', in *International Days of Sociolinguistics*, Rome, Luigi Sturzo Institute.

Cicourel, Aaron V., 1970, 'Basic and normative rules in the negotiation of status and role', in Hans P. Dreitzel, ed., *Recent Sociology*, 2: *Patterns of Communicative Behavior*, New York, Macmillan.

Cicourel, Aaron V. (forthcoming), 'Ethnomethodology', in Thomas A. Sebeok, ed., *Current Trends in Linguistics*, 12, The Hague, Mouton.

Cicourel, Aaron V., Kenneth Jennings, Sybillyn Jennings, Kenneth Leiter, Robert MacKay, Hugh Mehan and David Roth (in preparation), *Language Acquisition and Use in Testing and Classroom Settings*, New York, Seminar Press.

Deutsch, Martin, 1964, *Teaching the Disadvantaged Child*, Englewood Cliffs, N.J., Prentice-Hall.

Englemann, Siegfried, 1967, *The Basic Concept Inventory*, Chicago, Follet.

Friedman, Neil, 1968, *The Social Nature of Psychological Research*, New York, Basic Books.

Garfinkel, Harold, 1967, *Studies in Ethnomethodology*, Englewood Cliffs, N.J., Prentice-Hall.

Garfinkel, Harold and Harvey Sacks, 1970, 'The formal properties of practical actions', in John C. McKinney and Edward A. Tiryakian, eds, *Theoretical Sociology*, New York, Appleton-Century-Crofts.

Goodenough, Florence and D. L. Harris, 1950, 'Studies in the psychology of children's drawings', *Psychological Bulletin*, 369–433.

Gumperz, John J., 1972, *Language in Social Groups*, Palo Alto, Stanford University Press.

Herrnstein, R. J., 1971, 'I.Q.', *Atlantic Monthly*, 43–64.

Hunt, J. M., 1961, *Intelligence and Experience*, New York, Ronald Press.

Jensen, Arthur, 1969, 'How much can we boost IQ and scholastic achievement?', *Harvard Educational Review*, 39, 1–123.

Labov, William, 1969, 'The logic of non-standard English', in George Alatis, ed., *Linguistics and Language Study*, Monograph Series, no. 22, Washington, D.C., Georgetown University Press.

Mehan, Hugh, 1971, 'Accomplishing Understanding in Educational Settings', unpublished PhD dissertation, University of California, Santa Barbara.

Mercer, Jane R., 1971, 'Institutionalized Anglocentricism', in Peter Orleans and William R. Ellis, Jr., eds, *Race, Change, and Urban Society*, New York, Russell Sage.

Sacks, Harvey, 1967–70, unpublished lecture notes, UCLA, UC Irvine.

Schegloff, Emmanuel A., 1968, 'Sequencing in conversational openings', *American Anthropologist* 70 (6), 1075–95.

Schütz, Alfred, 1962, *Collected Papers I: The Problem of Social Reality*, The Hague, Martinus Nijhoff.

Shores, David L., ed., 1972, *Contemporary English*, Philadelphia, Lippincott.

Shumsky, Marshall, 1972, 'Encounter Groups: A Forensic Science', PhD dissertation, University of California, Santa Barbara.

Spearman, Carl, 1923, *The Nature of Intelligence and the Purposes of Cognition*, London, Macmillan.

Valentine, Charles A., 1971, 'Deficit, difference, and bicultural models of Afro-American behavior', *Harvard Educational Review*, 41, 137–58.

Wechsler, David, 1944, *The Measurement of Adult Intelligence*, Baltimore, Williams & Wilkins.

Williams, Frederick, ed., 1970, *Language and Poverty*, Boston, Markham.

Woodworth, Robert S. and Harold Schlosberg, 1954, *Experimental Psychology*, New York, Holt.

Zimmerman, Don H. and Melvin Pollner, 1970, 'The everyday world as a phenomenon', in Jack Douglas, ed., *Understanding Everyday Life*, Chicago, Aldine; Routledge & Kegan Paul, 1971.

16 Mock-ups and cock-ups: the stage-management of guided discovery instruction*

Paul Atkinson and Sara Delamont

Taking our cue from the title of this conference, we propose to discuss two varieties of educational practice which, in rather similar ways, stress the first-hand 'experience' of the student in the process of learning. We wish to strike a recondite harmony between two learning situations which at first glance may appear quite diverse. The two situations we consider are guided-discovery science at secondary school level, and the bedside teaching of medicine in medical school. The examination of these two areas derives from our own 'experience' as researchers. The paper is based upon research in an independent Scottish girls' school, 'St Luke's' (Delamont, 1973), and in the Edinburgh medical school (Atkinson, 1975). In discussing these two, apparently disparate, types of educational experience, we have been struck by a number of parallels; here we shall attempt to draw out some of these common themes, and to set them in a theoretical framework.

The curriculum development movement of the 1960s produced what purported to be a new way of learning at secondary level. Instead of the pupils being the passive recipients of lectures, or participating in drill-and-practice sessions, the new curricula posited a different relationship between teacher and taught, and a different mode of learning. Such new curricula as the Nuffield Science developments or the Schools Council Humanities Curriculum Project attempted to take away from the teacher what had hitherto been her primary role—imparting knowledge. Rather than the teacher delivering *ex cathedra* statements of fact, the new curricula envisaged that the pupils should retrieve information from a range of resources provided for them. The teacher's role was to be modified to a cross between just one more resource, a 'counsellor-and-friend', or a neutral chairperson.

Source: P. E. Woods and M. Hammersley, eds, *School Experience*, Croom Helm (forthcoming).

Such an approach was central to the ideology which informed changes in science curricula. In the development and implementation of 'Nuffield Science', it was a major principle that pupils should conduct experiments, analyse the results and draw conclusions from them. Whilst teachers would still demonstrate experiments and so on, far greater stress was to be placed on the pupil's *discovery* of the nature of things. The rationale of the new approaches had been articulated by Henry Armstrong at the turn of the century, with his advocacy of 'heuristic' approaches to science education (1898):

> Heuristic methods of teaching are methods which involve our placing students as far as possible in the attitude of the discoverer—methods which involve their *finding out*, instead of being merely told about things. It should not be necessary to justify such a policy in education . . . Discovery and invention are divine prerogatives, in some degree granted to all, meet for daily usage . . . it is consequently of importance that we be taught the rules of the game of discovery and learn to play it skilfully. The value of mere knowledge is immensely over-rated, and its possession over-praised and over-rewarded.

The new approaches should therefore stress pupils' engagement in 'real' experimentation and 'real' discovery, rather than the empty, unrealistic recapitulation of classic demonstrations. It was, therefore, hoped that such new curricula would involve the teachers and pupils in the joint production of something that was taken to be much more like the work of 'real' science. The authors of the Science Teacher Education Project (1974, p. 63) make this orientation explicit: 'For many of the teachers who were involved in the curriculum projects of the 'sixties and 'seventies it was in the hope of giving pupils an experience of the process of being a scientist.' Thus the activities of science education were to become more like the real-world activities of professional scientists (or rather, what were *taken to be* their activities). In this way the natural phenomena with which students worked would also become more 'real'. This aspect of the new science was encapsulated in the survey of teaching practices undertaken by Kerr *et al.* (1963). Although this study was done before the new curricula were in full swing, it does touch on important aspects of the emergent style of thought. The researchers produced a series of statements about practical work in school science, one of which was:

> To make biological, chemical and physical phenomena more real through actual experiençe. Practical work can improve appreciation of basic phenomena by providing opportunities for contact with actual equipment and processes.
> It is the reality of the experience with the actual thing that influences so much the level of understanding.

By virtue of these developments, pupils should learn to 'think scientifically'—that is, to design experiments, perform them and draw appropriate conclusions from their observations. Emphasis was to be placed on 'ways of knowing' rather than on the retention of 'facts'. This approach comes across clearly in the Scottish Integrated Science Scheme discussed by Hamilton (1975). The official documentation associated with the scheme—known as Curriculum Paper Seven—recommends, *inter alia*, that:

> The discovery method should be used wherever possible. (Recommendation 5)
> A much reduced emphasis on the retention of the factual content of the syllabus. Instead . . .
> pupils should be exposed to many other aspects of the work of the scientist . . . the experimental processes of thought by which he arrives at his conclusions and the language which he uses to communicate these conclusions to others.
> (Paragraph 8)

These recommendations and the ideology of the 'new' science were therefore shot through with these related themes: the importance of pupils' personal experience; the methods of discovery; the reality of science; the reality of natural phenomena. We shall go on to examine some aspects of how such approaches are worked out in classroom practice. At this point, we turn aside to consider our second type of instructional system.

While the science teaching we have outlined was innovatory, the system of medical teaching we discuss is a time-honoured one. But just as the science teaching was to bring 'learning' and 'practice' more into line, so it can be seen as analogous to the traditional methods of 'on-the-job' training characteristic of the 'clinical' phase of professional education. Such educational practices as clinical teaching on the hospital wards also stress the students' exposure to the 'real' work of the hospital: emphasis is placed on the

student's own first-hand 'experience' in accumulating practical knowledge. This is emphasised in the classic study of the University of Kansas Medical School (Becker *et al.*, 1961), where the notion of 'clinical experience' is used by staff and students alike to justify the importance of the student's first-hand involvement in work with the patients in the teaching hospital. Just as the science curricula we commented on contrasted pupils' experience and discovery with the rote-learning of 'facts', so the medical approach contrasts clinical experience with the pronouncements of textbooks (to the detriment of the latter). Whilst students chafe at learning the preclinical sciences (such as anatomy, physiology and biochemistry), they greet their entry into the teaching hospitals as marking a move towards the 'real work' of medicine. They are taught by practising clinicians and come into contact with real patients. Just as the science curricula are predicated on 'discovery', a similar concern informs much of the medical teaching: in this context, the students are often required to 'discover' the correct diagnosis by questioning the patient (taking a history) and examining his body. Indeed, this is the basic objective of clinical teaching in its early stages; considerations of management and treatment of patients tend to come in a little later.

We shall go on to discuss the nature of the 'reality' which is produced and reproduced in the two educational contexts.

Although it has changed somewhat in recent years, the underlying rationale of clinical teaching in medicine has remained largely unaltered since the eighteenth century. At root, the method stems from the apprenticeship approach to medical training whereby students learn 'on the job'. Students who are in the clinical phase of their course of study are attached to clinical units ('firms') and receive instruction from the doctors in the hospital wards, out-patient clinics, operating theatres and so on. The traditional view of this activity is that presented in Richard Gordon's *Doctor in the House*—where students tag along behind the consultant on his grand ward round: they shuffle along behind the entourage of junior doctors, ward sister, nurses and senior students. The doctor examines his patients, occasionally throwing scraps of information to the students or pausing to fire questions at them. Such a popular view is not entirely inaccurate: as Cramond (1973) remarks, the most notable aspect of *Doctor in the House* is its universality. However, the contemporary approach is somewhat different. Whereas, in the past, students were often attached to working rounds in this way, the Edinburgh teaching rounds described here were specifically scheduled as *teaching* rounds, pure and simple, and consisted of just one clinician and a group of students without any other courtiers or hangers-on. Thus the bedside teaching sessions did not form part of the management of the patient by the hospital staff: it was not a therapeutic situation. Thus the routine patient care done by hospital personnel and the teaching of junior students did not overlap.

This *bedside teaching* is in sharp contrast to another situation to which students are exposed in the hospital. These occasions are known as *waiting nights*. The hospital wards receive emergency patients on a rota basis, and on their weekly 'waiting night' (or 'receiving night'), students who are attached to the ward are expected to come in and attend for at least part of the evening. On such occasions the students can observe the patients as they are admitted in acute conditions. They see people come in with 'acute abdomens', or in the critical phase of a heart attack; they see hospital cases when they are 'fresh'. If the patients are up to it, students may take a history from those newly admitted and examine them. Alternatively they may merely observe while the admitting clinician works on the patient himself and offers a running commentary on what he is doing. In surgical units these occasions provide the students with much prized opportunities to go into the operating theatres where they can observe things like emergency appendicectomies—or even assist at such operations. Thus waiting nights— and the sort of experience they provide for the students—can be contrasted with the teaching rounds that are routinely conducted during the day. In the former context, the students are present while the 'real' work of the hospital is going on (and it would go on even if they were not present). Teaching rounds, on the other hand, are clearly separate from the hospital's routine work with the patients—and the students are their sole *raison d'être*.

The students recognise the distinction between these two varieties of teaching situation. Whilst they do not always employ the vocabulary, they occasionally label the distinction as one between 'hot' and 'cold' medicine. It is often applied to types of surgery: 'hot' surgery is that concerned with intervention in life-threatening crises, whereas 'cold' surgery covers the elective surgery for conditions such as hernias or haemorrhoids. It has also been employed in the arena of medical education by the authors of the Royal College of General Practitioners' report, *The Future General Practitioner*. They distinguish between two settings (p. 228):

(1) that which occurs at the time of the consultation, including discussion and observation immediately before, during and immediately after it.
(2) that which takes place at a time remote from the consultation, but employs material taken from it, based on memory or on written or on audio-visual recordings.

They go on to employ the vocabulary of 'hot' and 'cold' to evaluate these as effective educational occasions, i.e.:

The effective teaching of any objective often depends on a 'hot' situation: this focal point in

the consultation develops as a result of an unpredictable reaction between patient, doctor and teacher.

While the vocabulary in this context is applied rather differently, again it carries implications of actuality, and of a reality which is experienced at first hand, rather than through a *post hoc* reconstruction. For the medical students and their clinical experiences the contrast between 'hot' and 'cold' medicine was an important one and it concerned the nature of the 'reality' that they were experiencing.

One normal difference between the two contexts lies in the fact that the waiting night marks the beginning of a patient's hospital stay. By the time that students see them in the course of ward rounds, on the other hand, their 'career' as a hospital patient will be starting to take shape, or will be well under way. As a result of this, it is usually the case that when students see patients in the course of ward-work and bedside teaching, their trouble will routinely have been managed and/or diagnosed by the hospital personnel. Very often the patients' acute symptoms will have been treated—and any severe pain, high fever and so on will have been controlled (if possible) and may have disappeared altogether. Waiting nights provide the students with an exposure to patients whose illness is fresh. In this situation diagnosis will not yet have been done—and the students and the doctors are in a similar state of relative ignorance concerning the precise nature of the patient's presenting complaint. But when students see patients in the course of ward rounds, unless they happen to have seen them on a waiting night, then the distribution of knowledge is rather different. While the students are in a state of relative ignorance concerning the patient, now the doctor who is conducting the teaching round will already be acquainted with the patient's history and present complaint—either from his own work with the patient, or via the documentary evidence assembled in the case-notes folder.

From the point of view of the distribution of knowledge, then, the two teaching contexts differ. Yet the latter situation—that of bedside teaching— is designed to produce something which approximates to the sort of medical reality that is accomplished in the acute 'hot' situation. As we have said, it is a primary purpose of bedside teaching to provide students with practical opportunities to take histories, perform examinations and formulate diagnoses. The exercise may proceed upon the assumption that the patient's diagnosis is *not* already agreed upon by the clinical staff, or that management of the illness has not been initiated. The students may be (and often are) required to take the patient's history 'from scratch', as if the patient had not already given it—sometimes repeatedly—to the hospital doctors. This previous work that has been done by the hospital staff may, therefore, be discounted and the participants proceed as if it had not in fact been done. (This is generally possible because rather few of the patients will have been seen by students during the waiting night, as the students take turns to come in each week in twos or threes.)

This state of affairs can be illustrated in the following student's description of what happens when a student *has* seen a patient previously:

> After waiting nights, Mr Michael [the consultant surgeon] takes all students to see the new admissions. If you've already seen the patient, you keep quiet while Mr Michael plays games with the others, and sees how well they can make a diagnosis. Then you fill in the details—and try desperately to remember which abdomen it was when you've seen only a little bit of it in theatre.

This same student went on to develop his point about 'playing games'. He instanced a patient with jaundice. They could see she was yellow, he said, and they had been told already that she had cancer: they had had to take what he described as a 'very fake history', since they knew the answers to the questions anyway. He thought that the doctor who was teaching the group might just as well have said: 'There's a patient in that bed; she's got jaundice but she's got secondaries in her liver.' Here the student draws attention vividly to the way in which bedside teaching may be conducted 'as if' diagnosis of the patient's condition were starting afresh rather than having been already established by the doctors.

What we have been sketching here, in describing this aspect of bedside teaching, is a situation which is contrived in order to parallel some of the features of another situation. Clearly, it is not designed to reproduce *all* the possible features of 'real' or 'hot' medicine. The participants do not pretend that this 'really is' an admission on a waiting night: they do not feign rushing about, coping with emergencies, working against the clock and so on. (In fact this is one of the contrasts that students draw between the two types of situation—that the *pace* of the work is very different: 'cold' encounters can proceed at a much more leisurely pace.) In other words, the reproduction of 'hot' medicine in clinical teaching should not be confused with 'acting out' the situation (it is not a 'dress rehearsal' in that sense). It is designed to achieve a reconstruction of selected features in order to produce a plausible account of the supposedly 'real' situation for specific, practical purposes. We shall develop our comments on these lines subsequently.

Recalling our initial comments on the nature and practice of 'guided discovery' science teaching, it will be apparent that it shares some important features with 'cold' medical teaching; indeed, we might stretch the medical students' term and refer to it as 'cold' science. Of course, the school pupils do not have access to 'hot' science as do the medical students, but the parallel holds in so far as their school science is conducted in such a way as to replicate features of 'real' science. We concentrate on one particular area of school science—physics and biology—as taught to the fifteen-year-old girls at St Luke's. The O grade syllabuses in these subjects last for two years, and at the time of the fieldwork, the girls had completed one and a half terms of work. St Luke's was relatively unusual for a girls' school in that it had a strong science department run by enthusiastic, well-qualified teachers. The biology teacher (whom we shall call Mrs Linnaeus) and the physicist (Dr Cavendish) were both firmly committed to the 'guided discovery' ideology embodied in the O grade syllabuses, and it is their classes particularly which exemplify the nature of such 'cold' science.

A typical biology lesson would run as follows: Twenty-odd girls assemble in the laboratory (described in Delamont, 1976). Mrs Linnaeus asks someone to summarise the experiment(s) completed the previous lesson. She then asks for further hypotheses relating to, and following on from, that conclusion, which now need to be tested. The girls then suggest experimental designs to test these hypotheses. Methods are discussed and written up on the board. Then the class divide into pairs and all perform the same experiment(s). Practical work occupies some forty minutes, with the girls unprompted, writing-up in the lulls between bursts of work. When all, or most, of the pairs have completed the experiment, Mrs Linnaeus calls everyone's attention and asks each pair for their results. These are listed on the board, no comments being passed on their 'correctness'. When the list is complete, she asks what can be deduced from them. Pupils scan the results, comment on any that appear aberrant, and decide what the common, overall result is. They then consider whether or not the hypothesis is supported, and, often prompted or guided, produce a conclusion. Once this stage has been reached the formal part of the lesson is over, and the time remaining until the end of the double period is spent in tidying away apparatus, writing up the day's work, with the results and conclusions, and, for those who still have time, starting the homework assignment.

During the fieldwork, the classes were 'doing' photosynthesis—working through a series of controlled experiments to display the relative effects of light, chlorophyll, etc. We see this as paralleling 'cold' medicine. Just as the patient's condition has been diagnosed, so the biochemical processes of photosynthesis are well known. Just as the medical students are aware that a diagnosis exists, though they do not normally have prior access to it, so too the pupils are aware that biologists know about photosynthesis, though they do not normally have access to that knowledge themselves. The students operate a 'proper' procedure (taking a history, performing a physical examination and so on)—so too the girls go through the motions of stating hypotheses, designing rigorously controlled experiments and deducing conclusions. Neither situation is 'real', but both are parallels of 'real' processes. In both cases, it is important that the appropriate techniques be learned.

The problems faced by Mrs Linnaeus and Dr Cavendish in sustaining 'cold' science came mainly from the girls' 'failure' to perform experiments correctly. On the whole, they were able to steer the discussion into the right channels: the right hypotheses were usually formulated. Difficulties arose in the performance of the experiments themselves. Mrs Linnaeus taught two parallel biology classes. Whereas the girls in one group generally produced a set of results, in the other, the same experiments burned, boiled dry, boiled over or just failed to get finished inside lesson time. Thus, in the first class, Mrs Linnaeus usually had eight to ten sets of results to draw on; in the second, only two or three sets were generally available, or 'correct', and the ideal of scanning a *range* of results as a basis for the conclusion was rarely achieved. In this group, Mrs Linnaeus was always falling back on statements such as: 'If the experiment had worked, you would have been able to see . . .', 'Actually . . .'. Given these two classes, it was possible to see Mrs Linnaeus's 'cold' science succeeding and failing. Mrs Linnaeus believed strongly in guided discovery methods but, for her, the 'guiding' was extremely important. She steered the pupils' discussion firmly towards the right answers and 'stage managed' her classes with brisk efficiency. However, her strategy was not proof against pupils' potential failure to perform the physical manipulations necessary in the experiments.

The case of physics was rather different. Dr Cavendish also believed in a discovery-based approach to science teaching. However, she did not (or could not) do any 'guiding'. She provided a context in which discovery could take place—a laboratory full of apparatus and a textbook—and left the pupils to play at science as they would. While this may be closer to the situation of 'real' scientific discovery, it produced a high degree of anxiety and confusion among the pupils, to the extent that observation was an embarrassing, even distressing, occupation. The field notes taken at the time reflect some of this confusion:

Dr Cavendish sums up last week's experiments— in answer to queries from Fleur. Tessa and Lorraine write down this summary—tho' they were present at the lesson (Fleur was not). Tessa moves to check summary with Jackie on next bench. Dr C. asks simple question on basics—Eleanor answers right—Dr C. gives longish explanation of calculating acceleration. Girls then get out equipment to re-do experiment. Tessa, Mary and Fleur work near me—they discuss lacrosse teams—Mary says she's left the next table (where she's supposed to work) "cos they're trying to muddle me up.'

I move to next table where Charmian and Henrietta are explaining acceleration to Karen—

then Angela comes to Karen for help and is passed to Charmian for a repeat performance.

Throughout the field notes similar episodes— characterised by muddle, confusion and anxiety—are recorded. For example, the next week it was noted:

Dr C. starts lesson by announcing: 'Last week you discovered an important relationship.' Greeted by ironic laughs. Ignores this and gives explanations of relationship between force and mass . . . (later) Getting out equipment for an experiment started last time. Chorus of 'It didn't work!' After two experiments (on force, mass and acceleration) the class are still unsure of what they are doing and why. She gives detailed explanation again. Then says: 'A time will come (when they will understand it).' A chorus of ironic echoes of her sentiment.

Tessa, Lorraine and Fleur muddle around for some time with apparatus—eventually work out what they are doing from book and commonsense. Henrietta, Charmian and Michelle—much more together—have actually got some figures out of it!

Every lesson Dr Cavendish's attempt at summarising previous work would be greeted with dismay—the girls had always failed. The experiment had failed, or the mathematics were too hard, or the conclusions had simply not emerged. Dr Cavendish would be forced to re-explain, or would do the experiment herself, or re-work the maths. Many of the lessons 'worked' only because of a pupil, Charmian, who conducted tutorials at the back of the room using the textbook and her group's results!

This is clearly an extreme example of the problematic nature of such 'cold' science. But we would argue that such types of encounter are always precarious: they require a degree of careful creation and maintenance and the borderline between bringing them off and spoiling them is narrow. Even the usually well managed bedside teaching can easily be spoiled.

As we have pointed out already, patients may not be seen by the students until some time after the initial admission to the hospital ward. Now, although the teaching situation may be steered towards the diagnosis of the patient's trouble, by the time that bedside teaching takes place, the nature and the appearance of the illness may have changed. It is a normal trouble associated with 'cold' medicine that, with the passage of time, the initial signs and symptoms of the presenting complaint may abate or disappear altogether. Hence, when a teacher wishes to demonstrate a point of diagnostic observation and inference, the signs he wishes to show the students may well elude him. This contingency can be illustrated in the following field note extract:

Dr Muir reminded us that anaemic patients often have a dry, red, swollen tongue. He asked Miss Miniver to put out her tongue: it looked quite normal.

'I'm terribly disappointed,' the doctor said.
'On Saturday she had a red swollen tongue.'

There was no doubt that the patient was still to be considered 'anaemic', but the doctor had expected to provide a further example of diagnostic signs, as well as 'clinching' the diagnosis already arrived at. In the face of such events, the clinical teachers were observed to resort to 'repair' devices of various sorts. The two commonest variants were 'In fact . . .' and 'retrospective' clauses, both of which accomplish the same thing. In the example given above, the doctor uses a 'retrospective' appeal to a previous state of affairs that 'fitted' the order of things that he is putting forward to the students. Similarly, just as Mrs Linnaeus would attempt to repair the students' failings in their experiments and findings with her 'Well, actually . . .', the doctor would fill in what 'In fact . . .' should have appeared in the patient as a reflection of the underlying pathology. For example:

[In response to questioning from one of the students] the patient reported that he had not been having to pass water many times during the day. But Dr Massie commented, 'In fact, he reported frequency during the day as well'.

By means of such repair work, 'cold' medicine and science are once more brought into line with what is known about the phenomena of the 'real' world. The rationality and efficacy of scientific and medical inquiry are re-affirmed and demonstrated by the invocation of such appeals by the teachers concerned.

The successful accomplishment of 'cold' medicine and 'cold' school science depends upon the observation of context-specific conventions. In particular, sustaining the reality depends upon the participants acting 'as if' the answer to the puzzle were not already established. In the medical school, the teaching session may be threatened if a patient orients to the fact that the answer is already available to the doctor. Such a patient may protest about the students' inquiries, point out that the questions are irrelevant to his or her own care, and that the doctor himself can readily provide the answers (and more). Such a patient's 'grumbling' may not only spoil the 'bedside manner' of the doctor and students—it may also threaten the encounter by laying bare the nature of its contrivance.

Such disruption is also a consequence if the patient goes even further in this direction. Some patients will not only be aware that the doctor knows what is wrong with them—they may also know the diagnosis themselves. Failure to act in accordance with the tacit rules of 'cold' medical teaching may therefore lead them to divulge this information. In other words, they may treat a student's initial question as a direct request for this diagnosis, rather than an opening move in a sequence of questions and answers from which the diagnosis may be inferred by the students,

e.g.:

> *Student*: What brought you into hospital . . . ?
> *Patient*: Ulcerative colitis, the doctor called it . . .

In other words, if the bedside session is to come off as a successful recapitulation of 'real' diagnosis, then the work that has been done on the patient must be set aside by those 'in the know' (cf. Atkinson, 1975). Therefore, in conducting and 'stage-managing' such bedside encounters, the teaching clinicians may need to guard against such untimely disclosure of information. This can be illustrated from our field notes:

A girl student was exploring whether the patient [an elderly woman] had any signs of anaemia. As she was examining her eyes, the inside of her mouth, the creases in her palms, etc., the old lady chipped in: 'I've had a blood transfusion since I came in . . .' The doctor interrupted, 'Don't tell them too much! You're giving the whole show away—giving away the whole shooting-match!'

Giving away too much involves revealing the stage-management of cold medicine by making explicit the information which would otherwise remain unspoken.

A further field note extract also demonstrates how the clinician may guard against such an eventuality. In this case he invents a 'meta-game' in which to locate the rule that the patient is not to divulge data to the students.

The consultant began the teaching session by telling the students: 'Imagine that Mr— is an Eskimo who's deaf and dumb and mentally deficient . . .' In other words they were not to take a history, but were to proceed straight to the physical examination. As the various students took the patient's pulse, examined him for *oedema*, tested his eye movements, examined his thyroid, etc., the consultant commented to the patient that he was 'doing fine', and that he was using him as a 'male model'. The consultant then asked one of the students to examine the patient's *precordium*. When the student opened the patient's pyjama jacket, he exposed an operation scar on the left side of his chest.

> *Patient*:   'Do I tell them about that?'
> *Consultant*: 'No; as far as they're concerned that's a shark's tooth that tore you apart.'

In much the same way, trouble can occur in school science if the particular conventions of cold science are not respected. This can be illustrated in the following observation from a biology lesson, made during the girls' work on photosynthesis. (The experiment under discussion involved covering growing leaves with silver foil with several holes cut in it. After a few days the leaves are picked and tested for starch, which should be only present in the uncovered patches.)

Michelle: Mrs Linnaeus, I don't see how that will prove it—it could be all sorts of things we don't know anything about.

Mrs L.: (*Comes down the lab. to stand near Michelle, asks her to expand her problem—to explain what she doesn't see.*)

Michelle: Well you said if there was starch in the bare patches it would mean there was—it would be because of the light. But it could be the chemicals in the foil, or something we know nothing about.

Sharon: Of course it'll prove it—we wouldn't be wasting our time doing it if it didn't.

Mrs L.: I don't think that's a very good reason, Sharon! (*She laughs, then goes on into a long and detailed vindication of the experimental structure. This involves discussing the molecular structure of carbohydrates, and other phenomena. Few other girls bother to listen—Henrietta does.*)

We can note how both girls' exchanges are problematic, given the nature of cold science. Michelle treats it as 'hot' science—that the process really is one of scientific discovery in which the phenomenon under consideration is genuinely not understood. From the point of view of her learning the logic of science, the teaching may be regarded as successful—but it causes problems in the here-and-now situation of the classroom, since the teacher's smooth production of a lesson depends upon treating the 'experiment' at its face value. Sharon's interjection can be read as an attempt at a remedial exchange: she attempts to reaffirm the nature of cold science as really doing what is claimed for it. However, in doing so, she lays bare the stage machinery of the exercise—shows that it is a 'put-up job'. She explicitly orients to the teacher's prior knowledge: they would not be wasting their time. She sees that the enterprise has been managed in such a way as to produce an outcome in line with Mrs Linnaeus's intended result—the right answer. Sharon threatens the mock-up as a plausible situation. Mrs Linnaeus therefore denies that Sharon's approach is a 'reasonable' one and reaffirms the rationality of discovery methods. (Note, however, that she does not deny that Sharon is right.)

As a teaching strategy, 'guided discovery' in one of its forms is difficult to sustain. There are many points at which it can go wrong. Teachers using it need to engage in artful stage-management if they are to bring it off successfully. If the nature of this management is not respected by any of the parties, then trouble can ensue. By the same token, the interaction can become problematic if the 'stage machinery' becomes too visible in the course of the encounter. In either event, it becomes difficult for the participants to create and maintain the 'reality-like' nature of the exercise.

We should now like to develop our analysis of these varieties of teaching encounter, and the characteristic

modes of pedagogy associated with them, by reference to a game-theoretical approach. We wish to suggest that the sorts of teaching encounters that we have been commenting on can be usefully approached using the perspective of 'information-games'—an approach derived from Lyman and Scott (1970), Scott (1968) and Goffman (1970). The idea of an information-game is one of four game-theoretic analytical devices that derive from Goffman's commentaries on the conduct of everyday life. Scott summarises these 'gaming' notions in this way (1968, p. 159; emphasis as in original):

> In *face-games* each participant manoeuvers to maximize his own realization of a valued identity, while seeking an equilibrium that will permit others to do likewise. In *relationship-games*, the participants seek to create, maintain, attenuate or terminate personal relationships. In *exploitation-games*, the participants seek to maximize their position of power and influence vis-à-vis one another. In *information-games*, the participants seek to conceal and uncover certain kinds of knowledge.

As Scott himself points out, these may be treated as distinct for analytical purposes only. In concrete situations, they are 'empirically overlapping', and the possibility of the application of them all to educational encounters will be apparent.

The notion of an information-game has been applied in a particularly telling way in Scott's ethnography of race-track punters, and their attempts to discover 'tips' and reliable information concerning the horses in a race (1968). Similarly, it has been brought into play to analyse the process involved when blacks pass for white, or homosexuals pass for straight and so on (Lyman and Scott, 1970): they seek to ensure that information and aspects of their identity that may be discrediting shall remain undisclosed. In the same way, in Scott's work on horse-racing, whereas the punters will seek to uncover relevant information, so the owners, trainers and jockeys may be involved in covering up the information that the betting man seeks (e.g. whether or not a horse will really be trying to win the race). In the course of such information-games, the actors will be engaged in sequences of *covering* and *uncovering* moves. While one or more participants will seek to discover information, and so initiate uncovering strategies, these moves may be countered by covering up on the part of the actor or actors who have control of the information that is sought. In the course of the interaction, those engaged are involved in monitoring the 'information state' of the other actors in an attempt to gauge how much information they have gleaned, or how much they 'really know'. The process is one of 'strategic interaction', in Goffman's terms.

Our introduction of 'information-games'—in this form at any rate—may appear paradoxical or even perverse in a discussion of pedagogy. It is an 'obvious' feature of education that it is concerned with communication and the *transmission* or *presentation* of knowledge, and the rationale may appear to be quite the reverse of 'information-games'. Certainly, we need to modify Scott's formulation somewhat. Scott's discussions are addressed almost exclusively to situations where one or more actors are concerned that information should remain undisclosed. However, we can extend the notion to situations where the purpose of the action is that information should (or at least could) be disclosed and discovered, but where the *process of inquiry* is what is at stake. Consider, for instance, what goes on when the panel of a show such as *What's My Line?* try to guess the identity of a guest celebrity. Although the game is set up in such a way that the guest's identity is hidden, there is considerable chagrin and embarrassment if the panellists do not in fact arrive at the right answer. The fun of the game is not in the 'contest', but in the process of question and answer whereby the answer is arrived at. The same general principles apply to the 'cold' medicine and science that we have been discussing.

As we have shown, the successful conduct of these teaching encounters depends upon the successful discounting of already established knowledge. In medicine, bedside teaching proceeds on the basis that previously acquired knowledge about the patient's illness should be set aside so that the diagnostic exercise can proceed as it would under the 'normal' circumstances of 'hot' medicine. In the same way, school science proceeds on the tacit assumption that the pupils are engaged in the 'discovery' of phenomena which are already well known, and which the teacher has already set up as the end point of their endeavours. In other words, what is at stake in teaching situations of this sort is not so much that the relevant conclusions should *remain* undisclosed, but rather that they should appear in the appropriate manner and at the appropriate time. It is necessary that the parties should 'go through the motions' of correct medical or experimental procedure. The conduct of the information-games serves to ensure that an *orderly* production of knowledge should occur in accordance with the rules of appropriate 'discovery' methods.

In this regard, the sort of management of knowledge that we are describing is a regular feature of teacher-student interactions. Information-games of various sorts are normal features of classroom discourse. It is by no means the case that all 'teaching' implies the didactic *presentation* of knowledge. In various ways, the accomplishment of teaching may depend on the teacher's knowledge and information being temporarily kept back from the students. This has been noted by Sinclair and Coulthard (1974) and by Stubbs (1975). Stubbs, for example, suggests that many teachers' questions can usefully be described as 'pseudo-questions': that is, what pass as questions in the classroom are rather different from those usually encountered in other social contexts. Teachers'

questions are not rhetorical, in so far as they do require an answer of some sort, but they do not indicate ignorance on the teacher's part. For most of the time, when a school teacher asks her class: 'Who won the battle of Waterloo?', we would be wrong in assuming that the teacher herself does not know, and is expecting her pupils to instruct her in elementary history. Whereas most questioners' utterances will normally be treated as displays of their ignorance, teachers' questions will normally be grounds for the display of their knowledge—either in correcting pupils' answers or in acknowledging their correctness. Similarly, when a teaching doctor asks a student to produce a diagnosis about a patient, he is normally checking to see if he can do it successfully, rather than seeking the 'second opinion' of a colleague. In other words, the production of certain varieties of pedagogical device depends upon the suppression of the teacher's own prior knowledge of the 'correct' answer, so that students themselves may display it or elicit it for themselves, while the teacher may prompt the students towards the right answer. From this point of view, then, the devices of 'cold' medicine and science can be seen as such elementary gambits 'writ large', so as to provide the grounds for extended educational encounters.

We can now go on to consider briefly the nature of 'cold' medicine and science rather more precisely. These pedagogical practices can be seen as 'glossing' devices: that is, that they are ways of 'doing observable-reportable understanding' (Garfinkel and Sacks, 1970). These teaching practices are socially organised ways in which the participants produce something like a 'working model' of medical diagnosis or scientific experimentation in such a way as to make observable, teachable and reproduceable the methods whereby these things are normally done by competent members of the respective professions. Garfinkel and Sacks themselves suggest something of the sort in their discussion of glossing practices that they refer to as 'mock-ups', and they refer explicitly to working models as a concrete illustration (1970, p. 263):

Mock-Ups. It is possible to buy a plastic engine that will tell something about how auto engines work. The plastic engine preserves certain properties of the auto engine. For example, it will show how the pistons move with respect to the crank shaft; how they are timed to a firing sequence, and so on . . .
Let us call that plastic engine an account of an observable state of affairs. We offer the following observations of that account's features. First, in the very way that it provides for an accurate representation of features in the actual situation, and in the very way it provides for an accurate representation of *some* relationships and *some* features in the observable situation, it also makes specifically and deliberately false provision of some of the *essential* features of that situation.

In the same way, the 'mock-ups' that we have been concerned with are also made possible by the essentially false premise that 'discovery' is being done *de novo*, rather than the action being the stage-managed recapitulation of already known 'facts'. Garfinkel and Sacks continue later: '. . . the knowledge of the ways in which the account . . . makes false provision is for the user a controlling consideration in permitting it to be used as an account of the actual situation.' (ibid.) In the educational context, the teacher's prior knowledge of the end-point of the students' enquiries (one of the 'false provisions') provides the teacher with a resource in controlling the situation. Students' lines of inquiry and inference can thus be managed in such a way as to facilitate the appearance of the conclusion that was sought. In a similar manner, the students may use an understanding of the nature of the 'false provisions' as a resource in their own problem-solving. When medical students are aware that the patient has already been diagnosed, then they may try to ascertain the 'right answer' by investigating the end-of-the bed chart, the folder of case-notes or other ward personnel —thus short-circuiting the normal investigative procedure. Similarly, as we have discussed, pupils can invoke their understanding of the teacher's prior knowledge of the outcome of their experiments in justifying or querying the usefulness of certain courses of action.

What we are dealing with, then, are carefully managed 'versions' or 'reproductions' of certain types of reality, whose verisimilitude depends upon a degree of 'stage-management' on the part of teachers, and upon the systematic falsification or transformation of selected features of that reality. Goffman has recently commented on just this sort of transformation in his discussion of 'framing' (1975, p. 59):

> In our society, and probably in all others,
> capacity to bring off an activity as one wants to—
> ordinarily defined as the possession of skills—
> is very often developed through a kind of
> utilitarian make-believe.

And he goes on to comment that events which are encountered are ' "decoupled" from their usual embedment in consequentiality', which again draws our attention to the way in which the 'reality' must be re-created in 'unreal' circumstances if their authentic working is to be assured. The degree of abstraction and reconstruction involved can vary. Goffman cites the example from clinical medicine where modern techniques allow for the mechanical simulation of illness and treatment—for instance the use of manikins which reproduce the reaction of patients to the administration of anaesthetics (Levinson, 1970). This variety of 'bedside' teaching depends upon an extreme abstraction, whereas the clinical teaching we have been concerned with more closely approximates the personnel and appearance of normal medical work.

The relationship between 'reality' and 'mock-ups' or 'practice' is dialectical. It is particular features of 'reality' that are selected and reconstructed to produce the 'working model'. In the same way, the model itself provides an interpretive framework whereby the reality may in turn be understood. Through these 'reality-like' experiences, students amass a stock of typifications and recipes for action in typical circumstances in preparation for situations that are 'for real' (cf. Schütz, 1964).

The precise nature of the medical and scientific mock-ups lies in the way both provide occasions for the *methodic* reproduction of knowledge. Both medicine and science are socially organised ways of furnishing us with stocks of knowledge about the natural world and ways of handling it. They both consist of devices for determining *facts*—the facts of chemistry, biology or medicine. When we speak of factual propositions—for instance, as against 'opinions', 'beliefs', 'guesses' and so on, we treat 'facts' as being warranted in a way which does not apply to those other classes of knowledge (cf. Phillips, 1973). The status of such 'facts' is not something which is essential or inherent in the account of the world which they embody—but rather resides in the procedures and methods which are mobilised to produce and validate the knowledge. This view is summarised by McHugh (1971, p. 332):

> . . . nothing—no object, event, or circumstance—
> determines its own status as truth, either to the
> scientist or to science . . . an event is transformed
> into the truth only by the application of a canon
> of procedure, a canon that truth-seekers use and
> analysts must formulate in providing the
> possibility of agreement.

The place of such socially shared procedures for the production and evaluation of scientific knowledge is highlighted in Kuhn's discussion of stability and change in science (1970). For Kuhn, it is the scientific 'paradigm' (or 'exemplar') which is the ground for scientists' consensus over appropriate topics for inquiry, methodologies and the sort of answers that might reasonably be expected from investigations. The paradigms:

> . . . provide scientists not only with a map but
> also with some of the directions for map-making.
> In learning a paradigm, the scientist acquires
> theory, methods and standards together,
> normally in an inextricable mixture.

Hence the consensually-given 'facticity' of interpretations of states of affairs depends upon those 'facts' having been produced by the appropriate and agreed-upon methods. By the same token the efficacy of the conventional methods is constantly reaffirmed by the recurrent and reliable production and reproduction of recognisable 'facts'. The stage-management of 'cold' medicine and science furnishes occasions for the concrete display of the warranted production of factual knowledge. The methods of inquiry that are required of the students in these contexts parallel those of 'real' knowledge-production; the teacher is in a position to organise and control the situation in such a way that the requisite answer will be forthcoming for the students' investigations. Hence the warranted nature of the view of the world ('facts') and the distinctive way of looking at the world ('methods') are affirmed. What appears as 'discovery' is the recapitulation of the socially agreed nature of 'science', 'medicine' and the natural world.

Note

* Revised version of a paper presented at the Open University conference, 'The Experience of Schooling', Cranfield Institute of Technology, April 1975.

References

Armstrong, H. E., 1898, 'The heuristic method of teaching or the art of making children discover things for themselves: a chapter in the history of English schools', reprinted in W. H. Brock, ed., 1973, *H. E. Armstrong and the Teaching of Science*, Cambridge University Press.

Atkinson, P. A., 1975, 'In cold blood: bedside teaching in a medical school', in G. Chanan and S. Delamont, eds, *Frontiers of Classroom Research*, Slough, National Foundation for Educational Research.

Becker, H. S., Geer, B., Hughes, E. C. and Strauss, A. L., 1961, *Boys in White*, Chicago University Press.

Cramond, W. A., 1973, *Prescription for a Doctor*, Leicester University Press.

Delamont, S., 1973, 'Academic Conformity Observed', unpublished PhD thesis, University of Edinburgh.

Delamont, S., 'Beyond Flanders Fields', in M. Stubbs and S. Delamont, eds, *Explorations in Classroom Observations*, Chichester, Wiley, 1976.

Garfinkel, H. and Sacks, H., 1970, 'On formal structures of practical actions', in H. C. McKinney and E. A. Tiryakian, eds, *Theoretical Sociology: Perspectives and Developments*, New York, Appleton–Century–Crofts.

Goffman, E., 1970, *Strategic Interaction*, Oxford, Blackwell.

Goffman, E., 1975, *Frame Analysis*, Penguin.

Hamilton, D., 1975, 'Handling innovation in the classroom: two Scottish examples', in W. A. Reid and D. F. Walker, eds, *Case Studies in Curriculum Change*, Routledge & Kegan Paul.

Kerr, J. F. *et al.*, 1963, *Practical Work in School Science*, Leicester University Press.

Kuhn, T. S., 1970, *The Structure of Scientific Revolutions*, 2nd ed., Chicago University Press.

Levinson, D. O., 1970, 'Bedside teaching', *New Physician*, 19, 733.

Lyman, S. M. and Scott, M. B., 1970, *A Sociology of the Absurd*, New York, Appleton–Century–Crofts.

McHugh, P., 1971, 'On the failure of positivism', in J. Douglas, ed., *Understanding Everyday Life*, Routledge & Kegan Paul.

Phillips, D. L., 1973, *Abandoning Method*, San Francisco, Jossey–Bass.

Royal College of General Practitioners, 1972, *The Future General Practitioner*, London, Royal College of General Practitioners.

Schütz, A., 1964, 'The stranger: an essay in social psychology', in A. Brodersen, ed., *Collected Papers*, vol. 2, The Hague, Nijhoff.

Scott, M. B., 1968, *The Racing Game*, Chicago, Aldine.

Sinclair, J. McH. and Coulthard, M., 1974, *Towards an Analysis of Discourse*, Oxford University Press.

Science Teacher Education Project (STEP), 1974, *Theory into Practice*, ed. J. Haysom and C. Sutton, London, McGraw–Hill.

Stubbs, M., 1975, 'Teaching and talking: a sociolinguistic approach to classroom interaction', in G. Chanan and S. Delamont, eds, *Frontiers of Classroom Research*, Slough, National Foundation for Educational Research.

17 Cue-consciousness
C. M. L. Miller and M. Parlett

An important part of our study was to discover how students reacted to their exams and how they prepared for them. A key concept here is the 'hidden curriculum', a term perhaps more familiar in the United States than here. The hidden curriculum (Snyder, 1971) describes the implicit demands (as opposed to the explicit obligations of the 'visible curriculum') that are found in every learning institution and which students have to find out and respond to, in order to survive within it. It is part of the hidden curriculum, for instance, that the student has to decide which pieces of work can be 'selectively neglected' out of the mass of set work; or which particular method of doing problems will get him the highest marks. Finding out about these things can be thought of as almost an adaptive response—in the biological sense—to the learning system.

These kinds of activities are often referred to as 'playing the system' or 'using strategies', the students as 'game-players', and so on. These are terms that have by now passed into the folklore of university teaching, and are often used somewhat indiscriminately. Saying that some students manipulate the system is all very well, but it does not go very far. How exactly do 'strategies' operate? How do students practise them? Do all students 'operate' the system equally? If not, what kind of students do so or do not do so? Most significantly—how does responding to the hidden curriculum affect academic learning and responses to the visible curriculum?

It is clear from previous research (Snyder 1971, Becker *et al.* 1968, Parlett 1969) that this area is complicated but also highly important. Hidden curricula can run counter to the intentions of actual visible curricula, and discussions of forms of teaching and assessment need to recognize and take into account the 'hidden' implications of particular schemes. Ultimately it would be helpful to know sufficient about students' responses to hidden curricula to be able to predict the likely effects of introducing a new form of instruction or examining.

'Cues' and the consciousness students have of them

When we started interviewing final year Honours students in one of the departments studied, we were not concentrating particularly on *individual* differences in students' approaches to assessment: indeed, we were concerned more with what was common or shared. However, when we began the detailed analysis of the data at the end of all the interviews, individual differences began to show up strongly and could not be ignored. The chief distinguishing features were as follows. One group of students talked about a need to be perceptive and receptive to 'cues' sent out by staff—things like picking up hints about exam topics, noticing which aspects of the subject the staff favoured, noticing whether they were making a good impression in a tutorial and so on. These students seemed to believe that these factors were terribly important in what their final degree marks would be based on.

There was another, smaller, group of students who were further distinguished by having, over and above this receptiveness or perceptiveness towards cues, an *activity* component. Unlike the first group, they were not just content to pick up hints and to wonder if they were making a good impression. Instead they deliberately interacted with the system: they button-holed staff about the exam questions; sought them out over coffee; made a point of discovering who their oral examiner was, what his interests were, and, most of all, deliberately attempted to make a good impression on staff. This for them seemed to constitute a very large part of what the exams were all about. We

Source: C. M. L. Miller and M. Parlett, *Up to the Mark: a Study of the Examination Game*, Society for Research into Higher Education, monograph no. 21, June 1974, section 3, pp. 51–3, 55–6, 59–68, 72–5.

have called these people, who are characterized by their dynamic interacting way of behaving, 'cue-seekers'. The first group, who were perceptive without the activity component, we have called 'cue-conscious'.

The third group, and the largest, had neither perceptive nor active components—and we labelled them, perhaps rather unkindly, 'cue-deaf'. For them, it seemed that working as hard as you could was the ingredient for success. They believed that the impression they made on staff—if they did make one—would not affect the way in which they were marked. Nor did they speak of picking up hints.

The differences between students in what we decided to term their 'cue-consciousness' was something that we had not predicted and which emerged from analysis after the interviews. We should emphasize here that the three types (cue-seekers, cue-conscious and cue-deaf) are shorthand descriptive terms and not to be taken as rigid categories or as formally defined psychological types. Theoretically, a category system here, rather than a continuum, is somewhat artificial. Given that we found these three major types, that is not to say that there are not finer gradations between them. However, elaboration of these would necessarily depend on a more focused study than was warranted here. Cue-consciousness is a concept that extends previous ideas of the hidden curriculum in a useful way. (. . .)

Exam performance

One obvious question was whether the final degree class correlated with whether someone was cue-seeking, cue-conscious or cue-deaf. When we knew the results of the final examinations, we compared these with the cue-conscious categories already given us by our judges. Inspection of the data certainly seemed to indicate a connection—three of the cue-seekers getting Firsts. It seemed, too, that people who were cue-conscious tended to get Upper Seconds, and those who were cue-deaf got Lower Seconds. There was only one Third awarded in this class, and two Ordinary degrees.[1] Table 17.1 shows the results, and, indeed, the suspected relationship does hold up.[2]

Table 17.1

degree class	First	Upper Second	Lower Second/ Third[a] Ordinary[b]	totals
Cue-seekers	3	1	1	5
Cue-conscious	1	6	4	11
Cue-deaf	1	2	11	14
Totals	5	9	16	30

a One Third class.   b Two Ordinary degrees.

If one compares the aggregate final examination marks of the three types rather than the actual degree class awarded, one finds that the marks of the cue-deaf are significantly lower than those of both the cue-conscious and cue-seekers.[3]

This relationship between exam performance and cue type is an intriguing one, but we are not of course suggesting that the extent of cue-consciousness is the sole determinant (or even necessarily a causal determinant at all) of academic success or failure. It is merely a correlate, albeit perhaps an important one. One must remember, too, that there were several notable exceptions to the trend: one cue-deaf student getting a First and one cue-seeker getting a Lower Second. (. . .)

In [the remainder of this section] we present several short extracts from interviews, with particular students as examples of the three types; and, second, we go on to discuss a number of issues related to cue-consciousness.

Davidson: a cue-seeker

Davidson[4] was one of the most positive of the cue-seeking group. He hardly needed any questioning at all in the interviews—all his views on assessment came pouring out and it was obvious that he had given the subject of examining a great deal of thought. He certainly had a great abhorrence of finals exams. More than any other student he used metaphors—in referring to exams—such as 'the final death' and 'the great hurdle'. He said he had 'an absolute horror of them'.

> You can go through university for four years, two years doing Honours,[5] and really do quite well until you come to the stumbling block which is the final exam . . . all the ethos that surrounds it, the set time—that in three hours you must stop, and time runs out. It's so incredible.

A large portion of what he said was about 'playing the game'—which was his own term for it.

> I play the examination game. Two or three of us have invented it—the examiners play it, so we play it too. You talk in tutorials partly for the sake of talking, partly for the sake of getting known by the lecturers, trying to make sure of course that what you say is reasonably intelligent and isn't complete waffle.

Notice that he and his friends believe that they spontaneously 'invented' the examination game. He goes on:

> *I am positive* there is an examination game. You don't learn certain facts for instance, you don't take the whole course, you go and look at the examination papers and you say 'looks as though there have been four questions on a certain theme this year, last year the professor said that the examination would be much the same as before', so you excise a good bit of the course immediately, say I'm going to concentrate on four or five topics, the main ones to begin with—and there you are!

This is another part of the examination game, you're always prodding. You know if you can get a lecturer over a cup of coffee, you are always saying 'Have you written the examination paper yet?' you know, this sort of thing.

He seemed to use playing the game in part to cope with his fears of being examined, by 'objectifying it'—standing outside it and defining it as an 'artificial farce':

You know, this idea that you can actually view it objectively, if I do this, and if I avoid that ball there, don't bother about these people standing here, I should be able to get quite a few marks—this sort of idea. But it's simply because it's so artificial.

He described the differences between people:

Everybody does play the game in a sense, everybody's looking for hints, but some of us look for it or probe for it, rather than waiting for it to come passively. We actively go and seek it. It's so silly because it inhibits your contact with your lecturer and professor in a sense.

There seemed to be a sort of compulsion for him about playing the game. He didn't want to do it but somehow he 'had to'. He was very much aware that it had an adverse effect on what he learnt. He said:

If you get a *seen* paper and you know the questions in advance, then you can try and shove in as many references as possible, and again this is playing the game—the appearance of knowledge. This is what you do in essays as well, you know, you don't do it because you *want* to, it's because you have to.

Davidson was both determined and ambitious. He wanted very much to get a First, because he believed that you couldn't hold your own in academic life without one.

There are three points to make here. First, that this student has a pronounced fear of exams. This is based on the idea that he's got to show himself up brilliantly within one three-hour exam in a subject, a procedure he sees as extremely artificial. Second, he seems to use playing the game as a sort of defence mechanism, to the point even that he sees the techniques of the game as being tested, rather than himself. Third, there is his sense of compulsion: he knows it's not particularly good for the way he learns, but he *has* to do it. He says:

What is the purpose of the examination game? It becomes purposeless except for you, because you know you want to get a certain class of degree within the system, but as far as assimilating knowledge properly is concerned, it just doesn't work, because if you play the game properly you're choosing all the time, and not getting an overview because you know there will be a certain question you have to answer.

There were two other cue-seekers who had views remarkably similar to Davidson's, though obviously he was unique in certain respects. One, Scott, again makes the distinction between exam techniques and knowing what the work is about:

The technique involves knowing what's going to be in the exam and how it's going to be marked. You can acquire these techniques from sitting in the lecturer's class, getting ideas from his point of view, the form of his notes, and the books he has written—and this is separate to picking up the actual work content.

And on tutorials:

The impression you make on staff affects how they mark your paper and this makes me make particular efforts in classes—it's in a sense a rather cynical approach. I do this in Professor X's class—he tends to single me out from the rest of the class now and I don't think the others like it very much, but from my point of view it's very good and I hope it will affect how my papers are marked.

McKenzie: a cue-conscious student

Very alert, thoughtful, talkative, McKenzie was intrigued by the whole thing—the idea that in fact how you dressed, what you said to staff, might well affect your degree result. These were ideas of his that he brought up in the interview and which currently fascinated him. He was speculating about them, discussing them with his friends.

We (the students) were discussing the other day whether the impression we give to the staff has any effect at the examiners' meeting—whether you look tidy, whether you are liked and so on. Some people's names conjure up instant good reactions and others have the opposite effect. The same reactions are bound to work when the papers are being marked.

He was very aware of the cues that were being dropped and the possible importance of making an impression, but he wasn't at Davidson and Scott's stage of sophistication in accepting and *acting* on them. He talked about picking up hints, and the importance of self-confidence. He seemed on the threshold of realization, but lacking the certainty and determination that seemed to characterize Davidson and Scott

There is definitely an exam technique but I am not really sure what it consists of . . . identifying the technique is what you are here to do . . . something to do with taking exams in your stride . . . it's important to have a card index in your mind . . . writing neatly, not having too many crossings out so that the examiner likes your paper.

He is a good example of the type of student who is cue-conscious without the active 'seeking' component. He got a good Upper Second.

Dean is another example of someone who came into this category. 'The lecturer gets a picture of you and this impression must affect him as he's marking the papers, however impartial he tries to be.' Did some people then make a special effort to get themselves noticed in class? The reply was: 'I don't think they do, people only talk when they are interested.' Notice the conviction that staff *are* affected by the impression they already have of a student, but that students do not go deliberately out of their way to make any special efforts to this end—in other words, this student did not realize that Scott and Davidson and others were already doing this.

Nichols: cue-deaf

Nichols is a typical example of one of the cue-deaf group.

> I don't choose questions for revision—I don't feel confident if I only restrict myself to certain topics.

He went on to make a remark that seemed characteristic of the cue-deaf: 'I will try to revise everything'. To him, exam questions were 'deadly secret', and he did not seem to have the confidence even to question-spot, let alone to go out to seek information from staff:

> I would never ask staff if a certain thing is going to come up because they wouldn't tell you—I have always thought that exam questions were a deadly secret.

He had a strong faith in staff's question-setting—when asked how well he thought this year's work could be shown up in a three-hour exam, he said that 'the staff must formulate questions in such a way as to make you show up your work.' He added: 'But I don't know how they do it.' He definitely regarded the staff as being in control of the whole situation—they did what was best for you and you didn't have to think about it. He did not consider that staff members' personal impression of him could contribute to his result.

> I don't know (about staff getting an impression of students) although I suspect they probably do in case they have to give an opinion, although I don't think this counts as part of the degree.

Payne was another example of a cue-deaf student.

> I am a very poor question-spotter. What I think will come up, invariably doesn't, so I just go through everything I can. On the morning of the exam I concentrate on the subjects I think will come up—but invariably I am wrong.

Two exceptions

Before extending the discussion, it is instructive to look at two exceptions to the general trend: MacAllister and Hunter, whose degree results were other than those one might have 'expected' from their category of cue-consciousness.

MacAllister was a man who obviously was not a cue-seeker: he was classified by our judges as cue-conscious. However, he turned out to get a First, and was the only student in this group to do so. The result surprised some people, including himself. In some ways he seemed to be unique in this sample of students. He fitted into the stereotype of the 'bright student who did not have to bother to work'. He was the only person who talked a lot about acquiring a way of thinking about one's subject; he remarked that 'the facts are not important, it's how you think.' Although he 'wouldn't ask the staff what was in the exam, because they wouldn't answer', he certainly showed awareness about the importance of making a good impression and he was selective about his revision. But he says:

> I tend to spend a lot of time on things I am really interested in, so I won't get a good degree. If I swotted away diligently, I would get a better degree but I wouldn't be so intellectually broadened.

He said when he is not working he reads novels and composes music: 'I can get very involved in music and waste a whole day that way.' He was the only student to mention 'academic flair' and to wonder what it was, and how one acquires it in connection with his chosen subject. He thought it was some sort of spark that distinguished a particular type of mind and he was quite preoccupied with this idea.

When we saw him again after the exams, we asked him if he was surprised by his getting a First. He replied that he was very 'lucky' and he felt that he had a much wider view of the subject than some people who had also done well.

Hunter was an opposite case: a man defined as a cue-seeker by the judges (although not all the judges agreed), and a cue-seeker who ended up with a Lower Second. He was the only one to whom this happened. But it turned out to be a somewhat curious case. There was a prolonged discussion about this man at the examiners' meeting. What had happened was that he had walked out of one exam, explaining clearly on his paper that he'd had a mental block. This was discussed at some length at the examiners' meeting. There were a variety of opinions. Some argued strongly for counting him as 'an examination casualty' and not penalizing him at all: others argued that he should get zero and that this result should be averaged in with the rest—after all, 'You'll have chaps not turning up for exams the whole time.' There was more weight towards the former view, i.e. regarding him as an examination casualty, and they ended up by giving him a compromise degree. What actually happened to Hunter we learned from his retrospective questionnaire. He implied that the mental block arose from the fact that the complicated system of his question-spotting for the exam had gone completely awry: he had revised only specific topics and not a single one had come up; hence his 'mental block'. He certainly was an examination casualty but not, perhaps, in the way that the examiners envisaged. One other distinguishing feature about Hunter was that, *unlike* the other cue-seekers, he was extremely pessimistic about his degree class before the exams, saying that he would probably get a Third, and he certainly did not have the driving ambition of the others.

The three types and their academic efforts

For cue-seekers, examination performance consisted of a series of specialized techniques that had to be acquired. We have seen that this professionalized attitude was associated with the view that the assessment system was highly artificial. Failure (or even not getting the degree they wanted) was rarely spoken of by the cue-seekers. But the indications were that failure would have been attributed to a fault in technique not in themselves: in other words it would be *externalized*, as befits a system that is artificial.

The cue-deaf, in contrast, felt that if they performed badly it would be due to their intellectual inadequacy, in not being able to cover everything. The fear of failure was thus internalized and led to a good deal of anxiety and depression. The poor exam result they dreaded would confirm their sense of personal inadequacy.

The cue-conscious seemed to think that performance was based on a mixture of hard work and luck. Unlike the other two groups they tended to report a lot of mood swings before the exams—one day thinking they were doing fine and the next thinking 'but what happens if none of the right questions comes up?' This emphasis on 'luck' is revealing. Luck was never mentioned by the cue-seekers—it wasn't luck, it was technique. It was also rarely mentioned by the cue-deaf—for them it was hard work only that would show dividends. But luck was very often cited by the cue-conscious as an important factor in success and obviously relates to their only partially defined scheme of what was likely to turn up in the exams. MacAllister—who unexpectedly got a First—was certain that he was 'lucky' to do so.

A second point illustrated by the case studies is the difference in the perception of staff by students in the three groups and their views on staff/student interaction. Nichols, cue-deaf, certainly viewed the staff as authority figures from whom students absorbed knowledge. This suggests a totally different type of relationship between students and staff from that described by other groups. Nichols had far less direct interaction with staff than Davidson and Scott did,

as cue-seekers. Scott, for example, went out of his way to 'make a good impression' on one of the professors in tutorials. He described how he had to get that professor to the stage of singling him out in the class for attention as a favourite.

There was an interesting follow-up to this, in that Scott's efforts to impress the professor may have turned out later to have been crucial to his degree result. When it came to doing Finals, Scott was far more physically and mentally exhausted than he had anticipated. We saw him, deathly pale and barely awake, just before going in to tackle the paper set by Professor X—the one with whom he had made so many efforts in class. He wrote what he judged to be a very bad paper, far beneath his capabilities for what he saw as one of his best subjects. It is possible that Scott underestimated how well he had done the paper, but there were confirming comments from other students sitting near him on how little he had written. Professor X, however, gave him a First on the paper and this mark was crucial to Scott's getting the final degree class he wanted. It is not unlikely that this member of staff had appreciated the high standard of work of a student perceived as bright and conscientious during the year and had taken these factors into account in marking him.

From what has been said, it is clear that students who are as radically different as the cue-seekers were from the cue-deaf are obviously also going to be spending their time very differently in academic activities, and in turn, this will affect what and how they learn.

We can summarize the differences in the following way: the cue-seeker learns and revises very selectively indeed. (For example, both Scott and Davidson, having obtained the question topic, would write out 'original' answers to it and practise these.) Also they spend a good deal of time with staff but their relationship is constrained by the fact of the impending examination. The cue-conscious revise and learn selectively too, but not with the same degree of certainty. They therefore cover more topics, but are less prepared for any one of them. They apparently do not initiate as much contact with staff as do the cue-seekers, but when this does occur, presumably it is not so exam oriented. The cue-deaf tend to start learning and revision at the first page of their notes and go through methodically and may have virtually no informal contact with staff at all.

Interests and involvement

We have been aware in our study of a measure of conflict among some students between work for the purposes of doing well in examinations and the study of material of a course for its own interest—the two are not necessarily the same thing. Students who were highly cue-conscious, while believing that it was important to be very selective in learning for the exams, often also had strong interests in certain of their subjects. If they had pursued them fully, these interests would have competed with the heavy work-load they had allotted themselves for the exams. Paradoxically for the cue-seekers, their cue-seeking behaviour was often most marked in courses in which they were highly intellectually involved and wanting to do well in. Thus, intrinsic interest in the course work had not become submerged by examina-tion constraints; but there was certainly competition for attention.

We have also said that the cue-conscious' and the cue-seekers' attitudes to exams affected their relation-ship with staff. It should be pointed out, though, that almost certainly cue-seekers did not initiate discussion with staff solely for the purpose of finding out about examinations. But when there was opportunity for discussion there was also scope for questioning about examinations and for remarks of staff being taken as 'cues'. More opportunities for general discussion were likely to occur with those staff who taught the students' 'favourite' subjects or those in which they were especially interested. Many of these staff had come to be regarded by students as friends, in addition to their having respect for them, and informal con-versations took place on this basis.

Another missing piece in the jigsaw of cue-con-sciousness concerns the impact that friends' percep-tions of the exam system have upon each other. It was surely no accident that a very cohesive group of nine students who worked together for Finals were all cue-conscious. This group included three cue-seekers who got Firsts, and all the others except one got Upper Seconds. The group talked about assess-ment frequently among themselves and one wonders how many of them who were potentially cue-deaf were alerted by the rest. There is certainly evidence that they influenced each other to some degree One suspects that 'bright' students working together may spur each other on, and that they are likely to ex-change ideas. So although one would not want to conclude that the good degree results of that group are necessarily a function of their shared knowledge of cue-consciousness, the importance of friendship and communication in this context is evident. (. . .)

The variation between the students we studied had an interesting counterpart in certain staff differences. Students varied in the importance they attached to picking up and acting upon cues from staff about the exams; but staff also differed in how much they gave indications of likely exam questions in advance.

It was certainly not generally realized in one department how discrepant were the attitudes and practices of different staff members towards intimating the likely topics of the examination beforehand. At one end of the scale were staff who saw themselves as definite 'non-hinters':

'Oh no, I don't give them any idea of what's coming up in the exam.'
   'They have no idea what will be in the exam—

I don't decide myself till the last minute. Of course there's always a question on — (mentions a large subject area), but then there are at least 30 things I could ask about that!'

The fact that a lecturer had no intention of giving cues or hints did not of course mean that cue-conscious students made no inferences from what he *did* say. Indeed, a lecturer's apparent emphasis on certain references was taken as a 'hint' by some cue-conscious students. Other features, such as the amount of lecture time devoted to particular topics, or the frequency of allusions to a particular current theory, were also registered as indications.

Another, somewhat larger, group of staff acknow-ledged that they gave some hints. One of them remarked: 'I give them the odds, you know. Any intelligent student knows your hobby-horses.' This member of staff was clearly expecting 'any intelligent student' to make inferences. It is also a revealing comment in that he took for granted that the questions in his examination papers were likely to be on his 'hobby-horses'. So students in his course who were basing their guesses about exam topics on frequency of repetition and other marks of emphasis would certainly be on the right track.

A third (very small) group of staff believed in giving students more than just 'the odds':

'Oh yes, I make it very clear to them what to expect.'
   'I tell them pretty much what they're going to get. I'd be in favour of writing out the questions beforehand, giving them a "seen" exam.'

We have already suggested [in chapter 8 of the book from which this extract is taken] that the staff members' being explicit about the questions did not necessarily put an end to cue-seeking, although it may have reduced some of the pre-exam stress.

The fact that 'hinting' was usually a covert and unofficial activity, if a not uncommon one, and that there was such a discrepancy between the staff over how much they entered into it, led to students being somewhat confused. One of them remarked:

It's ridiculous, there's this sort of half-way house —they don't actually *say* what is coming up but they do this sort of hinting thing—at least some of them do, others wouldn't tell you anything.

Another described the process:

He sort of throws it away at the end of the lecture, very casual, 'Ah, by the way, you should look at this before June'—he never comes right out and says, 'you'll get a question on this.'

It may be that different attitudes of staff over hinting are connected with the relative emphasis they placed on their examination testing for 'breadth' versus 'depth'. The old distinction made between 'finding out what they *don't* know' and 'finding out what they *do* know' is relevant here. Breadth (or 'coverage'), is often considered of prime importance in 'professional' or certain 'basic' subjects. Thus one professor remarked:

They must know these basic facts and I want them to show that they have covered them at least once, even if they forget them the next day.

This member of staff saw the purpose of his examination as primarily to test factual learning over a wide area, and 'giving the game away' by hinting in advance would have been altogether incompatible with this general aim.

The reasoning, by staff who did give hints, seemed in part to be based on the notion that defining the topic meant that a student could concentrate his revision effort upon it. He would be able to go into some depth and detail, perhaps getting a good deal more out of the subject than if he were expected to cover a broader area.

It is important to realize that testing for depth of knowledge, or alternatively for breadth, is not a simple dichotomy. As one staff member put it:

I hear people talking about breadth. But what is 'breadth', for heaven's sake? If it means 'coverage', then how many coats of paint do you need before you decide that something is 'covered'?

From discussions with staff, we inferred that, for the majority, neither breadth nor depth predominated to the exclusion of the other. Nevertheless, there were extreme positions of the kind we have indicated—perhaps attributable in part to the type of subject matter the lecturer was teaching.

In conclusion, the connection between cue-consciousness and the intentional or non-intentional giving of cues by staff, is a complicated and also sensitive area. Both hinting by staff and the receiving and inferring by students, proceeds in a covert, untalked-about fashion. The practices were, however, unofficially condoned by many staff. Two of the cue-seekers thought that some staff were actually sympathetic to cue-seeking; and, moreover, that they had probably done it themselves as undergraduates. One head of department, when asked if he had any technique for taking his own first degree exams (which he sat, as he remarked, 'many years ago') said:

Oh! Good heavens no, I never worried about exams. Of course you put in the right references, that kind of thing, made sure you'd read your examiner's books and so on, but then everybody does that, don't they?

Notes

1 Students whose marks are not considered to be high enough for an Honours pass, may be recommended for an Ordinary degree.
2 A test of the degree class of perceptive/receptive students (i.e. cue-seekers and cue-conscious combined) against that of cue-deaf gives a significance level of $P < 0.05$ (Fisher's Exact Test, 2-tailed).
3 Cue-seekers $(n = 5)$ against cue-deaf $(n = 13)$, $P < 0.05$ ($n = 13$ and not 14 because n omits one honours student for whom we had only half his final marks because he was doing a combined degree); cue-conscious $(n = 11)$ against cue-deaf, $P < 0.05$; cue-seekers against cue-conscious, $P > 0.05$ (Mann–Whitney Test, 2-tailed).
4 We have used fictitious names for individuals.
5 The Edinburgh Honours degree normally takes four years, of which the final two years are devoted to the main Honours subject.

References

Becker, H. S., Geer, B. and Hughes, C., 1968, *Making the Grade*, New York, Wiley.
Parlett, M., 1969, 'Undergraduate teaching observed', *Nature*, 223, 1102–4.
Snyder, B. R., 1971, *The Hidden Curriculum*, New York, Knopf.

Section III   Pupil cultures

18 The Sisterhood*

Audrey M. Lambart

The Sisterhood was an inter-form element in the informal structure of the third-year pupils at Mereside, an unstreamed urban grammar school for girls which I studied as part of the research project carried out at Manchester, 1963–7, and already written up by Colin Lacey and David Hargreaves.[1] The Sisterhood is of interest for showing how factors determined both within and outside the school interacted through its formal and informal structures; it also suggests that factors of an unusual kind may be important in establishing associations.

Before discussing the Sisterhood itself, I shall comment briefly on the school and the city in which it was located, referring generally to areas of residence, social class, the formal structure of Mereside, and aspects of the informal structure of the third-year forms. Subsequently I shall comment more fully on these in discussing the Sisterhood's patterns of behaviour as perceived by staff and girls, and its academic standing and performance.

Mereside was situated in an industrial city, which had three main areas, probably of ancient origin, reflecting its social diversity. The Sisterhood was part of the intake of 1961, which had been drawn from the two areas most sharply in contrast to one another demographically and physically. Westwood contained the centres of the city's industry and was densely populated. Northfield was suburban in character; and whereas it had rather more than 10 per cent of its male labour force in *middle-class* occupations, Westwood had less than 4 per cent in this category. Conversely, 40 per cent of the male labour force in Westwood were in occupations categorised as *working class* against slightly under 30 per cent in Northfield. Non-manual workers who were categorised as *section i of the lower middle class* formed less than 10 per cent of the male population of Westwood and over 16 per cent in

Northfield. Nevertheless, the percentages of skilled workers and persons working on their own account varied little as between any of the three areas of the city, and were 44.08 for Northfield and 46.60 for Westwood. These were categorised as forming *section ii of the lower middle class* for the purpose of analysis.[2]

Although Westwood had more girls than Northfield eligible for selection to enter grammar school in 1961, entrants to Mereside from Northfield outnumbered those from Westwood by a ratio of approximately 2:1. The size of contingent from junior schools in the two areas also varied considerably. Northfield sent sixteen from one junior school; the largest number to come from a school in Westwood was eight.

These contingents were in any case broken up when the girls entered Mereside, for they were distributed among three forms (X, Y and Z) without reference to ability or achievement, and for their first year were taught entirely in these forms. Each numbered thirty plus. At the beginning of their second year, girls were placed in one of three sets—Latin, German or General, the last not taking a second foreign language. Although some element of parental choice was allowed, achievement in first-year French and English primarily determined the set to which girls were assigned. These also numbered thirty plus. At the beginning of the third year, girls were further placed in sets for science, mathematics and French; and in each case examination marks were used to decide which of four sets it should be. These varied in number and, of course, cross-cut forms.

Setting had replaced streaming several years before, because streaming had been accompanied by social as well as academic problems. Despite this, it could be argued that there was crypto-streaming in the intake of 1961, since of thirty-five girls in the third-year Latin set, only four were not in either the first or second set for French, mathematics and science; and none was in a fourth set for any of these subjects. Conversely, none of thirty-four girls in the General

Source: unpublished. Audrey Lambart is staff tutor in educational studies, the Open University.

set was in the top set for any of the subjects considered, and twenty-four were in the third or fourth set for all of them. The connection between membership of the Latin set and all-round academic achievement was maintained when I calculated each third-year girl's overall average mark in half-yearly examinations (excluding Latin and German marks so as to avoid penalisation of girls in the General set), and then made a tripartite division into levels of achievement, I, II and III, each containing thirty-three girls. In level I (the highest) there were twenty-four girls from the Latin set; in level III (the lowest) there were nineteen girls from the General set. Nevertheless, thirteen girls from this set were in level II, and two were in level I.[3]

Finally, in order to consider each girl's academic standing as closely as possible, I placed them in three combinations of subject sets: A mostly indicated membership of the Latin set and high sets in other subjects; B German and middle-range sets in other subjects; C membership of the General set and third or fourth sets in other subjects.[4] There was a large measure of agreement between subject combination and level of achievement, and this was widely recognised by the girls at Mereside. Nevertheless, scrutiny of the detailed figures showed interesting variations in the numbers of girls which each form had in subject combinations A, B and C, and levels of achievement I, II and III. The question why this should be became an intriguing one, since forms had been created in a manner calculated to discount differences of this kind, and had remained unchanged in composition overall. The third forms of 1963 were of roughly the same size (ranging from thirty-two to thirty-four), yet there were eighteen girls from 3Y in level of achievement III, whereas 3Z had half this number and 3X only six.[5] Analysis of observations and sociometric data suggested that the informal structure of each form was connected with these differences.

The existence of informal structures in 3X, 3Y and 3Z was established by observation and sociometric techniques. All three forms had observable groups of at least three girls, and pairs of friends (some of whom were isolated from the rest of the form; others who were part of the larger groups). There were also isolates in each form. Sociometric techniques were used to check observations and in some cases they revealed further patterns of association, or cases of isolation.

The informal structures of 3X, 3Y and 3Z were related further to social class and junior school attended, and it was demonstrated that both were shared factors among various groups and pairs in all three forms, but that neither factor fully explained the informal structure of any form. Social class and junior school were of course dependent upon the educational provision and social composition of the city. In contrast, two other factors which were considered—level of achievement and subject group—were determined at Mereside school, and the available evidence gave ground for claiming that these too were connected with the informal structure as it existed. In some cases indeed the academic standing of pupils provided a clearer basis for association than the externally determined factors. But it was noted in particular that a relatively high level of achievement as well as a relatively low one might be connected with difficulties in association.

Two further points should be made about the informal structure of Mereside's third forms. Although each was essentially of the same kind, there were differences of detail between them. Second, these were connected with behaviour as perceived by teachers and pupils, and with academic performances. I shall discuss the Sisterhood with reference to both, after setting it against the general background already given.

The nature and history of the group is perhaps best shown by quoting an account of it given to me by one of its main members. One (Janice Goodwin) told me there were thirteen, later adding two more and commenting on another pair of girls whom she thought aspirant members. Later, another main member (Joyce Green) wrote an account for me, which follows. Where code numbers are used it is because the girls concerned were named with reservations or by only one of these two informants.

The Sisters

At school we have a sort of family which nearly always plays together. There are quite a few girls in it their names are, Joyce Green, Geraldine Green, Christine Hobbs, Jessie Wallace, Alison Downs, Janice Goodwin, Patricia Matthews, Lesley Vernon, Rita Thomas, Diane Oliver, Penelope Rowson, Andrea Swift, Jennifer Hallen. The main ones in this are really Alison Downs, Janice Goodwin, and me. I play in class with Jennifer, Andrea, Penelope, Diane, and Rita, who are all in 3Z. Then in 3X Patricia, Janice, Lesley and Alison go together. And in 3Y Geraldine and Christine. Out of school I play with Janice and Alison the most, while Jennifer, Andrea, Jessie, Patricia, Christine and another girl 285 (who is not one of us really) play together. Lesley and Rita don't really play with anyone out of school because they live apart. Penelope and Diane play together with another girl 242 (who is not really one of us either). I myself do not play much with Jessie and a couple of others but they play with one of the sisters so they are counted in. The sisters have a good time at school. I suppose we might have a reputation among staff especially Janice and myself. But we do not mean to be naughty or awkward it is just that we like to have a bit of girlish glee but this is sometimes not appreciated by staff. Sometimes we have arguments but they nearly always get sorted out.

We go together because when you play in a gang you can have a lot more fun. We do not all go together all the time because some of us are on school teams in second year Christmas term it only affected me because I was the only one on a team. Then also there were house practices. But from Easter to midsummer it affected more of us because then Geraldine, Janice, Andrea and I were on it. Then this year it affects a few again because Geraldine and Alison are on the school hockey and Christine and I are on the school netball. Janice is netball reserve but she is a very good player. So we have a lot more fun really all the Sisters go to one another's houses quite a lot I am always at Janice's with Alison and Janice stayed with me for a full half term once and she stayed last Christmas Eve as well. Alison, Geraldine and I go to Janice's of a Saturday night and have a little feast we buy chips, chocolate and mineral and then we gorge ourselves (yum, yum). So don't you agree we have more fun than the average schoolgirl . . .

The possibility of the Sisterhood acting as a substitute family may be inferred from Joyce's statement. It was implicit also in a request made to me by both Janice and Joyce that I should act as its 'Mum'.

When I reluctantly agreed, Lesley Vernon of 3X remarked 'Who shall we get as Dad?'; and Janice's retort 'We can get plenty of Dads' was made poignant by my knowing that her mother was incurably ill. This fact led me to classify Janice as belonging to a broken home, and it is remarkable that no fewer than four of the other six girls in 3X whom I placed in the same category were named either by Joyce or Janice alone in connection with the Sisterhood: 285, 299, 296 and 284.[6] It will be noted however that, in naming the first of these, Joyce commented that she was 'not one of us really', and that 296 and 284 were included only because Janice thought they were trying to join the Sisterhood. She may have been the chief obstacle to the admission of these two aspirants. But I have no proof of the point, and her attitude to them was shared by other members of the Sisterhood. In the case of 296 in particular it provided a sharp insight into the standards required for membership and likely causes of exclusion. This may be illustrated by two incidents. The headmistress took Janice to task for doing a newspaper delivery round. Later, she confided to me: 'I use the money for clothes. We never wear uniform out of school.' I had noticed that Janice was careful of her appearance, and that the Sisterhood generally looked well turned out. The comment one made of 296 was telling: 'Her blouses are grubby.'

Table 18.1   Membership of the Sisterhood: play-groups, area of residence, junior school, social class and form

	area	junior school	social class	form
First play-group				
Janice Goodwin (main member)	Westwood	singleton	working	3X
Alison Downs (main member)	Northfield	singleton	lr. mid. (i)	3X
Geraldine Green	Westwood	singleton	lr. mid. (i)	3Y
Joyce Green (main member)	Westwood	High Street	lr. mid. (i)	3Z
Second play-group				
Pat Matthews	Northfield	Millfield	lr. mid. (i)	3X
Christine Hobbs	Northfield	Millfield	lr. mid. (ii)	3Y
Jessie Wallace	Northfield	Millfield	lr. mid. (ii)	3Y
Andrea Swift	Northfield	Millfield	lr. mid. (i)	3Z
Jennifer Hallen	Northfield	Millfield	lr. mid. (i)	3Z
285 ('not one of us really')	Northfield	Millfield	lr. mid. (ii)	3X
Third play-group				
Diane Oliver ⎱ added by Janice to	Northfield	Millfield	middle	3Z
Penelope Rowson ⎰ original list	Northfield	Millfield	lr. mid. (i)	3Z
242 ('not really one of us either')	Northfield	Millfield	working	3Y
Two girls said by Joyce not to really play with anyone out of school, because they live apart				
Lesley Vernon	Northfield	South Street	lr. mid. (ii)	3X
Rita Thomas	Northfield	non-regular	lr. mid. (ii)	3Z
Aspirants (named by Janice)				
296	Westwood	singleton	lr. mid. (ii)	3X
284	Northfield	South Street	lr. mid. (ii)	3X
Named as members only by Janice				
299	Northfield	non-regular	lr. mid. (i)	3X
278	Northfield	non-regular	working	3X

296 lived with one parent, and, to make matters worse, in an older part of the city: her difficulties were clear when she came up to me one day, full of laughter, to say: 'Me friend's given me bath salts for Christmas and we haven't got a bath.'

One other specific point of interest about the home situation of the Sisterhood's members concerns Joyce and Geraldine Green: it may be seen that 3Y was the only form which did not contain one of the girls whom Joyce considered to be 'main members', and it was to this form that her sister (Geraldine) belonged. The girls were twins, and differences between them were a matter of frequent comment, not only through this fact but also because Geraldine belonged to the Latin set and Joyce to the General. By her own account, Joyce played out of school 'the most' with Janice Goodwin and Alison Downs of 3X, the two whom she had named as 'main members' along with herself, and it is possible that, in her friendship with Janice in particular, who stayed at Joyce's house, she sought a substitute sister less academically inclined than Geraldine.

In discussing the Sisterhood's membership in connection with the *place of residence*, I relate the play-groups which Joyce had mentioned to the main areas and enumeration districts of the city. Table 18.1 also gives the *junior school* and *social class* of each girl. The name of a girl's *junior school* is not given where she was the sole entrant from it in her own form, or had not come to Mereside as part of the original intake (in this case the term 'non-regular' is used).

The play-groups were clearly connected with *place of residence*. Only three of the Sisterhood's members (and one aspirant) lived in Westwood; and in fact Joyce, Geraldine and Janice lived in enumeration districts of Westwood which marched with Northfield. Further, Alison Downs, who was named as going to Janice's home with the twins, lived not far within Northfield's borders. The first play-group, which these four girls belonged to, cross-cut form lines completely, since it contained two girls from 3X (Janice and Alison); one from 3Y (Geraldine), and one from 3Z (Joyce). It also contained the three 'main members' of the Sisterhood. A further point which may be made of this play-group is that, although Alison's home was near the enumeration districts in which Janice and the twins lived, it was even nearer to that in which Rita Thomas's home was situated; yet she was one of the two girls said not to 'really play with anyone out of school because they live apart'.

The second play-group detailed by Joyce consisted of Jennifer Hallen, Andrea Swift, Jessie Wallace, Patricia Matthews, Christine Hobbs and 285 ('not one of us really'). This also had girls from all three of the third forms in it, and they lived in enumeration districts of Northfield which adjoined each other. But, although Penelope Rowson lived in the same district as Patricia Matthews, Jessie Wallace and Christine Hobbs, she was yet noted as playing in a third group with Diane Oliver; and her home was located in an enumeration district which was not contiguous, though it was not far away. This is particularly interesting because Penelope and Diane were the two girls whom Janice had added to her original list, which suggests that they were apart from the others in her mind. Both belonged to 3Z and had, in fact, reciprocated first friendship choices, but 242, with whom they played (although she was 'not really one of us either'), belonged to 3Y. The importance of residence is suggested by the fact that her home was in the same enumeration district as Diane's. The second girl who was said like Rita Thomas not to 'really play with anyone out of school because they live apart' was Lesley Vernon of 3X; and it was the case that she lived in an enumeration district which had no other member of the Sisterhood in it. The importance of residence as a factor influencing association is, however, indicated by the fact that 284, one of the two girls whom Janice suspected of trying to get into the Sisterhood, lived in the same district as Lesley; especially since Janice had added that 284 and 296 had 'tried to take Lesley away from us'. 296, in fact, lived in Westwood, like Joyce and Geraldine Green, and Janice herself; but her home was in an enumeration district some distance away from those where they lived.

Since *junior school* and *place of residence* were likely to be associated factors, it is not surprising to find that all members of the second play-group (who lived in adjoining enumeration districts in Northfield) had been together at Millfield Junior School; so also had the three girls in the third play-group, who lived in near-by districts. Millfield had, in fact, sent the largest single contingent to Mereside in 1961, and these nine girls represented just over half of it. In contrast, the first play-group contained three girls (Janice, Alison and Geraldine) who were singleton members from their junior schools, in their own forms, though not necessarily in the intake of 1961 collectively: for instance, Geraldine, though a singleton from High Street in her own form, had attended it with her sister Joyce, and several other girls in 3Z. Of the two girls who 'live(d) apart', Rita Thomas was a non-regular entrant to Mereside School, and had, indeed, joined the school only in September 1963. This may explain why she was not part of the first play-group, although she did not live far from Alison Downs. Lesley Vernon, the second girl who 'live(d) apart' had been at South Street school with 284, near whom she lived, and 284 was one of the girls said to have tried to take Lesley away from the Sisterhood, as well as to be trying to join it. 296, who was also said to be trying to join the Sisterhood, was a singleton entrant from her junior school. Despite the preponderance of girls from Millfield, indeed, the Sisterhood was obviously not exclusively tied to the members of one junior school.

Besides claiming that 284 and 296 were trying to join the Sisterhood, and that they had tried to take Lesley away, Janice Goodwin had said: '296's one of those people who always talks out loud and makes you uncomfortable.' This may have implied that the Sisterhood was snobbish, but it may be seen that there were representatives of all four *social classes* in it and that none of the various play groups consisted entirely of the members of any one of them. To give detail: of the thirteen girls named by both Joyce and Janice, just over half (seven) came from section (i) of the lower middle class, and another was from the middle class. Four were from section (ii) of the lower middle class, and as a minor point of interest it may be noted that Janice was the only one from a working-class background. 296 was discussed above with reference to the general home situation of the Sisterhood. By father's occupation she was placed in section (ii) of the lower middle class

With reference to these factors determined outside Mereside, one may summarise the Sisterhood by saying that, although the play-groups it contained were clearly connected with *place of residence* in the majority of cases, the Sisterhood was not exclusively tied to any particular area of the city. Again, although most of its members had come to Mereside from the *junior school* providing the largest contingent in the intake of which it formed part, the remainder were drawn from several different schools and one girl had only recently entered Mereside. It may be reiterated that the Sisterhood was not exclusive to any *social class*, and that representation of the working class was minimal.

The Sisterhood's connection with factors determind *inside* Mereside School may be seen from Table 18.2, which gives the academic standing of the association's membership with reference to subject combinations, set and levels of achievement. Information is given also on third-form groups which the Sisterhood's members belonged to, and I shall refer to them in commenting on their behaviour as perceived by pupils and staff. For ease of reference, colour names were given to the groups, and these are used here. It may be seen that the Sisterhood contained representatives of all three of the main *subject combinations*, derived from information concerning sets, and it is of interest that, when I asked her how the Sisterhood had come into existence, Joyce said: 'It grew when we were put in sets. We used to be all in twos and threes before that.' Presumably, she spoke of the intra-form elements of the Sisterhood in her reference to 'twos and threes'; and allocation to sets at the beginning of the second year would have brought girls from all three forms into contact with each other for some lessons. A particular point which may be noted is that Janice

Table 18.2

form	subject combination and set	level of achievement	intra-form group, if any
3X			
Janice Goodwin (main member)	B (General)	II	*greens*
Alison Downs (main member)	B (German)	II	*greens*
Patricia Matthews	C (General)	III	*greens*
Lesley Vernon	C (General)	II	*greens*
3Y			
Geraldine Green	A (Latin)	I	*blues*
Christine Hobbs	A (German)	I	*blues*
Jessie Wallace	B (Latin)	II	*blues*
3Z			
Joyce Green (main member)	B (General)	II	*yellows* connected *blacks*
Andrea Swift	A (Latin)	I	*yellows*
Jennifer Hallen	B (German)	III	*yellows*
Diane Oliver	A (Latin)	I	connected *yellows*
Penelope Rowson	A (Latin)	I	connected *yellows*
Rita Thomas	C (General)	II	—
Named only by Joyce			
3X 285 ('not one of us really')	B (German)	II	—
3Y 242 ('not really one of us either')	C (General)	III	*browns*
Named only by Janice as members			
3X 299	C (General)	III	—
278	C (General)	II	—
as aspirants			
3X 296	B (German)	II	—
3X 284	A (Latin)	II	connected *greys*

Goodwin, Patricia Matthews and Lesley Vernon of 3X, 242 of 3Y ('not really one of us either') and, in 3Z, Joyce Green and Rita Thomas, all belonged to the General set. This excludes the third 'main member' (Alison Downs) whose setting was sufficiently like that of Janice and Joyce to place her in the same subject combination, but who, in fact, took German. She was also in the same level of achievement as these two other 'main members' of the Sisterhood.

Besides claiming that it had grown when its members were put in sets, Joyce Green had also told me that girls in the Sisterhood 'never come top because we've got brilliant people in all forms.' The implication that the Sisterhood existed as a focus for girls of mediocre ability is not borne out by the *levels of achievement* of its members if these are considered generally: five of the thirteen girls named by both Janice and Joyce were in level I. (Of the remaining eight, six were in level II and two in level III.) It may be seen, however, that none of the girls in level I was in 3X; and closer scrutiny of available evidence showed that, although Geraldine Green was at the top of 3Y's mark list, in the list for 3Z Penelope Rowson was second, Diane Oliver fourth, and Andrea Swift seventh. It may have been Geraldine's academic success which prevented her from being one of the Sisterhood's 'main members'; and it is of interest that Diane Oliver and Penelope Rowson whom Janice added to her original list had higher marks than Andrea Swift, their companion in 3Z, and had been named in reverse order to their specific academic standing. Even so, it was the case that the Sisterhood contained girls of varying levels of achievement and in all three of the main combinations of subject group, and that in general its members were above average in terms of ability.

Before discussing the association with reference to *patterns of behaviour* as perceived by pupils and staff, it may be helpful to comment further on characteristics which the Sisterhood's members had in common. Besides being well dressed and clean, they had a sense of fun bordering often on mischief; and they were careful of the 'respect' they gave to teachers.

At lunch-time, members ate together so far as possible, and seized any opportunity to disregard rules. Girls were supposed to walk quietly and in single file in corridors. The Sisters were given to walking to dinner arm in arm, three or even four abreast. Inside the dining-room, members had a nice system for giving favours to friends, and expressing hostility to others, in serving food. At the end of afternoon school, also, the Sisters would collect one another from various form-rooms and managed to misuse tunic girdles in a variety of ways: once, for instance, five tied themselves together. Another time, an aspirant member was fastened to a radiator, then left.

The attitude to teachers was expressed by a comment which was made to me of 299, who had won a medal for helpfulness. Alison Downs explained: 'That's for opening doors for teachers and things like that'.

I gained evidence about staff and pupil perceptions of *patterned behaviour* from questioning as well as observing. During my first few weeks of participant-observation, I was struck by the frequency with which girls named one another as pets or 'picked on', and when I sought information systematically on this point about the ninety-nine third-form girls, ten were named as pets, twenty-seven as victims and fourteen in both categories. Of the last, four were named more frequently as victims, giving a total of thirty-one in this category.

There was a clear connection of perceived victimisation with intra-form groups. Thirty-nine girls were members, or connected with them; and twenty-three of these girls were named as victims. The *greens* (3Y) were named in entirety, as also the *yellows* (3Z) and four members of the *blues* (3Y). Reference to Table 18.2 will show that these were groups which contained the Sisterhood's members. More specifically, it may be said that Joyce Green, Jennifer Hallen and Andrea Swift of 3Z, Janice Goodwin, Lesley Vernon, Alison Downs and Patricia Matthews of 3X, and Christine Hobbs and Jessie Wallace of 3Y were named as victims. So, too, were the two girls said by Joyce to be 'not really . . . of us'—242 of 3Y and 285 of 3X. Against this only two members of the Sisterhood were named as pets: Penelope Rowson of 3Z, who was, in any case, added as an afterthought, and Geraldine Green of 3Y.

Information on staff perception of behaviour was derived from two sources. First, mistresses were asked to name silly, naughty or demanding girls. The three main members of the Sisterhood appeared in the resultant list of seventeen deviants along with Patricia Matthews, 285 who was 'not really one of us', and the aspirant 296. There was a difference between forms, in that these girls were mostly in 3X and none of the Sisterhood's membership of 3Y was named. It may be noted also that the *greens* were the only group to be named in entirety amongst the deviants, as they had been in the victims, and to be included as a totality in the Sisterhood.

The second source of information about staff perceptions of behaviour consisted of the record of sanctions (reports) which they imposed for offences against discipline. Several of the Sisterhood's members were among the ten girls who received a disproportionate number of reports. Here again, however, there was a difference between forms. 3Y was unrepresented, while from 3X Alison Downs (main member), Patricia Matthews and the aspirant 296 were named. But neither of the other two main members, Janice Goodwin (3X) and Joyce Green (3Z), received a disproportionate number of reports. Joyce's supposition that 'we might have a reputation among staff, especially Janice and myself' is amply supported by one item of evidence, but not the other, and this probably reflects the fact that reports were not officially prescribed as a sanction against misbehaviour in class.

Additionally, the Sisterhood's members probably helped one another to avoid offences, such as failure to hand in homework, for which reports were prescribed. Moreover, the girls most likely to receive them were academically weak, and it has been shown that the Sisterhood contained many girls whose academic standing was above average. As in the case of victims, deviants and girls receiving disproportionate numbers of reports, however, there was an uneven distribution of the Sisterhood's members at different levels of achievement amongst the three forms. This was also the case if reference is made to the set to which its various members belonged. I illustrate the last point with particular reference to the General set, since I was able to observe it several times, and hence gain information on the patterned behaviour of girls in it.

Two of the Sisterhood's main members (Janice Goodwin and Joyce Green) were in the General set, together with three girls named by both and another three named by either Janice or Joyce (see Table 18.2). The collective representation of girls from the Sisterhood in the General set is significant because it was commonly considered weaker than the Latin and German sets, and contained nineteen out of thirty-three girls in the lowest level of achievement (III). But, among these, there were from the Sisterhood only Patricia Matthews and 299 and 242 named in connection with it. Lesley Vernon, Rita Thomas and 278, together with Janice Goodwin and Joyce Green, were in level of achievement II despite being in the General set.

Yet, in observing the General set, it was quite clear that Janice was a key trouble-maker. As I have explained, this set like others cross-cut forms, and it was notable how members of the Sisterhood who came together in it for lessons continued to sit close to one another. Joyce Green, in her original account, named 'especially Janice and myself' in stating her view that the Sisterhood 'might have a reputation amongst staff': my observations of the General set left no doubt that it was earned there, particularly by the behaviour of Janice. On occasion, I saw her throw books and pencil-case to the floor. She was also capable of dumb and not-so-dumb insolence of subtle sorts. For instance, in speaking of Janice, one mistress said of another girl who was, in fact, expelled from Mereside: 'She's not clearly so exasperating as Janice Goodwin. She says in a virtuous butter-wouldn't-melt-in-her-mouth voice: "You told us to tell you when we couldn't understand."' Janice was not, however, alone in misbehaviour in the General set. Patricia Matthews, Lesley Vernon and 242 provided strong support, expressed particularly through laughter which could become quite uncontrollable. The girl who was eventually expelled could generally be relied on to compound the disorder. My own feeling was that, in general lessons, the Sisterhood expressed resentment based on the feeling of inferiority which they suffered from belonging to this set, despite their level of achievement.

The Sisterhood was, however, made up from intra-form groups, and prolonged observation of these, supplemented by all available evidence, led me to the conclusion that these groups at Mereside School expressed differences grounded in its internal stress on academic achievement, as well as in social factors reflecting the diversity of backgrounds from which its pupils came. The intra-form groups were connected with the varying proportions each had of girls in the three levels of achievement, and its number of deviants. It should not be assumed, however, that a concentration of deviants in a form implied a low level of achievement overall.

3X, which had the most militant wing of the Sisterhood in Janice and the *greens*, also contained a group (the *greys*) whose members were all in level of achievement I and subject combination A. Hostility to this group may have motivated the *greens* to deviant behaviour when they were taught as forms. The balance of factors was complex in all cases. 3Y, like 3X, was dominated by two groups, but here the *blues*, which contained several of the Sisters, was academically stronger than the other main group (the *browns*). This was remarkable for being mainly in level of achievement III and largely composed of girls who had joined the intake of 1961 in its second or third year. Significantly, 242 ('not really one of us') was one of the two *browns* who had entered Mereside as part of the normal intake. She had come from Millfield junior school and her wish to belong to the Sisterhood may have been grounded in this, or in a desire to mix with girls whose level of achievement was higher than that of the *browns*. 3Y's very high proportion of girls in the lowest level of achievement was, of course, connected with this group. 3Y also suffered from having no girls of exceptionally high academic standing in association, and it was only in this form that one of the Sisterhood (Geraldine Green) was top.

Finally 3Z. This was less noticeably dominated by two groups, but had an exceptionally able pair to whom the *yellows*, strongly represented in the Sisterhood, were able to express hostility through deviance. It may also be noted that Joyce Green, the Sisterhood's main member in this form, was connected with another intra-form group called the *blacks*, for this contained several girls in level of achievement I who apparently also resented the exceptional pair, and sometimes joined forces with the *yellows* against them. This pair was effectively isolated within their relationship in the form, and it is interesting that one of them was the friend who gave 296 an unsuitable Christmas present of bath salts. Girls in association outside the Sisterhood seemed to be well aware of its numerical strength, and to seek supporters themselves if they could not join it.

Not everyone aspired to membership of the Sisterhood. Those who did had to meet requirements, some of which have been discussed. In conclusion, it should be stressed that, despite its deviance, the Sisterhood existed as a focus for girls with more than average ability. This feature can be added to its members' characteristic mischief and inherent disrespect for teachers. These may, indeed, have been a function of what some members of the Sisterhood probably considered relative failure. One recalls Joyce Green's statement that we 'never come top because we've got brilliant people in all forms.'

Nevertheless, when they came to O level, Geraldine Green from 3Y, Diane Oliver, Penelope Rowson and Andrea Swift passed in seven or more subjects; one of the main members (Alison Downs) had left, but of the other two, one secured four, and the other, three passes.

Notes

* This article is based on chapter 7 of an unpublished thesis submitted to the University of Manchester in 1970, under the title: 'The Sociology of an Unstreamed Urban Grammar School for Girls'.

1 Colin Lacy, *Hightown Grammar*, Manchester University Press, 1970; David Hargreaves, *Social Relations in a Secondary School*, Routledge & Kegan Paul, 1967.

2 Occupations were categorised according to the *General Register Office Classification of Occupations*, 1960. This gave sixteen socio-economic groupings of kinds of work (pp. xi–xii). Employers and managers were placed in 1, 2 and 13 of these groups, professional workers in groups 3 and 4, non-manual workers in 5 and 6, foremen and supervisors in 8, skilled manual workers in 9, persons working on their own account were placed in group 12 and farmers in group 14; group 7 contained personal service workers, 10 semi-skilled workers, and 15 agricultural workers. Unskilled workers were placed in group 11 and members of HM Forces in group 16. These were amalgamated into four classes: *middle* (groups 1, 2, 3, 4 and 13), *section i of the lower middle class* (groups 5 and 6), *section ii of the lower middle class* (groups 8, 9, 12 and 14), *working* (groups 7, 10, 11, 15 and 16).

3 The tabulation from which these figures were taken yielded $\chi^2 = 37.946$ with 4 degrees of freedom (d.f.).

4 More precisely, A covered Latin with sets 1/2 for French and maths/science, also German with set 1 for French, and maths/science. B covered Latin with any third set, German with sets 2/3, for maths, science and French, also General with a second set of any kind. C indicated membership of the General set and sets 3/4 for French, maths, science, and also German with French 4 and maths/science 3/4.

5 The tabulation from which these figures were taken yielded $\chi^2 = 11.470$ with 4 d.f.

6 Evidence on this point was difficult to obtain, and I counted as being from broken homes those whose record cards named only one parent, regardless of whether a reason was given for this; also those for whom there was evidence of separation or divorce, or one or both parents dead. Within a total of 286 girls who were in their first, second or third year of study at Mereside, I classified twenty-six as being from broken homes. Twelve of these girls were in the third-year forms, and of these at least half had suffered bereavement or other disturbance in home relationships after their entry to grammar school.

19   Interaction sets in the classroom: towards a study of pupil knowledge

Viv Furlong

Not all pupils 'know' the same things about their school lives. They do not all form the same common-sense judgments about their teachers or the curriculum; they do not all see other pupils in the same way. Because of this, a study of pupil experience or 'knowledge' of school life must begin by looking at the way some pupils come to share common perspectives, and how pupils influence each other in what they 'know'. In other words, we need a more detailed understanding of pupil interaction. Only when this process is fully understood will it be possible to go on to document what individuals or groups actually 'know'. This paper is therefore intended to provide the groundwork for a more detailed study of pupil knowledge.

The ways in which pupils influence each other, both in their behaviour and in their interpretation of their school experience, is of great interest to both teachers and parents. That interest is often expressed in phrases such as 'He's getting into bad company', or 'She's a good influence on her class.' Despite this interest, there has been relatively little research which examines pupils' informal school life. Most classroom observation, whether 'systematic' or 'anthropological', seems to be directed at throwing light only on the teacher-pupil relationship; this study is an attempt to redress that imbalance.

The field work was carried out in a secondary modern school in a large English city for two terms during 1972 and 1973. I had taught in the school since 1970. The data presented relate to one class of sixteen fourth-year girls, whose average age was fifteen.[1] The material has come from two main sources. First, notes made during my extensive observations of lessons with each of their ten teachers: I simply sat at the back of the class and wrote down what the girls did and said, concentrating in particular on situations where they communicated with each other. The

second source of data was tape-recorded interviews with groups and individual girls.

Many of the quotations selected for this paper relate to one particular girl, whom I call Carol. (All names of pupils and teachers in this paper are, of course, pseudonyms.) In this way the reader can build up a consistent picture of interaction as it takes place in the classroom. For this purpose, any of the girls could have been chosen, for Carol is not seen to be in any way unusual.

Of the sixteen girls, thirteen, including Carol, were of West Indian origin, although most of them had spent the majority of their school career in England.[2] This class was considered to be below average intelligence and they occupied a 'one from bottom' position in the streaming system. The general assessment of the staff was that they were 'difficult' but not the 'worst' class in the school.

The paper is divided into two main sections. The first part is devoted to building up an understanding of what interaction is, and how it takes place in the classroom. Patterns of interaction are seen to be related to how individuals or groups define classroom situations: what they 'know' about them. The second section develops this model, illustrating Carol's typical pattern of interaction, and typical ways of looking at classroom situations.

I begin by comparing my approach with some of the existing work on pupil interaction, most of which has been based on a key theory of social psychology: that of groups. I argue that the results are less than adequate.

The social psychological approach

Various authors[3] have applied a social psychological model to the study of schools. The process of pupil interaction in the classroom is assumed to take place within the context of peer groups or friendship groups. It is suggested that these groups have a 'culture' of

Source: M. Stubbs and S. Delamont, eds, *Explorations in Classroom Observations*, Chichester, Wiley, 1976, pp. 24–44.

norms and values which colour the pupils' whole school experience.

This approach does not, however, examine how the pupils *themselves* see their social relationships. Researchers have not asked how pupils actually interact with each other in the classroom, or examined the different action they see as appropriate in different circumstances.

The studies by David Hargreaves (1967) and Colin Lacey (1970) are probably the best known in this field. Their analysis is simple. They both believe that social interaction can best be understood by using the concept of the informal group. They assume that friends will 'interact' more frequently than pupils who are not friends, and that in so doing they will develop their own norms and values. Interaction is therefore understood only in terms of group membership, and it is a simple task, using a sociometric questionnaire, to discover exactly who is in the group. (A sociometric questionnaire is a means of obtaining quantitative data on the preferences of individuals for associating with each other. For example, Hargreaves asked pupils to write down the names of the friends they went around with at school. Pupils who chose each other were assumed to form a peer group.)

Once Hargreaves and Lacey have plotted their different groups, they proceed to 'measure' the norms and values associated with each. They assume that these groups form 'cultures' which will be consistent in their approach to the school, and Hargreaves goes so far as to identify the 'central norms' of each of the classes he studied. For example, the main value of his 4B is seen as 'having fun' while the values of his 4C are characterised in terms of delinquency (Hargreaves 1967, p. 27).

Conformity to these central norms is explained in terms of 'social pressure' or 'power'. Conforming to the demands of the group culture is something the individual must do if he is not going to sacrifice his social status. Those who do not conform are called 'deviants'.

There are three major difficulties with this model. First, interaction does not just 'happen' in friendship groups but is 'constructed' by individuals. When classes are observed, it becomes obvious that who interacts with whom can change from minute to minute, depending on a great many circumstances. Pupil interaction in a classroom will not necessarily include all friends at the same time, and will often involve pupils who are not friends at all.

The second difficulty with this model relates to the idea that norms and values will be consistent. It would be obvious, even to the most casual observer of classroom behaviour, that there is no *consistent* culture for a group of friends. Even the most delinquent pupils will be well behaved in certain circumstances.[4] Teachers do not always invite the same amount of conformity or hostility, and some lessons allow for greater feelings of personal achievement than others. Classroom situations change in the meaning they have

for pupils and, as they change, so will the pupils' assessments of how to behave.

Finally, the model suggests that there is a pressure on group members to conform to the group's demands. The culture is presented as an external reality, and social behaviour is shown not so much as an interaction between two or more individuals, but as one person responding to some reified group. The implication is that the individual has little choice in his action, as he is controlled by something outside him: the group.

This 'external' analysis of interaction is inadequate, because it misses the main point, that participants have to build up their own respective lines of conduct as they go along. They must continually interpret each others' actions, and therefore continually 're-define' the situation for themselves. Norms and values are significant only in so far as they are interpreted by the participants during the interaction process.

I am therefore arguing for an alternative understanding of classroom interaction, where the pupils are seen to be continually adjusting their behaviour to each other, where those actually interacting are always changing, and where norms of behaviour are not consistent. In these circumstances it is impossible to use the necessarily static methods implied by the social psychological model. Questionnaires and paper-and-pencil tests become inadequate, and it is necessary to observe pupils' interaction as it actually happens in the classroom. It is also important to record what the pupils say about their classroom situations, and to try and understand how they form rules for interpreting these situations. Anthropological observation must therefore become the major tool of analysis and cannot simply be used to resolve ambiguities as Lacey for example suggested (1970, p. 98).

Interaction

The object of this study, then, is to develop a more sensitive analysis of the way in which pupils influence each other, both in their understanding of their school experience and in the types of behaviour they consider appropriate. The assumption that this somehow 'happens' in groups is inadequate and it is necessary to study interaction as it takes place and as the pupils themselves see it.

By interaction, I mean situations where individuals come to a common 'definition of the situation' by drawing on similar commonsense knowledge, and make common assessments of appropriate action. That is, they 'see' what is happening in the same way and agree on what are appropriate ways to behave in the circumstances. This does not mean that those interacting will behave in the *same* way, simply that they behave in a way that can be interpreted by others as showing similar 'definitions of the situation'. Nor do pupils have to 'tell' each other how they see things, for their actions will symbolically tell this to the whole class.

In this way, running out of a class or shouting an answer to a teacher can be examples of interaction when the individual takes into account that he is being given support by smiles or laughter from others present. He knows by their support that they 'see' the classroom situation in the same way; they share the same commonsense knowledge about it. Here it is not enough to look at the individual on his own, for he is aware that his behaviour is a 'joint action'; that others are taking part; that he is interacting.[5]

The following example of interaction comes from my observational notes. The incident occurred after Carol had been told to leave the room because she had been rude to the teacher. My notes show her interacting with Valerie and Diane, and taking into account what they are doing in choosing her own action:

> She (Carol) wanders out slowly, laughing and looking round at Valerie and Diane, who laugh as well. She stands outside the door, looking through its window for a few minutes ... trying to catch the eyes of the people inside the room.

While she is walking out of the room, Carol is aware of Valerie and Diane and is making continual non-verbal contact with them. Even when she is outside the door, she maintains this contact for a few minutes, but after a while she gives up and wanders off out of sight.

In this example, Carol is communicating with two other girls in the room, each of whom 'see' what is happening in the same way. They symbolically communicate this to her by the way they act (laughing and looking at her) and therefore support her action. These three girls who are choosing their behaviour together form a group or a set. To distinguish those taking part in this sort of grouping from any other, I am going to call it an 'interaction set'. That is to say: the interaction set at any one time will be those pupils who perceive what is happening in a similar way, communicate this to each other, and define appropriate action together.

Now consider this example of Carol interacting with a much larger group of girls; she is aware of them and directs what she says to them all. They are all part of an interaction set.

> (Eight of the girls are sitting round the same bench in the science lab. Carol and Diane run in thirty minutes late and sit down with them all.)
> *Carol* (to the whole table): I went home to get some tangerines.
> *Mrs Newman*: Where have you been?
> *Diane* (aggressively): Dentist ...
> *Mrs Newman*: Where have you been?
> *Carol* (aggressively): None of your business.
> (Mrs Newman ignores or does not hear this remark.)

The interaction set in the second example is much larger than in the first: nine girls are involved, as opposed to three.

The descriptions above show that the girls are aware of each other in choosing their behaviour. This awareness of others is implied in the way they describe classroom situations. For example, in an interview, Carol uses the term 'we' rather than 'I': 'We sneak out of the class, or ask to go for a drink of water ... and we don't come back, we don't come back in again at all.'[6] This is a generalised classroom description, and Carol thinks in terms of herself and her friends; she does the same when describing specific situations: 'We had RE ... We had that stupid teacher, and he just sits there and gives us these stupid books to read, so I just sit there reading them ... so Anne says "Let's go out", so me, Jill, Linda and Diane just follow her out.'

A lot of Carol's classroom behaviour takes place in the context of an interaction set. She takes others into account in deciding how to behave, and is aware that they share a common definition of the situation. Similar observations were made for all the other pupils in the class. Each spends a great deal of her classroom time interacting rather than behaving individually.

Who is in the interaction set?

Consider the following descriptions of classroom situations, which show different interaction sets in operation. In the first, the set comprises Carol and Diane alone; they are late for the lesson and are talking to each other in the corridor. Angela tries to distinguish herself from them in the teacher's eyes by 'telling on them'.

> (When Mrs Alan comes in, Carol and Diane are missing, she asks where they are. Angela says they were in the last lesson.)
> *Angela*: Them lot are outside, Miss.
> (Mrs Alan goes out and sends in Carol and Diane who enter, laughing loudly, and start to sit down. They are followed in by Mrs Alan, who shouts, 'Stand at the front.' They continue to laugh and look round the room, though less confidently than before. Other class members are no longer laughing with them and Carol and Diane's eyes rove round the room, but come into contact with no one in particular.)

In this second example, the interaction set includes Carol and five other girls.

> Carol, Valerie, Diane, Anne, Angela and Monica sit round one of the benches in the science lab. There is continual talking throughout the lesson from these girls even though they carry on copying down the notes that Mrs Newman has written down on the board. At times the noise from these girls is so great that Mrs Newman can't be heard. The rest of the class, sitting round the other bench, are comparatively quiet.

It is obvious from these examples that quite different interaction sets are in operation. In the first situation Carol and Diane form a distinct unit. They are defined as an interaction set both by themselves and by others' assessment of their action, as shown by Angela's behaviour. In the second example, a much larger interaction set is in operation. Again, Carol, Valerie and Diane take part, but this time Anne, Angela and Monica participate as well, each legitimating the action of the others.

There are other situations which illustrate different patterns of classroom interaction. In the following example, which describes a test, the pattern of interaction continually changes.

> When the test begins, they slowly move to different seats without being told to . . . Linda does not know the answer to the first question and does not write anything. Diane whispers across the room to Carol, 'You doing it?' Carol holds up a blank piece of paper and giggles, she hasn't been able to do the first two questions either. Miss Lane asks the next question: 'Name a common cooking cheese' . . . Linda smiles, looks round the class and does not write anything. Next question: 'Name one use the body puts calcium to.' Linda behaves differently. She writes, then looks up to the ceiling for a moment, and then writes again. 'Name a common egg drink.' Linda and Jill's eyes meet; they both seem to know the answer and quickly look away, covering their papers from each other with their arms.

Here the girls are moving in and out of interaction, depending on whether or not they know the answers. When they know the answer they act alone, when they do not, they interact.

The changing pattern of interaction is reflected in the way the girls describe each other. For example, in an interview, Carol, Valerie and Diane discuss who they are 'friends with' in the class:

> *Carol*: Yes we're all friends together, really . . . not Monica though, she's not really with us.
> *Valerie*: No, she works too hard, she's too good.
> *Diane*: Well, she used to be last year.
> *Carol*: Well I suppose she is most of the time.

They seem confused about whether Monica is or is not a 'friend'; observations show that Monica interacts with these three girls only at certain times, but at others she has nothing to do with them, often sitting on the other side of the room.

Patterns of interactions can vary a great deal. Sometimes these girls act quite alone without obvious communication between them, apparently defining situations for themselves. At different times interaction sets form, involving varying numbers of girls and occasionally the whole class. Each interaction set relates to a specific definition; all of the girls interacting share the same commonsense knowledge of the situation.

Norms and values

A great many researchers have tried to study the 'culture' of different adolescent groups by trying to identify both the norms of behaviour and the underlying values to which members subscribe.[7]

I have already argued that action cannot be understood in terms of friendship groups, for these are not the same as interaction sets where membership can vary from minute to minute. Consistent groups do not exist in reality, and observation has also shown that there is no consistent culture for a group of pupils. Norms and values relate to specific definitions of the situations and to typical interaction sets, rather than to a particular group of friends. We have already seen that there is a great variety of behaviour in the class—a variety too great to be described in terms of a consistent 'culture' as the word has traditionally been used. This diversity is even more strongly brought out by the following description of some girls going to two different lessons on the same afternoon.

> (The girls are standing in the corridor talking to me before the beginning of a commerce lesson.)
> *Mary*: Quick—Mrs Alan!
> (She runs violently into the class, smiling. The other girls all enter quickly and find their places and sit talking.)
> *Mrs Alan* (through the noise): Good afternoon 4G.
> *Girls in unison*: Good afternoon.
> (There is silence as they wait for the register to be taken, each girl answering her name as it is called. They then wait quietly for the lesson to begin.)

Contrast this with the beginning of the science lesson that followed immediately afterwards:

> The girls all enter the lab. Carol, Valerie, Diane, Debbie, Monica, Anne and Angela are talking, shouting and laughing. They find their places, and continue talking, all completely ignoring the teacher, Mrs Newman. She takes the register, but is not able to call out the names as there is too much noise, and she spends a considerable time looking to see who is there.

The way the girls behave in these two situations is quite different: different norms are being used, and different interaction sets are in operation. In the first example the whole class shares a common definition of the lesson, whereas in the second example, seven girls form one specific interaction set.

The following examples relate to history, but with two different teachers. They bring out just how varied behaviour can be:

> Carol, Valerie, Diane and Mary are sitting close together, though there is no visible interaction between them, verbal or non-verbal . . . Mr Marks moves to the back of the class and talks to me in whispers for the last ten minutes of the lesson.

None of the girls show any signs of hearing us, they all seem too involved in their work to notice us.

As Mary says, in an interview: 'We all love it, it's our favourite subject . . . we all like history.'

During my period of observation, the history teacher, Mr Marks, left. Carol describes an incident with the new teacher who replaced him. 'I just started to laugh and he hold my collar until I get out of the chair so I hit him . . . then I push him and he fall down.' Extreme behaviour like this is very rare, but the girls are quite frequently rude and hostile to their teachers, and sometimes do not bother to turn up to lessons at all.

The idea that different norms and values are appropriate at different times is borne out by what the teachers wrote on a questionnaire about the pupils. Take for example the comments made about Carol by two teachers, Mr Marks, the history teacher, and Mrs Newman, who taught science.

Mrs Newman: Carol is restless, awkward and often very noisy . . . I can get a lot more done when Carol isn't there.
(Mr Marks wrote after he had left: 'amenable to discipline and not at all unintelligent'.)

Obviously these teachers saw very different 'sides' of Carol in their lessons and, for this reason, the girls' behaviour cannot be described as a 'culture' in the normal use of the word. The range is too great and at first glance, at least, their actions often look contradictory. Carol can arrive one day at a lesson and work quietly and well, and the next day not bother to turn up at all for the same lesson.

I am not suggesting that the action of these girls is random: there are patterns and common ways of behaving, as will be shown below. Yet these patterns are much more complex than has been implied by other researchers. Norms of behaviour relate to specific definitions of classroom situations. People who interact regularly function with a limited number of typical definitions, and there will be typical patterns of action related to each. Before discussing norms and values for any one girl, therefore, it is necessary to examine how she sees situations, what she 'knows' about them, and who else shares that knowledge. Only in this light can her specific actions be interpreted.

The individual and the set

A large proportion of the classroom behaviour of the girls observed took place in the context of interaction sets; there was a great deal of joint rather than individual action. In these circumstances it is important to examine the relationship between the individual and the other interaction set members. Are pupils 'forced' to act in a certain way simply by being a member of an interaction set, or do they choose their action for themselves?

There are two ways of examining the relationship between the individual and the set. The first is to look at the behaviour of pupils when they are not in interaction: when they define situations in a different way from those around them. The second method is to look at the variety of action that takes place in any one interaction set.

Individual action Most of Carol's classroom behaviour is interactive, but sometimes she acts alone. On these 'individual' occasions she shows the same types of behaviour as when part of a set. What is different is not the behavioural content, but the times when Carol considers that behaviour appropriate. Carol can be seen as having the same 'repertoire'[8] of classroom behaviour in individual or interactive situations. For example she can be just as hostile to a teacher when acting alone as when part of an interaction set. When she 'greeted' her new history teacher by pushing him over, she was acting alone. Other girls describing the same incident seemed slightly shocked by the extremity of Carol's action; they were not participating or supporting.

A quite different example of very individual action comes in a cooking lesson: 'Carol . . . works alone, all lesson; she talks to no one, not even to Dorothy who is working at the same table.' In an interview, she explains how she sometimes acts alone: 'Valerie . . . and them lot sometimes start to muck about, you know, and I says to them all, "Why can't you lot behave?"—you know, start to tell them off. Sometimes I just sit down in the corner, you know—just sit down by myself.' Carol can therefore be extremely hostile and disruptive in some lessons, but at other times is very work-orientated. In the examples above she was acting alone, defining situations for herself. Yet, as is well documented below, she frequently shows exactly the same type of behaviour in interactive situations.

Particular 'pieces' of behaviour can, then, be displayed in both social and individual settings. Action should therefore be considered not so much a product of a social situation, in some way 'manufactured' by it, but much more 'facilitated' by that situation. The choice of action remains with the individual, and belongs to her. Only the general situation is interactively defined.

Variety of action Girls who assess situations in a similar way and define appropriate actions together do not necessarily act in the *same* way. When Carol and Diane run in late to a science lesson, it is Carol who makes most of the comments to the teacher, saying 'None of your business' when asked where they have been. Diane, on the other hand, is much quieter, and begins getting out books and finding out what they have missed. Despite the fact that they are in full communication with each other, each legitimating the action of the other, they negotiate different 'social identities', Carol being outspoken, and Diane being supportive. Similar examples occur in less hostile situations. For example, Carol often shouts out answers to questions, or wanders round the room, while Diane and Valerie support her by watching and laughing. They seldom, if ever, take over this sort of action themselves.

Thus joint action does not always imply the same action. It simply demands behaviour that can symbolically communicate to another a particular definition of the situation; it must show that interactants have the same commonsense knowledge. Thus the range of any one individual's joint action can, theoretically at least, be quite varied, as long as it symbolically implies a common definition. It is the willingness to take others into account and share interpretations and definitions of situations that is important. Carol chooses her own action, but is dependent for support on others. She does not act in the same way as she would if she were alone, but decides how to behave in the light of commonly negotiated definitions of the situation.

Definitions of classroom situations

Goffman (1959) has suggested that definitions of the situation tend to be 'idealised'. That is, a group's or interaction set's definition of the situation is likely to differ to some extent from the individual's own. Establishing a common point of contact demands compromise from all. Action itself may be drawn away from what the individual wants to what is appropriate to the idealised definition. Goffman has also pointed out that most groups function with a limited number of 'typical' definitions: people 'see' situations in certain set ways. Of course, individuals can extract themselves from interaction, and groups as a whole can establish new definitions. Goffman is simply suggesting that this will not be the usual experience.

In this section, I illustrate some of the 'idealised' and 'typical' definitions of classroom situations that Carol often subscribes to. That is, I will examine some of the criteria she uses in making assessments of situations and show some of the more common interaction sets related to these.

Before proceeding, a number of points should be made. First, my objective will be to provide a series of simplified 'ideal/typical' definitions, so that the interaction sets associated with them can be specified. These definitions are not intended to be rigid categories for analysing behaviour, since real life situations would be unlikely to correspond to any of them exactly. Second, the pictures to be presented will necessarily be static. The more abstract knowledge Carol uses to move from one definition to the next is beyond the scope of this paper. Finally, it must be remembered that these definitions relate only to Carol and her interaction sets. It is not suggested that they have wider validity.

For Carol and those she interacts with, the most significant factor involved in making definitions of classroom situations is the teacher. Many of her criteria of assessment related to teachers, both in the way they taught, and in the methods they used for controlling the class. The following example comes from a group interview:

> *Question*: When you work in class, is it because you like the subject, or is it the way the teacher teaches?
> *Diane*: It's the subject.
> *Carol*: Mmmmmmmmmm. It's the teacher as well, isn't it?

In another interview:

> *Question*: Why do you think you all muck about so much?
> *Carol*: The teachers look for it, if you ask me.
> *Question*: Why?
> *Carol*: I don't like no subjects, they're boring, they make me feel like going to sleep.

Obviously, then the teacher was very important. How was he assessed?

'Strict' and 'soft' teachers One of the major distinctions between teachers was between those who were seen as 'soft' and those who were 'strict' or 'tough'. Valerie often interacts with Carol; in an interview, she says:

> 'Some of the teachers are soft, you could stand up and they don't teach you nothing, they don't teach you anything that way.'
> *Question*: What would you do if you were a teacher, and you came in and everyone was mucking about?'
> *Valerie*: Well it would depend on what sort of teacher I was. If I was a tough teacher, I'd go 'Sit down'. You know, once you hit one of them, the rest are frightened, and everybody just do the same thing just sit down.

As criteria of definition, though, 'soft' and 'strict' are not adequate. Take, for example, two teachers, Mrs Alan, who taught commerce, and Mrs Newman, who taught science. Both of them were characterised as 'soft' by Carol. But she and her friends responded quite differently when these two teachers told them off for something. In a lesson with Mrs Alan, Carol, Valerie and Diane had arrived late, and were instructed to stand at the front of the class. They were then severely told off. The three girls became extremely hostile, and made abusive comments to the teacher. Mrs Alan ignored these for a while, but when Carol called her an 'ignorant pig', she was asked to leave the room.

This example can be contrasted with Carol's interactive behaviour when being told off by Mrs Newman for coming in late. When asked where she had been, she simply said 'None of your business', and continued discussing what she had been doing with seven or eight of her friends.

Carol, Valerie and Diane seem to take the 'telling off' from Mrs Alan far more seriously than from Mrs Newman. Even though both teachers were thought of as 'soft', one seemed to pose a more serious threat to the girls than the other, and their response was different. Other girls in the class also defined these situations differently. In the first instance, the rest of the class was quiet, and avoided contact with Carol, Valerie and Diane. In the second case they eagerly participated, and were keen to listen to Carol's latest exploits. Obviously, some teachers were 'softer' than others!

'*Learning a lot*' Carol made further distinctions between teachers. She readily admitted that while taught by Mr Marks, history was her best subject. 'You can't talk in Mr Marks' lesson, you just have to work . . . so after a while you work, and you enjoy it because you're learning a lot.' This may be compared with her comments on her new history teacher who came after Mr Marks had left. He was also 'strict', but 'he don't make sense, I don't understand nothing.' There is obviously an additional criterion being applied, for Carol seemed to be concerned about how much different teachers actually managed to teach her. For example,

> *Question*: What do you think about teachers who aren't strict, but who are really soft?
> *Carol*: Some of them are all right. I learn a lot from some of them . . . Mrs Alan's soft, but I learn a lot from her, because it's kind of funny the way she gives jokes.

Obviously, 'learning a lot' was important to Carol, but we must ask what she actually means by this. It seemed to be important that teachers 'explain'. 'Mr Marks would talk to us as well. Not talk them big words you know; talk words we understood.' But the new history teacher 'talks and writes things on the board, like diagrams, names, and you're supposed to keep them in your head, and then after he talks, it don't even make sense.' Also important was whether she was actually involved in doing something rather than just listening.

> *Carol*: I can't stand people talking when I'm not doing anything!
> *Diane*: Yes, like Mr Stacks, in art. He puts you to sleep. We have him on Wednesday, and he just talks and talks for two lessons.

Actually giving these girls a feeling of 'learning a lot' was extremely difficult for any teacher, whether defined as 'soft' or 'strict'. Linda probably best sums up the difficulty:

> 'I don't like doing maths. I can't do it, it's too hard. I don't know how to add. Well, I know how to add, but I don't know how to do the other sums. They're too hard anyway. I don't do nothing in maths lessons, I've always got a

headache . . . I enjoy doing things I know, I can sit all morning doing that, but when something's hard and I don't really know how to do it, I don't *want* to do it. I don't even want to try. I get bored.'

Linda expresses her difficulty in trying to learn when she does not really understand. She must learn immediately or not at all. The whole class seemed to have very little interest in their subjects *per se* and were strongly dependent on the learning context provided by the teacher.

Members of staff who did not live up to Carol's particular criteria of assessment—that is those who 'can't teach you nothing'—were 'written off'. Carol approached their lessons 'knowing' that she was not going to learn anything.

Naturally, this is a simplified assessment of what classroom situations meant to Carol. Nevertheless, if particular lessons are looked at in terms of a combination of the simple criteria of definition (that is 'strict/soft', 'effective/ineffective'), then typical interaction sets and patterns of behaviour emerge.

Typical patterns of interaction

Teachers who were assessed as potentially 'effective' and able to provide some lessons where it was possible to 'learn a lot' were approached in a very different style from those who were considered 'ineffective'. Naturally, 'effective' teachers were not always successful in providing the right learning context for the girls, but when they were, a fairly standard pattern of interaction emerged.

'*Successful*' *lessons* In lessons where the context enabled the girls to 'learn a lot', they would act as a unified group, and the whole class was included in the same interaction set. Although they were not always in verbal contact, each girl was aware that the others defined the lesson as one where they could 'learn'. In these circumstances it was irrelevant whether the teacher was 'strict' or 'soft'. Mr Marks was considered 'strict' and the whole class worked quietly and well. Miss Keene, on the other hand, was 'soft', yet in 'successful' lessons no one took advantage of this fact. Consider this example of a typing lesson with Miss Keene.

> (Miss Keene is teaching the girls how to file alphabetically. It is a revision lesson, though evidently the girls do not understand the principles fully.)
> *Miss Keene*: Carol, how would you file 'The Borough of East Hamilton'?
> *Carol*: Under H. (She obviously does not realise that the name is *East* Hamilton) . . .
> *General question*: How would you file Miss Mary Brown-Curtis? (Someone says 'C', not realising it is a double-barrelled name.)

Carol: M. (She is going to the other rule they have just learnt which says that if it does not go under the surname as a person, it must be the name of a company, and therefore goes under the first name. She seems to be trying to apply rules as she understands them, but is still confused) . . .
Miss Keene: 20th Century Films Limited.
(Carol says 'C', then 'F', applying the rules she knows. But this is a new one. As 20th is short for twentieth it should go under 'T'.)

Here the girls are willing to take risks, struggle to understand and consistently keep applying rules to make sense of what they are being told even though they make a lot of mistakes. They take into account that others are behaving similarly in choosing to act in this way.

When the girls assess a lesson in this way, they will often ignore attempts to 'redefine' it. In the example below, everyone in the class but Debbie is working, and her attempts to communicate with the other girls are ignored.

Debbie is eating an ice lolly. Mrs Alan tells her to put it in the bin, but Debbie refuses and turns round in her seat to face the rest of the class. Mrs Alan grabs the hat Debbie is wearing, and says: 'Right, you are in school to do as you are told. When you have put your sweet in the bin as I asked you can have your hat back.'
Debbie: You give me that hat back. I paid for it. Give it back to me!
As she says this she looks towards Diane and Carol, but they continue with their work. Debbie sulks for the rest of the lesson, making no attempt to do any work whatsoever. She is totally ignored by the rest of the class, who carry on working enthusiastically.

Here, it is only Debbie who sees her action as appropriate. The rest of the class are too interested in their work. They form an interaction set, but Debbie is left outside it.

Judgment of 'effective' teachers Lessons as 'successful' as those shown above were very rare, but the ability of teachers to provide such a context, even occasionally, was extremely important in the girls' eyes. When a teacher was considered 'potentially effective', the girls seemed more likely to approach the lesson with an open mind, and reserve their judgment until they had seen the content of the lesson. Of course, with 'strict, effective' teachers, this was not so important, for as Carol says of History, 'you just have to work'. With 'soft, effective' teachers, specific lesson content becomes much more significant. An extreme example of the sort of assessment that took place was shown in domestic science. These lessons were often 'successful', particularly when the girls were actually cooking, rather than learning theory:

Valerie, Jill, Diane, Carol and Linda are all missing at the beginning of the lesson. Carol rushes in and says to Monica: 'What have we got to do, write notes?'
Monica: Yes.
Carol: I'm going out then. (She runs out . . .)

Writing notes in domestic science was considered a 'non-learning' situation.

'Non-learning' situations Two factors seemed to lead to a lesson being defined as a 'non-learning' situation. The first was when teachers who were judged 'potentially effective' did not provide an adequate learning context. The second was when teachers were considered 'ineffective'. In these latter circumstances the specific content of the lesson was irrelevant. The judgment had already been made, and the girls would arrive 'knowing' they would not learn anything.

This was Carol's most frequent definition of the situation. Most lessons were not able to provide her with the sort of learning context she wanted. Her interactive behaviour at these times could be called mildly anti-authoritarian. It involved joking, laughing, talking on topics such as boys and clothes, while at the same time, at least nominally, carrying on with the classwork. The interaction set usually included nine or ten girls. They were: Carol, Valerie, Diane, Debbie, Anne, Angela, June and Monica, with Linda and Jill taking part when present.[9]

An example of this sort of interaction with a 'potentially effective' teacher comes in a typing lesson. Carol is interacting with a large group of girls who all sit close to each other. Although they are working they still manage to make jokes among themselves.

Miss Keene has asked the class how to go about 'tabulating'. She says: 'How many spaces do you go in?'
Various people shout out answers, all of which are wrong; eventually Debbie gives the right answer. After it has been said, Carol jumps up and shouts out the right answer again, looks round the room, and giggles.
Anne (out loud to the class): Oh, God, she waits till someone else has said it.
(All of the girls sitting near by laugh.)

It is to this type of interaction that Carol is referring when she says of her class 'we're all friends together really', and Valerie says 'You get a lot of fun, a lot of jokes in the classroom.' Valerie points out that Carol is best at making jokes, but also says that others are involved: 'She's good at making jokes (pointing at Carol) and she (Diane) . . . and Anne and June . . . and this other girl, Debbie, she's good at laughing'.

The next example comes from an RE lesson which Carol considers a 'waste of time' and 'boring'. It is an example of how they behave when they consider the teacher 'ineffective'.

Carol, Valerie, Diane, Jill, Debbie, Anne, Angela and Monica are sitting close together. Debbie is playing with one of Carol's shoes; Valerie and Diane are reading comics and Carol is combing her hair and occasionally making jokes quietly to those around her. By and large no one in the class seems very interested in the content of the lesson ... eventually the teacher 'notices' that Valerie and Diane are reading comics and demands to have them. Diane quietly gives hers up, but Valerie says 'Oh no sir, please don't take it.' The teacher insists and takes it away until lunchtime. Carol immediately gets out another magazine from her bag, turns round to Valerie and Diane, and they all start looking at it.

When a particular teacher's lessons were defined in this way, it was fairly irrelevant what specific material they presented. They always met the same style of interaction. By Easter of her fourth year, with the typing and history teachers leaving, Carol had 'written off' six out of her ten teachers in this way. Most of these assessments were shared by several of the other girls in the class.

'*Bunking it*' Another response when it was not possible to 'learn' was to run out of the lesson or not bother to turn up at all—in their terms, they would 'bunk it'.

This involved a different interaction set, as only Carol, Valerie, Diane, Jill and Linda would 'bunk' lessons.

In an interview, Carol explained how 'bunking' was related to specific definitions.

'With Mr Marks in history, them lot sometimes say "Let's muck about", or "Let's bunk it", and I say "Yeah", and then I goes in the lesson and them lot comes in and calls me "snide". If I don't feel like bunking it, I don't. But now (i.e. with the new history teacher) if they tell me don't go to history, I don't go.'

She describes how they make the decision to miss a lesson:

Question: When you and your friends say 'Let's bunk a lesson', who actually suggests it?
Carol: When we don't want to go nowhere, like if we say we don't want to go to this lesson ... Valerie comes up and says 'Let's bunk it.' Sometimes Diane do, sometimes I do. I say, 'Let's bunk it' and they all agree.

This interaction set is far more specific than the others described. Carol, Valerie, Diane, Linda and Jill were the only girls in the class who would 'bunk' lessons. They also formed a separate interaction set when teachers who were regarded as 'soft' tried to become 'strict'.

Teachers who become 'strict' When a 'soft' teacher

tried to become 'strict', for example if he threatened to discipline the girls in some way, a specific pattern of interaction emerged. This situation occurred regardless of whether teachers were considered 'effective' or not.

In the following example, Valerie and Jill had arrived late for science.

Mrs Newman (to Valerie and Jill): Where have you been?
Carol (aggressively): Shut your mouth.
(This is said loud enough for Mrs Newman to hear, but she ignores it.)

Another time, Carol, Valerie, Diane, Jill and Linda arrived late for domestic science and became aggressive.

Miss Lane: I think one of you ought to go and tell Mr Kraft (*Deputy Head*) where you've been.
Valerie (aggressively): I ain't going nowhere. (She turns to talk to Carol ...)
Carol (to those round her): Where's Monica?
Linda: Oh! she's at the front (of the class).
Carol: Oh! look at that lot. She's too brainy for me. (They all laugh.)

In this example the girls who arrived late sat physically separated from the rest of the class and at each successive 'joke' they laughed heartily. Even though the rest of the pupils and probably the teacher could hear what they said, none of them laughed or made any comment.

Again, it was only Carol, Diane, Valerie, Jill and Linda who would interact in this manner. On these occasions, the rest of the class sat very quietly, seldom interacting with anyone but the teacher. Carol and her friends were defined as an interaction set by themselves and by the rest of the class.

I have shown that interaction sets represent shared knowledge among a group of pupils and are associated with regular patterns of behaviour. But the definitions presented above are necessarily incomplete, as is shown by the way Carol will sometimes, for no apparent reason, extract herself from a common definition and act alone. A very good example of this sort of 're-definition' came in a science lesson. The rest of the class were chattering and laughing in their usual way and not taking much notice of what the teacher was saying.

Carol and Diane sit at the top of the bench, farthest from the board. They are correcting or finishing a diagram of a skeleton, and seem very engrossed in it. Carol says 'and this is the arm, the femur ...'
Eventually they put their folders away and then begin writing the notes written on the board.

Here, for some reason, the girls were willing to extract themselves from their typical definition of science and establish new appropriate behaviour. Obviously, additional criteria of assessment are being applied and a new pattern of interaction emerges.

Why is it that Carol will come to one science lesson and work very hard, while the next day she will take part in a common definition and 'bunk it' completely? Why is it that even with teachers who are assessed as 'able to teach', some lessons are more 'successful' than others? Obviously more detailed analysis of pupil knowledge is necessary before these questions can be answered with any certainty.

What can be said, however, is that 'how to define the situation' is a constant problem for these girls and one that demands continual negotiation. Unlike the successful grammar school pupil who knows how to look at his school experience, these girls constantly have to make sense of frustrating and often confusing situations. This, together with the fact that all inter-action sets tend to function with a limited number of definitions, makes it progressively difficult for individuals to extract themselves from their usual way of seeing things. Attempts by teachers to reach these girls were effective only when they conformed to the girls' own standards of assessment. They no longer blindly accepted all teachers as the grammar school pupil might do. Presumably because of their own unsuccessful learning experiences they had established their own criteria of judgment. They seemed to want to learn quickly, effectively and, at least to begin with, with the minimum of effort. Teaching these girls in the way they wished to be taught was something which many members of staff (myself included) found almost impossible.

Conclusion

Pupil knowledge about school life is differentially distributed. An interaction set presents a static picture of a group of pupils making the same commonsense judgments about classroom situations. Their behaviour is chosen in the light of what they agree they 'know' about that situation. The fact that different pupils take part in interaction sets at different times simply illustrates the point that they do not always agree about what they know. Teachers, subjects and methods of teaching mean different things to different pupils. A study of pupils' knowledge must take this fact into account and begin by specifying situations where pupils do agree. Only then would it be possible to ask what they agree about—what they know.

In describing some of Carol's definitions, I have already illustrated some of the things she knows about school life and pointed out which girls agree with her and when. Unfortunately, the whole concept of 'definition of the situation' is a static one.;[10] What is now needed is an understanding of Carol's abstract knowledge so that we can tell how she goes about classifying situations in the typical ways I have shown.

Both teachers and researchers seem extremely ignorant of what school life means to pupils. The present study already brings into question some of the more popular beliefs amongst teachers about 'non-academic' adolescents. There is a common assumption that such pupils will only be interested in subjects that will be immediately relevant to their life when they leave school. It is for this reason that many time-tables are heavily laden with 'practical' subjects such as typing, domestic science, woodwork, metalwork, and (if all else fails) games. Yet the girls described in this paper were much more concerned with 'learning', no matter what the subject. History or typing could be of equal interest to them if they provided the sort of learning situation that they looked for. Further case studies of pupil knowledge will not only be of interest to sociologists, but may even be some practical use to teachers, both in preparing their material, and in understanding their pupils.

Perhaps the last words should be left with Carol herself:

Question: What do you think the teachers think of you as an individual?
Carol: I don't think they like me much . . . I'm not a good girl anyway . . . I don't blame them; if you've got a child and she's rude, you can't like her very much . . . I mean, if I was in their place, I wouldn't like *me* 'cos the way I act—you know, I won't learn, keep making jokes and muck about. I don't blame them, but I'm not worried at all you know!

Acknowledgments

I would like to begin by thanking the pupils of 4G for allowing me to observe their lessons and for their open and frank discussions with me; without them there would have been no paper. I am grateful to the Local Education Authority for allowing me to carry out the research, and to the staff of the school where I have worked for four years. The continued co-operation and interest of many teachers, particularly those who allowed me to observe their lessons, was a great help. I would also like to thank Dr Ed Sherwood and Dr Diana Leat for their encouragement and support throughout my research. For financial support, I am indebted both to the Social Science Research Council and to the Lawrence Atwell Charity, administered by the Skinners' Company. For comments on the first draft of this paper, I am grateful to Dr Diana Leat and to my wife Ruth.

Notes

1 Because of the high proportion of 'immigrant' pupils, the staff/pupil ratio was considerably better than in many neighbouring schools. Most of the 'lower ability' classes comprised twenty pupils or fewer.
2 About 50 per cent of the school population were classed as 'immigrants' by the Local Education Authority; i.e. they had not been born in Great Britain or Ireland. The majority of these 'immigrants' were West Indian. The remainder of the school were mainly working-class English or Irish.
3 See for example Hollinshed 1949, Coleman 1960, Hargreaves 1967, Sugarman 1966, 1967, 1968, and Lacey 1970.
4 See for example Lacey's (1970) discussion of a pupil called Short (p. 98), or some of the comments made to Hargreaves about maths (pp. 99–100).
5 For a fuller discussion of 'joint action' see Blumer 1965.
6 One of components of Bernstein's (1971) 'restricted code' is a strong sense of loyalty to the group, as is implied here.
7 See in particular Cohen 1955.
8 The notion of 'repertoire' in behaviour is developed in Goffman 1959.
9 As part of the 'remedial group', Linda and Jill did not take all of their lessons with the other girls.
10 This limitation on the usefulness of the concept of 'definition of the situation' characterises the distinction between ethnomethodology and symbolic interactionism. For a useful comparison of these two approaches on these lines, see Zimmerman and Wieder 1970.

References

Bernstein, B., 1971, *Class, Codes and Control*, Routledge & Kegan Paul.
Blumer, H., 1965, 'Sociological implications of the thought of George Herbert Mead', *American Journal of Sociology*, 71, 535–44.
Cohen, A., 1955, *Delinquent Boys: the Culture of the Gang*, Chicago, Free Press.
Coleman, J. S., 1960, *The Adolescent Society: the Social Life of the Teenager, and its Impact on Education*, New York, Free Press.
Dale, R., 1973, 'Phenomenological perspectives and the sociology of the school', *Educational Review*, 125 (3), 175–89.
Filmer, P., Phillipson, M., Silverman, D. and Walsh, D., 1972, *New Directions in Sociological Theory*, Collier Macmillan.
Goffman, E., 1959, *The Presentation of Self in Everyday Life*, New York, Anchor Books; Penguin, 1969.
Hargreaves, D., 1967, *Social Relations in a Secondary School*, Routledge & Kegan Paul.
Hollinshed, A. B., 1949, *Elmstown's Youth: the Impact of Social Class on Adolescents*, New York, Wiley.
Keddie, N., 1971, 'Classroom knowledge', in M. F. D. Young, ed., *Knowledge and Control: New Directions for the Sociology of Education*, Collier Macmillan.
Lacey, C., 1970, *Hightown Grammar: the School as a Social System*, Manchester University Press.
Sugarman, B. N., 1966, 'Social class and values as related to achievement in school', *Sociological Review*, 41, 287–302.
Sugarman, B. N., 1967, 'Involvement in youth culture, academic achievement and conformity in school', *British Journal of Sociology*, 18, 151–64.
Sugarman, B. N., 1968, 'Social norms in teenage boys' peer groups—a study of their implications for achievement and conduct in four London schools', *Human Relations*, 21, 41–58.
Werthman, C., 1963, 'Delinquents in schools; a test for the legitimacy of authority', *Berkeley Journal of Sociology*, 8(1), 39–60.
Werthman, C., 1970, 'The functions of social definitions in the development of delinquent careers', in P. E. Garbedian and D. C. Gibbons, eds, *Becoming Delinquent*, Aldine, 1971.
Young, M. F. D. and Keddie, N., 1973, 'New directions: is there anything happening in sociology?', *Hard Cheese*, no. 2, May 1973, 29–36.
Zimmerman, D. H. and Wieder, D. L., 1970, 'Ethnomethodology and the problem of order: comment on Denzin', in J. D. Douglas, ed., *Understanding Everyday Life: Towards the Reconstruction of Sociological Knowledge*, Routledge & Kegan Paul.

20 The meaning of 'trouble'

Elizabeth Rosser and Rom Harré

It is no easy matter to understand social action. The difficulty is revealed in the disparity between much that is said about the social actions of young people and what can be revealed about those actions by allowing the actors themselves to provide our understandings. The reasons for this kind of disparity will become clear as we go along.

Our first undertaking must be to think about the nature of social action itself, what it is that we are required to understand. A social action by an individual person is part of a more elaborate structure of actions which is a mutual creation by certain people acting together in a co-ordinated way. It is important to remember that social actions may be perfectly co-ordinated in hostile, or friendly performances, so that co-ordination of action must not be thought to imply that there is no rivalry, opposition, or even hatred, involved in the performance. People are related to their performances by a variety of personal attributes, including their abilities, their practical knowledge of what is required to achieve certain social acts, and even some theoretical understanding of what sort of sociality those acts achieve. The task of the ethogenic scientist attempting to understand social action includes not only an external description of a pattern of action and of the social act that it seems to perform, but also a specification of the abilities required of the actors, and some attempt to reveal the practical knowledge and theories of sociality involved in the competent performances of social life.

In order successfully to analyse social episodes into their component actions and to discern the structure that links them, it is necessary to have a correct idea of what social actions actually are. There has been much confusion on this matter, particularly in social

Source: article commissioned for this volume. Elizabeth Rosser is a postgraduate research student in the Department of Educational Studies, University of Oxford; Rom Harré is a Fellow of Linacre College and lecturer in the philosophy of science, University of Oxford.

psychology, where, despite an official recognition of the weakness of behaviourist psychology, investigators have continued to treat the components of social action as externally defined behaviours. But it is abundantly clear that this approach involves a serious error. The nearest concept we have to an accurate expression of the nature of social action is that of 'meaning' in its most generalized sense. The point of saying that the components of social episodes are meanings can be seen in an example. It is only as a meaning that a gesture (a particular behaviour) is an insult, for example. The difference between the insult as meaning and the gesture as the vehicle of that meaning can be seen by reflecting on the fact that the same insult can be given by a variety of different gestures and, of course, by a verbal device which may involve no gesture at all. Equally, it is disconcerting to find that the same gesture may, in different cultures, have quite a different meaning, and what is an apology in one may be an insult in another. In order, then, to analyse a social episode into its component actions, we must learn the meanings that are ascribed to certain speeches and gestures and postures, etc., in a given culture. It is only among meanings that we can expect to find some kind of cross-cultural order appearing in social life.

We have already emphasized the fact that social episodes involve structures of actions; that is, they are orderly sequences of meaningful speeches and gestures. How is it, then, that the mutual creation of orderly sequencing of actions can be achieved? It is a central principle of the ethogenic theory that we should begin the investigation of the achievement of orderliness by applying the idea of following a rule. We know, with certainty, that there are cases of formal interaction, such as a ceremony where the sequencing and orderly production of structure is the product of conscious rule-following by the actors. A central idea of ethogenics is the general application of the concept of rule-following as a model for understanding social events which would otherwise be mysterious. This is not just a model. As we shall show, even in those cases where our participants are not carrying out ceremonial or formal action-sequences, they are, nevertheless, acting according to rules which are well understood by them and shared in their community. How is it that we can find out such a fact? To understand that we must briefly set out the main features of the ethogenic method in social investigations.

Having set out what we understand by social action and what we are looking for in ethogenic research, we must ask how scientific understanding should best be achieved. Clearly, two converging forms of investigation are required. One, microsociological analysis, looks at a social interaction from the outside, so to speak, taking an observer's point of view and imposing an observer's concepts. However sensitive such an analysis may be to the appropriate level of meaning of the components of the interaction, it nevertheless involves the imposition of a conceptual framework upon actions which may be quite differently understood by those who perform them. Furthermore, if on the basis of our microsociological analysis we frame hypotheses about the social competence and social knowledge of the people who have performed these actions, at the best we are *attributing* knowledge and competence. The radical approach of ethogenics centres on taking the accounts given by the participants in the action seriously as contributions to social and psychological understanding of those actions and how they are generated. Account analysis extracts participants' concepts and builds sociological and psychological theories in terms of them. The hypotheses that are formed about social competence and social knowledge in the course of account analysis are not attributions but *revelations* of social knowledge and competence.

It might seem that account analysis should have priority over microsociological analysis as revealing 'the truth' about the action pattern and its genesis, but this would be too simple. The giving of accounts is itself a social action and people use their capacity to create accounts as ways of changing the action itself. Both forms of analysis are required for an adequate socio-psychological science, since they home in on the individuals and their knowledge from two different but supporting directions.

Sometimes, however, it is the case that one or other of these forms of analysis has priority. We could say that when microsociological and account analysis support one another, then the analyses converge, and this is very frequently the case. Sometimes, however, particularly where the microsociology is a folk sociology, as employed for example by teachers, journalists, adults and others, we find the analyses divergent. The reality conjured up in observer's accounts of the action are seemingly very different from that conjured up in the participant's account of the action. In these circumstances of divergence, the ethogenic standpoint demands that participants' accounts have priority.

Trouble in school is a case of divergence and, in our view, is a very clear example of the sort of case where the accounts of the participants are to be taken with great seriousness. This does not mean that observers' accounts are to be taken lightly. On the contrary, as themselves parts of the social world, external descriptions have practical power in that it is often in terms of them that programmes of amelioration or repression are conceived. Where observers' and participants' accounts diverge and observers' accounts are the basis of practical programmes, it is no wonder those programmes almost always fail.

Not only are the accounts of the people involved given equal status as contributions to the socio-psychological understanding of the episodes of social life, but the final general theory of action in those situations in that culture (and we make no wider claim) is to be constructed in terms of the available concepts in the local culture. In this respect ethogenics differs from macrosociology, since in the latter a suprapersonal view is obtained and invites, quite properly, the *introduction* of concepts.

Both the production of and accounting for action, we suppose, derive from individual cognitive resources and local knowledge of the rules and meanings of action. A preliminary schematization of these resources, which derives both from meaning-oriented microsociology and from the analysis of real life accounts, is based upon groups of four elements; situation, actor, arbiter and rule system. Each group of elements is represented in an individual's knowledge of sociality and serves as a resource for acting, planning action and prospective and retrospective commenting upon the action; that is, in people's accounts.

Our study was ethogenically oriented and involved recording conversations with pupils from two comprehensive schools. One group were seen in their youth club, the other group in their school. The material was analysed, as far as possible, in terms of categories that emerged from the pupils' speech itself, and revealed a knowledge of social rules and of types of situations that were recognized as socially distinct.

Distinct situations (as recognized by our participants) called for distinctive presentations of self involving distinctive demeanours to others. Correct behaviour is not just a matter of following the rules, but of appearing to be the appropriate kind of person. In each situation, action and self-presentation are determined by the judgments of others, whether real or imaginary. We came to see that two of these situations, home and school, were treated in a very similar way, and that the reality of these situations, as the pupils conjured them up in speech, was remarkably different from the reality we had seen reported by parents and teachers.

A good example of a teacher's view is revealed in an article by Tim Devlin in *The Times* of 6 May 1975, quoting the speech of a woman teacher who had been driven out of school, or, as Devlin put it, 'forced to resign'. The reality conjured up in her speech involves some important social attributions to the schoolroom in which she found herself. For example, she says, 'I tried to get some kind of order but could not make myself heard above the din.' In describing what the girls were doing, she conjures up a disorderly, meaningless situation in which all kinds of unrelated activities were taking place. Order was *wanting* and *wanted* by her, a characteristic of the situation she 'tried to get', but 'failed'. Her speech gives a vivid and gripping account of her situation, yet in our investigations we unearthed another reality in the accounts of members of classes like hers, people with whom she seems to have had little real contact. It never seems to have occurred to this unfortunate lady that she worked within an official theory of the institution and that order of another kind *already existed in the class*.

The existence of disparate accounts of what went on raises all kinds of important issues. We would like to express the matter in terms of one kind of contrast, that between official and unofficial theories of an institution and its activities, in this case, the school and schooling. The official theory is made available to us in all kinds of publications and talk. The unofficial theories are more difficult to come by. Clearly, the teacher in Tim Devlin's article subscribed to the official theory. Schools are places provided by a benevolent state for the benefit both of society and individual children. Schooling involves the 'transmission of culture' and the acquisition of skills, and is a key process in readying the young for adult life. Teachers are skilful and knowledgeable, pupils are clumsy and ignorant. Disorderly and anomic situations lurk as threats on the borders of reality and appear as and when discipline breaks down. Order is the product of social work by teachers on children. It is this latter proposition that is a central feature of the perception of schooling of Tim Devlin's teacher.

But if we want to understand schools and schooling, this theory and its associated rhetoric will not do as a *comprehensive* account. Since there are many times the number of pupils than there are teachers, administrators and helpers, and in general the undistinguished citizenry do not share the official theory but have a clutch of theories of their own, we need to reveal these theories, understand their associated rhetorics, and pay attention to the *orderliness* of the social landscape viewed from their standpoint. It is also worth emphasizing that ethogenic techniques reveal the theories held by the folk, whatever they may be, and accord them respect. So that from this standpoint a well-meaning but naïve young radical teacher who proposes a Marxist rhetoric is offering a competing *official* theory, an imposition from outside the social reality addressed by us as problematic. *Any* official theory, of whatever political colour, is, for ethogenics, a problem, not a resource! For all we know, each reality, as constituted, is an aspect of a composite social world and is a truth.

We were concerned in our study not with what happened, but with the way what happened was understood, justified and conceived. It is clear that the pupils have their own complex system of rules by which they account for their behaviour in school and at home, but their interpretations in certain circumstances can differ between groups of pupils as well as between pupils and their elders.

Our participants fell into two sharply distinguished groups, from geographically distinct areas and having somewhat different ways of life. Those we call group A lived in a recently constructed industrial suburb of a middle-sized country town. Their parents worked in a very large factory where 'industrial relations' were bad. Many families in this suburb had emigrated from other parts of Britain but not usually in the lifetime of our participants. Without detailed sociological investigation, it is difficult to make sweeping statements about the parental society of group A participants, but we think it can be said safely that the result of the mixing of markedly different British sub-cultures was a fairly anomic and bland common sociality. Our participants attended a large comprehensive school, which had been built at the same time as their industrial suburb. The speech of our group A participants tended to a widespread use of glottal stops, of unstressed consonants and non-standard vowels, though only one spoke in a marked regional dialect. Most of them were not taking exams at the time of their discussion with us but they had made some attempt on the examination system in the past, at the CSE level, one having succeeded in as many as eight subjects.

Our second group, B, lived in a country town but one which had very little industry. They attended a new local comprehensive and were the first-year intake brought in to begin the school. The parents of our participants worked mostly in predominantly managerial jobs. Our participants' speech tended to be careful, with only a trace of local accent. They were much engaged in the taking of examinations, and over half had recently taken from six to nine O levels and the rest from three to seven CSEs. Unlike our group A participants, group B had well-articulated conceptions of future careers and the steps needed to achieve them.

For group A, neither school nor home were considered 'serious'; that is, people participating in these social places were not living fully in accordance with the official rhetoric for that type of institution. For most of these pupils, official tasks such as learning seem to involve highly conventional behaviour fulfilling a meaningless ritual. This is not just an arbitrary theory they have developed but is derived from their seeing themselves as having been written off. 'They [the teachers] sort of couldn't care less if you were going to leave at the end of the fourth year. All their time was spent on the ones that were going to stay on, so ones that were going to leave were never there and nobody sort of worried about them.' Several of these pupils clocked in at the beginning of the school day and then left. One even went off to work.

The more academically oriented group (group B), on the other hand, were more willing to accept the official school rhetoric. These pupils came largely from supportive families whose parents had primed them for success in school in general, and as a means to a professional career. 'I've been brought up to think that school-work comes first, you know, if you want to get anywhere.' In addition, this group experienced a school atmosphere close to their expressed ideal, and had the considered advantage of being the first-year intake in a new school. 'You got a lot of responsibility. A lot is expected of you but I think there's more advantages than disadvantages. I think it encourages people. You want to achieve what people expect of you.'

Despite the differences between the two groups, their criticisms of school organization and atmosphere had much in common. Furthermore, both groups judged their teachers by reference to a similar set of criteria. To their way of thinking, classes were not disorderly and anarchic but rule-bound, and these are the same classes which teachers and journalists describe in terms of total chaos.

Our students shared a system of justification for what they did which involved two major components: the first, an elaborate categorization of occasions of offence, the second, some quite specific principles by which retribution for the offence was meted out.

The first category of offence was rather vague. In the home it was widely referred to as 'getting on my nerves' (A) or 'going on' (B). For group A, that phrase was occasionally used in school, but much more frequently the pupils referred to the same category of generalized offence at school as 'being boring'.

The second category of offence involved more specific actions. We would identify them in our form of speech as 'forms of contempt'. A somewhat generalized offence which occurred in both home and school was recognized as 'treating me like a kid'. Group B seemed more fortunate in this respect, having teachers who did not offend so frequently. 'They [the teachers] speak to you as a person, not as a little kid as they do in junior school. They speak to you more like they would do at college, more like you're somebody . . . as if you know something. It builds your confidence.'

Another more specific form of contempt was being given teachers who for one reason or another were classified as 'a load of rubbish', 'useless'. Both groups agreed that poor teachers were those who 'treated teaching as a nine to five job, after that forget it. They don't pay any attention, do what they got to do and get out'; those who 'go on as if they were never young and did things we do'; those who 'feel it's below them to explain', or were unable to put the subject matter over well.

It was important to them to be recognized as persons each in their own right. It was thought to be deeply contemptuous to be treated as anonymous. 'If you're just another person in the classroom you don't get on half as well.' Not surprisingly, the failure of group A's headmaster to know their names was deeply resented. 'You can go in there and he'll say, oh yes, and try and think of your name. He doesn't know who you are but he'll say he knows you. He doesn't know any individual apart from the ones that are in there every day.' Group B said of their headmaster, 'He takes an interest in you, which helps.' We came to see that group B recognized in their teachers, and in their school situation as a whole, many of the qualities which group A found to be lacking in theirs.

One of the worst categories of offence was indecision or weakness of will by those they expected to be strong. Although both groups considered it 'natural to play the teachers up', this proposition was qualified by group B who felt that playing around was 'worse in the third and fourth forms, not so bad in the fifth year', and that unruly pupils were 'not in the O level group'. For the O level people, and those who just wanted to work, mucking around was seen to be unfair both to them, because it held them back, and to the teachers; 'they seem to think they're there to punish the people. They're there to teach. If you don't want to listen, get out.' Playing up was also seen by group B to take a different, more subtle, form in later years.

> 'It's more trying to get the better of him or her. I suppose it helps both, doesn't it really, because if you're trying to catch the teacher out that means you've got to know your lesson pretty well, because otherwise if you try to catch the teacher out and yet you've been proved wrong, you've had it really. For the teacher, it's quite easy to snap back at you, and the teacher's always on his guard.'

Both groups made it clear that the 'soft' teacher's offence was to provoke more playing up. 'The more meekly they reacted, the more we go on. Well, those that could stop us did so in the earlier years and we never played them up again. Those that didn't, that was it for them.' These young people found mere feebleness by those they expected to respect particularly offensive. Part of the explanation we think is that it is perceived as a way of not taking them seriously. For example, in the home, 'He's not like a father as you'd sort of think as a father . . . well, they're supposed to be protective, aren't they. He couldn't care less what I do as long as he knows where I am. I mean, you know, if I said I was going to an orgy, he'd say, oh allright, as long as I know where you are.' In the same way, teachers who the pupils felt should 'show they're the boss', but were unable to do so, received rapid and at times violent retribution.

Equally, if not more offensive, acts were those where someone who had been feeble 'comes on strong' and then, when challenged, gives in. Examples of this form of insult appeared both at home and at school for group A, but only at school for group B, for whom parental discipline seemed to be more effective. In group A we have the father who, after conniving at a fifteen-year-old daughter going out every night for eight consecutive weeks, tried to assert his authority. She answered back ('it's allright, I've got him under my thumb really') and he abandoned his position, giving her a pound for spending money. Or the soft teacher who attempted to assert her authority and was condemned, not for trying to be strong, but for being unsuccessful.

> 'She tried kicking me out of the classroom. I'd been mucking around. And none of my mates liked that. They just started getting mad with her and chucking blackboard rubbers, smashing up the lightbulbs and everything, and in the end she just went in to the store cupboard, crying her eyes out, and we locked her in'.

The offence of weakness on the part of teachers seems to be very much bound up with the pupils' own theories about the value of discipline. Not only did they disrespect parents and teachers for not meting out punishment when deserved, but it was clear that they wished for discipline in the structure of their everyday lives. Although group B expressed a great liking for the friendly relaxed atmosphere of their school, they were nevertheless critical that it was often too lax. This viewpoint was reinforced by the observations of those pupils who had attended grammar schools for a while and had found the 'stuffy' regimes, where 'you don't have any feelings towards somebody . . . where you have to sit in silence in neat rows' to be distasteful. Discipline to our people was seen to be essential. 'Well, if I do an essay, I like it to be marked. Whereas if the teachers just don't mark it, just give a comment, or just tick it, I tend to get lazy'. 'It's an unusual thing to say, but I think probably if it was stricter it'd get better results.' 'There's no discipline. Well, if there was people would learn something a bit more'. Both groups agreed overwhelmingly on the necessity to strike a balance between freedom and natural behaviour and complete rigidity in the classroom. 'You know you want someone who's pretty strict but who'll let you feel a bit free.' 'I think you've got to hit a medium where in the class it's not so strict. I mean silence doesn't help, but too much talk tends to hold you back.' A good teacher, in their view, 'is someone who'll take a good joke but will make us work', 'subtle control, everybody's happy and you don't realize you're getting the work done.'

A third category of offence is that of overt insult. Our pupils regard this category as very much less wounding, largely, we think, because in these offensive stances they are being treated as equals. These involve arguing, verbal insulting, and, in the case of group A, hitting.

Finally, there are offences of unfairness. Recognition of pupils as individuals was a major concern. A deeply wounding cause of offence involved a teacher or parent treating a student in a manner which suggested that he or she was the same sort of person as an older sibling who had either offended in some way or was being offered as a worthy model. 'Other teachers got it in for me because my brother [a trouble-maker] went there before me.' 'I'm a bit rowdy and I'm compared with him and that annoys me. He's done so and so, he's got so and so . . . and I, you know, feel as if, well, I'm not exactly thick, I think, I'm just that little bit lower. Well, when he did his exams he did O levels, whereas I'm doing CSEs.'

Unfairness was also seen to stem from the helplessness of their position as children/pupils as opposed to parents/teachers, where, by definition, parents/teachers hold ultimate authority. As such, pupils often felt themselves 'put down', trapped in their position.

> 'On my report they write that I'm a bit too chatty, that I talk too much to everybody, friends and teachers. One comment on it said, "I talk to the teacher, that is good." Well, I'm the one who gets everyone else going . . . it starts the discussion. And another comment said, "I tend to wear the teacher's patience talking." So I said to them, well, if I didn't talk you'd say I was withdrawn, and they didn't know how to answer that. It's true.'

In the home we see this offence operating in the way parents make moral judgments for their children and dictate their choice of friends.

> 'I had a boyfriend . . . and my parents didn't like him, so they broke it off . . . the boy had come for a visit with his prospective second stepfather and my parents didn't like the boy, well, they liked him, but they didn't like his parents. Well, they thought they were lower class. They didn't like their background. D— had been in a home for children for three years. He [Dad] wrote to his stepfather and said he didn't want me to see D— again. I liked them.'

There are a number of principles of retribution which are used to explain the sorts of response which the offences bring forth. These fall into two broad categories: principles of 'reciprocity' and principles of 'equilibration'. A principle of reciprocity requires that one gives back whatever one has received, so that in a simple case of verbal insult one returns verbal insult or on being hit one hits back. As one girl put it, 'And if they turn nasty, well, we can turn nasty too.' Hitting as a form of interaction was largely unknown to group B both at home and at school.

In the second main form of reciprocity the reciprocal action does not take the same form as that insult. The phrase most commonly used for this by group A was 'storming out', but the reaction of walking out was shared by both sets and we have many accounts of such occasions; but because there is less freedom of action at school, this, unlike simple reciprocity, seems to be confined to home. Protection of self seems to be involved in walking out. Our people didn't want their parents to see they had been upset. 'Then if I want to feel upset, I'll go and feel upset somewhere where they can't see me.' 'Well, I try not to [show emotion] anyway, you know. You put on a good front as you might say, you know.'

In categorizing the occasions of offence, we emphasized the importance that the pupils attached to forms of contempt. But the principle of reciprocity is not applied in dealing with this kind of offence: they do not see themselves as returning contempt for contempt. The accounts seem to involve an equilibration; that is, when they feel themselves put down, treated without seriousness, they behave in such a way as to restore themselves as mature beings. This then defines the form of their response.

Over and over again we find that in talking about such an occasion they describe themselves as making a dignified or non-demeaning withdrawal into a silence. 'I just go quiet and that annoys them even more.' 'Yes, ignore them, I'm very good at that. I just switch myself off, play some Pink Floyd in my head, look at the ceiling.' 'I just wait until they've finished, you know. It just happens like an alarm, or something, and it's going to keep going until it's finished, and that's it. Might as well not have happened, you know'.

There are occasions when equilibration is achieved by some positive action. We see the girl who is indignant with her father 'for ever warning me about coming home pregnant' not only retaliating verbally, 'What do you think I am? Do you think I just stand on corners and wait for them to go past or something?', but also using her indignation to provoke his fury by pretending that the pain of a suspected ulcer is in fact a sign of pregnancy. 'Anyway it plays up now and again, and I goes, "Oh, my stomach" and I say, "Oh Dad, I'm pregnant." He goes up the wall.' Nevertheless, withdrawal, rather than positive action, seems to be the most frequent response, as they account for their lives, and the commonest means by which equilibration is achieved. This suggests that forms of contempt are perhaps the commonest readings which our people give to things which happen to them, and which they can attribute to the actions of others. It is not surprising, therefore, to find Tim Devlin quoting the teacher as saying, 'The worst thing they did was to ignore you completely.' Looking at it through their rhetoric, of course, they were not ignoring their teacher at all. From their point of view they were restoring a measure of dignity, conceived to have been taken from them, by withdrawal into injured or strategic silence.

Who are the arbiters of the propriety of social action? Both sets of participants, as might be expected, refer to their peers as the audience and critics before whom their dramatic performances are staged, and whose judgment they defer to. There is a faint hint, which we have been unable to follow up, of one or two members of each group having a special prominence in this regard. Peer arbitration is clearly described in the two following extracts:

'The situation demands it, I suppose. You can't very well sit there. You've got a whole class of thirty-five people sat round absolutely mucking about, chucking books, ripping up books, everything like that and the teacher stood out in the classroom writing a load of work down on the blackboard. You can't really work, so you've got the choice. You either stand up and walk out and go to a different class, or you join in. If you walk out of the class you get called all the names under the sun, "Cissy" and "Pouff" and all that crap, so you just join in ... Anybody that works in a lesson that you doss about in, that you know you're going to doss about in, that's it, you get called "Ponce" and everything'.
'I'm what's generally known as a "creep" actually. But there are "creeps" and "creeps". J—, he's known generally just as a "swot". He is a "swot" so he takes that position. I'd be defined as someone who works hard but who can also fool around.'

But additionally, and given the enormous importance attached to the equilibration of dignity, it is not surprising to find a form of self-arbitration, where what they have done and said is judged by reference to their own conceptions of the integrity and dignity of themselves, regardless of 'popular' opinion, or the arbitration of specific others.

In one respect members of school A showed a marked difference in arbiters from members of school B. Parents and teachers count for nothing as arbiters in group A. Their judgments of propriety are scorned or ignored, and their good opinion is not sought. Group B, however, take parents' views of propriety fairly seriously, though they certainly do not take them as absolute in the arbitration of proper action and correct portrayal of character.

A typical group A reading of attempts at parental authority ran thus:

'Theirs is the old-fashioned style. Do everything by the book, the book's it and that, you know. That's life and you should go by that and there's no other way. But I want to live my life how *I* want to live it ... My Dad keeps on how his life was hard and everything and I should have the same. It just gets on my nerves and I just get up and walk out and don't come back at all for two or three days.'

Relationships between group B people and authority were very different: 'I respect my parents because they respect me and I don't cause trouble or anything.'
And the clear acceptance of the parental standards by the speaker shows in:

'We don't row. We never row except when my brother's home. It's my mother and brother usually. They get on very well, but it's just that sometimes my brother gets on her nerves. She likes everything to be just so. She likes everybody to eat properly and not to make a noise. And he is very rowdy. He is a very rowdy, unruly person, and so Mum's always raising her voice at him.' (What about you?) 'Oh, its easy to keep in line.'

And is equally clear in:

'When I was going out with a bloke, Mum said, "Be in by ten", and I thought, "Well, they've let me go out with this boy, why can't they let me have a bit longer, you know?" And of course if I came in late they said, "We'll chop it down." So therefore, that way I think it's right because I've got to learn that I've got to come in at a certain time.'

However, in certain circumstances the claim to at least an equal place in decision-making does emerge: 'Me? I'm a back-room lawyer in many respects. My sisters won't stand up for themselves. However, I do. I don't stand on any decision if it's unfair. I won't accept it.'

The accounts we have analysed so far are concerned with short-term cycles of offence, retribution and reciprocity. The orderly and rule-bound action-sequences whose structures we have revealed above are over in a matter of minutes. But both groups describe occasions of much longer term cycles of interaction. An adult moves a proposal of some sort, involving an offence of some kind. The long-term cycle involves four phases, (i) violent rejection of the proposal *as insulting or demeaning*, (ii) arguing from some basis, constituted as rational for the occasion, against the proposal, (iii) a withdrawal in the course of which the challenged persona is maintained according to a local convention (e.g. door slamming, head-tossing, etc., the fine structure of 'storming out'), (iv) ignoring the offence because no resolution is possible: experience has told them that none of the reactions shown in the previous phases is in any way effective against a repetition of the offence. We see this cycle in a description given by one boy as a result of his parents 'getting on at him'. At first he reacted

'Violently . . . just generally went mad, strolled in and out when I wanted. Didn't work at home. Just walked in, dumped my stuff, got changed and walked straight out again. Cheeky and things like that.' (And after a while) 'Oh, I just played along then, let them think they was having a good time . . . Just let them get on with it . . . They had upset me but they didn't realize it.

They put me into stinking moods sometimes. I just don't care any more . . . They can do what they want. I'm never at home.'

The structure of the discussion phase (ii) is different in the two groups. As the dominant organizational theme of the discussion, group A report such matters as accusations, counter-accusations, castings of the other into demeaning categories and the like, while the *issue* is not addressed. Group B, on the other hand, report the second phase as dominated by rational criteria, and the issue is addressed seriously. A further empirical study should be made to reveal the conceptions of rationality involved, since we cannot take it for granted that they will be 'logical' in the strict sense.

Our analysis has produced a striking contrast between the accounts of classroom situations given by those attempting to impose a reality conjured up by the official rhetoric used for talking and writing about schooling and the accounts generated by those who use explanatory schemata and ways of speech available to people who do not subscribe to or perhaps do not even know what the official rhetoric is.

On the basis of this study, we can offer some tentative suggestions about the 'problem of disorder in our schools'. Official explanations such as 'the decline of the family' do not seem to fit the 'reality' revealed in the speech of our participants very well. The central issue for them seems to be the unseriousness of the institution and its practices and the depersonalization and contempt meted out to those who see it as such. The clash between the effect of the unrealistic present school-leaving age, the available curricula and the school scene as viewed from within generates a 'trialectic' of contempt, depersonalization and reciprocal retaliation which underlies and is the meaning of 'disorder' from the viewpoint of our participants. The school itself, which is, after all, a comparatively new social invention, is officially construed according to a conception of disciplinary and academic relationships which is very hard to sustain against other and conflicting renderings. Something has to give. Perhaps the 'school' could become a community resource, where those who *seek* knowledge and skill could find it, regardless of age and official attainments. And the apprenticeships to violence, which our schools now offer as a major part of the informal curriculum, particularly to those whose physical maturity is denied by the official theory of schooling, could be eliminated from the real curriculum, by letting those who will go free.

Peter Woods

The importance of laughter to pupils

Many pupils' assessment of school is predicated on the amount of laughter they can derive from it. Remarks abound like 'we get a good laugh, generally you know in the long run', 'we'll miss the teachers because we have a lovely laugh with them, we won't get them so much', 'school isn't so bad, we can have a good old laugh here.' The importance of laughter to them might also be inferred from the eagerness and delight which they took in recounting certain incidents to me. In this respect, the discussions I had with pupils were laughs in themselves, which I shall discuss later. This enthusiasm is difficult to recapture but the following transcript gets near to it.

(I am talking with a group of six girls, Kate, Tracy, and four others.)
Kate: I remember Mr Gantry calling Tracy 'my pet goat'.
Tracy: Always in trouble, me and Kate.
Kate: Lazy, horrible lot, pests he used to call us. Lazy.
Tracy: You ain't 'eard 'is new saying have you? 'e says to Joanne Mackie, don't sit there looking pretty will you, so Joanne says, one thing I look a sight better than you. (*Loud shrieks of laughter and suckings-in of breath from girls.*)
Kate: We used to play 'im up in the third year just so's he'd give us a lecture and we wouldn't have to do no work.
Tracy: 'orrible, miserable lot, he used to say. Lazy.
Kate: Yeah, we used to laugh at 'im.
Tracy: What about when 'e made us go outside and made us march back in properly.
Kate: What about when me and you fell out and I threw your book across the classroom and 'e sent me down to Miss Judge.

Dianne: What about when Mr Bridge stood just outside the door.
Tracy: Dianne fell off a chair first and as she went to get up, she got 'old of me skirt, she was 'aving a muck about, and there was I in me petticoat, me skirt came down round my ankles and Mr Bridge came in (*great screams of laughter from girls*). He'd been standing outside the door.
Kate: 'e told her she'd get suspended.
Tracy: He 'ad me mum up the school, telling her what a horrible child I was.
Kate: Nobody will marry you said Miss Judge.
Tracy: Oh yeah, Miss Judge sits there, 'n 'nobody will want to marry you Jones', she said. I said 'well you ain't married anyway.'
(*Shrieks of laughter from girls.*)

Types of school laughter

Laughter can be an instrument of policy, its aim to forge better relationships and to create an atmosphere judged to be conducive to the achievement of the aims of the school. Laughter can also be a reaction against authority and routine, a socially divisive and disturbing element made in the interests of the preservation of one group and the destruction of the other.[1] Both of these are chiefly teacher-initiated. We can find both, of course, in the same school. In a previous paper on pupils' perceptions of teachers, I noted the importance pupils of all abilities attached to teachers being able to share a joke and have a laugh with them.[2] During such incidents, teacher and pupil were seen to transcend the institution and become human. This seems apparent in remarks of teachers like 'he's more natural', and 'he's more like your friend than a teacher'. Conversely, a prominent feature of teachers disliked was their lack of fun and propensity to laughter (e.g. 'he's always moaning').[3] I am not concerned here with the first type of teacher-initiated laughter, since my focus is on the pupils. Among them,

Source: unpublished. Peter Woods is lecturer in educational studies, The Open University.

I discerned two broad types of laughter, which I shall call 'natural' and 'institutionalized' laughter.

Natural laughter

Laughing seems a natural function. The young especially like to laugh, so we can assume there will be a certain amount seeking to push through the institutionalized constraints to the surface, whatever the character of the institution. However, there was plenty of evidence that much school laughter had its own peculiar characteristics. The pupils themselves distinguished readily between 'natural' and 'institutionalized' laughter.

> *Sandy*: It's different when we're outside, isn't it? When you're mixing with other people that are older than what you are, can't act stupid then.
> *PW*: You act with a ladylike deportment, do you.
> *Tracy*: Eh?
> *Gill*: Well, we have a laugh when we go out.
> *Sandy*: I mean we don't muck about like we do at school.
> *Gill*: No, we don't stand there throwing bottles and plimsolls about.
> *Sandy*: We have a good laugh when we go out anyway.
> *PW*: What and still be sort of 'ladylike'?
> *Sandy*: Yeah, and still have a good laugh. When we are out of school uniform, it's a lot different.
> *Gill*: I don't know, when you go out you sort of act your age and I don't know.
> *Sandy*: We aren't silly at home, not very often anyway. You act silly at school for a laugh.
> *Gill*: Yeah, not all the time, but we muck about.

Many of the examples that appear in my notes I would interpret as natural laughter. Much of the laughing and joking with teachers (as opposed to against teachers) and between groups of friends I would place in this category. The content of this type of laughter is often extra-institutional. Girls, for example, make capital out of their evening social engagements. I would also include, as natural, certain high-spirited activities which occur, and never come to the attention of staff. During my stay at the school, two that came to my attention were 'mass rapes' and 'FPs'. Mass rapes were calculated systematized 'assaults' on certain girls by one group of boys. 'FPs' were 'funny positions', which simply involved boys falling on top of each other, the aims seeming to be to do this in as bizarre a situation or in as massive a pile as possible. No doubt the fact that such activities are contrary to official norms adds extra piquancy to the enjoyment, but I feel that this type of laughter owes more to 'boys being boys' and 'girls being girls' than to any institutional factor beyond the part it plays in bringing them together. Many of these activities might be conceptualized as 'side involvements' in that they are peripheral to the main official activity of the school and do not impinge on it.[4] The same is true of some other laughs dependent on the pupils' own interaction, such as those which involve socialization into a subculture.

Institutionalized laughter I: mucking about

Institutionalized laughter takes two main forms: (1) 'mucking about', a kind of seemingly aimless behaviour, often labelled by teachers as 'silly' or 'childish' and (2) subversive laughter aimed—deliberately or not—at undermining the authority structure of the school or the status of a particular teacher. Both forms of laughter seem to vary among pupils in proportion to their commitment to school. Examination pupils generally were less bored and made less mention of having a laugh than non-examination pupils. This was confirmed by my observations. Examination pupils were more circumspectly behaved and officially oriented. Non-examination pupils seemed to exercise their minds mainly in devising their own forms of amusement, thus transforming the reality of the school. Laughter is an excellent vehicle for this. Erving Goffman has observed that joking is a way in which the individual makes a plea for disqualifying some of the expressive features of the situation as sources of definition of himself; and to participate with a group of one's similars in this kind of activity can lend strength to the show of role distance and to one's willingness to express it.[5] This, incidentally, illustrates the caution we must exercise in interpreting positive answers to asking children if they like school. Many of them might say yes, but only after having transformed the reality of it.

In their conversations with me, one particular form (5th form non-examination) talked to me about their life at school. There was a remarkable contrast between, on the one hand, a set of factors which could be subsumed under 'boredom' and, on the other, those relating to fun and laughter. The former made for dour, grim recounting while we talked within the official definition of the school. Many regretted not having been allowed to take examinations. Some had lost out by choices in the third year. The 'work' they were doing and had been doing since the beginning of the fourth year was too 'boring', too 'simple'; they were simply repeating work; or did 'useless', 'meaningless' work or 'nothing'; lessons were not 'helping for the future'; they were 'ignored', 'forgotten about', 'practised upon', 'made use of'; some teachers agreed with them, others 'didn't care', 'picked on them', 'took it out of them'.

The following examples are given to demonstrate how ingrained this boredom is within these pupils.

Example 1

> *PW*: Do you get anything out of school subjects?
> *George*: No, not very helpful I don't find them, just boring.
> *Len*: Some of them interest yer.

Harry: Everybody likes an easy time, don't they? Like our English group now, it's mad ain't it? He tells you the answers before you ever do anything. Says 'Oh well, I'll write it up on the blackboard first and then I'll copy it out.' Huh! rubbish!

Len: It's like Mr Brown, you don't learn nothing on that, you just copy off the board.

Harry: Blackboards and blackboards of writing, it's just meaningless. You write it down. Can you tell me what we done last week?

George: Done nothing.

Len: I wasn't here last week.

PW: What use do you make of this writing, do you ever read it again, are you ever tested on it?

Len: No.

Harry: We haven't 'ad an exam in two years, it's pointless.

Example 2

Kim: I can do it, I just don't like it, it's too boring. The maps we are doing now are so simple really.

Christine: I've not learnt anything these past two years. The English we're doing is exactly the same as my sister's doing in the first year, and the maths work, she's doing 'arder work than what I'm doing.

Kim: What I'm doing is fractions, but 'alf of this work is only second form stuff, I just sit around doing nothing either because it's too easy or because I'm not bothered about it.

Christine: See, we're not learning anything, we've done it all before. I wish they'd give us some work, some proper work to do. It's so boring. We have two lessons with Mrs Nelson, that's interesting because she talks to us about life and things like that. Nobody plays about there because it's interesting. In chemistry the boys sit around and throw things about.

Example 3

Sally: I'm repeating work, it's making me sick because I can remember doing it before and it was quite exciting then but now we're painting and washing up and everything else.

Susan: . . . ever so easy . . . (*All talking at once in agreement.*)

PW: Isn't there anything you enjoy doing?

Joanne: Art, and that's about all—for a laugh.

Example 4

John: There's nothing to do here. There's a long dinner hour, not that we mind that but us being fifth years, we can't have a room to ourself where we can talk. If you go in the cloakroom you might be suspected of stealing if something goes wrong, but if we had us own room we could go in there and talk, but we're all outside bored stiff, there's no activity to do, it really does depress you. We 'aint got nothing to do, you're just waiting for the next lesson and when it comes, you're bored stiff.

Example 5

PW: Looking back on school, what do you think you're going to remember about it most?

Paul: Boredom, of all the lessons and that. Same thing day after day. I liked primary school better, there were more things to do and I seemed to get on better there.

Example 6

Alan: When they had speech day everyone started ripping off these bits of foam under their chairs and started throwing them about. Suddenly I noticed a line of teachers at the door taking names, everyone in the hall, you know, spaced out, sort of gestapo, spaced out, standing up for the interrogation . . . 'Did you throw?' . . . 'Were you in?' . . . some people got the cane, but it was so *boring* it weren't true speech days. If you're sat there for a whole afternoon with nothing to do you do get bored, don't you?

Example 7

Simon: It's not a bad school really, you know. I don't mind it you know, but . . . coming every day doing the same old thing one day after the other, same lessons, you know, gets a bit sickening. You can't wait until the end of the week or the end of the day, you know, when you get here.

PW: Do you find the work difficult?

Simon: No, it's not difficult, it's boring. You just sit there with a whole lot of work to do.

PW: What do you do, say in English?

Simon: Wednesdays, teacher reads to you which you nearly fall off to sleep, I do anyway. You get so bored with it you know.

PW: What else do you do?

Simon: It's hard to think. I remember once I got so bored I did fall off to sleep in English. Yeah, so bored with it.

Example 8 From field notes 5 March 1975; art—periods 1 and 2, 4th form. Carol, Janice and Susan seem lost for anything to do. 'Have you any jobs sir?' The three of them shimmy idly over.

Teacher: 'How am I going to find jobs for you three for all of next term?' (Teacher sets them arranging magazines in a file, the three exchange looks of resignation.) Teacher tells me they're not interested in art. They came to him for negative reasons. He sees some of them three times a week, twice for half days. There are four more terms to go yet.

A considerable amount of 'mucking about' was mentioned in association with expressions of boredom, itself often connected with routine, ritual and regulations. Thus speech days, assemblies and other forms of ritual which the vast majority of pupils I spoke to described as 'boring', 'useless', 'meaningless', 'a waste of time', taxed their ingenuity in remaining sane. I witnessed many assemblies. On the surface they seemed rigid, militaristic, well-drilled affairs. Pupils filed in by form, were inspected for uniform as they passed through the door, and lined up in serried ranks. Teachers ordered them, squaring off rough corners, tidying up lines, filling up spaces. They stood among them at strategic points while those not on 'duty' mounted the platform. There followed, usually, a talk, a hymn, prayers, then announcements. The beginning and end were monopolized by the band. For most of the pupils I spoke to in the senior school, it was twenty minutes of standing boredom. Here are some typical reactions:

'Assemblies are a waste of time. For religious people they're OK, it's a good morning's start, but there aren't many religious people in the school. You're all in there together, it's a great temptation to kick somebody's legs and make them fall down just for a laugh, just temptation to trouble.'

'No, we don't listen in assembly, we just muck about. Sing to drown everyone else and that.'

'Useless, rubbish.'

'The boys keep tickling yer . . . All mucking about . . . boys pulling your hair and that.'

'Waste of time I reckon, 'cos while you're standing there you might as well have an extra ten minutes on your lessons. All you do is sing a song and say a prayer, and that's it, you're out again. You could do that any time, couldn't you, at home?'

Among the pupil assembly activities that I observed were the mutilating of hymn-books, whispering messages along the row, general scuffling, teasing the nearest teacher, communicating by coughs, making faces at the teachers on the stage. The hymns seemed to be quite an exciting affair. Among the competitions I witnessed were trying to be the last one to finish a verse, getting a word in in the middle of a pause (the most amusing one I heard was a cacophony of 'harks' in the pauses between the lines in 'Hark the Herald Angels Sing'), trying to drown the senior mistress, inventing new words for the hymn as you go along, mutilating your hymn-books some more.

Pupil rules: the backdrop to subversive laughter

Pupils not only make their own amusement during assemblies, they have their own sense of order determined by status among themselves. If this is disturbed by teachers, there is great annoyance.

Look, as far as I can remember, ever since the first year the 5L used to stand at the back didn't they Frankie? Back at the left hand side, so you work your way up the school and you get there and you got to move and then we get moved. (*All talk heatedly at once.*) Why should we suddenly get moved? All the other fifth-years have been back there.
PW: I don't follow.
Well you ought to be able to find your own position, walk straight up at the back but you have to be lined up, lined in half way down, form by form . . .

Similarly, if their 'laughs' are seriously curtailed by an over-zealous member of staff, they might bear him particular resentment since he is forcing them back into boredom. It is a kind of second-order annoyance. They have accepted the boredom and have invented certain ways of coping with it. These are similar to Goffman's 'secondary adjustments'— the ways the individual stands apart from the role and the self, taken for granted for him by the institutions and by which he 'makes out', 'gets by', 'plays the system' and so on.[6] The maintenance of social order in the school depends on staff not seeing, ignoring or accepting this. They are, in fact, 'hidden norms'. Behind the apparently sterile officially ordered facade, there is operating another system developed by the pupils through time which transgresses the general rules of the institution without appearing to do so. It is 'concealed deviance' from an official point of view. But, from a pupil's point of view, time, tradition, lack of detection and spiritual and physical necessity have legitimated such activity. Studies of deviance usually take an official line whether it is regarded as a qualitative activity, one that is so labelled, or one phenomenologically conceived, but pupils, commonly disregarded because they have less power, also have their notions of deviance.

The usual interpretation of rituals, that their chief function is to reinforce social order, is, of course, uni-dimensional. It assumes a passive assembly who receive the ordering and an active staff who impose it. I am saying that, despite first appearances, everybody is active but in different milieux. The pupils have their own rules. H. L. Foster has noticed this in another educational setting, namely that involving urban lower-class black children in the United States.[7] He suggests that one of the reasons why the education of such children is not working is that urban educators have been playing the game of teaching and learning by the wrong rules.[8]

The formal organizational rules of the urban teachers and administrators are not working. The rules actually running the schools are the informal rules set by the students which evolve from lower class urban black male street corner behavior and life style.

However, there was nothing in my study to suggest anything remotely like 'street corner behavior'. This was a rural area and there were no signs of any integrated behaviour as in an inner city, though there are undoubtedly class differences between pupils and teachers, and this is connected with the development of group perspectives. The in-group of course does not need laughs as much as the out-group. For the latter, therefore, there are structural connotations but their behaviour, unlike Foster's 'street corner behavior', is much more institutionally produced. It is a response to circumstances and those circumstances shape and condition the response.

How do pupil rules work during lessons? In these micro units individuals have more influence and can vary from teacher to teacher and in accordance with their own composition.[9] I think it true to say, however, that there is a pupil-institutional core norm which all new teachers discover and adjust to. Some of them never succeed and spend their time and energy in misguidedly trying to establish official rules. This infraction of pupil rules and norms can promote 'heavy' conflict, displayed in anger.

Lorraine: We 'ad a lady teacher and she picked on Angela and we all sort of went against 'er. We were shouting at her, moaning at her, telling her why was she 'itting Angela for nothing. You know she was 'itting Angela, and we just turned round, chucked our pencils all over the place, said right, we're not doing no more work, and we sat there, didn't we?
Yvonne: Yeah. We all slammed our pencils down and just sat there.

Here is another group of girls' account of the same incident:

Lisa: Some teachers say we're uncontrollable, like Miss Yates.
Others: You can't talk to her . . . No you can't . . .
Tracy to Lisa: When she 'it you, it weren't even you were it?
Lisa: No, she 'it me for nothing.
Beryl: They all started shouting at 'er and she said 'sorry'.
Lisa: She said 'I'm ever so sorry.'
Tracy: Someone said 'you didn't 'ave to 'it 'er.' She went off her rocker, so she grabbed 'old of Lisa, slapped her face and 'you'll come down to the (*senior mistress*)', got to the door and there was a riot.

This teacher told me that she never understood these girls. As a new teacher she had tried to impose an inflexible static order on her classes, 'starting as she meant to carry on' in the folk wisdom of the trade. If my theory is correct, this could be dangerous practice. It shows an ignorance of powerful sociological forces. We must distinguish between school norms, teacher-class norms, and teacher-individual norms. As pupil and school come to terms with each other, so does each teacher and class and each teacher and individuals in each class. This is why starting teachers are in such a difficult position. They don't know the school norms and are often misled by seasoned teachers instructing them in their own class and individual norms. Their initial approach, therefore, could either be firm, and possibly misplaced, or tentative, in which case, in repressive schools, the sponge-rubber behaviour of the pupils, traditionally suppressed, will naturally spring back at them, pupils taking what advantage of the negotiation they can.

Another illustration of the consequences of infraction of pupil rules came during a discussion about pupil antics I'd observed during certain lessons (such as walking over desks, swinging from beams, playing tape recorders, soft and loud, and playing 'find it' with the teacher, connecting bunsen burners to water taps and directing fine jets to the ceiling, leaving the room and returning by various routes, etc.). Invariably, they did these things just 'for a laugh', but occasionally to annoy a teacher.

'. . . say if he's taken a pack of cards off someone, say, and we're just trying to get our own back to try and annoy him—we'd do everything we could think of to annoy him.'

Much of this reaction takes the form of subversive laughter, which I discuss below.

Aided colonization: the avoidance of subversive laughter

There was every indication that in my study, at least, pupil norms and rules were taken into account. I certainly found two groups in the school, one oriented officially, the other unofficially. The latter was not distinctively anti-school.[10] The pupils in this group were more 'colonizers'.[11] Now these were in some ways encouraged in the formation of a 'culture' which in ethos is pro-school by the staff. An interesting case in illustration of this is 'the smoking game'. There is a school rule against smoking, supposedly strict, but not explicitly against the possession of cigarettes. Many in the upper school are compulsive smokers. They must have their cigarettes, so they must smoke secretly. A club formed behind the swimming-pool, but that was highly dangerous because of the presence of oil, so the area was put out of bounds. This was strictly enforced. The club reconvened behind the potting shed, another formed on the far side of the playing-fields, and these were disregarded. Clearly, it is more important to the staff that pupils should not blow themselves up than that they should not smoke. But they also realize that the smoking game is, in fact, one they cannot win, and that attempts at strict enforcement will only lead to unproductive trouble. 'There goes Michael for a smoke', said one teacher to me during a lesson. 'What can you do?'— said with a humane grin rather than a tone of despair. I witnessed another teacher having an elaborate game with the boys in one class focused on the detection of cigarettes. 'Come on Dogsbody where are they, I know you've got some?' and searching a boy's clothing amid jocular protests; finding some and confiscating them in mock triumph, only to return them with an indulgent grin at the end of the lesson. Pupils played the smoking game in my presence—teasing each other about the possession of cigarettes, threatening to light up in my presence and so forth.

'Give us a fag, scruff.'
'I don't smoke.'
'What are these then?' (*Fumbling in his pockets.*)
'Do you want a light?'

I took this to mean that I was entering into the same kind of tacit conspiracy with them as some teachers were, in recognition of their own norms and rules. Rule infraction is good substance for a laugh, especially if those associated with official rule-making implicitly join in. In this sense pupils and teachers occasionally transcend the institution and find common cause in a common humanity.

In this respect teachers as law-enforcers are acting in a similar way to E. Bittner's skid-row police.[12] They do not employ a strict interpretation of the rules, rather basing their discretion on 'a richly particularized knowledge of people and places'. They recognize that the law can be unjust. They often 'play by ear', using their own rules. We might regard this kind of teacher-pupil interaction as 'reciprocal indulgence', following N. W. Braroe's concept of reciprocal exploitation.[13] Children are refused the privilege of playing adult roles (teachers are allowed to smoke, wear jewellery, they have freedom of movement, speech, etc.), therefore children must define the self along defensible lines but in a way to permit validation of this self by teachers. Hence, for example, they smoke in secret. To some teachers, pupils are childish, irresponsible and stupid. The pupils, because they can bend the rules so easily and trick teachers, see themselves as taking the advantage. This suggests that bad feeling in a pupil might be caused more by teacher rejection of self as presented by the pupil than because of the specific instance. In other words, the many deep-felt complaints from certain pupils about being 'picked on' may not have anything to do with the actual justice of the matter but rest in the teacher's denial of the pupil's desired presentation of self. This is a delicate matter requiring keen teacher perception. Pupils offer an image of self consonant with a consensual definition of the situation supporting a social structure which includes the superordination of teachers over pupils. If this image of self is not recognized or accepted, then the consensus may fall.

School is 'not so bad', therefore, for many pupils so long as they can 'have a laugh', primarily to relieve the boredom of the official programme. The lesson for teachers would appear to be that if they cannot make the programme more interesting to these pupils, they must take into account their need for creating their own interest to enable them to get through the day.

Teacher types: laughter initiators

This, however, does raise the question, considering classroom laughs, of wide differences among them depending on the teacher. The non-examination group I studied did have a few likes—mainly de-institutionalizing activities such as community service or social studies, 'when we go on trips and that', but mostly the official programme was dead for them. They seemed to see teachers in four categories:
1 Those that keep you working.
2 Those you can laugh and joke with.
3 Those you can work and have a laugh with.
4 Those that just don't bother.
Those in category 3, according to my thesis, would appear to be showing most sociological awareness. In Bittner's terms they are using their knowledge of the pupils to mediate the school policy. Those in category 1 are seeking to impose it more literally. The difference is brought out in the following conversation.

Jane: Sometimes you can hear him shouting in the other room. He won't laugh, you see, they try to get him to laugh, they do these stupid things and they just want . . . If he'd laugh they'd be allright, he won't, you see.
Anne: Oh yeah, they'd do anything to try to make him laugh. He puts them in the report book and everything. They don't care.
Deirdre: Every lesson somebody is going down for it.
Jane: Yeah.
Deirdre: He put one girl in twice in one day. They do it on purpose. If he was to be more friendly with them like Mr Lennox is, 'cos he'll have a laugh with you.
Jane: You see, he won't smile and have a laugh with you like Mr Lennox will.
Deirdre: 'Cos we can have a joke with him, can't we?
Jane: Yeah, and we do work as well, but in there they play about and don't do any work.

Here the 'authoritarian' teacher intent solely on 'working' gets his come-uppance directly. A more 'successful' (in his own terms) authoritarian teacher usually succeeds in displacing it towards the category 2 type teacher. Let us examine this more closely. The teacher whom you can both work and laugh with is a respected person, who knows his job, can keep control, teaches them something sometimes, but above all retains his human qualities in the classroom. His perception of teacher role does not require of him any different behaviour pattern than that of human being role. He has no problems of role distance and correctly perceives the pupils' desired presentation of self through the constraining and dehumanizing institutionalized morass.

The authoritarian teacher frequently adopts a different role from choice.

Kathleen: What about when we 'ad Mr Bullet? He made us stand up straight when we walked in the classroom.
Deirdre: Like being in the army that was.
Kathleen: He made us march out, if anyone spoke, he made us write about three essays out.
Sally: There was a different side to him though 'cos me and Tracy used to go in his room at break times—he was ever so nice—didn't have to march in then, just sit on desks and chat to him, he was ever so nice.

This reminds us, as T. Burns noted, of the discreteness of status positions and the schizophrenic nature of our society.[14] I also perceived a marked change in some teachers between classroom and staffroom or between on-duty and off-duty. This suggests that many teachers' classroom attitudes are open to change. However, such is the nature of secondary school teaching today that control is valued above transmission. In other words, the authoritarian teacher enjoys high esteem because of his ability to perform the custodial function, while others struggle in varying degrees. This is usually taken to be because of either their own deficiencies or the evil and difficult nature of the children. No doubt some teachers have more 'trouble' than others. It would be foolish to deny that they affected the situation and this would be particularly true of 'weak' or 'wet' teachers. But it is part of the thesis of this paper that these difficulties, which largely take the form of the pupils 'having laughs', originate from the boredom they experience from the total institution. The authoritarian stamps out 'side involvements' and 'secondary adjustments'. There are no laughs in his lessons. If they are a bore, the students would need to take and make more elsewhere.

Institutionalized laughter II: subversive laughter

Thus, having a laugh can come to assume a political nature. Reaction against authority can be stirred by the authoritarian teacher, possibly in reaction to a laugh against boredom, and invariably fulfilled on the weak. When pupils get at the teacher directly, by for example putting pins on his chair, making strange noises, sitting on whoopee cushions, letting off stink bombs, ventriloquizing nicknames and playing other sorts of games deliberately to annoy, they are seizing opportunities to get at the stereotypical teacher rather than that teacher personally. Certainly they will exploit what personality idiosyncrasies they can, but

they are subsidiary to the major sociological factor.

There are several forms of subversive laughter. One of the most common is 'subversive ironies'.[15] Among schoolchildren, one form of this is name-calling. Attaching nicknames to staff in depiction of character forms a status bridge which by displacing it in humour belittles it. Thus the headmaster and his deputy might be known as 'Dick Dastardly' and 'Side-kick' and the senior mistress as 'Nellie' or 'Flossie'.

Unfortunate facial characteristics or behavioural habits or postures are seized on with alacrity and teachers are rapidly transformed from Mr or Miss So-and-So or 'Sir' to 'Deputy Dawg', 'Captain Pugwash', 'Cheetah', 'Fruitie', 'Beefy', etc. From this it is a short step to having them engage in all sorts of unlikely activity—usually illicit sexual activity. Numerous jingles, poems and anecdotes decorate the pupils' 'quarters'. Interestingly, sexual prowess and parts seem to conform to the staff hierarchy. Much of this is closed humour, that is to say it is used only within, from one's own culture or to oneself, for the purposes of making the enemy appear ludicrous and boosting one's own status and self-esteem. Many behind-the-hand sniggers occur in coactive teaching situations. There is a more open technique which has the effect of making the enemy appear ludicrous in his own eyes as well as everybody else's. This would include shouting out the teacher's nickname, firing missiles at him and arranging booby-traps.

The authoritarian teacher, jealous of his status and sensitive to assaults on it, often tries to detect or anticipate subversive ironies. However, they are not easily detectable and he may pick on a form of natural everyday laughter by mistake.

Wendy: Remember when we were discussing . . .
All: Oh yeah! (*Much laughter.*)
Sharon: That was in the third year, he went off his rocker at us didn't he?
Wendy: What was it, I know we were talking about Christmas pudding and my mum said me Nan's knickers caught fire (*great laughter*).
Sharon: I remember, Wendy . . . it weren't very . . .
Wendy: We were both sat on the front desk chatting away . . .
Sharon: He went barmy, I told him he shouldn't be really listening (*general laughter*).

Here, a teacher has invaded a private area and earned a rebuke accompanied by laughter which could have done nothing for his self-esteem.

Another form is 'confrontational laughter'. On one occasion, one girl, unaware of the senior mistress's presence, shouted for the television set to be turned up because 'I can't 'ear the bloody thing.' This immediate confrontation of cultures from which the senior mistress felt obliged to retreat produced much laughter, as did another occasion when a girl in anger told the senior mistress to 'get stuffed'. Both these incidents show the pupils' culture impacting against the teachers' culture to the detriment of the latter. It also illustrates the important role of vulgar language, which here helps the pupils to sustain their own definition of the situation and blocks a construction of the 'official' one. Such occasions provide superb and dynamic material for laughs in the countless retelling of the incidents which will take place. The relating of them to me was yet another one of these occasions for laughter.

Subversive ironies in number could be regarded as 'gallows humour', a response to an atmosphere of tension and unease wherein people seek an intellectual and emotional escape from disturbing realities.[16] Gallows humour can become a means of social control in boosting the morale of the victim and at the same time undermining that of the oppressors.

There is another form of subversive laughter which I would call 'symbolic rebellion'. Some people make a career of open resistance, in their terms 'playing teachers up'. As above with gallows humour, success depends on response.

George: Jones 'e isn't worth playing up because he don't do nothing.
Alan: He don't like me, he picks on me. The other day in activities we were all sitting around the table playing dominoes and he came over and clouted me. The others were doing the same.
George: Jones just goes a bit red, it's not worth the effort of playing 'im up unless you're going to get a response. Mr Cook goes livid.
PW: Do you plan what to do in advance?
Pete: We don't often plan. We sometimes go in late, that always gets their goat. Mr Diamond gets the chin, he knows all these big words, he called George 'a churl'. We just laugh at him.

Symbolic rebellion can also take the form of destruction of school property. Thus two glasshouses, which it had taken one class of non-examination boys a full term to repair and make functional, were destroyed by the same boys in the space of five minutes, only a few weeks after completion of the task. Another example that occurred during my stay was the blazer-ripping incident. Of all the symbols of school authority and their own oppression none is more detested by the pupils, generally speaking, than school uniform. It is precisely because it is so closely associated with school norms and teacher authority that enforcement and conformity is pursued with vigour. After years of inspections and remonstrations about their clothing a tradition had developed among boys who were leaving that others would tear his blazer literally to shreds. During my stay one boy's blazer was duly ripped early during his last week. The detection, prosecution and punishment of the offenders was executed with exceptional vigour by the teachers. I took this as evidence of the extent to which teachers were sensitive to the symbolic assault on their authority. To the pupils, the teachers' case seemed unreasonable, unfair and altogether out of proportion to the event.

'What's one blazer, it wasn't all that good anyway.'

'They'd been writing all over blazers, writing their names on them, it's a traditional activity at the end of yer school days.'

'They all get ripped on the last day anyway. You can't do much about it. Last day they all come round and cut chunks out of your hair, tie up your hair, half cut up your blazer and then messing about all the way home, sticking scarves out of the window and things like that, but they can't do much about that because you've left.'

Once leavers are clear of the school they can do what they like, but this blazer-ripping, occurring at the beginning of the week in which pupils left, impinged too much on school time and became, therefore, in the teachers' view, not only a violation of school rules and norms and their authority but also an over-stepping of the bounds of discretion most of them usually employed. Again, a situation redolent with laughter turned into heavy conflict, characterized by anger.

Conclusion

'Having a laugh' is not always enjoyable by any means. As a cure for painful experiences it is only partly efficacious. When it comes to leaving school, many, particularly the girls, may feel sad, even cry, forgetting the bad times, remembering the laughs, even summoning affection for those who have hurt them the most; possibly because the treatment led to particularly memorable laughter-making devices. Thus might authoritarian teachers be given more cause for self-congratulation. But, in the existential situation of the classroom, the laughter might have arisen from constraining situations in response to boredom or in reaction to oppressive authority. The question of accounting for the boredom in its total and blanketing effect on some pupils is a much broader one involving structural and historical factors. There are also questions unanswered about the nature of the laughter and its incidence among the pupils. For example, to what extent is it a response or reaction to the dominant culture, and/or how far is it an expression of their own culture? These are matters requiring further investigation. Neither must psychological aspects be forgotten: for example, laughter as tension release.

What I have endeavoured to show is that pupils have their own norms, rules and values and that their school lives are well structured by them in ways not immediately apparent and not always based on official criteria. In their lives, laughter has a central place either as a natural product or as a life-saving response to the exigencies of the institution—boredom, ritual, routine, regulations, oppressive authority. Inasmuch as the latter predominate in a school, the laughter will not be consensual, contributing to control, but obstructive, subversive and rebellious, contributing to conflict. Despite the severe constraints teachers work under, it is surely not beyond their power to harness at least some of this ingenuity, creativity, brilliance and joie de vivre as a contribution to, rather than an antidote to, schooling.

Notes

1 *Previous work on laughter.* Sociological work on humour and laughter might be seen as leaning towards either of two models, conflict or control.[17] Among the latter, which focus on the way laughter mellows the abrasive qualities of institutions, joking relationships between teachers and pupils have been explored by Walker, Goodson and Adelman.[18] They show that joking is heavily situated; that is, it might not be appreciated by an outsider unfamiliar with the history and general context of the relationships under observation. This in itself suggests there might be more humour in schools than meets the eye. Using conversations with teachers as leads and as illustrations, Walker and his colleagues suggest various ways in which joking might facilitate the teacher's task; mainly it has to do with establishing personal relationships with students, but jokes can also 'mark areas of vulnerability in the frame'.[19] However, as observers, they were mostly impressed by the way 'jokes short circuit social situations in a way that allows them to become personal and unique. Joking is one way in which social structures are made human.' Fifty years ago, D. Hayworth was advancing a theory that laughter was originally a vocal sign to other members of the group that they might relax with safety.[20] A similar point is made by J. Emerson with regard to hospitals, when she talks of joking being the negotiation of a private agreement to suspend a general guideline of the institutional setting, bargaining to make unofficial arrangements about taboo topics.[21] Other features of bureaucratization have been seen to be assailed by humour. R. L. Coser, for example, found that 'negative democratization' encourages a colleague-type of relationship between nurses and doctors rather than a service one—'hence the banter and joking which help further to cancel out status differences and the relative frequency of interaction.'[22] Anthropologists have noted how among primitive societies joking seems to maintain equilibrium among persons and groups who, because of their relative positions and social ties, might otherwise feel antagonism toward each other and threaten the disruption of the society.[23] This function is claimed to have been identified in a London department store.[24] On the conflict side, Coser elsewhere suggests three main social functions of laughter among hospital inmates—the alleviation of boredom, elevation of status and the counter-action of ritual and routinization with expression of individuality.[25] Freud remarked that 'what is fine about humour is the ego's victorious assertion of its own invulnerability'.[26] A. J. Obrdlik made a similar point on a nation-wide scale in his study of 'gallows humour', which he claims arises in difficult and dangerous situations and which might be taken as an index of strength or morale on the part of oppressed peoples; it could have a disintegrating effect on those toward whom it is directed.[27] In these situations, the humourist triumphs over his own weakness and gains added strength from a collective nature of the victory.

It can strengthen boundaries and demarcate separate cultures. The relevance of such work to schools will immediately register with anyone familiar with them.

2 P. E. Woods, 'Pupils' views of school', *Educational Review*, 28 (2), 1976.

3 I talked with nearly all the pupils (over 300) in the 3rd, 4th and 5th years at least once, mostly twice, and sometimes three times in the course of my involvement with the school. This does not include the innumerable informal chats held with them, nor the observations which informed and reinforced the discussions.

4 E. Goffman, *Behavior in Public Places*, Collier-Macmillan, 1963.

5 *Encounters*, Bobbs-Merrell, 1961; Penguin, 1972; see also R. A. Stebbins, 'The meaning of disorderly behaviour: teacher definitions of a classroom situation', *Sociology of Education*, 44, spring 1970.

6 E. Goffman, *Asylums*, Chicago, Anchor Books, 1961; Penguin, 1968.

7 *Ribbin', Jivin', and Playin' the Dozens*, Cambridge, Mass., Ballinger, 1974.

8 ibid., p. 179.

9 Viv Furlong has discussed the changes in general behaviour within one class both among different teachers and according to the composition of the class; see 'Anancy goes to school: a case study of pupils' knowledge of their teachers', in P. E. Woods and M. Hammersley, eds, *School Experience*, Croom Helm (forthcoming).

10 As some groups were purported to be in D. H. Hargreaves, *Social Relations in a Secondary School*, Routledge & Kegan Paul, 1967 and in C. Lacey, *Hightown Grammar*, Manchester University Press, 1970.

11 Goffman, *Asylums*.

12 'The police on Skid Row: a study of peace-keeping', *American Sociological Review*, 32 (5), October 1967, pp. 699–715.

13 'Reciprocal exploitation in an Indian-white community', in H. A. Farberman and E. Goode, eds, *Social Reality*, Englewood Cliffs, Prentice-Hall, 1973.

14 'Friends, enemies and the polite fiction', *American Sociological Review*, 18, 1953, pp. 654–62.

15 Goffman, *Asylums*.

16 A. J. Obrdlik, 'Gallows humor: a sociological phenomenon', *American Journal of Sociology*, 47, 1942, pp. 709–16.

17 M. L. Barron, 'A content analysis of intergroup humor', *American Sociological Review*, 15, 1950, pp. 88–94; J. H. Burma, 'Humor as a technique in race conflict', *American Sociological Review*, 2, 1946, pp. 710–15; R. M. Stephenson, 'Conflict and control functions of humor', *American Journal of Sociology*, 56, 1951, pp. 569–74.

18 R. Walker, I. Goodson and C. Adelman, 'Teaching That's a Joke', paper presented at the Open University conference on 'The Experience of Schooling', Cranfield, 1975.

19 B. Bernstein, 'On the classification and framing of educational knowledge', in E. Hopper, ed., *Readings in the Theory of Educational Systems*, Hutchinson, 1971.
20 'The origin and function of laughter', *Psychological Review*, 36, 1928, pp. 367–84.
21 'Negotiating the serious impact of humour', *Sociometry*, 32, 1969, pp. 169–81.
22 'Authority and decision-making in a hospital; a comparative analysis', *American Sociological Review*, 23, 1958, pp. 56–63.
23 A. R. Radcliffe-Brown, *Structure and Function in Primitive Society*, Cohen & West, 1952.
24 P. Bradney, 'The joking relationship in industry', *Human Relations*, 10, 1957.
25 'Some social functions of laughter', *Human Relations*, 12, 1959.
26 'Humour', in *Collected Papers*, Hogarth Press, 1950, pp. 215–21.
27 op. cit.

22 The class significance of school counter-culture[1]

Paul Willis

This new type of school . . . is destined not merely to perpetuate social differences but to crystallize them in Chinese complexities. (Antonio Gramsci on 'democratic' educational reforms in Italy during the early twenties[2])

The existence of anti-school cultures in schools with a working-class catchment area has been widely commented upon.[3] The raising of the school-leaving age has further dramatized and exposed this culture, often in the form of a 'new' crisis: disruption in the classroom. Teachers' unions are calling more and more vehemently for tougher action against 'violence' in the classroom, and for special provision for the 'unruly' minority. The 'reluctant fifth', difficult 'RSLA classes' and young, 'always in tears' (usually female) teachers, have become part of staffroom folklore.

The welter of comment and response, has, however, served to conceal certain crucial features of this culture: the profound significance it has for processes of job selection, and its relation to the wider working-class culture. In what follows I want to draw attention to these omissions. Concretely I want to make two suggestions. (1) Counter-school culture is part of the wider working-class culture of a region and ultimately of the nation, and, in particular, runs parallel to what we might call shop-floor culture. (2) The located anti-school culture provides powerful informal criteria and binding experiential processes which lead working-class lads to make the 'voluntary' choice to enter the factory, and so to help to reproduce both the existing class structure of employment and the 'culture of the shop floor' as a segment of the overarching working-class culture. My argument is, then, that the stage of affiliation with the counter-school

group carries much more significance than is usually acknowledged. I therefore go on to examine, in the latter part of this chapter, when, how and why this process occurs. I will conclude with some comments on the meaning and status of this general class culture, of which the school and factory variants are part.

Studies of the transition from school to work, which might have made the connection between the school social system and the world of work, have simply been content to register a failure of the agencies and their rational policies—derived basically from middle-class preconceptions. The matrix of inappropriate middle-class logic—self-development, self-knowledge, matching of lifestyle/career profile—overlying the located, informal cultural processes in the institutional practice of the Youth Employment Service and the relentlessly descriptive set of the main writings on the 'transition',[4] have effectively obscured the essential connectedness of working-class experience for the young male proceeding from school to work. Studies of the school[5] have been absorbed by the cultural divisions in the school itself, and have, implicitly at any rate, isolated the school from its surrounding networks. Consequently they have failed to address the central question of the determinancy of counter-school culture—is it the institution or the class context, or what mixture of both, which leads to the formation of this culture? In general the omission of the context in which the school operates would seem to imply that the institution be given primacy in the determination of the social landscape of the school.

My own research suggests that there is a direct relationship between the main features of working-class culture, as it is expressed in shop-floor culture, and school counter-culture. Both share broadly the same determinants: the common impulse is to develop strategies for dealing with boredom, blocked opportunities, alienation and lack of control. Of course the particular organization of each located culture has its

Source: article commissioned for this volume. Paul Willis is attached to the Centre for Contemporary Cultural Studies, University of Birmingham.

own history and specificity, and worked-up institutional forms. The institution of the school, for instance, determines a particular uneven pattern of extension and suppression of common working-class themes. In one way a more protected environment than the shop floor, and without the hard logic and discipline of material production, the school is nevertheless a more directly face-to-face repressive agency in other ways. This encourages an emphasis on certain obvious forms of resistance specific to the school. In one sense this is simply a question of inverting the given rules—hence the terrain of school counter-culture: smoking, proscribed dress, truancy, cheek in class, vandalism and theft.

At any rate, the main cultural and organizational aspects of shop-floor culture (at least in the Midlands industrial conurbation where I did my research), and for the moment ignoring the range of historically and occupationally specific variants, bear a striking similarity to the main features of school counter-culture. I concentrate here mainly on shop-floor culture, since the other chapters of this volume deal mainly with aspects of school culture.

The really central point about the working-class culture of the shop floor is that, despite harsh conditions and external direction, people do look for meaning and impose frameworks. They exercise their abilities and seek enjoyment in activity, even where most controlled by others. They do, paradoxically, thread through the dead experience of work a living culture which is far from a simple reflex of defeat. This is the same fundamental taking hold of an alienating situation as one finds in counter-school culture and its attempt to weave a tapestry of interest and diversion through the dry institutional text. These cultures are not simply foam paddings, rubber layers between human and unpleasantness. They are appropriations in their own right, exercises of skill, motions, activities applied towards particular ends.

More specifically, the central, locating theme of shop-floor culture—a form of masculine chauvinism arising from the raw experience of production—is reflected in the independence and toughness found in school counter-cultures. Here is a foundry-man talking at home about his work. In an inarticulate way, but for that perhaps all the more convincingly, he attests that elemental, essentially masculine, self-esteem in the doing of a hard job well—and to be known for it.

I work in a foundry .. you know drop forging ... do you know anything about it .. no .... well you have the factory know the factory down in Bethnall Street with the noise ... you can hear it in the street ... I work there on the big hammer ... it's a six-tonner. I've worked there 24 years now. It's bloody noisy, but I've got used to it now .. and its hot ... ... I don't get bored .. there's always new lines coming and you have to work out the best way of doing it .. You have

to keep going .... and it's heavy work, the managers couldn't do it, there's not many strong enough to keep lifting the metal ... I earn 80, 90 pounds a week, and that's not bad is it? ... it ain't easy like .. you can definitely say that I earn every penny of it ... you have to keep it up you know. And the managing director, I'd say 'hello' to him you know, and the progress manager .... they'll come around and I'll go .. 'all right' (thumbs up) ... and they know you, you know .... a group standing there watching you .... working .. I like that .... there's something there ... watching *you* like .. working .... like that .. you have to keep going to get enough out.

Here is Joey, this man's son, in his last year at school, and right at the heart of the counter-culture:

That's it, we've developed certain ways of talking, certain ways of acting and we developed disregards for Pakis, Jamaicans and all different .., for all the scrubs and the fucking ear—'oles and all that (..) There's no chivalry or nothing, none of this cobblers you know, it's just .. if you'm gonna fight, it's savage fighting anyway, so you might as well go all the way and win it completely by having someone else help ya or by winning the dirtiest methods you can think of like poking his eyes out or biting his ear and things like this.

There's a clear continuity of attitudes here, and we must not think that this distinctive complex of chauvinism, toughness and machismo is anachronistic or bound to die away as the pattern of industrial work changes. Rough, unpleasant, demanding jobs *do* still exist in considerable numbers. A whole range of jobs—from building work, to furnace work to deep sea fishing—still involve a primitive confrontation with exacting physical tasks. The basic attitudes and values developed in such jobs are still very important in general working-class culture, and particularly the culture of the shop floor; this importance is vastly out of proportion to the number of people involved in such heavy work. Even in so-called light industries, or in highly mechanized factories where the awkwardness of the physical task has long since been reduced, the metaphoric figures of strength, masculinity and reputation still move beneath the more varied and richer, visible forms of work-place culture. Despite, even, the increasing numbers of women employed, the most fundamental ethos of the factory is profoundly masculine.

The other main, and this time emergent, theme of shop-floor culture—at least in the manufacturing industries of the Midlands—is the massive attempt to gain a form of control of the work process. 'Systematic soldiering' and 'gold bricking' have been observed from the particular perspective of management from F. W. Taylor[6] onwards, but there is evidence now of a much more concerted—though still informal—attempt to gain control. It does happen, now, sometimes, that the men themselves actually run production. Again this is effectively mirrored for us by working-class kids' attempts, with the resources of their counter-culture, to take control of classes, insert their own unofficial timetables, and control their own routines and life spaces.

> *Joey*: (. .) of a Monday afternoon, we'd have nothing right? Nothing hardly relating to school work, Tuesday afternoon we have swimming and they stick you in a classroom for the rest of the afternoon, Wednesday afternoon you have games and there's only Thursday and Friday afternoon that you work, if you call that work. The last lesson Friday afternoon we used to go and doss, half of us wagged out o' lessons and the other half go into the classroom, sit down and just go to sleep, and the rest of us could join a class where all our mates are.
> *Will*: (. .) What we been doing, playing cards in this room 'cos we can lock the door.
> *PW*: Which room's this now?
> *Will*: Resources Centre, where we're making the frames (*a new stage for the deputy head*), s'posed to be.
> *PW*: Oh! You're still making the frames?
> *Will*: We should have had it finished, we just lie there on top of the frame, playing cards, or trying to get to sleep.
> *PW*: What's the last time you've done some writing?
> *Will*: When we done some writing?
> *Fuzz*: Oh ah, last time was in careers, 'cos I writ 'yes' on a piece of paper, that broke me heart.
> *PW*: Why did it break your heart?
> *Fuzz*: I mean to write, 'cos I was going to try and go through the term without writing anything. 'Cos since we've cum back, I ain't dun nothing. (*It was half-way through term.*)

Put this against the following account from the father of a boy who was in the same friendship group as the boys talking above. He is a factory hand on a track producing car engines, talking at his home.

> Actually the foreman, the gaffer, don't run the place, the men run the place. See, I mean you get one of the chaps says, 'Allright, you'm on so and so today.' You can't argue with him. The gaffer don't give you the job, the men on the track give you the job, they swop each other about, tek it in turns. Ah, but I mean the job's done. If the gaffer had gid you the job you would . . . They tried to do it, one morning, gid a chap a job you know, but he'd been on it, you know, I think he'd been on all week, and they just downed tools. (. . . .) There's four hard jobs on the track and there's dozens that's , . . you know, a child of five could do it, quite honestly, but everybody has their turn. That's organized by the men.

Of course there is the obvious difference that the school informal organization is devoted to doing nothing, while in the factory culture, at least, 'the job's done'. But the degree of opposition to official authority *in each case* should not be minimized, and production managers in such shops were quite as worried as deputy heads about 'what things were coming to'. Furthermore, both these attempts at control rest on the basic and distinctive unit of the informal group. This is the fundamental unit of resistance in both cultures, which locates and makes possible all its other elements. It is the zone where 'creative' attempts to develop and extend an informal culture are made, and where strategies for resting control of symbolic and real space from official authority are generated and disseminated. It is the massive presence of this informal organization which most decisively marks off shop-floor culture from middle-class cultures of work, and the 'lads'' school culture from that of the 'ear-'oles' (the name used by the 'lads' of my research to designate those who conformed to the school's official culture).

The solidarity, and sense of being 'in the group', is the basis for the final major characteristic of shop-floor culture that I want to describe here. This is the distinctive form of language, and the highly developed humour of the shop floor. Up to half the verbal exchanges are not serious or about work activities. They are jokes, or 'piss-takes', or 'kiddings' or 'wind-ups'. There is a real skill in being able to use this language with fluency: to identify the points where you are being 'kidded' and to have appropriate response in order to avoid further baiting.

This badinage is necessarily difficult to record on tape or represent, but the highly distinctive ambience it gives to shop floor exchanges is widely recognized by those involved, and to some extent re-created in their accounts of it. This is a foundry-worker talking at home about the atmosphere in his shop:

> Oh, there's all sorts, millions of them (*jokes*). 'Want to hear what he said about you', and he never said a thing, you know. Course you know the language, at the work like. 'What you been saying, about me'; 'I said nothing', 'Oh you're a bloody liar', and all this.

Associated with this concrete and expressive verbal humour is a developed physical humour; essentially the practical joke. These jokes are vigorous, sharp, sometimes cruel, and often hinge on prime tenets of the culture such as disruption of production or subversion of the bosses' authority and status. Here is the same man:

> They er'm play jokes on you, blokes knocking the clamps off the boxes, they put paste on the bottom of his hammer you know soft little thing, puts his hammer down, picks it up, gets a handful of paste, you know, all this. So he comes up and gets a syringe and throws it in the big bucket of

paste, and it's about that deep, and it goes right to the bottom, you have to put your hand in and get it out (. . . .) This is a filthy trick, but they do it. (. .) They asked, the gaffers asked—to make the tea. Well it's fifteen years he's been there and they say 'go and make the teas'. He gus up the toilet, he wets in the tea pot, then makes the tea. I mean, you know, this is the truth this is you know. He says, you know, 'I'll piss in it if I mek it, if they've asked me to mek it.' (. . . .) so he goes up, wees in the pot, then he puts the tea bag, then he puts the hot water in. (. . . .)—was bad the next morning, one of the gaffers, 'My stomach isn't half upset this morning.' He told them after and they called him for everything, 'you ain't makin' our tea no more,' he says. 'I know I ain't not now.'

This atmosphere of rough humour and horseplay is instantly recognizable among the 'lads' in working-class schools, and obviously missing from the more hesitant 'polite' exchanges amongst the 'ear-'oles'. The ethnography of school cultures is full of similar —virtually interchangeable—incidents. There is the same felt desire to brighten grey prospects with a 'larf'. Certainly for the group of 'lads' who were the focus of my 'main' case study, reliance on the group, verbal humour and physical trickery, was the continuous stuff of their informal relations.

Joey: You know you have to come to school today, if you're feeling bad, your mate'll soon cheer yer up like, 'cos you couldn't go without ten minutes in this school, without having a laugh at something or other.
PW: Are your mates a really big important thing at school now?
—Yeah
—Yeah
—Yeah
Joey: They're about the best thing actually.
Spanksey: You like to come to school, just to skive, 'cos you get bored at home. You'd rather come here and sit in the Youth Wing or summat.
Joey: (. .) You'm always looking out on somebody (*when skiving*) and you've always got something to talk about, . . something.
PW: So what stops you being bored?
Joey: Talking, we could talk for ever, when we get together, it's talk, talk, talk.

There is no space to pursue the point any further, but in more detailed ways, from theft, vandalism and sabotage to girlie books under the tool-bench or desk, it is apparent that shop-floor culture and school oppositional culture have a great deal in common.

The parallelism of these cultures suggests, of course, that they should both be thought of as aspects of the larger working-class culture, though a fuller account would obviously further differentiate regional, occupational and institutional variations. The fundamental point here is to stress that anti-school culture should be seen in the context of this larger pattern, rather than in simple institutional terms. This wider connection has important and unexamined implications for the school's management of the 'disruptive' minority. Put at its most obvious, strategies conceived at the institutional level will not overcome problems arising from a profound class-cultural level. In fact the concerned teacher may be effectively boxed in, since the undoubted level of institutional determinancy— which I am not denying—may well block those strategies which do take into account the wider working-class culture. I mean that the teacher who tries to use working-class themes or styles may be rejected because he's a teacher: 'there's nothing worse than a teacher trying to be too friendly', and that a teacher who innovates organizationally—destreaming, mixed ability groupings, etc.—can never prevent the emergence of oppositional working-class themes *in one form or another*. It is the peculiarly intractable nature of this double determinacy which makes this form of working-class culture present itself as a 'crisis'. It shows up in high relief some of the unintended consequences and contradictions inherent in the state's ever-expanding attempts to make inroads into located working-class culture.

I do not wish, here, to go into the complex questions concerning what makes working-class culture—in all its variety and sectionalism—what it is. Nor—having, I hope, established the similarity between shop-floor and anti-school culture—do I want to claim any simple causation between them. My aims are more limited; my immediate text is that of job choice among working-class lads. What I want to argue about the parallelism I have described is that it accomplishes—in practice—a continuity between the two cultures, between work and school, in terms of the experiential passage of the working-class individual and his group. Processes within the school culture generate unofficial and deeply influential criteria which guide kids to similar, though expanded, situations: i.e. the shop floor. These unofficial criteria make a much more compelling case for particular job choices than does any amount of formal guidance.

Before looking at these located criteria, though, let us look at the manner in which the counter-school culture blocks, or reinterprets, the formal information concerning work with which it is saturated. All official communications about careers and work are importantly filtered through the group. By and large what might be termed as the *denoted*[7] messages from teachers and careers officers are most heavily filtered. This is the manifest content of particular communications concerning either the practical details of specific jobs or general principles about the best form of approach to work. Unless an individual has already decided to do a certain specific job, information about it is simply not taken in. It is certainly not true that new information is fed into a rational grid system which matches job profile with ability profile, or lifestyle/with/ job/ambition profile. If things are remembered, they are picked up by some highly selective living principle of the counter-cultural school group. The following discussion is on careers films:

Perc: I wonder why there's never kids like us in films, see what their attitude is to it? What they'm like and what we'm like.
PW: Well, what sort of kids are they in the films?
Fuzz: All ear-'oles.
Perc: All goody-goodies.
Will: No, you can tell they've been told what to say. They'm probably at some acting school or summat y'know and the opportunity to do this job—film careers for other kids—and you gotta say this, 'Wait for your cue', 'Wait till he's finished his lines.'

Information that is given to the kids concerning what might be thought of as an ideology of getting a job, and of getting on in a job, is either blocked, interpreted into unrecognizable forms or simply inverted. The following conversation is from a discussion on careers sessions:

Spanksey: After a bit you tek no notice of him, he sez the same thing over and over again, you know what I mean?
Joey: We're always too busy fucking picking your nose, or flicking paper, we just don't listen to him.
PW: How about the speaker who came from the College of Education?
Fred: They try to put you off work . . Joey, he says to him, 'Do you want to be a painter and decorator, painting a wall, you can get any silly cunt to paint a wall', or 'Do you want to do the decorative pieces, sign writing.'
Spanksey: Got to be someone in society who slops on a wall . . . I wanted to get up and say to him, 'There's got to be some silly cunt who slops on a wall.'

In terms of actual 'job choice', it is the 'lads'' culture and not the official careers material which provides the most located and deeply influential guides for the future. For the individual's affiliation with the non-conformist group carries with it a whole range of changes in his attitudes and perspectives and these changes also supply over time a more or less consistent view of what sorts of people he wants to end up working with, and what sort of situation is going to allow the fullest expression for his developing cultural skills. The located 'lads'' culture supplies a set of 'unofficial' criteria by which to judge not individual jobs or the intrinsic joys of particular kinds of work—indeed it is already assumed that all work is more or less hard and unrewarding—but generally *what kind* of working situation is going to be most relevant to the individual. It will have to be work where he can be open about his desires, his sexual feelings, his liking for 'booze' and his aim to 'skive off' as much as is reasonably possible. It will have to be a place where

people can be trusted and will not 'creep off' to tell the boss about 'foreigners' or 'nicking stuff'—precisely where there were the fewest 'ear-'oles'. Indeed it would have to be work where there was a boss, a 'them and us', which always carried with it the danger of treacherous intermediaries. The experience of the division 'ear-'ole'/'lads' in school is one of the most basic preparations for the still ubiquitous feeling in the working class proper that there is a 'them' and an 'us'. The 'us' is felt to be relatively weaker in power terms, but also somehow more approachable, social, and, in the end, more human. One of the really crucial things about the 'us' which the 'lads' wanted to be part of was that they were in work where the self could be separated from the work task, and value given to people for things other than their work performance—the celebration of those independent qualities which precisely the 'ear-'oles' did not have. Generally, the future work situation would have to be one where people were not 'cissies' and could handle themselves, where 'pen-pushing' is looked down on in favour of really 'doing things'. It would have to be a situation where you could speak up for yourself, and where you would not be expected to be subservient. The particular job would have to pay good money fairly quickly and offer the possibility of 'fiddles' and 'perks' to support already acquired smoking and drinking habits. Work would have to be a place, most basically, where people were 'all right' and with whom a general culture identity could be shared. It is this human face of work, much more than its intrinsic or technical nature, which confronts the individual as the crucial dimension of his future. In the end it is recognized that it is specifically the cultural diversion that makes any job bearable. Talking about the imminent prospect of work:

Will: I'm just dreading the first day like. Y'know, who to pal up with, an er'm, who's the ear-'oles, who'll tell the gaffer.
Joey: (. .) you can always mek it enjoyable. It's only you what makes a job unpleasant, . . I mean if you're cleaning sewers out, you can have your moments like. Not every job's enjoyable, I should think. Nobody's got a job they like unless they're a comedian or something, but er'm . . , no job's enjoyable 'cos of the fact that you've got to get up of a morning and go out when you could stop in bed. I think every job's got, has a degree of unpleasantness, but it's up to you to mek . . to push that unpleasantness aside and mek it as good and as pleasant as possible.

The typical division in school between the 'lads' and the 'ear-'oles' also has a profound influence on thoughts about work. It is also a division between different kinds of future, different kinds of gratification and different kinds of job that are relevant to these things. These differences, moreover, are not random or unconnected. On the one hand they arise systematically from intra-*school* group oppositions and, on the other, they relate to quite distinct job groupings in the *post-school* situation. The 'ear-'oles'/'boys' division becomes the skilled/unskilled and white-collar/blue-collar division. The 'lads' themselves could transpose the divisions of the internal cultural landscape of the school on to the future, and on to the world of work outside, with considerable clarity. Talking about 'ear-'oles':

Joey: I think they're (*the 'ear-'oles'*) the ones that have got the proper view of life, they're the ones that abide by the rules. They're the civil servant types, they'll have 'ouses and everything before us (. . .) They'll be the toffs, I'll say they'll be the civil servants, toffs, and we'll be the brickies and things like that.
Spanksey: I think that we . ., more or less, we're the ones that do the hard grafting but not them, they'll be the office workers. (. . .) I ain't got no ambitions, I doe wanna have . . I just want to have a nice wage, that 'ud just see me through.

Not only does the 'lads'' culture and its opposition to conformism provide criteria for the kind of job which is relevant to them, it also possesses internal mechanisms—the 'kidding', the 'piss-take', the 'larf'—to enforce a certain view of appropriate work. In a discussion on what jobs they wanted:

Eddie: I wanna be a jeweller.
PW: A what?
/Laughter/
Eddie: A jeweller.
PW: I dunno, what's the joke. What's funny about a jeweller.
/Laughter/
—he's a cunt.
—he's a piss-taker.
—'im, he, he'd nick half of the jewels he would.
Spike: He wants to be a diamond-setter in six months.
Derek: He'd put one in a ring and six in his pocket.
PW: Do you know anything about jewellery?
Eddie: No.
/Laughter/

Altogether, in relation to the basic cultural ground-shift which is occurring, and the development of a comprehensive alternative view of what is expected from life, *particular* job choice does not matter too much to the 'lads'. Indeed we may see that, with respect to the criteria this located culture throws up, most manual and semi-skilled jobs *are* the same and it would be a waste of time to use the provided middle-class grids across them to find material differences. Considered, therefore, in just one quantum of time—the last months of school—individual job choice does indeed seem random and unenlightened by any rational techniques or end/means schemes. It is,

however, confusing and mystifying to pose the entry of working-class youth into work as a matter of *particular* job *choice*—this is, in essence, a very middle-class construct. The criteria we have looked at, the opposition to other more conformist views of work, and the solidarity of the group process, all transpose the question of job choice on to another plane: these lads are not choosing careers or particular jobs, they are committing themselves to a future of generalized labour. Even if it's not explicitly verbalized, from the way many of the kids actually get jobs and their calm expectation that their jobs will change a lot, they do not basically make much differentiation between jobs—*it's all labour*. In a discussion on the jobs they had arranged for when they left:

Perc: I was with my mate, John's brother, I went with 'im to er, . . he wanted a job. Well, John's sister's boyfriend got a job at this place, and he sez to Allan, he sez, 'Go down there and they might give you a job there', and he went down, and they sez, 'You're too old for training', 'cos he's twenty now, he sez to Allan, he sez, 'Who's that out there', and he sez, 'One of me mates', he sez, 'does he wanna job', and he sez, 'I dunno.' He sez er'm, 'Ask him.' He comes out, I went back in and he told me about it and he sez, 'Come back before you leave if you want it.'
——: What you doing?
Perc: Carpentry, joining. And a month ago I went back and, well, not a month ago, a few weeks ago and I seen him.
PW: Well, that was a complete accident really. I mean had you been thinking of joinery?
Perc: Well, you've only got to go and see me woodwork, I've had it, I ain't done woodwork for years.

In a discussion of their future:

Eddie: I don't think any of us'll have one job and then stick to it, none of us. We'll swop around.
Spike: It just shows in your part-time jobs don't it, don't stick to a part-time job.

Shop-floor culture has, as we have seen, an objective dimension which gives it a certain strength and power. Now this quality chimes—unexpectedly for some—with the criteria for acceptable work already thrown up by the counter-school culture. The young adult, therefore, impelled towards the shop floor, shares much more than he knows with his own future. When the lad reaches the factory there is no shock, only recognition. He is likely to have had experience anyway of work through part-time jobs, and he is immediately familiar with many of the shop-floor practices: defeating boredom, time-wasting, heavy and physical humour, petty theft, 'fiddling', 'handling yourself'.

There is a further, perhaps less obvious, way in which the working-class boy who is from the 'lads' is drawn in to the factory and confirmed in his choice. This is in the likely response of his new employer to what he understands of the 'lads'' culture already generated at school. The reverse side of the 'them' and 'us' attitude of the 'lads' is an acceptance by them of prior authority relations. Although directly and apparently geared to make some cultural interest and capital out of an unpleasant situation, it also accomplishes a recognition of, and an accommodation to, the facts of power and hierarchy. In the moment of the establishment of a cultural opposition is the yielding of a hope for direct, or quasi-political, challenge. The 'them' and 'us' philosophy is simultaneously a rescue and confirmation of the direct, the human and the social, and a giving up—at any conscious level—of claims to control the under-workings of these things: the real power relationships. This fact is of central importance in understanding the peculiar density and richness, as well as the limitedness and frequent short-sightedness, of counter-school and shop-floor culture.

Now, curiously enough, those conformist lads who enter the factory unaided by cultural supports, diversions and typical, habituated patterns of interpretation can be identified by those in authority as more threatening and less willing to accept the established *status quo*. For these lads still believe, as it were, the rubric of equality, advance through merit and individualism which the school, in its anodyne way, has more or less unproblematically passed on to them. Thus, although there is no surface opposition, no insolent style to enrage the conventional onlooker, there is also no secret pact, made in the reflex moment of an oppositional style, to accept a timeless authority structure: a timeless 'us' and 'them'. Consequently, these kids are more likely to *expect real* satisfaction from their work; to expect the possibility of advance through hard work; to expect authority relations, in the end, to reflect only differences in competence. All these expectations, coupled frequently with a real unhappiness in the individual unrelieved by a social diversion, make the conformist lad very irksome and 'hard to deal with'. In manual and semi-skilled jobs, then, those in authority often actively prefer the 'lads' type to the 'ear-'ole' type. Underneath the 'roughness' of the 'lads' is a realistic assessment of their position, an ability to get on with others to make the day *and production* pass, and a lack of 'pushiness' about their job and their future in it. Finally, the 'lads' are more likeable because they have 'something to say for themselves', and will 'stand up for themselves', but only in a restricted mode which falls short of one of the 'us' wanting to join the 'them'. It is precisely this parlous ground upon which the conformist often unwittingly and unhappily stands. For one of the 'lads', not only is the shop floor more familiar than he might expect, but he is also welcomed and accepted by his new superiors in such a way that seems to allow for the expression of his own personality where the school had been precisely trying to block it—this is an

initial confirming response which further marks up the 'transition' from school as a liberation.

What is surprising in this general process of induction into the factory is the voluntary—almost celebratory—nature of the 'lads'' choice. The recognition of themselves in a future of industrial work is not a question of defeat, coercion or resignation. Nor is it simply the result of a managed, machiavellian process of social control. It is a question, at any rate in part and at least at this age, of an affiliation which is seen as joyous, creative and attractive. This fact is of enormous importance to us in understanding the true complexity of the reproduction of our social order: there is an element of 'self-damnation' in the acceptance of subordinate roles.

It is the partly autonomous functioning of the processes we have been considering which surprisingly accomplishes the most difficult task of state schooling: to 'direct' a proportion of kids to the unrewarding and basic tasks of industrial production. The word 'direct' is carefully chosen here since it need not have connotations of coercion, but it does make the unequivocality of the destination clear.

Pierre Bourdieu[8] argues that it is the exclusive 'cultural capital'—among other things, skill in the symbolic manipulation of language and figures—of the dominant groups in society which ensures the success of their offspring and so the reproduction of their class privilege. This is because educational advancement is controlled through the 'fair' meritocratic testing of precisely these skills which 'cultural capital' provides. We can make a bleak inversion of this hypothesis and suggest that it is the partly 'autonomous' counter-cultures of the working class at the site of the school which 'behind the back' of official policy ensure the continuity of its own underprivilege through the process we have just been considering. This process achieves the reproduction of underprivilege much more systematically than could any *directed* state policy. Of course state policy *says* it is doing the opposite. In this case, then, 'autonomous' working-class processes achieve the 'voluntary' reproduction of their own conditions *in spite of* state policy. We cannot unravel this complex knot here, save to observe that the widespread *belief* in the egalitarianism of state policy—not least among teachers themselves—may be an essential prerequisite for the continual functioning of those *actual* processes which are working to the opposite effect.[9]

We have looked at aspects of the process whereby some typical working-class kids come to regard their future in the factory as natural, inevitable, and even freely chosen. We have seen the pivotal importance of the 'lads'' counter-school culture in this process. Analytically, therefore, the most basic parameter in terms of so-called 'job choice' is affiliation or non-affiliation with this group, rather than the more or less random (correctly recorded in the major studies) influences—official and other—operating during the specific period of the actual passage from school to work. From my own work it is perfectly clear that this affiliation with the counter-school group can happen at any time from the second year onwards. I want to term this important process of affiliation *differentiation*: the separation of self from a pre-given system.[10]

Even where there had been some form of social division in the junior school—and there is plenty of evidence in 'ragging of teacher's pets', that there was, —in the first years of the secondary school everyone, it seems, is an 'ear-'ole'. Even the few of those who come to the school with a developed delinquent eye for the social landscape behave in a conformist way because of the lack of any visible support group. On 'coming out' as a 'lad':

> *Spike*: In the first year . . . I could spot the 'ear-'oles'. I knew who the fucking high boys was, just looking at 'em walking around the playground—first day I was there (. . .) I was just, was just quiet for the first two weeks, I just kept meself to meself like, not knowing anybody, it took me two years to get in with a few mates. But, er . . . after that, the third years was a right fucking year, fights, having to go to teachers a lot.

Still, whether the process is resumed or starts from afresh in later years, what can we understand of its elements and nature? Basically I suggest that we should understand *differentiation* not as some quality or change within the individual but as a *change in the relationship*—at a greater or lesser speed—between staff and pupils. The founding relationship between teacher and pupil in our society, and one which can endure for the entire pupil career of some individuals, is of superior/inferior established in the axis of institutionally-defined qualities—knowledge, development, effort, probity—and on the destruction, suppression or suspension of 'private' or 'other' axes of knowledge and control. This is something of an ideal type, and has been hardened here for the sake of clarity. Certainly some reformists might argue that there is more now allowed under the school roof than a conventional model of this type. Be that as it may, in terms of how schools are *actually* run in working-class areas, and certainly the ones I saw, this axial definition gives us the most useful paradigm for understanding actual behaviour. In a very obvious sense, despite much vaunted curriculum reform, teachers control what is taught in classes—most certainly in the early school years. This model, and especially what it tells us about the attitude to privacy, becomes most valuable, however, when we come to look at face-to-face relationships—and remember that the school is the agency of face-to-face control *par excellence*. The stern look of the inquiring teacher; the relentless pursuit of 'the truth' set up as a value even above good behaviour; the common weapon of ridicule; the accepted arrangements for tears after a caning; the stereotypical deputy head, body poised, head lowered, finger jabbing the culprit; the un-

expected head bearing down on a group in the corridor: 'Where's your tie, think you own this place?' are all tactics for exposing and destroying, or freezing the private. What successful conventional teaching cannot tolerate is private reservation. And in the early forms in virtually any school it's plain to see that most kids are reciprocating in this relationship. The eager first-form hands reaching and snapping to answer first are all seeking approval from an acknowledged superior in a very particular institutional form. And in the *individual* competition for approval, the possibility of private reservations becoming *shared* to form any oppositional definition of the situation is decisively controlled. The teacher is given formal control of his pupils by the state, but unless he can exert his social control through an *educational* paradigm, his position would become merely that of the prison guard.

For the members of the 'lads'' culture, of course, that is exactly how the teachers are seen and, for the teacher, the change in relationship this implies makes his situation increasingly untenable and one of survival rather than of education. *Differentiation* is where the teacher's superiority is denied because the mode in which that superiority is expressed is delegitimated —there are *other* ways of valuing oneself. This valuation comes from those 'private' areas, *now shared* and made visible, which were held in check before. These resources are mobilized to penetrate the nature of the teacher's previous authority and to develop forms of resistance. The following is a classic statement—albeit exaggerated—of an attempt by a teacher to act against the 'private' or 'independent' area of the pupil's life, and of a resistance born of an essential belief that the teacher's authority is arbitrary, and predicated on an illegitimate suppression of other meanings and activities. In a discussion on teachers:

> *Joey*: (. .) the way we're subject to their every whim like. They want something doing and we have to sort of do it, 'cos, er, . . er, we're just, 'cos, er . . ., we're under them like. We were with a woman teacher in here, and 'cos we all wear rings and one or two of them bangles, like he's got one on, and out of the blue, like, for no special reason, she says, 'Take all that off.'
> *PW*: Really?
> *Joey*: Yeah, we says, 'One won't come off', she says, 'Take yours off as well.' I said, 'You'll have to chop my finger off first.'
> *PW*: Why did she want you to take your rings off?
> *Joey*: Just a sort of show like. Teachers do this, like, all of a sudden they'll make you do your ties up and things like this. You're subject to their every whim like. If they want something done, if you don't think it's right, and you object against it, you're down to Simmondsey (*the head*), or you get the cane, you get some extra work tonight.

And of course once this pupil analysis develops it soon moves off from a defensive resistance to an offensive one.

> *Joey*: It's a sort of a challenge, coming to school thinking, 'How can I outwit the teachers today?', like. The teachers're the establishment, they've done things to you, you don't like what they've done, how can you get back?

During this period of *differentiation* and after, one really decisive way of blocking the teacher's attempts to penetrate that which is private and informal is to be 'ignorant': to be uninterested in what the teacher has to offer. In a system where knowledge, and the educational paradigm, are used as a form of social control, 'ignorance' can be used in the same way as a barrier to control. The traditional notions of the causality of counter-school culture in low (measured) intelligence would, perhaps, be better reversed.

If the conventional paradigm of the teaching relationship is expressed powerfully in face-to-face situations, so is the differentiated resistance of the 'lads'. There is a particular overall style which communicates quite clearly to any teacher that 'this guy is not going to be pushed about'. It's a surly, disdainful look; a way of standing in the corridor as an obstruction though it could never be proved; a foot-dragging walk; an over-friendly hello; an attention on ties, fingers, shoes, books, anything rather than the inquiring eyes of the teacher which might penetrate too far.

For those involved the process of becoming a 'lad', is seen as a definite step towards maturity; it's 'coming out of your shell' or 'losing your timidness'. Diligence, deference, respect—these become things which can be read in quite another way.

> *PW*: Evans (*the careers master*) said you were all being very rude, (. .) you didn't have the politeness to listen to the speaker (*during a careers session*). He said why didn't you realize that you were just making the world very rude for when you grow up and God help you when you have kids 'cos they're going to be worse. What did you think of that?
> *Joey*: They wouldn't. They'll be outspoken. They wouldn't be submissive fucking twits. They'll be outspoken, upstanding sort of people.
> *Spanksey*: If any of my kids are like this, here, I'll be pleased.

That area which I have called 'private' or the 'independent', which the teaching relationship attempts to suppress and which *differentiation* liberates, is, of course, the input to the school social system which derives most clearly from the outside. Fairly obviously, in a working-class area it derives from the working-class culture of the neighbourhood. In the accounts of the boys in the crucial period of affiliation with the 'lads', the external (to the school) content of their experience is evident. Often physically outside of the school, these incidents also draw on codes of conformism to delinquent or oppositional values which are not those of the school.

> *Spike*: I'll tell you how it first started. It was Joey, Bill, Fred and Farmer (*all from his year at school*), they come round for me and I was . . never been out with them and I was fucking shittin meself. I was scared I was. I was only twelve or thirteen. Joey picked a crate of bottles up, threw a bottle to each of us, and said, 'throw 'em' and we fucking threw 'em and Joey threw the crate and it led from there to throwing bricks into train windows, dropping fucking big boulders on to trains, running from the screws, smoking. The reason I say this smoking was to be big. I thought 'Oh, fucking hell, I'm thirteen, here I am, y'know, great, fucking smoking.'
> *Bill*: We all got together and started knocking about and realized that we got to go up a bit like, you know, we started to grow up a bit, bit more sensible things you know . ., the third-years was the main, the main year for us, when all the Crombies, and all the Skinheads all started really, and we used to knock about together up the (*name of a football ground*).

It will readily be seen that there is a huge reservoir of located cultural meanings and possibilities for experience on the streets open to the 'lads' which is fundamentally working class. This is the basic material which fuels the growing 'private' and 'independent' sector of school experience. Understanding something of how these working-class materials are taken up in the school, and into relationships with teachers, it can be seen that counter-school culture is a particular, worked-up, form of working-class culture taking on specific appearances at the institutional level. We have, in the school counter-culture, a classic case of the circle of entanglements which can occur between state institutions and a situated class.

The very typical bottle-smashing incident described above cannot reasonably be thought of as a *determining* instance of allegiance to counter-school culture. Rather it should be thought of as a *crystallization* of a basic shift in attitudes and loyalties. The boys, themselves, very rarely identify for us any deep causes for the changes they describe so vividly. Apparently, for them, it really is a question of *accidental* causality— sitting by so-and-so in class, meeting 'the lads' at night by chance or being 'called for' unexpectedly. Of course what these accounts do testify to is the importance of the group, and the sense in which, for particular individuals, the group always seems to have been in existence. It is very clearly the strength and presence of the group which allows the 'private' and previously reserved areas within the individual to be expressed and become public.

Attempts to uncover the basic determinants of school counter-culture are fraught with difficulties. It is here that we skirt the deep waters of the determinacy of basic class cultures. Certainly we should be wary of simplified causal explanations. We can, however, suggest some of the possible factors which first break the individual from the mould of the conventional teacher/pupil paradigm—and once opposition is born it is amplified through group processes and staff reaction, and ultimately becomes self-justifying.

Though it is only rarely verbalized, and though it is finally expressed only at the level of action and cultural involvement, we can discern at the heart of the 'lads'' culture a fundamental assessment of the real conditions facing them. At some basic level they weigh up and compare the likely outcomes of the possibilities facing them. Now since many of the boys involved enjoy a considerable native intelligence, we cannot assume that the outcome of taking the 'conformist road' is reckoned to be academic failure and obloquy. There is, therefore, at some level, an estimation of how even the *successful* outcome of the 'conformist road'—CSE, perhaps GCE passes and an office job—measures up to the results of taking the 'non-conformist road'—independence, social collectivity, celebration of direct experience. In one way these are, of course, the obvious and immediate pay-offs, the 'instant' as against 'deferred' gratifications. It *seems to be* these interests, as such, which win the day. In a discussion on 'ear-'oles':

> *Joey*: (. . .) We wanna live for now, wanna live while we're young, want money to go out with, wanna go with women now, wanna have cars now, and er'm think about five, ten fifteen years' time when it comes, but other people, say people like the 'ear-'oles', they'm getting their exams, they'm working, having no social life, having no fun, and they're waiting for fifteen years' time when they're people, when they've got married and things like that. I think that's the difference. We are thinking about now, and having a larf now, and they're thinking about the future and the time that'll be best for 'em.

However, I want to argue that this is not the thick-headed animal choice for the nearest bale of hay but the result of a collective and individual cultural process of some maturity which takes a sensible wager on the meaning and pay-offs of *several* possibilities over time.[11] The possibility of reaching up to the highest strata of employment through the school system as it confronts them in the working-class area seems to be so remote as to be meaningless.[12] The route of *relative* success—an office job—through conformism is more possible. Such an achievement, however, is viewed in a very ambivalent light. The 'real world', they felt in their bones, was not quite like the school account of it. The institution might give you a few CSEs but what did that matter if you were an 'ear-'ole'. 'Immediate gratification' might be the basis for the development of highly necessary *long-term* skills. It does not pay to be too 'timid' in the strange, modern, industrial metropolis. In a discussion of 'ear-'oles':

> *Spike*: Well, they've got no push, I tell yer. Jones, Percival, or . . ., they've got nothing inside 'em to get up there, (. .) If they've got nothing inside 'em—no spunk to give 'em the push—they've gotta have somebody behind 'em to push 'em all the time, and that's no good. You can't survive like that.

In a specifically *cultural* mode, then, I am suggesting that the 'lads' make some basic assessment of their situation: most obviously of where their *immediate* interests lie, but also of the distinction between 'how things really work' and how the state institution of the school says they work;[13] of how actually to survive in the society which *they know*. Their own analysis is, in many ways, superior to that given to them by their teachers, and it clearly exerts a determining pressure upon the extent of allegiance to the 'lads'.

Another more obvious determining factor on this allegiance is the influence of parents. Involved in some form of shop-floor culture themselves, it is hardly surprising that their attitudes help to influence the behaviour of their offspring. Certainly for the 'lads' there is a widespread sense that their behaviour, in particular their opposition to the school and scorn of the weak and conformist, fits into a larger pattern, is expected of them in some way, and is part of an alternative pattern of being supported and protected by their parents against more official views; much in the way that they collectively supported their own alternative culture against the pressure of the school. In a discussion on 'ear-'oles':

> *Spanksey*: (. .) you know, he ain't a mastermind (*his dad*) you know. He was a ruffian when he was younger you know, he's a larf you know. I couldn't. I don't think he'd like to see me, his kids, you know, me or our Barry or me little sister, ear-'oles, you know what I mean.
> *Will*: Yeah, and with me, our old man, he was brainy like, but soon as he left school, started to work at the brewery, used to get the booze down him like you know I dare say, that influenced me.
> *Spanksey*: What's that school on the way to the football Petty Coat Lane, something like that, that was a real rough school that was, in our dad's time, you know what I mean, and he's rough.

At the institutional level, it's also possible to suggest a possibility for how the *process* described above is initiated. In what might be called an act of 'cultural prolepsis', staff often put kids into a double-bind situation which can be broken only by fulfilling the *worst* expectations of the teacher. Often the teacher upsets his own conventional teaching paradigm by assuming *too early* that particular groups or individuals reject his superiority and the standards by which it is maintained—and who can grudge him this cultural assumption, faced with what has happened massively in the past? This means, however, that the pupil is presented with a goal which he is simultaneously told he can never reach. This is a very characteristic attitude of teachers towards kids on the edge of, or heading towards, or even actually in, counter-school culture: to make exhortations for behaviour of which it is denied the recipient is capable. In a discussion on recent urges by the staff:

> *Derek*: (. .) They say you'm adults and that and yet, some things they, they'll say you're adults and then they'll say you'm responsible and all this, and then the next thing they'll turn around and say er, 'Walk down the corridor quietly in a line' and they'll treat us like children.

Since, apparently, it's impossible to be good, why not, at least, enjoy the devil's tunes.

The preceding has over-neatly divided the two categories of conformist and non-conformist. Any living school year is a complex mixture of individuals somewhere between these two points. Furthermore, it is also true that staff do not necessarily rate *very* conformist behaviour highly. Their own institutional axis of approved values registers a certain kind of obedience as 'girlishness', so that they often see a watered-down 'lads'' influence in a positive light. Certainly, there is a very important zone between the 'ear-'oles' and the 'lads' not dealt with in this paper, where the staff are able to control a certain independence, with its roots in the 'lads'' culture by the exercise of curriculum areas and practices which include elements of both the conventional teaching paradigm and the oppositional culture. Sport is the obvious example here, and the following extract comes from a boy who is precisely on this middle ground.

> If it was true I wouldn't mind admitting I was an ear-'ole, but I think I come somewhere in between . . I suppose in the first year I was a bit of an ear-'ole, you know, and, like more, I've got on with the sports teachers, because I enjoy me sport and I've progressed, because I don't mind having a joke. I don't take it too serious but sometimes I crack a joke about the teachers, you know to their face sort of thing, and they see the funny side of it all. They don't seem to have relationship like that with the ear-'oles. They teach 'em, nice, good lads. They seem to treat me as somebody to talk to like.

I have been stressing the 'cultural level' and the way in which 'semi-autonomous' processes at this level have profoundly important material outcomes. In order to do this I have necessarily emphasized the 'creative', independent and even joyous aspects of working-class culture as it is, anyway, for the 'lads' during the 'transition'—they may well have different views a few years *into* work. Certainly we need to posit the attractiveness of this culture to avoid simple determinist and economist views of what makes kids go to the factory, and to establish properly the level

of the 'voluntarism' by which these lads go to a future that most would account an impoverished one. However, we should be careful not to lionize or romanticize our concept of working-class culture. School counter-culture and shop-floor culture are fundamentally limited and stop well short of providing any fully worked-out future which is an alternative to the one they oppose. Indeed, in certain fundamental respects, we are presented with the contradiction that they actually—in the end—*do the work of bringing about the future that others have mapped for them*. The basic shortcoming of these cultures is that they have failed to convert *symbolic* power into *real* power. The real power thus still creates the most basic channels along which symbolic meanings run so that the symbolic power is used, in the end, to close the circle the *actual* power has opened up, and so finally to *reinforce* the real power relationships. The insistence of a human meaning which must justify its situation, but which does not have the *material* force to change its situation, can simply operate all too easily to legitimate, *experientially*, a situation which is fundamentally alien to it. To put it more concretely, the school counter-culture, for all its independence, accomplishes the induction of manpower 'voluntarily' into the productive process, and its mate, shop-floor culture, encourages an accommodation to, rather than a rejection of, the *fundamental* social relations there.

Something in the spirit of betrayal implicit in this kind of powerful and intensive, but formally limited, cultural organization is often caught in the semi-mythical, apocryphal, cultural folk wisdom of the shop floor. The following is an explanation of why young lads want to go on the shop floor given to me by a middle-aged worker in an engineering factory.

> I was thirteen, like, an impressionable age, I s'pose, and this is something I've never forgotten. I was with my old man and we were at the zoo, and we saw a crowd up on the 'ill like, people were clapping, and all crowding around a gorilla's cage. We pushed to the front, like, Dad was more curious than me, like, he got right to the front, and there was this gorilla clapping and stamping, and lookin' around like, havin' a good time. All the people were clapping, egging him on like. Then he suddenly come to the front of the cage and spat a mouthful of water all over our old man. He'd been goin' to the back of the cage, like, gettin' a mouthful of water, comin' forward, clapping like, then spitting the water out all over 'em.
> My old man stood back really shocked like . . . then he went back in the crowd and waited for some other silly buggers to push forward. I didn't realize then, like, I was only a kid, what it meant like . . ., but I do now. We don't all grow up at once, see, that's life, we don't grow up at the same time, and when you've learnt it's too late. It's the same with these kids comin' in

the factory, every time, they think its great. 'Oh, what's this, I wanna be there', y'know what I mean. You'll never change it, it's the same with everything, comin' to work, getting married, anything—you name it.

There is a fairly clear theory here about what makes kids want to start work, as well as a long-suffering, half-amused, typical working-class fatalism. There is also the ironic dynamic of the morality play. What is most noticeable, however, is a naturalized sense of timelessness: 'life's like that'. It's nobody's fault, nobody's failure, that makes the gorilla spit, or shop-floor life kill with monotony, or the wife nag to an early grave. It's simply the grim reality that humans have *always* faced. The same principle of the treacherous appearance disguising—and leading to an entrapment in—the real situation below is common to many aspects of working-class culture, and particularly in people's attitudes to the main transitions of life: birth, death, marriage, retirement, religious conversion. Even sometimes, it seems, death will turn out not to have been worth the trouble, though of course, the compelling unity of the drama means that the full ritual of the funeral cortege, plus cars bigger than ever were ridden in during life, must be gone through. We may suggest, however, that this final powerlessness before nature might be less of a universal law, and more a product of a specific, historic and continuing failure of working-class culture to achieve a basic modification of the conditions which brought it in to being. For all its symbolic resistance, the moving spirit of working-class culture till the present has been accommodation to a pre-given reality, rather than an active attempt to change it.

The reasons for this basic limitation stretch right back to the history of the world's first industrial proletariat and we cannot go into them now, but two contemporary factors might be mentioned specifically in relation to shop-floor culture. The trade union is the institutional extension of the culture of the work-place, the form in which culture and its meanings might have become more visible and the vehicle through which really concrete attempts have been made to transform *symbolic* into *real* control.

Trade unions, however, can be seen in their modern function merely as a mediation between shop-floor culture and the dominant managerial culture. Unionism negotiates the space between them and, in this negotiation, gives up much that is really central to the shop floor for what is often simply an accommodation in managerial interests. The nature of unionism and its organization is not, however, evenly textured. While the union bosses adopt a form of managerial culture and join the main industrial establishment,[14] the shop stewards and local organizers are still very much of the local culture. While trying to achieve union and organizational aims, they use specifically cultural forms of communication—spectacle, bluffs, drama, jokes, sabotage, to mobilize the man.[15] The union structure, then, is a complex and varied institution which strikes different degrees of appeasement at its various levels. The power of shop-floor culture determines at least the *form* of union activity at plant level, but the higher administrative level has completely lost that detailed binding-in with the lived culture of the work-place which was the original guarantee of true representativeness. To put it another way, the unions have lost touch with, even betrayed, the real roots of working-class radicalism—the culture of the shop floor.

From the side of capital, one of the most important controls on the power of shop-floor culture to challenge its own conditions is the practice of management science and human relations. Under the banner of a 'neutral' humanization of the work process, it has been one of the most formidable techniques of social control ever developed. Essentially, human relations rest on a simple and obvious discovery: informal groups exist. This is precisely, of course, the area covered by the culture of the shop floor. Hard on the discovery of this territory came techniques for colonizing it. Techniques of 'employee-centred supervision', 'consultation', 'open door relations' can neutralize oppositional shop-floor culture on its own grounds by claiming the informal group for management ideology. This can unbend its springs of action. The sense of control given to the workers by these techniques is usually illusory—the basic structures of power remain—and yet the located, rich, potentially dominating culture of resistance is being destroyed.

Whatever the final balance-sheet drawn of strengths and weaknesses in shop-floor and working-class cultures,[16] the point of this article has been to stress the continuity of school culture with the wider class culture, and to draw attention to the deep-moving processes of regeneration among this class—some of the most important of which occur at the site of the school. These processes should not be mistaken, in the sociology of education, for mere institutional flux or localized disturbance. What is *not supposed* to go on in school may have more significance for us than what is *supposed* to go on in school.

Key

( )	background information	
(inaudible)	part of sentence inaudible	
/ /	description relating to collective activity	
. . . .	long pause	
. . .	pause	
. .	short pause	
. . ,	phrase incompleted	
, . .	phrase completed, then pause	

(. .)	phrase edited out
(. . .)	sentence edited out
(. . . .)	passage edited out
—	speaker interrupting or at same time as another speaker
- - -	transcription from a different discussion follows
——	speaker or name not identified

Notes

1 This article is based on the findings of a project at the Centre for Contemporary Cultural Studies between April 1973 and June 1975, financed by the SSRC, on the 'transition from school to work' of white working-class average to low ability boys in a Midlands industrial conurbation. It used intensive case-study methods and participant observation based on a number of schools and factories in this region. The 'main' case study was of a friendship group of twelve boys as they proceeded through their last four terms in a single-sex secondary modern school (it was twinned with a girls' school of the same name). The school was adapting itself organizationally—mixed ability groupings, time-table blocking, destreaming, etc.—in preparation for an expected redesignation as a comprehensive school which finally occurred only after the case study group had left. All of the parents of the lads were interviewed in depth, and a period of participant observation was spent with each of the lads at some point in the first six months of their respective work situations. The full results of this work will be available in *Learning to Labour: How Working-class Kids get Working-class Jobs*, forthcoming from Saxon House.

2 A. Gramsci, *Selections from the Prison Notebooks of Antonio Gramsci*, ed. and trans. Q. Hoare and G. Nowell Smith, Lawrence & Wishart, 1971, p. 40.

3 D. H. Hargreaves, *Social Relations in a Secondary School*, Routledge & Kegan Paul, 1967; M. D. Shipman, *Sociology of the School*, Longman, 1968; Ronald A. King, *School Organization and Pupil Involvement*, Routledge & Kegan Paul, 1973; Michael F. D. Young, *Knowledge and Control: New Directions in the Sociology of Education*, Collier-Macmillan, 1971; Colin Lacey, *Hightown Grammar*, Manchester University Press, 1970.

4 See for instance M. P. Carter, *Into Work*, Penguin, 1969; Kenneth Roberts, *From School to Work: Study of the Youth Employment Service*, David & Charles, 1972.

5 For instance the admirable and pioneering D. H. Hargreaves, op. cit.

6 *Scientific Management*, Greenwood Press, 1972; first published 1947.

7 For a fuller explanation of this concept and its relation to the 'connoted', see Roland Barthes, *Mythologies*, Cape, 1972; Paladin, 1973; Barthes, *Elements of Semiology*, Cape, 1967. Basically the difference between *denoted* and *connoted* refers to the difference between the direct and intended message of a particular communication, and the indirect, often unintended messages which are communicated, at the same time through such processes as association, generalized suggestion and use of available cultural stereotypes. I consider the important 'connoted' level of careers information elsewhere, see *Learning to Labour*.

8 Pierre Bourdieu and Jean-Claude Passeron, *La Répro-duction; éléments pour une théorie du système d'enseigne-ment*, Éditions de Minuit, 1971.

9 *Learning to Labour* deals more fully with these questions.

10 I argue elsewhere that this is a fundamental principle of working-class culture in general: 'Human Experience and Material Production: the Culture of the Shop Floor', University of Birmingham, Centre for Contemporary Cultural Studies (duplicated).

11 A mathematician could tabulate these possibilities in the form of a non-zero-sum-game and come up with very similar results.

12 And surely figures for university entrance amongst the working class proper support them in this.

13 This bears an interesting relationship to the Marxist distinction between the 'state' and 'civil society', as does the 'lads'' *cultural* concept of generalized labour to the notion of general labour power, and as does the folk wisdom notion of false appearances (described later) bear a relationship to the Marxist notions of real relations/phenomenal forms. I develop the meaning of these 'coincidences' for a notion of advanced proletarian 'consciousness' in *Learning to Labour*.

14 Tony Lane, *The Union Makes us Strong; the British Working Class, its Politics and Trade Unionism*, Arrow Books, 1974.

15 H. Beynon, *Working for Ford*, Allen Lane, 1973.

16 These questions are taken up more fully in *Learning to Labour*.

23 Reactions to labelling
David H. Hargreaves

Labelling theory asserts that deviance arises in the interaction between two parties: the labeller and the labelled. We may conceive of this social process in terms of three elements. *First element*: the commission of some act by the first party. *Second element*: the interpretation of that act as rule-breaking by the second party, leading him to define the first party as deviant and to accord him an appropriate treatment. *Third element*: the reaction of the first party to the second element. In my own recent research into deviance in school (Hargreaves, Hester and Mellor, 1975), the predominant concern was with the second element. In this paper I wish to redress the balance and consider the third element. It can be no more than a sketch of some possibilities.

Every major psychological and sociological theory of deviance exists in a popular or lay version. It can, of course, be argued that the social scientific theories are themselves derived from common sense. On this view the social scientist elaborates and sophisticates one strand of what everyone knows in the common-sense world. However, once the social scientist has developed and published his theory in a scientific form, it passes back into common sense and to some degree transforms it. (For this reason we need to investigate the impact of different deviance theories on teachers.) The lay version of labelling theory argues that people become deviant because they are so labelled by others. This is, of course, a distortion of the theory. The fact that a deviant label is applied by teachers to a pupil does not mean that he will necessarily accept that label as a valid and legitimate account of him, nor will he necessarily respond to the labelling by the commission of yet more deviance. We need to examine very carefully the reactions of the pupil to being labelled by teachers and examine the conditions under which he comes to accept the label and respond

Source: unpublished. David Hargreaves is Reader in the Department of Education, University of Manchester.

to it in particular ways. I discuss four of the factors which might influence the pupil's acceptance of the label.

1 The frequency of the labelling

A pupil who is called a 'chatterbox' or a 'trouble-maker' on one or two occasions is not likely to accept this label as part of his identity, even though he may accept the label as legitimate within the specific context in which it is applied. We are all 'called names' many times by many different people without any deep or long-term effects. But if one particular label is repeatedly applied by a variety of teachers in a wide variety of situations, then at minimum the pupil will be under no illusions with regard to the teachers' conception of him, and part of the groundwork for the acceptance of the label by the pupil has been laid. At school I was repeatedly (and justifiably) labelled as a 'chatterbox'; as an adult I have converted deviant talkativeness in school into the professional skills of a lecturer. It would be too much to claim that the labelling of me as talkative by the teachers caused me to become a lecturer, but they were certainly the social audience who helped me to define myself as a 'talk-ative' person.

2 The extent to which the pupil sees the teacher as a 'significant other' whose opinion counts

If the pupil cares about the teacher's opinion of him, then he is more likely to accept the legitimacy of the teacher's label, whether it is a 'conformist' or 'deviant' label. In the case of the (middle-class?) pupil who values the teacher's opinion, his *early* acceptance of the legitimacy of the deviant label may actually help to insulate the pupil from acquiring a deviant identity and from commiting further acts of deviance, since he will alter his conduct so that the teacher no longer has grounds for applying the deviant label to him.

201

Here the teacher's intention in performing the labelling, namely social control, is realized. In the case of the pupil (working-class?) who sets a lower value on the teacher's opinion, he may be able to discount the deviant label in its early application ('I don't care what he thinks'), thus avoiding the need to reform his conduct. Here the teacher's attempt at social control by labelling fails. However, this pupil may be constrained to accept the label at a much later stage when the application of the deviant label has become frequent and a matter of routine. What can be discounted in the short-term may prove to be more pervasively troublesome in the long term.

3 The extent to which others support the label

Sometimes a single teacher finds a pupil 'difficult' or a 'problem', but none of his colleagues shares the view that this pupil is in any way deviant. At other times all the teachers to whom a pupil is exposed will agree that the pupil merits a deviant label. We may call these two types, respectively, 'idiosyncratic' and 'consensual' deviants. It is certain that idiosyncratic deviants do exist in schools. They tend to remain hidden because teachers learn to recognize that the grumbling about a pupil whom nobody else finds 'difficult' will be taken by colleagues as a reflection on the teacher's competence rather than as evidence of pupil misconduct. The informal gossip and eternal discussions about pupils in staffrooms facilitate the development of a consensus about deviant pupils. One learns which pupils to grumble about in staffrooms. The consensus appears to be greater than it is, in part because those teachers who do not find the pupil 'difficult' tend to keep silent lest their overt denial that they find the pupil 'difficult' be interpreted by others as a form of boasting. One important consequence of the emergence of consensual deviants is that a teacher may acquire a preconception that a pupil is deviant, based on staff gossip, *before* he has actually taught a pupil. Phillipson (1971) has noted that delinquency rates of schools are associated with high rates of staff turnover. Part of the explanation of this may be that where there is a constant stream of teachers who have little knowledge of the pupils they are forced to rely on 'reputations' of classes and pupils as conveyed to them by the less transitory members of staff. Deviant labels would thus tend to be accepted and used by such teachers—'I've heard all about you, Smith'—who might not remain long enough in the school to test the validity of these labels and thus be in a position to revise them.

The informal staff gossip serves other important functions, including the dissemination of what Sudnow (1965) has called 'normal crimes'; that is, those deviant behaviours which occur regularly and which acquire typical features concerning the situations in which they occur, the manner in which they are committed, the characteristics of the perpetrator and of the victim (if any), and so on. An important aspect of the socialization of the new teacher is the learning of these attributes of the 'normal crimes' of schools, so that he can recognize them and deal with them quickly. A new teacher has to learn to recognize cases of 'cheek', 'playing the fool' and 'taking the mick'—the interpretation of pupil acts in such terms is more complex than it looks to the experienced teacher.

The extent of the acceptance of the label by other adults in the pupil's environment may also be important. If the pupil's parents and neighbours also apply the label which is consensual among the teachers, then the pupil will be under greater pressure to accept its legitimacy. Here again the middle-class pupil may be at an advantage. First, because of their greater interest in their child's schooling, parents are more likely to discover that the pupil is being labelled as deviant; and second, they are likely to investigate the events leading up to the labelling and make a considered judgment upon it. If the parents think that the labelling was justified, they will censure the child as well and seek to ensure that he commits no further deviant conduct. They will reinforce the teacher's social control attempts. If they think the labelling was unjustified, they will help the pupil to neutralize the labelling with such comments as: 'Well, the teacher was probably angry and upset and didn't really mean it. Just make sure that you keep out of trouble.' In extreme cases, such parents might make an official complaint against the school. The working-class parent on the other hand may hear of such events less frequently and make a generalized response rather than investigating the details. A response such as: 'I'm not surprised—your dad and your older brother were just like that at school, always up to some mischief', when the pupil feels that the labelling was unjustified, or a response such as: 'Never mind what the teachers say, love, I never liked them either', when the pupil knows that the labelling was justified, may help to undermine the teachers' labelling as attempts at social control.

4 The public nature of the labelling

When a pupil is labelled before a large public, such as in the school assembly or in front of a large class, the psychological effect is likely to be more severe than when the labelling takes place in a private setting such as an interview with the teacher at the end of a lesson. It is the same as the difference between an appearance in court and a confrontation with a policeman on the street-corner. Public labelling tends to take on the character of a degradation ceremony (Garfinkel, 1956) and can constitute a trauma to the pupil's self. Woods (1975) examines how teachers 'show up' pupils as a form of social control, and the research material vividly indicates how deeply some pupils resent this and take it as evidence that they are being 'picked on'. Public labelling humiliates, and it also disseminates. The larger the audience who witness the labelling, the greater the number of people to whom the label is communicated and the greater the chance that some of the audience will use that label and treat the pupil in accordance with it.

We must now examine in greater depth the consequences of the labelling and try to plot other aspects or stages of the reactions of the deviant who finds himself labelled. One might, to use a concept that is currently very popular in sociology, speak of the *career* of the deviant in school. Goffman (1961) indicates some of the values of this concept.

> One value of the concept of career is its two-sidedness. One side is linked to internal matters held dearly and closely, such as image of self and felt identity; the other side concerns official position, jural relations, and style of life, and is part of a publicly accessible institutional complex. The concept of career, then, allows one to move back and forth between the personal and the public, between the self and its significant society, without having to rely overly for data upon what the person says he thinks he imagines himself to be.

A useful starting-point here is the distinction between primary and secondary deviation as defined by Edwin Lemert (1967), who is one of the most noted of the labelling theorists. The importance of this distinction lies in the fact that it calls attention to the significance of the labelling in the generation of deviance. It helps to explain how the imputation of deviance by the labeller can have important consequences for any subsequent deviation.

> Primary deviation is assumed to arise in a wide variety of social, cultural, and psychological contexts, and at best has only marginal implications for the psychic structure of the individual; it does not lead to symbolic reorganization at the level of self-regarding attitudes and social roles. Secondary deviation is deviant behaviour, or social roles based upon it, which becomes a means of defense, attack or adaptation to the overt and covert problems created by the societal reaction to primary deviation. In effect, the original 'causes' of the deviation recede and give way to the central importance of the disapproving, degradational and isolating reactions of society.

We all commit primary deviations and for an infinite variety of reasons. All of us, for instance, have at some time told a lie or stolen something. Yet most of us do not think of ourselves as liars or thieves. Probably we were labelled by others, or labelled ourselves, as deviant; we stopped indulging in such conduct, perhaps; generally we forgot about our deviance. In other words, such actions and the labelling of them as deviant produced very few problems. In short, in many cases the labelling has a social control effect: we are deterred from committing further

acts of deviance. We act; the act is defined as deviant by a labeller; we avoid such conduct in future in order to avoid such labelling and any treatment meted out by the labeller.

An alternative response to the deviance is to justify or disavow the deviant conduct. This is usually referred to as *normalization* or *neutralization*. For example, one might tell a lie, in full knowledge that such conduct is usually defined as deviant, because on this occasion such conduct is not really a lie, but a 'white lie' which is justified because the intention behind the lie is an attempt to avoid hurting someone's feelings. There is a vast range of normalizing or neutralizing techniques by which in our avowals to ourselves or to others we manage to avert the problems we would experience if we ourselves labelled the act as truly deviant. We are all familiar with, and make use of, such phrases as 'I'm afraid I wasn't myself this morning', or 'I honestly just don't know what made me do that', or 'I don't usually say things like that.' Through such phrases we explain and manage our conduct without having to perceive ourselves as more than marginally or temporarily deviant. It is as if we can encapsulate our deviant action and locate it at an outer fringe of our self and our history where it can do us no damage.

The third possibility, which Lemert calls secondary deviation, arises when the labelling does not deter and cannot be normalized. Instead the labelling itself causes many problems for the labelled person which he copes with by committing yet further acts of deviance. The reaction of the labeller, his indignation and his punitive orientation, generates further deviance in the sense that this labelling fails in its intended purpose (to deter, to punish etc.) but creates problems for the labelled person which are, paradoxically, partly solved by further deviance. In secondary deviation the person's life and identity begin to be organized around the facts of the deviance, which cannot be normalized. An obvious example is the effect of prison. The intention is to punish and deter the offender—and to deter others. The effect may be that the prisoner finds life in prison unbearable unless he conforms to the criminal subculture of his fellow prisoners; when he comes out of prison he cannot get a job because everyone knows that he is an 'old lag'; he can survive most easily by committing a further crime of theft; he is caught and is sent to prison again, where he is now classified as a 'persistent offender' and the cycle repeats.

We see, then, that there are three possible consequences to the labelling of an act as deviant. It may deter; it may be normalized; it may set in chain a process which leads to the amplification of the deviance. In applying labelling theory to schools, we need to know under what conditions the labelling has each of these three effects. This is an empirical question to which we have at present no clear answer. We can do no more than attempt to sensitize ourselves to some possibilities.

So far I have used the term 'labelling' somewhat loosely to cover the reaction of the labeller. I must now distinguish two aspects of the labelling. The first is the process of defining, classifying or categorizing the deviant. It is what the labeller *calls* the deviant. The second is the treatment that the labeller metes out to the deviant; what he *does* to the deviant. We can refer to this as the process of *stigmatization*, by which the deviant is discredited, derogated, humiliated, degraded, insulted, mocked, paraded, rejected. Stigmatization involves a differential treatment as a result of the imputation of deviance. As we shall see, the treatment that the labeller defines as 'the official punishment' is only one part of the stigmatization.

We must bear in mind that the reaction of the labeller to minor acts of deviance hardly merits the term 'stigmatization'. For a pupil in school to be subjected to the processes of stigmatization, it appears that he must (1) have committed a very serious offence, or (2) have repeatedly and persistently committed minor offences, or (3) have given the teacher grounds for thinking that he is potentially a 'problem' pupil; e.g. he comes from a family which has a reputation as a 'problem' family.

The labelling and the stigmatization assign the pupil to a new and deviant status. In Becker's (1963) words:

> The important consequence is a drastic change in the individual's public identity. Committing the improper act and being publicly caught at it place him in a new status. He has been revealed as a different kind of person from the kind he was supposed to be.

That is, he is no longer a 'normal' or 'ordinary' pupil, but a 'troublemaker', a 'nuisance' or a 'thug'. This lays the groundwork for the transformation of identity by which the person can begin to see *himself* as centrally, pivotally, essentially or 'really' deviant. The labelling and stigmatization do not simply 'cause' the pupil to become more deviant. Rather, they change the meaning of the deviant acts in the life of the pupil, and they also change the meaning of that person in the eyes of all those who are aware of the labelling and stigmatization. As Matza (1969) phrases it:

> To be signified a thief is to lose the blissful identity of one who among other things happens to have committed a theft. It is a movement, however gradual, toward being a thief and representing theft.

He is no longer merely a person who once or twice committed a deviant act, but a person who *is* a thief who happens to spend quite a lot of his life refraining from committing theft. Instead of the act being just part of the person, the deviant act comes to engulf the person.

It is through the stigmatization that the labeller's conceptualization of the pupil as a deviant person comes to make its impact on the pupil's identity. The teacher has transformed his conception of the pupil; he was once 'normal' but now he is 'deviant'. In the process of stigmatization, the teacher unwittingly teaches the pupil to transform his conception of himself, and unwittingly imposes problems on the pupil which make it increasingly difficult for him either to think of himself as, or to be, 'normal'. Clearly we must examine the process of stigmatization in some detail.

Once the teacher defines the pupil as a deviant or potential deviant, then he will be treated as untrustworthy and as a target for *suspicion*. He loses his former right as a 'normal' to be treated as 'above suspicion'. The teacher is to some degree wary of everything he says and does. All his accounts to explain his untoward behaviour are carefully scrutinized and checked by the teacher, who is much more likely to see them as 'excuses', prevarications and even lies than as 'valid reasons'. He is seen as a person with 'something to hide'. It therefore follows that he must be kept under *surveillance*—'You have to keep an eye on Smith', says the teacher, and additional restrictions are made on his freedom of movement and autonomy. A pupil who is labelled a truant may be required to have a piece of paper signed by his teacher at the beginning of every lesson, be refused permission to leave the school premises at lunch-time or be denied permission to go to the lavatory unaccompanied in the middle of a lesson—rigorous controls that are not imposed on 'normal' pupils.

In addition, he is subjected to *exclusion* or *isolation*. He is seen as dangerous, contagious and contaminating. He must be separated from 'good' pupils lest he contaminate them and play the role of the one bad apple who ruins the whole barrel. He cannot be put in prison, our traditional method of excluding criminal deviants, but teachers can go to considerable lengths to prevent his deviance from spreading. They can make him work alone in a corner; they can discourage other pupils from associating with him; they can put all the 'problem' pupils into a common environment or a 'special unit'.

The deviant pupil is, in short, denied 'the ordinary means of carrying on the routines of everyday life open to most people' (Becker, 1963). In the light of the suspicion, surveillance and exclusion to which he is subjected, it would be surprising if he did not react with hostility and frustration. He cannot buck against the additional restrictions imposed upon him without validating his imputed deviant status. To demonstrate that he is not deviant, he has to follow a code which requires less deviation than that of normals who are never subjected to these special controls. Even if this deviant does abide by this new restrictive code (apologies to Basil Bernstein!), there is a chance that he will be suspected of shamming or insincerity. Moreover he becomes the target of techniques which seem liable to promote self-fulfilling prophecies. Compare the 'I just knew it would be you, Smith', addressed to the deviant, with the 'I'm surprised at you, Jones!' addressed to the normal.

It thus becomes increasingly difficult for the person to sustain a definition of himself as non-deviant. The mirror of social life, through which we all learn who we are, reflects back a deviant identity. As David Matza (1969) suggests with great insight:

> He is *unable not to* see or glimpse himself as he appears in the eyes of another. As Mead taught, that is the way the subject is put together and thus part of the human nature. It is quite a capacity, but sometimes it is more usefully conceived as an incapacity or flaw.

Once the label is applied by the teacher and accepted by the pupil, it points backwards and forwards in time for both of them. It points to the past in that the teacher can give retrospective interpretations to events prior to the application of the label and thus reconstruct the pupil's biography in terms of current 'facts'. These can take the form of:

> 'It all makes sense to me now . . .'
> 'I always knew there was something fishy about that girl . . .'
> 'I could see it all coming, really . . .'

Similarly, the pupil may be led to re-interpret his own history. The label points to the future in terms of prospective predictions that the behaviour implied by the label will be repeated. The teacher nurses an expectation of future offences that may become self-fulfilling. Similarly the pupil may come to see himself as destined or fated to repeat his deviance. It is by no means uncommon for the labelled pupil to be subjected to suspicion when the perpetrator of a deviant act is unknown; he is seen as a likely candidate, checked at an early stage and easily subjected to *false accusations* as well as to correct ones.

There is certainly good evidence that stigmatization sometimes takes the form of a very real social discrimination. In my own Lumley study (Hargreaves, 1967, pp. 95–6), the deviants, who were largely in the lower two streams of the fourth year, were subjected to very real discrimination, even though this was, from the teachers' point of view, understandable.

> The selection of prefects, for example, shows a very heavy bias, since it is predominantly A and B stream pupils who are considered most suitable for appointment . . . When the school organized holidays, the number of applications frequently exceeded the number of available places. Once again the bias towards high stream boys appears. In order to reduce the length of the list, the teacher in charge would consult other members of staff about applicants. Boys who received unfavourable reports were deleted from the list and would be told at a later stage that they had been 'unlucky in the draw'. Another way in which 'undesirables' could be excluded from the holiday was to publicize the projected journey primarily to A and B stream boys, who would be actively encouraged to join the school party. The teachers justified themselves on the grounds that the difficult low stream boys were a potential threat to the success of the holiday . . .

In examining the stigmatization, discrimination, injustices, etc. to which deviant pupils are subject, we must take care that we do not confine ourselves to cases which are obvious only to teachers and observers. We must also investigate pupil claims in this regard; what is justice to a teacher and observer may be seen as an injustice by the pupil. Carl Werthman's (1963) work is a brilliant example of a researcher who catches and analyses the pupil perspective. Werthman notes that the majority of pupils in the American high school accept the teacher's authority at face value and believe that the teacher has a legitimate right to pass judgment on practically all behaviour that takes place in school. Members of delinquent gangs, on the other hand, take a different view. They do not *a priori* accept the authority of any teacher; their judgment and reaction is contingent upon whether or not the teacher exercises his authority over areas they regard as appropriate and on grounds and in a manner they consider proper. For instance, delinquents do not grant the teacher an absolute right to punish certain forms of minor classroom misbehaviour such as talking to neighbours, gazing through the window and chewing gum, even though they accept that there are good reasons for banning such acts. Further, these pupils believe that under no circumstances may a teacher give official attention to race, dress, hair-styles and mental capacities. Finally, these pupils are extremely sensitive to the style in which the teacher's authority is exercised. The use of commands rather than requests is resented. Werthman shows that when teachers breach this code, the delinquents simply refuse to grant any legitimacy to, and therefore ignore, their authority. Their intention then becomes to demonstrate that they no longer grant such teachers any right to exercise any authority over them, and this they realize by misbehaving in the classes of these teachers. At the same time, these pupils may behave well in the classes of those teachers to whom they grant legitimate authority. In a sense, then, it can be said that certain teachers provoke these pupils into deviant conduct which would not be exhibited if the teachers behaved differently.

When the experience of the deviant pupil is looked at from his point of view, rather than the point of view of the teacher or adult, we can begin to understand (though not necessarily justify) that the deviant easily feels a pervasive sense of injustice. In short, he feels *victimized*. 'You're always picking on me!' is his angry (counter-)accusation against the teacher. For the most part teachers treat this as an illegitimate claim; but when we consider the suspicion, surveillance, discrimination, derogation and false accusations, we have to concede that the claim is not entirely without foundation. However it is the teacher who is the main reality-definer; it is the teacher who is high in what Becker (1967) calls the 'hierarchy of credibility'. The effect is that it is the teacher's view which prevails, which becomes the official reality and which is believed by others, such as the headteacher and parents.

With the sense of victimization there grows a sense of *impotence*—the deviant can never win by these rules. At first, reform is seen as pointless because it offers no pay-off. Reform attempts are too often greeted by teachers with suspicion and incredulity, which is as damaging to him as it is understandable to us. He is pressed back into the mould of his deviant label, being in a position where he has to persist for a very extensive period as a 'super-normal' person, in the face of constant distrust, merely to become regarded as normal. Later, he sees reform as impossible; and having reached the point where he perceives no possible alternatives, the likelihood of his accepting a pivotal or centrally deviant identity is greatly increased.

The key element now becomes the provision of social support for the deviant identity and it is here that some of the earlier subcultural theorists, especially Albert Cohen (1955) have made such a notable contribution. He points out that

the crucial condition for the emergence of new cultural forms is the existence, in effective interaction with one another, of a number of actors with similar problems of adjustment.

This may well be a possibility for those individuals in school who are labelled as deviant and come to see themselves as having a *common* problem. Cohen goes on to suggest some of the mechanisms by which a group solution can occur. His main interest is in gang delinquency, but the ideas can be readily adapted to pupils in school. It is held that members with the same problem come together and make 'exploratory gestures'; that is, probing and tentative moves towards a solution to their problem. By a process of mutual exploration leading to joint acceptance, the group creates a deviant subculture as a solution to their problems. It is hard for any single pupil deviant to 'go it alone' in school; the teachers are often punitive and derogating. The deviant needs reassurance and encouragement and so he must, according to Cloward and Ohlin (1961), find help by 'searching out others who have faced similar experiences and who will support one another in common attitudes of alienation

from the official system.' In many situations, the deviants do not have to seek one another. The school actively places them in a common environment, such as a low stream or a 'special unit'. They learn that they are not alone and that they can create a subculture which inverts the official culture of the school —one now achieves group status by being deviant.

Howard Becker (1963) describes this late stage of the deviant career in general terms.

From a sense of common fate, from having to face the same problems, grows a deviant subculture: a set of perspectives and understandings about what the world is like and how to deal with it, and a set of routine activities based on those perspectives. Membership in such a group solidifies a deviant identity. Moving into an organized deviant group has several consequences for the career of the deviant. First of all, deviant groups tend, more than deviant individuals, to be pushed into rationalizing their position ... Most deviant groups have a self-justifying rationale (or 'ideology') ... Whilst such rationales do operate, as pointed out earlier, to neutralize the conventional attitudes that deviants may still find in themselves towards their own behaviour, they also perform another function. They furnish the individual with reasons that appear sound for continuing the line of activity that he has begun. A person who quiets his own doubts by adopting the rationale moves into a more principled and consistent kind of deviance than was possible for him before adopting it.
  The second thing that happens when one moves into a deviant group is that he learns how to carry on his deviant activity with a minimum of trouble. All the problems he faces in avoiding enforcement of the rule he is breaking have been faced before by others. Solutions have been worked out ... Every deviant group has a great stock of lore on such subjects and the new recruit learns it quickly.

It is at this point that the teacher finds the deviant pupil most troublesome. The teacher's dominant experience of the pupil is this recurrent and incurable deviance; he tends to forget the complex deviant career which preceded it. With respect to deviant careers official notice is paid to the last stages, not the first steps. And it is at this point that the pupil cannot, and often does not want to, get off the escalator of deviance.

References

Becker, H. S., *Outsiders*, Free Press, 1963.

Becker, H. S., 'Whose side are we on?', *Social Problems*, 14, 1967, pp. 239–47.

Cohen, A., *Delinquent Boys*, Free Press, 1955.

Cloward, R. A. and Ohlin, L. E., *Delinquency and Opportunity*, Routledge & Kegan Paul, 1961.

Garfinkel, H., 'Conditions of successful degradation ceremonies', *American Journal of Sociology*, 61, 1956, pp. 420–4; reprinted in E. Rubington and M. S. Weinberg, eds, *Deviance; the Interactionist Perspective*, Macmillan, 1968.

Goffman, E., *Asylums*, Doubleday, 1961; Penguin, 1968.

Hargreaves, D. H., *Social Relations in a Secondary School*, Routledge & Kegan Paul, 1967.

Hargreaves, D. H., Hester, S. K. and Mellor, F. J., *Deviance in Classrooms*, Routledge & Kegan Paul, 1975.

Lemert, E. M., *Human Deviance, Social Problems and Social Control*, Prentice-Hall, 1967.

Matza, D., *Becoming Deviant*, Prentice-Hall, 1969.

Phillipson, C. M., 'Juvenile delinquency and the school', in W. G. Carson and P. Wiles, eds, *Crime and Delinquency in Britain*, Martin Robertson, 1971.

Sudnow, D., 'Normal crimes: sociological features of the penal code', *Social Problems*, 12, 1965, pp. 255–70; reprinted in E. Rubington and M. S. Weinberg, eds, *Deviance; the Interactionist Perspective*, Macmillan, 1968, and P. Worsley, ed., *Problems of Modern Society*, Penguin, 1972.

Werthman, C., 'Delinquents in school: a test for the legitimacy of authority', *Berkeley Journal of Sociology*, 8, 1963.

Woods, P., '"Showing them up" in secondary school', in G. Chanan and S. Delamont, eds, *Frontiers of Classroom Research*, Slough, NFER, 1975.

24 Physical context influences on behavior: the case of classroom disorderliness*

Robert A. Stebbins

Schools and schoolrooms are, among other things, physical contexts, which like other physical contexts, communicate messages from their makers to their users. Sometimes the users accept the makers' messages and act in harmony with their (the makers') reasons for shaping a context as they have. At other times the users reject the messages; although their actions still may be compatible with the makers' aims. In general, one category of users of schools and classrooms—the teachers—are more likely than another category of users—the pupils—to accept the makers' messages or reject them in ways still compatible with the makers' reasons for constructing the contexts.

Pupils, as Waller (1932, 196) noted, have their own aims, which often are at odds with those of school authorities. Moreover, they generally have only a negative interest in the social and physical orders of the school. They seem to have few reservations about how they use the school and its classrooms to realize their nonconformist interests (nonconformist from the standpoint of school authorities).

The relationship between the physical educational environment and disorderliness has been little studied. Indeed, there has been only moderate attention paid to the relationship between that environment and learning (for a review of portions of this research, see Sommer, 1969, ch. 7; Stebbins, forthcoming, ch. 2). Even in a period of heightened consciousness about the physical teaching and learning milieu as manifested in open-plan schooling, social scientific studies linking that milieu with pupil misconduct are practically nonexistent. Only six of the eighty-three items in the Ontario Institute for Studies in Education (1970) bibliography on open education report empirical investigations on this subject. None of these focuses directly on disorderly behavior. There is an abundant literature on educational architecture and especially on recent innovations there (see, for example, McCor-

mick and Cassidy, 1953; Castaldi, 1969; Caudill et al., 1967; Gross and Murphy, 1968). And there is no shortage of research and discussion on disorderly behavior at school (see, for example, Cutts and Moseley, 1957; Fuchs, 1969). But the situation today is as Sommer (1969, 101) saw it four years ago: 'Thus far, the interface between education and design has remained relatively unexplored—educators being mainly concerned with student behavior and designers with aspects of the physical environment.'

The chief aim of this paper is to present hypotheses generated from observational data on how certain physical conditions in classrooms encourage disorderly behavior there. Consideration of these conditions must be deferred, however, until additional theoretical, methodological, and descriptive background has been presented. We turn first to a brief statement of the importance for this study of the concept of the definition of the situation. In the section that follows the rudiments of a theory of physical context influence on behavior are sketched.

Importance of the definition of the situation

Purely objective examination of the physical conditions of student misconduct, examination carried out by an observer trained to disregard individual viewpoints, is impossible. Classroom behavior is disorderly when defined as such by the teacher or the pupils concerned. True, some student behavior would be identified as in violation of schoolroom rules by any participant in the situation familiar with the etiquette of teacher-pupil and pupil-pupil interaction in the Western world; for example, telling the teacher to shut up or fighting with another student. Other activities, such as reading a novel, playing with a pencil, or digging in one's purse, are labeled as disorderly only at certain times during the class session; and that depends upon certain personality and social characteristics of teachers and students.

Source: *Environment and Behavior*, 5 (3), 1973, pp. 291–314.

It is doubtful, in short, that valid data collection on and analysis of the physical conditions of disorderly behavior can be mounted without knowledge of how teachers define the situations in which such behavior occurs. All disorderliness considered here, was defined as such by the teachers involved (compare Stebbins, 1971). That is, they defined student behavior as disorderly when it was seen as impeding their teaching effectiveness, impeding the student's learning potential, simply violating the rules of classroom conduct, or any combination of these three criteria.

Theoretically, the teacher's definition of behavior as disorderly is one of two explanatory conditions that intervene between the physical contexts of the school and the schoolroom and the student behavior they influence. The other intervening condition is the student's definition of the same situation, wherein he interprets the circumstances as calling for certain behavior that could possibly be labeled disorderly by his teacher. Neither of these subjective viewpoints, however, is treated systematically in this paper. They have been mentioned in order to show that, without them, complete understanding of the influence of physical contexts on behavior is impossible. Here we will be concerned predominantly with the more objective (typically extracommonsense) links between context and behavior: certain kinds of educational contexts frequently encourage student behavior defined by teachers as disorderly.

Toward a theory of physical context influence on behavior

In this section, I wish to sketch the rudiments of a theory of physical context influence on behavior, which can then be used, among other purposes, to organize much of our discussion about the behavior of teachers and pupils in their physical environment.[1] A physical context is the nonhuman part of the immediate sociophysical situation that we perceive with our senses of sight, hearing, touch, smell, and, perhaps, taste and balance. Any physical context a human being has had a hand in constructing functions as a message communicated by that human being to the user of the context. A man-made context, even if it is no more than a few stones arranged to form a parking lot or four walls to form a room, is a message in a special type of social interaction between maker and user. With the stones the maker tells the user he must park within them; with the walls he tells the user he must not, indeed cannot, go beyond them.

Though they are sometimes difficult to separate in analysis, there are at least two reasons why makers want to construct or modify a context in a particular way; one or both reasons may guide their activities. First, makers may wish to influence the user's definition of that situation (and ultimately his behavior or feelings). Second, they may wish to express some personal characteristic or predisposition, such as an artistic idea, an interest, a sentiment, a skill, an atti-

tude, a wish, or an end. Within or around the physical context constructed or modified by the maker, users carry on their various activities without making alterations to that context.

The roles of maker and user engender different orientations.[2] Makers are oriented toward communicating a message through a physical medium, whereas users are oriented toward carrying out their various activities and usually only incidentally concerned with the physical context, if they are concerned with it at all. It can happen, however, that the context is somehow unusual enough to command a user's full attention (see Assumptions 12 and 13 in Proshansky *et al.*, 1970, 36–7).

Three categories of people are concerned with physical contexts: designers, staff, and clients. They act either as makers or as users or, at times, in both capacities simultaneously. Thus, the roles of maker and user can be differentiated as in Table 24.1.

Table 24.1

	designers	staff	clients
Makers	designer-makers	staff-makers	client-makers
Users	designer-users	staff-users	client-users

The first person associated with any particular context is its designer. The designer-maker is the one who plans and builds the context or has it built by someone else according to his (the designer's) plans. Though rare in the specialized urban life of the twentieth century, there are times when a person who designs a context also uses it. He is a designer-user, epitomized today in the man who builds his own home.

Subsequently, staff assume responsibility for the designer's physical context. Depending on what sort of context it is, they, as staff-users, work in it or on it or, possibly, reside in it. Staff may also adopt the role of staff-maker in order to influence other users' definitions of the situation or to express a personal characteristic or predisposition or to do both.

Once staff have assumed responsibility for a physical context, clients, unless it is strictly private, may start arriving. Their main role is client-user of the context and the services provided there by the staff. As with staff, clients may also adopt the role of client-maker in order to influence other users' definitions of the situation or to express a personal characteristic or predisposition or to do both.

Though makers often hope to influence users' definitions of the situation while they are in the makers' physical contexts, users occasionally refuse to accept the messages communicated. At other times, users define the situation, and therefore act, in ways never intended by the maker, ways that may be compatible or incompatible with his reasons for constructing or modifying the context in the first place.

The theory of physical context influence on behavior focuses not on the ways man positions himself in space vis-à-vis others nearby, for the purposes of communicating with them, but on the way he interacts directly with the relevant man-made aspects of the situation, for the purposes of adjusting his goals to those aspects or adjusting those aspects to his goals. True, he sometimes adjusts himself in particular ways to his physical surroundings in order to affect his goal of interacting with others. For instance, people move chairs around in public rooms so as to converse better with their friends or they turn chairs toward the walls in libraries so as to avoid such contact. But there are many occasions, as we shall see, when interaction with others is, at that moment, only a distant aim, a subsidiary aim, or no aim at all. Even when one is using the fixed and semifixed features of space directly for the purpose of communicating with other people, our theory suggests a new analytic slant by calling attention to our simultaneous interaction with the context makers.

The observations and discussion reported in this paper focus on two general research questions as they bear on the physical context of schools and school-rooms:

(1) When and how do users of a particular type of context fail to accept the maker's message?

(2) When and how do users of a particular type of context use it in ways never considered by the maker? Are those ways compatible or incompatible with the maker's reasons for constructing or modifying the context in the first place?

Research methods and sample

The data on which our discussion of the physical conditions of disorderly behavior is based were collected as part of the larger study of how teachers define certain classroom situations. From October 1969 through June 1970, I observed for approximately two hours each seventy-one teachers at work in their classrooms. My principal aim was to note their reactions to instances or situations of disorderly behavior, academic performance, and tardiness. Thirty-six male and female teachers of grades three, four, seven, eight, ten, and eleven in the amalgamated Protestant school system of St John's, Newfoundland, Canada, participated in the study during the first part of the academic year, 1969–1970.[3] The number instructing in each grade was roughly equal. Another thirty-five teachers, both male and female, were observed in Kingston, Jamaica. At the elementary and junior high school levels, these teachers taught in the private preparatory schools and the government-supported primary and junior secondary schools. The senior secondary school teachers taught in a government-aided although privately operated school, there being no other form of education at that level outside of the technical colleges. The grades they taught were, in general, the same as those taught by the St John's

teachers, although one grade five and four grade nine classes were also observed in order to broaden the basis for comparison. I was unable to observe any fifth form or grade eleven classes in Kingston because the general examination period began two weeks earlier than I had expected.

In the classrooms, I observed and recorded 145 instances of disorderly behavior. Many additional instances simply were observed without being recorded. Since the chief focus of the research was on the ways teachers define these situations, 95 of the observed and recorded instances were discussed with the teachers concerned in an interview that followed no later than the end of the school day.

Choice of teachers for the project was nonrandom. Its exploratory nature and subjective focus dictated that it was important to have participants who were more or less interested in the research and who were ready to communicate to the best of their ability their definition of each situation. Thus, only those teachers were observed and interviewed who volunteered to participate after the investigator had described the study in detail.[4] The sample groups were limited further by the condition that each teacher have at least two full years' experience in his profession, so that his ways of reacting to classroom events could be said to be relatively fixed. In fact, a large majority of the participants had experience in excess of five years.

Additional information about the research procedure of the project is available elsewhere (Stebbins, 1971; 1969). It is possible that some of the methods and controls adopted for study of teachers' definitions of classroom situations are unnecessary for—perhaps even adverse to—objective examination of the physical and temporal antecedents of disorderly behavior. They have been presented, because, for better or for worse, they constitute the methodological strengths and weaknesses of the present paper.

It should be clear by now that interest in the physical conditions of disorderly behavior emerged during the course of the research, instead of (as usually happens) prior to it. That there even is a physical dimension to disorderliness did not occur to me until I started observing Kingston schoolrooms, roughly halfway through the project. There the openness of school construction, smallness of classrooms, and bigness of classes, when compared with the educational scene in St John's, offered sharp contrasts. The amount of activity inside and outside the classroom, the level of noise, the close-quarter conditions, the numbers of pupils, and perhaps even the heat gave the impression of general disorder in some of the schools observed. These dissimilarities in the two education environments struck me immediately. And I realized at once that certain physical characteristics of their classrooms, such as the placement of three or four students in a two-student desk or the absence of one or more walls, offered Kingston children opportunities for disorderly behavior never dreamed of by their counterparts in St John's.

Thus, the chief aim of this paper is to present hypotheses generated from observational data on how certain physical conditions in classrooms encourage disorderly behavior there. With such a goal rigorous verification of these hypotheses is precluded at this time.[5] Therefore the reader must assume every finding is tentative, unless more systematic verificational research is cited in support of it. The findings, however, are presented in the present tense, often as if they have universal application; this is the form that most readily lends itself to testing.

Since the schools in St John's are, for the most part, like schools elsewhere in North America, we need only describe those in Kingston in order for North American readers to perceive the contrast. For those who are interested the St John's schools are described in Stebbins (forthcoming, ch. 2).

Kingston schools: a description

Kingston schools differ from those in St John's in numerous ways. Indeed, if a North American happened onto a Kingston school after school hours when pupils and staff were away, he would probably have great difficulty, were it not for the blackboards and desks, identifying it as a school. First, it is much less common to find a single massive rectangular school building. Those few schools constructed in this fashion are private. Instead, the typical school is composed of a set of comparatively small rectangular buildings positioned near each other, one floor high at the

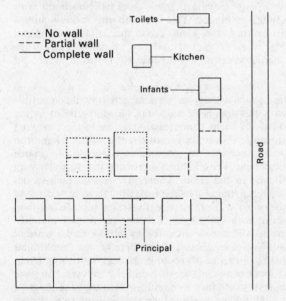

Figure 24.1 A Kingston primary school

elementary level and one or two floors high at the secondary level. Normally, each building contains three or four classrooms. Such a plan seems to facilitate ventilation, while cutting building costs. The external arrangements of buildings in three Kingston

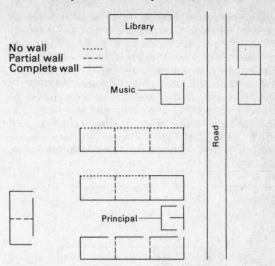

Figure 24.2 A Kingston junior secondary school

schools visited by the author are presented in Figures 24.1 through 24.3.[6] They may be compared with the floor plan, presented in Figure 24.4, of a typical inner-city elementary or junior high school in St John's.

As Figures 24.1 through 24.3 show, Kingston schools generally have no halls. Instead, the classrooms in each rectangled unit open onto one side of a passageway, which may or may not be covered. On the other side, the passageway is bordered by a grass or cement courtyard, a stretch of lawn (usually parched in spring and summer), a patch of bare earth, or a driveway.

Kingston schoolrooms, like those in North America, are little boxes within larger ones. Though generally smaller than those in St John's (perhaps by as much as one-third), they must serve many more pupils, the average enrollment being around fifty.[7] Equally significant, these little classroom boxes, except in the

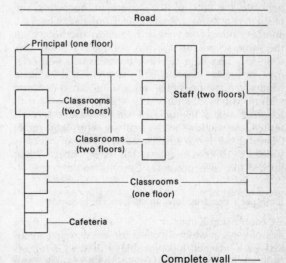

Figure 24.3 A Kingston senior secondary school

senior secondary schools, are never completely enclosed. Here, too, the designer's aim was probably to achieve adequate ventilation, while economizing on construction and labor costs. In the government-supported schools, there is, typically, no wall on the side of the room bordering the passageway. Or, if there is a wall, it is only 3 feet or so high. In the private (preparatory) schools this wall may be a sieve-like structure made of ornamental cinder blocks, which, although it fails to prevent auditory distractions, does allow ventilation and limits visual diversion.

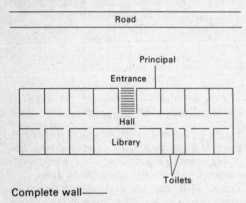

Complete wall———

Figure 24.4 A typical inner-city elementary or junior high school, St John's

The government-supported schools are only somewhat more likely to have walls at the front and back of their classrooms than they are to have them on the passageway side. Usually the rooms are partitioned by a line of portable blackboards and tack boards. Sometimes a concrete wall reaches approximately four-fifths of the way to the roof, leaving more than enough space for the sounds of lessons in neighboring classrooms to escape. Only those classrooms situated on the ends of the building have a true wall. The wall opposite the side of the classroom bordering the passageway varies considerably from one school to another, indeed from one classroom to another within the same school. In the more affluent schools this wall, too, may be a sievelike concrete structure or it may be solid concrete with several large jalousie windows. Sometimes this wall is simply solid concrete with no windows, with a very small window, or with louvered vents. In some of the secondary schools visited, the windows in this wall are set in large metal frames divided into smaller sections each of which is supposed to contain glass, but rarely does. When opened they swing outward from the room.

Designer's constructions and disorderly behavior

By contrasting Kingston and St John's schools, three sets of ways in which students use the designer's context in a manner incompatible with certain of his original aims became apparent. The first stems from the proximate location and use of several small buildings to form a school; the second stems from the construction of classrooms that lack doors and one or more walls; the third stems from the impingement of outside visual and auditory stimuli. The first two are found only in Kingston schools. The third is a problem in schools in both cities, but is most prevalent in Kingston. It is safe to assume that the designer, in interaction with his student users, intended his constructions to communicate to them the message to stay within the walls and doors and concentrate on official activities; even though, in Kingston institutions, there are fewer walls and doors within which to stay.[8] Of course, he may also have striven to communicate other messages through this type of context, messages that can only be discovered by interviewing him.

(1) *Kingston schools designed on the order of* those presented in Figures 24.1 through 3 are usually located among numerous large shade trees. The combination of several buildings huddled together beneath a number of trees whose leaves darken the grounds and whose trunks obstruct vision, makes it possible for those students so motivated to be in school but not in class. In schools constructed in this fashion (whether elementary or high schools), students may hide among the buildings and elsewhere on the school property for one or two hours or even the whole day. In the high schools, these truants talk with each other, perhaps engage in games, even study. In the elementary schools, they seem to do much the same things they would do were they playing in their own neighborhood with similar resources. That is, with the usual youthful exuberance, they chase each other, climb trees, fight, play various games, and, as we shall see, disturb ongoing classroom proceedings.

(2) *The absence of one or more walls* in a classroom leads to a variety of student activities incompatible with the designer's aims. One incompatibility is the relatively free conversational exchange between students inside and outside the room. Kingston youngsters will peer around a wall or a row of portable blackboards behind the teacher and talk furtively with friends in the class. Apparently, some teachers, although irritated by such behavior, have ceased trying to control it. For instance, I watched a grade four boy shout to a companion in the class behind (the two groups were not separated by blackboards) without drawing so much as a glance from his teacher. Similar behavior can be observed in the high schools in Kingston. One student carried on a brief conversation from outside a window on one side of the classroom with a friend outside a window on the opposite side. Within this crosscurrent the teacher struggled, without comment, to present a geometry lesson.

A second incompatibility, closely related to the first, is the tendency for the pupils at large on the school grounds to hang around the classrooms while lessons are in session. Unlike the conversations between students inside and outside the room, which are usually brief, the silent group of spectators may linger for as long as a teacher will tolerate such observation. These onlookers apparently make elementary and junior high school teachers uncomfortable, for in all cases noted they attempted to drive them off. Frequently, they were only momentarily successful. Shortly, the gallery would reassemble often with new spectators joining it, in effect replacing those who had seen enough and had set out in search of more stimulating sights to view. In the senior high school similar groups of onlookers were observed, but they never were told to leave. Perhaps teachers there felt those outside could benefit as much from their lessons as those inside.

Another incompatibility stemming from the openness of construction is the attraction of people to the classrooms who have no official right to be there. Two instances were observed in a junior high school in which youths, roughly the age of the students and identifiable as outsiders by the absence of a school uniform, passed by the classroom in which I was observing. In the first, a pair of teenage boys who were chasing a girl across the school grounds, paused to contemplate me and the fact of my presence there. In the second, a single male, slightly older than the students in the class, walked by the room twice and gave a low whistle at a couple of the girls. The teachers in these classes made no effort to remove the boys or have them removed from the school.

Still another incompatibility is that without walls, students—even though they lack official permission to do so—can leave the classroom at will. Frequently, such desertions take place when, for example, the teacher must turn his back to the class to erase the blackboard. When he does this, as many as three or four youngsters, close to the outer edge of the room, have been observed to slip quietly from it. In one low-ability elementary class, which is held under a large tree, there is for the students an additional advantage made possible by the total absence of walls: When their teacher reaches for them with the belt in order to administer punishment for an instance of misconduct, they simply bolt from the class area, chase around the school grounds, and reappear when they believe she has forgotten the infraction or for other reasons is unlikely to administer the punishment. On one occasion two boys settled the question of whether a strapping would take place by seizing the belt itself and lighting out with it for the freedom and safety of the school grounds.

One incompatibility—really an extension of the practice of students outside the classroom talking to those within it—is actual entry into the room. In one Kingston primary school where several classes are held under a large tin roof supported only by four wooden posts (see Figure 24.1), tardy pupils en route to classes elsewhere in the school will occasionally walk through one or more of the class areas while lessons are being conducted. It is also common for

students to enter a schoolroom, with or without seeking the teacher's permission, to give a message, books, money, and the like to a friend or brother or sister. That there is no opposition expressed toward such intrusions means, in this case, that Kingston teachers do not regard it as disorderly or regard it as only a mild form of disorderliness.

There is one aspect of Kingston classroom life that, although unintended by the school designer, is probably compatible with his aims. Openness of the classrooms permits them to be entered by both birds and dogs. But, perhaps because their presence is so common (especially the birds), they disrupt class business very little. This stands in contrast to life in St John's schools where the spontaneous appearance of any animal life in the classroom is quite rare. In St John's when a dog strays into a classroom, it forces an abrupt change of focus; ongoing activity is stopped temporarily while students and teacher attempt to eject the animal. However, students are often ambivalent about such occurrences. They would like to help their teacher; yet, that a dog is loose in the room probably has caused more interest and excitement than most other events of the year. So, in general, students treat the animal well, by petting it, talking to it, and making a less than genuine effort to catch it. Especially if the dog has no collar, it may take several minutes before he can be cornered and led from the room. The psychological return to lessons probably takes even longer. Since dogs manage to wander into St John's schools (undoubtedly aided by students) despite the schools being closed, being closed, in this instance, becomes a disadvantage; it prevents the presence of dogs from becoming routine and therefore incapable of disrupting seriously classroom proceedings.

The final incompatibility concerning the openness of classrooms is the difficulty such a condition poses for establishing whether a pupil is tardy. Technically speaking, tardiness is arriving in the classroom after the time at which official activities begin there. In many classrooms around the world, this time is marked by ringing some sort of bell. In St John's the bell always rings at this appointed time because it is electronically regulated. And the nearly universal response by teachers to this stimulus is to shut the classroom door. Students coming through the door after it is closed generally are defined as late and dealt with accordingly. Thus, the time at which school starts in St John's is a highly precise matter, acknowledged by the shutting of classroom doors. This makes tardiness manifest.

In Kingston the bells rung are handbells, the ringing of which is subject to the vicissitudes of memory and the accuracy of the watch of the teacher responsible for the tolling. Moreover, latecomers are sometimes difficult to spot in government-supported schools, owing to the openness of their construction and the amount of extraclassroom activity that occurs after official class business has begun. As we have seen, classroom doors are nonexistent in most Kingston schools, except those at the senior secondary level. Here, they may or may not be closed, depending on the teacher's orientation to such matters. Thus, although there is also a standard starting time for each school in Kingston, its de facto starting time tends to be much less precise than that of a typical school in St John's. And there is usually no arrangement such as a closed door to publicize lateness.

The incompatibilities of student use of school and classroom discussed in this section are fostered, in part, by the openness of school and classroom construction and by the arrangement of several small buildings on a large, tree-shaded plot of land. Adding walls and doors to the school plan would solve some of these problems. But such modifications probably would only create other problems that come from confining, for the greater part of each school day, large numbers of unmotivated youngsters in a space the size of a classroom. A far more efficacious solution, pedagogically, would be to reduce class sizes to manageable teaching units and introduce new instructional techniques and content that better hold the students' attention. The absence of walls and doors, in itself, is not objectionable, so long as the official business of the classroom is significantly more interesting to the student than what he might do if allowed to escape to the school grounds. How all this relates to open-plan education is considered in Stebbins (forthcoming, ch. 5).

(3) *No matter how closed*, no classroom is impervious to all external visual and auditory distraction. In this sense any classroom is open to some extent. Every teacher is aware of the momentarily disruptive effects of lightning, thunder, rain, snow, high winds, airplanes, firetrucks, ambulances, and the like. One St John's elementary teacher points out the sea gulls when they accumulate in sufficient number to attract her students' attention. This way she partly controls the effects of this visual stimulus that destroys the continuity of the presentation of her lessons by distracting the students. In another instance, a helicopter took off from a nearby field, buzzing a Kingston primary school in which I was observing. Immediately, the childrens' attention was diverted from their teacher's lesson in arithmetic as they rushed to the opened windows (one of the few classrooms to have windows) in order to observe. It took the teacher several minutes to persuade them to return to their seats, to calm them, and to resume treatment of the morning's arithmetic problems.

Whether their classrooms are open or closed, such events are overpowering enough to command the attention of grade school pupils everywhere. Openness only admits a greater variety of distracting stimuli, which, again, is incompatible with the designer's aims. For example, a boy in a Kingston primary school ambled along one of the passageways blowing what sounded like a duck call into each room he passed.

Or, consider the behavior of the following junior high school student:

I was observing in a grade eight English class while the pupils there wrote an essay for their teacher. A rare late spring rain poured down outside the door of the room, dripping noisily off the eaves onto the cement courtyard beyond the passageway. Rain discourages classroom deserters from circulating as much. Instead, they seek shelter under the trees, at the sides of buildings, under the eaves, and even in the classroom. Suddenly, a boy who had been standing outside the door to the classroom in which I was seated shouted to a friend taking refuge elsewhere on the school grounds. The teacher did nothing at first, assuming apparently that the message shouted would be the end of this form of communication. He was wrong. Soon a boisterous conversation was underway between the two, which complete with laughter, echoed through the enclosed classroom like gunfire. The teacher who could tolerate no more took action. 'What are you doing?' he rasped, as he poked his head from the room. 'What class are you from?' The boy, obviously startled, muttered that he was from 9A6. 'And where is 9A6 meeting?' the teacher inquired. The boy informed him it was meeting in its regular room. The teacher, seeing no reason either for the shouting or for the boy being away from class, flew into a rage. 'Why aren't you there?' he roared. 'Get your hands out of your pockets and stand up straight!' The boy slowly complied. 'Go over there and stand till your teacher comes!' The boy hesitated. 'Go on, get over there and stand!' Reluctantly, perhaps defiantly, the boy shuffled through the rain to the other side of the courtyard and waited under the eaves for his teacher. He was still there when the class period ended roughly twenty minutes later.

Whatever the strengths and weaknesses of classroom openness, many teachers seem to prefer a closed learning situation. This proposition is supported further by a case study of windowless classrooms in which teachers are reported to favor overwhelmingly the absence of windows as one way of reducing the misbehavior caused by distractions (Architectural Research Laboratory, 1965, 1–60). As for the children in these rooms, they were, in general, little interested in whether their rooms had windows or not. If a windowless educational environment has any effect on achievement, this research demonstrates it is very small.

In sum, school designers' constructions, especially in Kingston, inadvertently contribute to the enactment of a variety of forms of undesirable behavior. Much of this behavior is defined by teachers as disorderly. It ranges from inattention caused by distracting external stimuli; through mischievousness, often manifested as talking; to bad behavior, as seen in skipping school or class. Still, it should be noted that, although skipping school or class is defined as bad behavior by teachers in St John's and senior secondary and preparatory school teachers in Kingston, it appears to have only the status of mischievousness in the government-supported primary and junior secondary schools in Kingston. No wonder—it is so frequent that, like common forms of disapproved behavior elsewhere in society, it cannot be condemned and sanctioned too harshly.

One intriguing question that should be raised at this point is how many of the variances in the rate and kind of disorderliness and other forms of undesirable behavior observed among St John's and Kingston students are due to cultural differences and how many are due to differences in the physical context? Unfortunately, this study was not designed to consider this question, which can be most effectively answered by placing St John's students in a typical Kingston school and placing Kingston students in a typical St John's school. There are, however, at least three observations that suggest that cultural background is not as significant a determinant of the student behavior discussed here as physical context. First, in the most physically closed institution visited in Kingston—the preparatory school—disorderly behavior took much the same form as in St John's. Second, the one open-plan elementary school in St John's, though of too recent origin to make any definitive statements, appears to be facing disorderliness similar to some of that encountered in the Kingston primary schools. Third, other data from the same project being reported here indicate that teachers, who are usually from the same culture as their students, hold definitions of classroom situations remarkably similar to those of their colleagues in the other city (see, for example, Stebbins, 1972, 38–40).

Conclusions

This paper proposed to present hypotheses bearing on the physical context influences on disorderly behavior along the lines of two research questions associated with our theoretical statement. Turning to the first question, it was assumed that the designer's constructions intend to communicate to students the message to stay within the walls and doors and concentrate on official activities. The findings show that students in St John's abide the first part of this message, whether they like it or not, while some of those in Kingston fail to. What other messages schoolhouse makers might be communicating, if any, can only be discovered by talking with them.

With respect to the second question, the data indicate that students in schools and classrooms in St John's and Kingston frequently use them in ways never considered by the makers, ways that are incompatible with the makers' aims. In reality, it is probably true that when students use an educational environment in ways never considered by its maker, their behavior will nearly always be incompatible with his aims. Until we have more information on what aims these makers have—what messages they are trying to communicate through their constructions or modifications—this question, like the one above, remains only partially answered for the schoolroom context.

Notes

* This is a revised version of a paper presented at the Annual Meeting of the Council on Anthropology and Education, Montreal, Quebec, Canada, April 1972. The Institute of Social and Economic Research, Memorial University, provided the travel and subsistence grant that made the Jamaican portion of this research possible. I wish to thank Jeffrey W. Bulcock and John J. Figueroa for their most helpful comments on an earlier draft of this paper.

1 Space limitations preclude presentation of the more detailed version of this rudimentary theory and its associated literature, which, however, can be found in Stebbins (forthcoming, ch. 1).

2 Referring to makers and users as roles may appear to some as an unwarranted use of this sociological term. But there are sets of expectations or rules in many societies that apply to how people ought to construct physical contexts and how other people ought to use them. Certainly, we should feel these rules were violated if the maker of the dwelling in which we lived had only a 4-foot-high entrance or if the commode were placed at the same height. At least in some circles, users of certain physical contexts are expected to refrain from putting their feet on the walls or spitting on the floor. Just how these two roles articulate with other positions or social identities in the social structure, remains to be considered.

3 There is no public school system in St John's. Most of the Protestant schools have amalgamated recently under one administrative arrangement, which parallels the other major system in the city: that of the Roman Catholic Church. Although the study was designed initially to include observation of teachers in this latter system as well, the investigator was denied access to it and so had to be content with a religiously homogenous sample.

4 The author is well aware of the aversion some teachers have for observers in their classrooms. Willingness to participate in this study was expressed in varying degrees by those in the sample groups. Teachers for whom the thought of being observed is extremely repugnant failed, of course, to volunteer. How this sampling bias affects the results can only be determined by further research where randomness of respondent selection is striven for.

5 Scientifically, the study of the influence of physical and temporal conditions on disorderly behavior is at the exploratory stage, wherein research strives to generate what Glaser and Strauss (1967) call 'grounded theory'.

6 Since Figures 24.1 through 3 were constructed from memory, the arrangements of buildings in these three Kingston schools may not be depicted entirely accurately. At the time of observation, I could see no use for such details.

7 Class enrollments in Kingston schools range from around thirty to over eighty. One class in Kingston had an official enrollment of eighty students, but many were absent each day, thus cutting the effective enrollment to around sixty. At the elementary level, large classes are the rule throughout Jamaica (see Murray, 1968, 8–9).

8 This assumption is part of the overall commonsense perspective of Western man, for whom schools and schoolrooms have been part of life since the Middle Ages (*Encyclopaedia Britannica*, 1968). Until recently, we simply have known no other way to educate groups of children, and even adults, than by herding them into a room and instructing them. Historically, school designers, being part of society, have been strongly influenced by this cultural axiom. As Sommer (1969, 72) puts it: 'The school house is not simply the result of accident and inadequate theorizing; it arose in response to a certain type of teaching (sit and learn) in a certain type of society.'

References

Architectural Research Laboratory, 1965, 'The Effect of Windowless Classrooms on Elementary School Children', Ann Arbor, Mich., University of Michigan Department of Architecture.

Castaldi, B., 1969, *Creative Planning of Educational Facilities*, Chicago, Rand McNally.

Caudill, W. W. *et al.*, 1967, 'What works and what fails in school design', *Nation's Schools*, 79 (March), 85–116.

Cutts, N. E. and Moseley, N., 1957, *Teaching the Disorderly Pupil* New York, Longmans, Green.

Encyclopaedia Britannica, 1968, 'Educational architecture', pp. 1021–5 in Vol. 7, Chicago, Encyclopaedia Britannica.

Fuchs, E., 1969, *Teachers' Talk*, Garden City, N.Y., Doubleday.

Glaser, B. G. and Strauss, A. L., 1967, *The Discovery of Grounded Theory*, Chicago, Aldine.

Gross, R. and Murphy, J., 1968, *Educational Change and Architecture*, New York, Educational Facilities Laboratories.

McCormick, P. and Cassidy, F., 1953, *History of Education*, New York, Catholic Education Press.

Murray, R. N., 1968, 'Organization of the education system in the West Indies', presented at the Caribbean Educational Seminar, Jamaica, July/August.

Ontario Institute for Studies in Education, 1970, 'Open-Plan', *Current Bibliography*, no. 2, Toronto, Library, Reference and Information Services (October).

Proshansky, H. M. *et al.*, 1970, 'The influence of the physical environment on behavior: some basic assumptions', in H. M. Proshansky *et al.*, eds, *Environmental Psychology*, New York, Holt, Rinehart & Winston.

Sommer, R., 1969, *Personal Space*, Englewoods Cliffs, N.J., Prentice-Hall.

Stebbins, R. A., 1969, 'Studying the definition of the situation: theory and field research strategies', *Canadian Review of Sociology and Anthropology*, 6 (November), 193–211.

Stebbins, R. A., 1971, 'The meaning of disorderly behavior: teacher definitions of a classroom situation', *Sociology of Education*, 44 (spring), 217–36.

Stebbins, R. A., 1972, 'The Meaning of Tardiness: how Teachers Define a Classroom Situation', paper presented at the annual meeting of the Canadian Sociology and Anthropology Association, Montreal, June.

Stebbins, R. A., forthcoming, The Disorderly Classroom: its Physical and Temporal Conditions, St John's, Newfoundland, Committee on Publications, Faculty of Education, Memorial University.

Waller, W., 1932, *The Sociology of Education*, New York, Wiley.

25   The delinquent school

David Reynolds

Sociologists, criminologists and educational researchers have expended an enormous amount of time and money in their search for the causes of youthful problems like juvenile delinquency. In this search for what is almost the criminological equivalent of the 'Holy Grail', these researchers have lavished attention on delinquents' families, their physical type, their IQ, their personality and even on the sanitary amenities of their homes—they have concentrated on explaining deviance and delinquency as a consequence of individual, familial, cultural or neighbourhood pathology.[1]

One societal institution which has escaped much of the attention that criminologists have lavished upon children and upon their families is the institution of the school. Certainly some notice has been taken of the way in which the educational system may impose certain stresses and strains on large numbers of its working-class children. The blocked goal attainment hypotheses of Cohen (1955) and Cloward and Ohlin (1961) suggest that the educational system and the middle-class teachers that staff it may, because of their middle-class assumptions as to what constitutes the 'good pupil', deny working-class pupils status within the schools because these pupils have not been socialised to fulfil the status requirements of middle-class society. Delinquency outside the school may thus be a working-class child's solution to his problem of status frustration within the school, a solution that, as work by Hargreaves (1967) suggests, may be made even more likely by specific school practices such as streaming by ability.

However, the interest which sub-cultural theorists have shown in the educational system as a 'generator' of delinquency has yet to be marked by any rigorous analysis of exactly how it is that the educational system actually manages to produce the problems that it is said to produce. C. M. Phillipson, writing on the

same theme, argues that 'Throughout the literature the reference is to the school rather than to particular schools; sociologists seem to be operating with highly abstract models of the school which rest on their intuitive hunches about what schools are really like' (1971, p. 239).

Even the recent emergence of the 'interactionist' school, with their insistence on the importance of studying the social interaction between rule breakers and those who label them, has—with the exceptions of the work of Werthman (1967) and that of Cicourel and Kitsuse (1963)—generally neglected to study the key social problem defining agency of the school. Ritual mention is often made of the 'importance' of the school in the lives of delinquents, yet such mentions are rarely followed by anything more than informed gossip about the nature of within school social life and within school social interaction.

The result of our general ignorance as to exactly how the process of within school interaction is producing the problems that it is said to be producing is that we are still operating with the implicit assumption that all schools of a particular type are the same in the type and quality of this interaction and therefore in their effects—as Phillipson (1971, p. 239) notes:

> The implicit suggestion is that all schools are sufficiently alike to produce a standardised response from their pupils. The idea that there may be considerable differences between overtly similar schools, that some schools may facilitate and others hinder the drift into delinquency does not seem to have occurred to writers on delinquency.

Since children spend much of their time in schools and since few sociologists would dare to talk of 'the family' as if all families were the same, yet regularly talk of 'the school' as if all schools were the same, it is worthwhile trying to discover why there has been so little examination by researchers as to whether

Source: article commissioned for this volume. The author is lecturer in social administration, University College, Cardiff.

217

different schools may have the effect of producing or generating pupils with different rates of deviance.

The principal reason for this neglect appears to be the general societal conviction that education—by definition—exerts at best a worthwhile influence and at worst a neutral influence on the young people that undergo the process, a belief which tends to defy qualification and rejection. Whilst such a belief as to the value of education may be understandable amongst élite groups who have profited from the educational system—one government report argued that problems like delinquency 'may arise not because boys are at school but because they are not at school enough' (Central Advisory Council for Education, Crowther Report, 1959, para. 63)—many social researchers have simply taken the school regime as something given. They have individualised the explanation of institutional problems by concentrating on the family background, ability and personality of the deviant child without ever looking at the nature, quality and operation of the school regimes from which he or she is held to deviate.

A good example of how educational research often takes for granted the institutions and explains their problems as resulting from the pathologies of their children, is provided by some research into truancy. One study (Tyerman, 1958) compared a group of truants and so-called 'normal' children and concluded:

> Few of the truants had a happy and secure home influence. Most of them came from broken homes or homes where there was open disharmony. In general, the parents set poor examples and were unsatisfactory characters. They neglected their children, were ineffective in their supervision and took little interest in their welfare. The view of many writers that the truant is born in an inferior environment seemed to be confirmed.

Even where some of the truants gave reasons connected with school—such as fear of the teachers—as the explanation for their behaviour, the author comments (p. 220):

> These reasons may to some extent be valid but it is unwise to accept truants' excuses at their face value. The limits of self deception are wide and it is easier to blame other people than oneself. Parents and children look for scapegoats and teachers are often chosen.

An alternative view of truancy, delinquency and rebellion at school is to see them as a form of rational rebellion against a system which the children feel has little to offer them. Working-class children may thus see the school as an alien institution whose middle-class teachers deny them status, and may therefore rebel against their schools by exhibiting what to the schools is problematic behaviour. Rather than discounting the reasons and motivations given by the problem children and truants for their own actions as the products of 'abnormal' personalities, it may be worthwhile to pay some regard to the reasons that lie behind these deviant acts, since the problem behaviour may simply be a reaction to what the children see as unsatisfying environments within some of their schools.

While one can understand the reasons for the existence of this normative belief as to the value of the education our society provides, the effects of this belief have been, in general, to stultify the asking of critical questions about the nature of our educational processes.

The second reason for this basic lack of research into secondary school regimes and their possible effects in producing deviance and delinquency amongst their pupils is that the organisations which control research workers' access to the schools have seen this type of evaluative research as a great threat. Local education committees have been worried that any variability in the quality of the service they run may be exposed to public view and teacher unions have been concerned that evaluative research of this sort smacks of the hated 'payment by results' philosophy of the 19th century. Michael Power's work into differences in delinquency rates amongst Tower Hamlets secondary schools, called by some reviewers the most important work on delinquency for decades, was in fact stopped by London teachers and by the Inner London Education Authority. Certainly some organisations like the Schools Council have found it easy to secure access to schools for the purposes of doing research, yet this type of research—usually in the area of curriculum development—has been marked by its generally unquestioning approach to the organisation of schooling. Quite simply, there is very little work on the organisational effectiveness of different schools because very little work has ever been allowed (Power, 1967).

A third reason for the lack of evaluative research is the severe practical and methodological problems that are encountered when undertaking the research. Much of the information that is needed—school delinquency rates for example—requires a laborious effort to obtain. The demise of the standardised eleven plus exam and its replacement by teachers' estimates; and the increasing use of internally moderated school leaving exams means that schools' data on academic input and output is not of use since it is not strictly comparable from school to school.

Such research into school factors is furthermore very broad ranging—if we find that school A in the suburb has a low delinquency rate and school B in the slums a much higher rate, then we need to find out whether these schools are receiving similar children from similar neighbourhoods before we can ever presume that we need to investigate what is happening in their schools. Research into school factors and differences, then, is simply unscientific without comparable research into family factors, neighbourhood factors and pupil factors.

Research into within school interaction is also invariaby difficult research because of the absence of any substantial body of knowledge or satisfactory theoretical basis to inform the research. Certainly recent years have seen a growing interest by educational researchers in the processes whereby pupil success and pupil failure is produced within schools and within classrooms (Hargreaves, 1972; and for a recent review of developments see Chanan and Delamont, 1975). There are certainly valuable insights to be found in this type of work which emphasises how the quality of pupil/teacher interaction and teachers' definitions of their pupils may affect the success and failure of individual pupils and perhaps of whole classes. But the literature within this area tends to be rather more satisfactory in generating hypotheses than in testing them and, as one authoritative review of the sociology of school learning concludes, 'We are still in the conjecturing stage as far as identifying the aspects of in school experience and the kinds of in school interaction which contribute most to academic success' (Boocock, 1972).

Research into differences between schools as learning environments is therefore both difficult and wide ranging in its scope. Because educational researchers have looked at the easiest areas of their discipline first, no substantive sociology of the school exists to guide and help research into school variation. The result of this is that we probably know more about the relationship between the absence of internal toilets and children's reading ability than we do about the sort of school experience that may inhibit or promote pupil delinquency and other problem behaviour.

The fourth—and most important—reason for the absence of much research into this topic is that the educational research that has been undertaken suggests that the individual school is only a weak influence on pupils' behaviour, attainment and attitudes when compared to the strong influences of family social class and neighbourhood environment. The American Coleman Report, the British Plowden Report and the summary of recent research in Jencks's *Inequality* all agree that different schools do not have greatly different effects on their pupils' academic development, whatever the variation in their quality. In fact, Jencks's conclusion was unequivocal (1973, p. 256):

the character of a school's output depends largely on a single input, namely the character of its entering children. Everything else—the school budget, its policies, the characteristics of the teachers—is either secondary or completely irrelevant.

School differences, in other words, make no great difference.

However, these studies such as Coleman and Plowden are subject to important criticisms (Dyer, 1968; Corwin, 1974). They tend to include in their analyses very few school variables by comparison with the number of family variables and those that they do include are usually simple resource based indicators, such as the age of the school buildings, size of the playground or the number of books in the school library. Pupil/teacher relationships, teacher character or headteacher competence do not figure prominently as possible school 'factors'. Furthermore, the studies use only one measure of output—cognitive ability on non-verbal or verbal tests—on which children's performance is likely to be substantially determined by home background and family social class. Whether or not schools affect pupils' self-conception, self-esteem, deviance rates, attendance rates or vandalism rates does not appear to be a question that these researchers have ever posed.

So far, it has been argued that research into those factors that generate delinquency has concentrated on children's family background, neighbourhood and character as their explanatory variables. Researchers have mentioned 'the educational system' as having delinquency producing potential but do not examine if there are variations in this potential within the system. This neglect reflects the ideology that education solves, not creates, problems; the difficulty of ensuring access to the schools; the practical and methodological problems of doing the research and the absence of any body of theory to guide enquiry into this highly complex field. This neglect is further explained by the ready and uncritical acceptance of the view that the individual school has, in any case, little independent effect of its own upon its pupils' development.

However, over the past few years a small but increasing body of knowledge has gathered, which suggests that our neglect to develop any sociology of the school has greatly limited our understanding of the process of adolescent social and educational development. Michael Power's work already referred to showed wide variations—from 0.8 to 17.0 per cent per annum—in the incidence of delinquency (defined by a guilty court appearance) in the secondary modern schools of Tower Hamlets; variations that he could not explain by simple factors such as school size or the age of school buildings. Furthermore, Power suggested (1972) that the school rates were largely independent of neighbourhood characteristics and that, therefore, the school itself was an important influence on whether pupils drifted towards delinquency.

Recent work by Rutter in the primary schools of South London also suggests the existence of substantial 'school effects' and that there is something about certain schools in themselves which is associated with low rates of educational attainment and high rates of behavioural deviance among their children, a conclusion that is echoed by Gath, whose researches have revealed large differences between schools in their delinquency rates and child guidance referral rates (Rutter, 1973; Gath, 1972). Further research from the United States has also suggested that the academic climate of high schools is an important influence on pupils' scholastic attainment. Not surprisingly, students have been found to make better progress in schools where teachers and fellow students place a high value on achievement (McDill and Rigsby, 1973). Although we can therefore conclude that the individual school may have an important independent influence on its pupils' attainments and behaviour, the size of this influence and the precise features of the schools that may make their pupils different are, as yet, unknown.

Over the past three years work has been going on in our research community to see if, in fact, some schools are managing to prevent—and others promote —the growth of deviancy amongst their pupils and to see what it is about the successful schools that may help them excel. The particular community itself has two great advantages for this type of research, concerned as it is to sort out the relative effect of family, school and neighbourhood factors upon pupils' development. It is, firstly, a relatively homogeneous former mining community, with very small differences in the social class composition of the people who live in the catchment areas of the different schools. Any differences between the schools of the area in the sort of pupils they are producing are therefore more likely to reflect differences in the effects of their schools and less likely to reflect initial differences in the type of children the schools are receiving.[2]

The second advantage of this community is, quite simply, that the headteachers, staffs and education committee concerned agreed to allow the research in the first place. At a time when sociologists often emphasise the reluctance of official bodies to allow research into 'sensitive' areas such as the organisational effectiveness of aspects of the social services, it says much for the schools of the area that they should grant a researcher virtually unrestricted freedom to ask whatever questions he wants and also write what he wants about them and their schools.

Although this action may surprise some of their critics of the 'school as hell' or 'teacher as imperialist' variety, the teachers of this community, at least, appear keen to know how they can help—and how they may hinder—the development of their children.

Our work has concentrated so far on a group of nine secondary modern schools and on boys only within these schools. We have found large differences between the schools in the characteristics of their output of pupils, assessed in terms of rates of attendance, academic attainment (going on to the local technical college after leaving school) and delinquency (being found guilty before a court or officially cautioned by the age of fifteen). As Table 25.1 shows, the school with the top attendance rate averaged 89.1 per cent attendance over the years and the bottom school only 77.2 per cent. One school gets over half its pupils into the local technical college—which is regarded locally as the key to obtaining an apprenticeship or craft— and another manages to get only 8.4 per cent. The school with the highest delinquency rate has 10.5 per cent of its boys recorded as officially delinquent each

Table 25.1 Secondary modern school performance, academic years 1966–7 to 1972–3 (per cent)

school	delinquency (first offenders per annum)	attendance	academic attainment
A	10.5	79.9	34.8
B	8.6	78.3	26.5
C	8.3	84.3	21.5
D	8.1	77.2	8.4
E	7.4	89.1	30.4
F	7.2	81.3	18.5
G	5.2	87.0	37.9
H	4.5	88.5	52.7
I	3.8	83.6	36.5

year and the school with the bottom rate only 3.8 per cent per year. All the schools also exhibit a remarkable consistency in their relative performance over the years—the Kendall coefficient of concordance for the nine schools' attendance rates over seven academic years is 0.85 and that for academic attainment is 0.56. Even with national social change, local population movements and with seven different intakes of pupils, the relative performance of the schools remains substantially unchanged over time. As Table 25.2 shows for the attendance figures, year after year the 'effective' schools retain their effectiveness. The school differences are furthermore remarkably consistent with each other—schools high on delinquency are low on academic attainment ($r = -0.526$) and low on attendance ($r = -0.579$). The nine schools are therefore producing children who appear to be very different, to be consistently different over time and to be consistently different on three separate indicators.

It is possible that these officially generated statistics may reflect not just differences in behaviour between groups of pupils at the different schools but also variations in the administrative methods and definitions which are used to produce the statistics (Kitsuse and Cicourel, 1963), yet it is difficult to explain the differences in this way. The attendance registers were collected in the same way in all the nine schools and all of them used an identical system of 'processing' of their truants by means of Educational Welfare Officers. Further work to be published (Reynolds, 1977) also shows that the differences between the schools are not explicable by variations in the size of their catchment areas or by differences in the amount of illness amongst the pupils at the different schools. The academic attainment figures of numbers carrying on with their education at the local technical college, the entry to which is dependent on four passes in the local School Leaving Certificate, are of course dependent on the numbers of children that the individual schools enter for the various exams. Although it is possible that differences between schools may reflect not real differences in the academic performance of

Table 25.2 Attendance rates for boys at secondary modern schools by year and school, academic years 1966–7 to 1972–3 (per cent)

school	1966–7	1967–8	1968–9	1969–70	1970–1	1971–2	1972–3
E	88.5	89.7	90.9	90.6	90.0	87.5	87.2
	1[a]	1	2	1	2	2	2
H	88.0	87.3	91.6	88.9	90.1	88.2	85.7
	2	3	1	2	1	1	3
G	87.1	84.4	86.5	88.4	87.6	86.2	88.2
	3	5	3	3	3	3	1
I	86.3	87.9	84.2	84.6	83.0	80.0	80.0
	4	2	5	4	5	5	5
C	85.0	85.9	84.5	82.0	83.2	83.5	85.2
	5	4	4	7	4	4	4
F	83.9	82.8	83.5	82.5	80.6	77.3	79.0
	6	7	7	6	6	8	7
A	83.2	83.3	84.0	82.6	77.6	75.4	75.1
	7	6	6	5	8	9	9
B	82.7	75.4	81.3	77.5	73.0	79.0	79.3
	8	8	8	9	9	6	6
D	74.9	74.8	77.7	79.7	78.2	78.5	76.5
	9	9	9	8	7	7	8
annual average attendance for all nine schools	83.8	82.3	84.1	83.1	81.1	80.7	80.9

Kendall coefficient of concordance = 0.85 ($P < 0.001$ significant)

[a] Ranking of school in each year.

their pupils but simply the fact that some schools enter a higher proportion of their pupils for the exams than other schools, who enter only their most able children, this does not explain these findings. If the entry policy of the school were the determinant of its results, we would expect schools entering only the most able of their children to have higher pass rates than those entering a greater proportion of their ability range. This does not happen—school D, whose total fourth year of sixty-five pupils were entered only for 60 different exams in the 1972 School Leaving Certificate, achieved an overall pass rate of 47 per cent, whereas school H, whose fourth year of only twenty-seven pupils were entered for no less than 130 exams, achieved an 85 per cent pass rate. Since schools entering a small proportion of their pupils achieve the greatest failure rates of all, it is unlikely that the differences between the schools represent anything other than the fact that some schools are producing pupils who cannot—or more likely will not—show much academic ability.

The statistics of delinquency are perhaps those most open to doubt, since these rates may reflect variations in the processing of offenders by the local police force (Cicourel, 1968). It is easy to see how a school with a high delinquency rate may get a bad name with the local police, who may in turn patrol its catchment area more intensively and be more likely to 'book' offenders in that area rather than use their powers of discretion to warn them. Differences between schools may therefore be exaggerated by the results of differential police action. We know that area police based in the catchment areas of two of the schools have, in fact, been proceeding informally with offenders from those two schools—school A and school F—by taking them to their school for punishment, rather than by taking them through the formal legal processes, yet both these schools already have official delinquency rates that are above average. Since it is possible that other sources of bias might also be operating, we are currently studying the patterns of police patrolling to see if certain areas are 'over patrolled' relative to other areas and are also giving self-report studies of delinquent behaviour to samples of pupils in the schools as a check on the validity of the official records as indicators of the total amount of delinquency committed by their pupils.

Accepting that these statistics reflect real differences in the relative performance of the schools, further large differences in the pupils' performance are also in evidence even after they have left their schools. Table 25.3 shows the pupil unemployment rate for

Table 25.3 Pupil unemployment rate and overall school performance

overall rank	school	pupil unemployment rate (per cent)[a]
1[b]	H	1.4
2	G	0.0
3	I	1.9
4	E	1.3
5	C	1.0
6	F	2.6
7	A	5.4
8	B	7.0
9	D	no information

[a] Pupil unemployment rate is the proportion of all leavers (boys and girls) in summer 1972 who had not found employment by the beginning of January 1973.
[b] In this and following Tables, rank number 1 represents the most successful school.

the various schools, compared to an overall ranking order for the schools, which has been calculated by simply averaging each schools' relative position obtained on the tables of the three measures of output. The clear indication is that those schools which have the lowest relative success rates with their pupils also tend to have the highest rates of unemployment among their school-leavers ($r = -0.714$). Whether this is due to the fact that—because of their poor academic performance—some schools' pupils cannot get jobs, or whether this is due to the fact that some schools' pupils do not wish to find jobs in any case, we cannot be sure. All we can say is that—given the link between unemployment, low income and the generation of other social problems—some schools are sending out into life pupils whose life chances appear disturbingly poor.

The crucial factor is, of course, whether these large, consistent and associated differences between the schools in their success rates simply reflect the fact that some schools are getting a more 'problem-

Table 25.4 Social class of catchment area and overall school performance

overall rank	school	proportion of population in social classes 4 and 5 (per cent)
1	H	37.5
2	G	42.5
3	I	42.9
4	E	42.2
5	C	43.9
6	F	43.4
7	A	44.8
8	B	38.1
9	D	38.9

prone' intake of children. Since the nine schools draw their pupils from geographically separate areas of the community and since they take a fixed two-thirds of the full ability range in each case, it has been possible to assess the social characteristics of the pupils at the schools by looking at census data on the individual wards from which the nine schools take their pupils. Table 25.4 shows the overall school performance ranking, compared to the proportion of the employed population in each catchment area who are semi- or unskilled manual workers. Although a high proportion in these latter social groups could be the explanation for some schools' inferior performance, since the correlation between overall school performance and the proportion of the catchment area who are of low social class is low ($r = -0.134$), we can conclude that our schools' outputs vary virtually independently of the social background of their catchment area.

Further evidence to support our hypothesis as to the independent effects of the secondary school regimes comes from an analysis of the academic quality of the intake to the nine schools. Table 25.5 shows the mean

Table 25.5 Academic quality of pupil intake and overall school performance

overall rank	school	mean raw IQ score of intake (1974)
1	H	34.3
2	G	33.1
3	I	34.0
4	E	35.4
5	C	34.7
6	F	34.5
7	A	33.2
8	B	35.5
9	D	no information

raw score[3] on Raven's Standard Progressive Matrices test of non-verbal intelligence (Raven, 1960) obtained by the boys of the autumn 1974 intake that went to the secondary modern schools. Since there appears to be no suggestion that the more successful schools were receiving academically more able children,[4] we must conclude also that the reasons for some schools' evident success and other schools' manifest failure can hardly lie in the relative ability of their pupil intakes.

Since it appears that the schools of our area do have an independent effect of their own, do we know what it is about the school that can so dramatically affect the social and academic development of its pupils? Over the past three years, a programme of research has been undertaken in eight of the nine schools in an attempt to find out what it is about these schools that makes a difference for their children and what it may be about some schools that may make their children different and deviant. Apart from the collection of routine data on the resources, rules and organisation of each school, this work has included interviews with headteachers and staffs, and assessments of the social climate of the schools, the system of rewards and punishments used, the quality of the teaching, and the type of pupil (and teacher) subculture to be found in each regime. Further important insights into the school regimes' operation have come from the observation of the day-to-day functioning of the different schools conducted over two years by the writer and by a specially trained participant observer. This observer—who was not told the relative success rates of each school—spent a considerable time in each school taking lessons, observing classroom interaction in other teachers' lessons, talking to staff and pupils and assessing the nature of each schools' educational and social ethos. Full details of this work are described elsewhere (Reynolds, 1977) and this analysis is concerned only with the analysis of basic demographic data on each school, and on part of the participant observer's studies on the nature of each schools' educational and social ethos.

The first set of clues to explaining the relative success and failure of the schools are provided by analysis of the simple demographic data on school size, class size, adequacy and age of buildings and staff turnover. As Table 25.6 shows, there is evidence that the more successful schools tended to be smaller ($r = -0.634$), a suggestion which fits well with the available literature on the relationship between the size of educational institutions and their capacity to mobilise their pupils towards acceptance of the schools' educational and social goals (Boocock, 1972). The explanation for this finding is not altogether clear —teachers in the small schools tend to say that their school size means that they can know more pupils as individuals than is possible in the larger schools. If this is true, then it is likely that the close primary relationships possible in the small schools may lead to greater identification of the child with the teacher and perhaps to greater knowledge of their children's problems by the teachers.

As Table 25.6 also shows, staff turnover tends to be higher in the least successful schools ($r = -0.549$) although whether this finding indicates that the staff turnover was causing some schools' lack of success or whether the lack of success was causing the teacher turnover, we cannot be sure. It is likely, though, that high staff turnover functions to produce an adverse pupil response to their schools by its adverse effects on their level of identification with the teaching staff— as Phillipson notes (1971, p. 247):

> A high staff turnover means that pupils are regularly faced with different authority figures who make different and often conflicting demands upon them; the lack of steady, stable relationships will tend to result in a confusion among pupils about how to respond in similar situations to a constant flow of different teachers. A regular turnover of teachers provides a setting for the growth of cynicism among pupils about the worth of their school; one result may be a steady decline in the evaluation by pupils both of the school and of themselves.

Whereas these findings on school size and teacher turnover rates are—in view of existing research findings—to be expected, our findings on the relationship between class size, the quality and age of school buildings and the overall success rate of the schools are more surprising. Although a reduction in class sizes has been a priority of governmental policy for years and although teacher unions strongly support such a policy, research has tended to suggest that class size is not a crucial variable in terms of influencing pupil success and failure. In fact, several studies have shown children in large classes to make better than average scholastic progress (Little *et al.*, 1971; Davie *et al.*, 1972). Our data show that successful schools tend to have smaller class sizes ($r = -0.549$); interestingly, class size appears also to have the most marked effect on the academic attainment of pupils ($r = -0.78$), rather than on attendance ($r = -0.34$) or delinquency ($r = +0.38$). Whilst it might appear that this finding would support recent evidence on the

Table 25.6 School characteristics and overall school performance

overall rank	school	number of pupils (1974)	mean class size (1973)	staff turnover (1973–4) (per cent)	age of main building	adequacy of facilities or buildings
1	H	136	22.5	0.0	1904	poor
2	G	263	28.8	18.2	1906	poor
3	I	176	23.3	22.2	1905	fair
4	E	201	26.1	25.0	1903	poor
5	C	182	29.1	0.0	1903	fair
6	F	355	30.2	37.5	1914	poor
7	A	299	26.5	12.5	1912	poor
8	B	233	23.9	10.0	1937	good
9	D	264	31.7	42.9	1966	good

importance of the resources available to each school as crucial determinants of pupil success rates (Byrne and Williamson, 1975), the differences in class sizes among these schools at least tend to reflect the fact that some schools cannot get staff to come and teach in them, not simply that they have less staff posts available in the first place. Once some schools have posts they cannot fill and therefore have also above average class sizes, it seems likely that this will affect the overall level of success of the school, making it more and more likely that the school, because of its reputation and lack of success, will continue to be able to utilise less resources per pupil than others. A school with problems, then, will tend—by this cyclical process—to remain a school with problems, because rising class sizes will perpetuate its lack of success.

Our findings on the influence of the age and adequacy of school buildings are also somewhat surprising. Certainly findings from Britain (Plowden, DES, 1967), America (Coleman *et al.*, 1966) and Michael Power's Tower Hamlets study (1972) all suggest that the age, state of repair, adequacy and amenities of school buildings are of negligible importance in determining pupil success or failure, but in fact our findings suggest that the best schools tended to have older buildings and to be—according to the Director of Education's ratings as given in Table 25.6 —in less adequate accommodation. Although it is best to be wary of the importance of findings such as this (the implication is, in fact, that making buildings less adequate will make schools more successful!), it is perhaps worth saying that educational policies which assume that the provision of ever more luxurious buildings will necessarily result in greater pupil success are—according to these findings—in urgent need of critical analysis.

So far, then, it is clear that basic data on the schools suggests that the more successful schools tended to be smaller, have lower staff turnover, smaller class sizes and to be situated in older and less adequate buildings. Further work is in progress to establish both the relative importance of each of these factors and also the precise ways in which these factors appear to have their effects.

Analysis of both the organisational properties of the schools and the nature of the educational and social ethos that may explain their relative success rates is currently only in its early stages. This analysis is of course fraught with difficulty, not only because of the obvious complexity of studying the institution of the school and the practical problems of observer bias that are inherent in the use of the technique of participant observation, but also because the schools appear, at first analysis, to be very similar regimes. All had very similar curricula, because preparation for the exams their pupils sat imposed very similar demands on their teachers. Only one of the schools—the relatively successful school E—had what can be remotely described as a parent-teacher association, and this was merely a hesitant and intermittent experiment rather than a manifestation of a radically different school-teacher ideology. None of the schools had school counsellors—all used the traditional form master as their mechanism of pastoral care. All the schools used corporal punishment, all had formalised morning assemblies. In fact, the nine schools appear—as they are—rather 'unprogressive', traditional working-class secondary modern schools, closely modelled on the grammar schools that have had such high prestige within the educational system of Wales.

In most of the school rules that they attempted to enforce, too, the schools appeared very similar. All the schools banned swearing in class, cheeking teachers, going out of the school grounds without permission, and fighting in the school buildings. All of them tried to stop their girls from wearing jewellery and all of them encouraged their girls to play separately from their boys at break and lunch times. Yet in spite of the apparent similarities in much of what the headteachers and staffs enforced, close observation of the schools has revealed subtle, qualitative differences in some areas of school interaction that can begin to enable us to account for the quantitative differences

Table 25.7 Aspects of school regimes and overall school performance (participant observer's 'blind' ratings)

overall rank	school	uniform years 1, 2 & 3	uniform years 4 & 5	prefect system	enforcement of no chewing gum rule	enforcement of no smoking rule	institutional control	corporal punishment
1	H	yes	yes	yes	low	low	low	very low
2	G	yes	no	yes	medium	low	very low	very low
3	I	no	no	no	low	medium	medium	medium
4	E	yes	no	yes	low	low	low	low
5	C	yes	no	no	low	low	low	low
6	F	no	no	no	high	high	high	high
7	A	no	no	no	high	high	high	very high
8	B	no	no	no	high	high	very high	very high
9	D	no information available						

in the rates of deviancy and pupil problems that each school is producing.

As Table 25.7 shows, the schools differ widely in the strategies that they use to orientate their pupils towards their goals. Successful schools appear to be more likely to use prefect systems, although precisely how this may make for a school's success is not clear. Part of this method's effectiveness may be due to its pervasiveness as a form of social control within the school, since the presumably pro-school prefects will be in informal interaction with both their peers and also younger children at many times when staff authority may be absent—in school G, for example, two prefects from the fifth year stopped some younger children from the second year smashing school windows. In addition to splitting the pupil sub-culture of the fifth year by the creation of a generally more pro-school prefect faction, these pupil authority systems are believed by the schools to be effective as methods of 'rescuing' deviant children—school G, for example, makes eleven or twelve prefects a year out of a year of forty and usually attempts to make at least half of these appointments from the 'B' stream. The aim, as the headmaster put it, is 'To try to sort out the difficult ones.' All the evidence from these schools would suggest that the prefect system also acts as an unrivalled form of social control over those elevated to the position.

The occupants of the role appear to derive some personal pride from it and also some status within the more pro-school peer group of the 'A' stream—the usual green 'Prefect' badges are invariably worn. To be a prefect is also widely thought to confer advantages, in terms of a better reference and recommendation, upon individual pupils. Thus the pupils' commitment to this 'leadership' role gives the school a further symbolic sanction—the removal from office—that it can use to ensure the good behaviour of its pupils. One prefect in school H, for example, who was found to have written various slogans on the school walls and in the toilets, was simply stripped of his prefectship, an action which—being committed to the role—deeply hurt him and embarrassed his parents.

A prefect system, then, acts as a means of social control for the school in general and for the prefects in particular, since being given responsibility for the administration of part of a social structure leads people to shift in their attitudes towards an increasing adoption of the values of that formal system.

A further method that the successful schools tend to use to try to orientate their pupils to identify with their schools is the wearing of school uniform. In the schools that enforce this rule, it is seen as a method of promoting pride in the school and an identification with it, although, as Table 25.7 shows, only one of these schools really tries to enforce this rule with their fourth- and fifth-year pupils. School G, which enforces a school blazer, regulation colour pullover and trousers with its first three years, attempts to enforce a school tie only with the fifth-year boys and girls.

By enforcing a uniform on years 1, 2 and 3 and then not really attempting to continue to fight battles over uniform that they cannot win with their fourth and fifth years, the successful schools believe that they are gaining what they see as the benefits of this enforcement with little of the trouble that is often assumed to accompany it.

While the successful schools appear to be characterised by their use of school uniform and school prefect systems, they are remarkable because of the relatively high degree of autonomy that they give their pupils in other areas of school life. Elsewhere (Reynolds, 1976) I have argued that a 'truce' between teachers and taught appears to operate in the successful regimes, a truce which lays down boundaries beyond which the participants in the schools will not carry their conflict. This truce is in the nature of an unofficial arrangement for the mutual convenience of both sides of the school, made between working-class pupils of low aspirations who seek a stress-free time within their schools and teachers who realise that many of the rules and regulations which should, in theory, govern the interaction between them and their pupils would, if applied, only make their task as teachers more difficult.

The acceptance of the 'truce' situation by the staff is usually manifest in decisions about how hard to enforce three crucial rules—those against smoking, chewing gum and outside school behaviour—which are concerned to limit the autonomy of their pupils, and particularly of their senior pupils. Schools where the truce exists tend not to put great store on the enforcement of 'no chewing gum' rules—at school G, less than a quarter of the staff ever bother to observe this rule at all, whereas at school B it is universally observed. The punishments meted out for its use also reflect the different orientations of the staff—the punishment at school G is simply putting the gum in the bin, whereas at school B the usual punishment is to be hit round the head or arms and then be told to put it in the bin.

In their attitude towards pupil smoking, too, the schools differ in the autonomy they allow their pupils. Some—like schools A and B—try to stop this deviant behaviour and use special smoking patrols by the staff at break and at lunchtimes to root out the 'smokers' corner' which usually assembles round the playground wall or in the boys' toilets. School B has a quite remarkable ritual in which two members of staff go out round the playground wall following the customary group of smokers and lookouts, who go themselves from corner to corner, keeping a hundred yards between them and their enemy. As could be expected, the importance which the schools attach to their pupils not smoking is reflected in the punishments meted out to them if they do—school G merely confiscates the cigarettes of its caught smokers, whereas the staff of schools A and B usually hit or cane them, as well as confiscate their cigarettes. Since the schools where there is a rigorously enforced no smoking rule are those where there is the highest rate of smoking by the pupils and since the pupils at the schools appear to have very similar rates of smoking outside school (Reynolds, 1977), it seems likely that making an issue of whether the pupils smoke may only serve to increase the numbers who do. Quite simply, the more that a school seeks to restrict the within school autonomy of its senior pupils in this way, the more that these pupils may decide to commit the acts that the school has defined as deviant.

The unsuccessful schools, who do not appear to be motivating their pupils to conform and who are restricting some of their autonomy within school, are likely to be faced with increased cohorts of children whose opinion of their teachers and their school environment is unfavourable. In the absence of much normative commitment to the institution's demands that can ensure obedience, these unsuccessful schools appear subsequently forced to apply a much higher level of organisational control in the attempt to reach their goals and maintain commitment. Table 25.7 shows that 'institutional control', which includes such factors as the degree to which silence rules are enforced in lessons, and the existence of various restrictions on movement and activity, is higher in the more problem-prone schools (for further details of these scales see Reynolds, 1977). Schools B and F, for example, force their pupils to line up in silence in their playgrounds. In school B the pupils, having been distanced from each other by putting their arms out to their side, are then marched in single file through the corridors of the school, where members of staff wait to try and ensure that no-one talks and to hit anyone if they do. The same school's lessons are rigorously repressed— little more than copying out of books is ever attempted because of the fear that a more 'informal' or 'relaxed' classroom atmosphere may weaken the control that the staff believe to be so tenuous. In the lessons of school G, though, there is likely to be more noise, even more pupil misbehaviour such as talking to another pupil in the next desk, yet there is also likely to be more teacher participation in the lesson and also greater pupil acquisition of knowledge. In school G, as is to be expected, there is no ritualised lining up after breaks and before morning and afternoon school begins and there are no rules that pupils should walk on one side of the corridor when entering or leaving school buildings.

The conflict between staff and pupils in the schools where there is no truce and no easing up on the enforcement of some rules by teachers, is continually fuelled by the attempt of the staff to exercise control in areas of the pupils' lives where they expect autonomy, such as in their behaviour outside school. One boy from school B described what this means:

If they see you smoking in the night or in the pictures they get you when you come back to school. I remember one incident when me and my friends went to the pictures on a Saturday night and we had all been drinking before we went, and as the ice-cream woman came around we all got up to buy ice-cream, and as we were buying it one of the teachers in our school came over and asked to smell my breath and he smelt my breath and he said he will see me Monday morning. So I went home that night and told my mother what happend she gave me a scolding for drinking with the boys but she said it's nothing to do with the teachers. If we had more time I think I could go on for ages writing about the things about our school.

The acceptance of the truce by the staffs of the successful schools, on the other hand, means that the teachers accept that their authority does not extend outside the school gates or outside school hours. Drinking in a pub under age will be ignored by the teachers in schools such as school G, as will smoking going to and from school and various petty misbehaviour such as fighting in the street.

It is worth saying quite simply that the evidence from these schools suggests that the more a school seeks high control over its more senior pupils by increasing organisational compulsion and decreasing pupil autonomy, the more these pupils may regard their schools as maladjusted to their needs. Rebellion within and delinquency without will be the result of the failure of the pupils and their teachers to declare a truce.

The unsuccessful schools' problems in the control of their pupils which led them to attempt high organisational control in the first place are also in evidence if we consider the type of punishments that they use and the frequency with which they use them. Whereas in the successful regimes, with their more pro-school peer groups, a simple telling-off by the teacher or the occasional clip on the head may be enough to punish deviants and ensure pupil conformity, the unsuccessful schools cannot use these strategies successfully because they do not have the same type of normative commitment from their pupils. In fact, in some of these schools, to be told off by the teacher is likely to have the effect only of increasing the status of the deviant in his peer group. Where teachers cannot use verbal sanctions because they are not effective, these schools tend to use physical punishment to try to control their pupils. As Table 25.8 shows, there is a consistent tendency for the unsuccessful schools to use physical punishment as their normal punishment for rule-breaking—punishment which may include formal canings by the headmaster, informal canings by the staff or informal hitting of children around the head or on the arms. As we would expect, then, and as Table 25.7 shows, physical punishment of children of a formal and informal nature is highest in the least successful school regimes. It is possible, of course, that this association of physical punishment with high rates of 'problem pupils' reflects nothing more than the fact that some schools, having more problem-prone

Table 25.8 Typical punishments for breaking school rules and overall school performance

school overall rank	rules		
	no smoking	no fighting in school	swearing aloud in class
Hª	cigarettes taken and told off	told off	told off
G	cigarettes taken and told off	told off	told off— rarely caned
I	cigarettes taken and told off	told off and occasionally caned	told off
E	cigarettes taken and told off	told off and occasionally caned	told off— sometimes caned
C	cigarettes taken and told off	told off	told off
F	cigarettes taken, hit and caned	told off and hit	told off and caned
A	cigarettes taken, hit and caned	told off, hit and caned	told off and caned
B	cigarettes taken, hit and caned	told off, hit and caned	told off and caned
D	no information available		

ª Most successful.

pupils on entry, are forced to use physical punishment to control them. But since the intakes of the schools appear so similar in terms of their ability and social class background, a more likely interpretation of these findings is that high rates of physical punishment may actually generate or cause an adverse response to their school regimes from the pupils in these schools. Such findings, which agree with other surveys (Clegg and Megson, 1968), would suggest, as the Newsom Report (DES, 1963) commented, that 'Corporal punishment is likely to delay, rather than promote, the growth of self-discipline and it is humiliating for staff and pupils' (Newsom Report, quoted in Berg, 1968). Quite how high rates of physical punishment may have this adverse effect is not clear—maybe the extensive use of violence as a means of control may set an example of dealing with problems by means of aggression to the children. Perhaps high rates of physical punishment affect children's sense of self-worth or self-esteem. Whatever the reason, the successful school does not appear—or does not need—to use high levels of corporal punishment with children.

To summarise and conclude the analysis so far, we can take an example of a regime that is relatively unsuccessful—school B—and see how the various aspects of pupil's school experience in this regime are inter-related. School B has no prefects to diffuse the authority system and no school uniform to promote an identification with the school in the pupils' early years. There is no 'truce' in the school and social relations between teachers and pupils are consequently characterised by hostility and by the low regard in which pupils hold their teachers.

'I want teachers which associate with us pupils. The teachers like — can't take a joke or have a laugh.'

'Mr—, he's hard. He's more of an assassin than a teacher. I want teachers who can take a joke and understand you.'

Because of their lack of commitment to the teachers and their unwillingness to see them as 'significant others' in their lives, the teachers need to apply increased coercion to ensure their control.

'They hit you around like you were dirt here. Billy goes mad with you—he grabs your hair, pulls down your head and knees you in the stomach.'

The increased coercion is likely to produce lower commitment to the school on the part of the pupils and—as a consequence—lower expectations of the pupils on the part of the teachers.

'I don't like a few of our teachers. Some if you don't know what to do they don't help you and if you go out to ask them they just say why aren't you working why don't they help us? I think that's because we are in B that they haven't any time for us B boys.'

'Some teachers just tell you what to do and if you ask a question says "Work it out yourselves" and calls you a lout.'

'Only two or three teachers teach us our work properly. Others just write things on the board for us to copy. That way we don't learn anything for ourselves.'

The conflict between pupils and teachers is continually fuelled by the attempt of the staff to exercise control in areas of the pupils' lives where they expect autonomy, such as in their behaviour outside the school, and in some aspects of their behaviour inside it. In the schools like this one that have no truce, there are many pupils who wish for one.

'The rules that I don't agree with are no smoking and no talking in class. The rule of no smoking in the school is pathetic as if they stop us smoking in school we will only smoke outside or behind the teachers' backs so is it worth punishing boys that do smoke as there are plenty more behind their backs.

And if they stop you talking in class—it's a load of rubbish. All boys will talk in class so is it worth bothering to keep this rule. Besides they can never stop you talking. You are punished for asking the boy you sit by what page is next in maths.'

Where there is this sort of conflict in a school such as school B, there will invariably be vandalism within it, truanting from it and delinquency outside it. Such a reaction from the pupils of these schools is likely to reflect a weakening of the 'moral bind' which ties the child to conventional adult life and institutions and indicates that where the initiation of the child into the accepted ways of life of the adult community that the school undertakes is perverse, then so too will be the child's response. An initiation that the pupils are likely to regard as perverse is produced by the attempt of the teachers to exercise control over the pupils in areas of their life where they feel they should have some autonomy. The attempt by the school to exercise control in this area is likely to set in motion a circular process of deviancy amplification—the pupils will regard the teachers as using illegitimate authority and will be less likely to defer to their wishes in other areas of school life. Teachers, perceiving increased opposition, may intensify their efforts to ensure compliance with their rules, which will invariably mean the increased use of coercion, as the teachers are less likely to receive the normative commitment of their pupils. Such coercion is unlikely to reduce the total amount of misbehaviour exhibited by the pupils, and may only increase it, since informal social status within an increasingly alienated student body will increasingly depend upon pupils doing things which are wrong in the eyes of the school.

The successful school, on the other hand, does not fight battles over chewing gum, smoking and out-of-school behaviour that it knows it cannot win, and does not even attempt to enforce the wearing of school uniform when that enforcement becomes problematic. It does not use high rates of physical punishment and is not harshly authoritarian in its mode of control. The school that produces conformity in its pupils, like the family that produces conformity in its children, is small and diffuses responsibility among its members. This type of school is not non-directive or permissive in the classical sense of the term, since it is clearly directive about some things. The important thing about these schools is not whether or not they are directive, but is rather in which areas of pupils' lives they attempt to direct and how they attempt to do so.

Conclusions

The outline above, based upon our participant observer's ratings of the schools, is of course only tentative and poses almost as many questions as it answers. We need to know why the teachers at the different schools are using different methods and the ideological underpinnings and rationale that they may have for their use. We need to know about the process of within school and within lesson interaction whereby the beliefs and expectations of the teachers are mediated to their children. Most important of all, we need to know why the children appear to be so different at the various schools and why the children at some schools appear to be so 'deviant'. Are the self-perceptions of the cohorts of children at the different schools different, as they should be if some of the schools have encouraged the growth of a delinquent or deviant self-identity among their children? Further work to answer these questions is in progress.

But even though we are still discovering what it may be about the individual school that has the effect of promoting deviance or conformity to societal norms, we know from this study and from the other studies mentioned earlier, that the individual school does have a substantial effect on the sort of young people that its children turn out to be. What, then, are the implications of these findings?

The first important implication concerns the practice of educational research and the areas of their subject matter which educational researchers have viewed as worthwhile areas of investigation. When faced with the need to explain pupil problems, researchers have sought their causal explanation in the nature of the pupils' home and neighbourhood culture, but rarely in the nature of their schools, so that discussion of school deviants is rarely based on any examination of the institutions from which the deviants deviate. As a consequence, much educational research of recent years (Davie *et al.*, 1972) tells us only what we knew to be the case already—namely, that certain children from 'disadvantaged' homes are at higher risk of educational failure. The type of regime that may exacerbate, or help, the process is rarely discussed because it is a question that is never explored.

In recent years the emergence of the interactionist approach in the sociology of education has meant that increased attention has been given to the 'micro' level of the school and to the generation of classroom success and failure. Far more than before, the attempt is being made to understand why certain children should fail and others succeed, an attempt that is based upon an analysis of the teachers' own beliefs as to what constitutes 'educable' or 'ineducable' children. It is this whole neglected area of school life—the sociology of schooling—that needs further development if we are to advance our knowledge of the process whereby adolescent self-perception and identity are socially formed. In brief, then, it is perhaps time that more educational researchers brought schools back into their work.

Second, if the school is—as I believe—an important influence upon its own pupils' levels of truancy, delinquency and educational failure, we should perhaps consider the direction of some of our current educational policies. When confronted by social problems like truancy, delinquency or so-called 'behavioural disorders', our automatic tendency has been, and still is, to appoint more educational psychologists, employ more advisers and introduce more school based social workers. A veritable army of members of the 'helping' professions now exists to 'help'—or rather, force—the child to adjust to the reality of his school existence, irrespective of whether the reality is worth adjusting to.

Instead of continually merely treating the deviant and delinquent children, we should perhaps begin to look and see if the reason for their rebellion lies squarely in the nature, process and operation of some of the schools that we offer them. If the reason does lie there, then perhaps we ought to seek changes in some of our delinquents' schools.

Notes

1 Parts of this analysis have appeared in an earlier form as 'When teachers and pupils refuse a truce', in *Working-Class Youth Culture*, G. Mungham and G. Pearson, eds, Routledge & Kegan Paul, 1976.

2 The schools all take from defined areas of the community, as there is no system of parental choice of school or any overlap of school catchment areas.

3 Raw scores are used, rather than age-adjusted scores, because the age distribution of the pupil intakes of the different schools was very similar.

4 In fact, the correlation between overall school position and ability of intake is slightly negative ($r = -0.454$), suggesting that the more successful schools tended to have lower ability intakes than the unsuccessful. Further tests given to the intake have been concerned with verbal and mathematical ability, and analysis is proceeding to see if these tests indicate the same rather surprising results.

References

Berg, L., 1968, *Risinghill*, Penguin.

Boocock, S., 1972, *An Introduction to the Sociology of Learning*, Boston, Houghton Mifflin.

Byrne, D. & Williamson, B., 1975, *The Poverty of Education*, Martin Robertson.

Central Advisory Council for Education, 1959, *15 to 18* (Crowther Report), HMSO.

Chanan, G. & Delamont, S., 1975, *Frontiers of Classroom Research*, Slough, NFER Publishing.

Cicourel, A. V., 1968, *The Social Organisation of Juvenile Justice*, New York, Wiley.

Cicourel, A. V. & Kitsuse, J. I., 1963, *The Educational Decision-Makers*, New York, Bobbs Merrill.

Clegg, A. & Megson, B., 1968, *Children in Distress*, Penguin.

Cloward, R. A. & Ohlin, L. E., 1961, *Delinquency and Opportunity*, Routledge & Kegan Paul.

Cohen, A. K., 1955, *Delinquent Boys*, Chicago, Free Press.

Coleman, J. S., 1966, *Equality of Educational Opportunity*, Washington, Office of Education.

Corwin, R. G., 1974, *Education in Crisis*, London, Wiley.

Davie, R. *et al.*, 1972, *From Birth To Seven*, Longmans.

Department of Education and Science, 1963, *Half our Future* (Newsom Report), HMSO.

Department of Education and Science, 1967, *Children and their Primary Schools* (Plowden Report), HMSO.

Dyer, H. S., 1968, 'School factors and equal educational opportunity', in *Harvard Educational Review*, 38(1), 38–56.

Gath, D., 1972, 'Child guidance and delinquency in a London borough', *Psychological Medicine*, 2, 185–91.

Hargreaves, D. H., 1967, *Social Relations in a Secondary School*, Routledge & Kegan Paul.

Hargreaves, D. H., 1972, *Interpersonal Relations and Education*, Routledge & Kegan Paul.

Jencks, C., 1973, *Inequality*, Allen Lane.

Kitsuse, J. I. & Cicourel, A. V., 1963, 'A note on the use of official statistics', *Social Problems*, 11, p. 131.

Little, A. *et al.*, 1971, 'Do small classes help a pupil?', *New Society*, 18(473), 769–71.

McDill, E. L. & Rigsby, L. C., 1973, *Structure and Process in Secondary Schools*, Baltimore, Johns Hopkins Press.

Phillipson, C. M., 1971, 'Juvenile delinquency and the school', in W. G. Carson and P. Wiles, eds, *Crime and Delinquency in Britain*, Martin Robertson.

Power, M. J., 1967, 'Delinquent schools', *New Society*, 19 October 1967.

Power, M. J., 1972, 'Neighbourhood, school and juveniles before the courts', *British Journal of Criminology*, 12, 111–32.

Raven, J. C., 1960, *Guide to the Standard Progressive Matrices*, H. K. Lewis.

Reynolds, D., 1976, 'When teachers and pupils refuse a truce', in G. Mungham and G. Pearson, eds, *Working-Class Youth Culture*, Routledge & Kegan Paul.

Reynolds, D., 1977, *Schools that Fail*, Routledge & Kegan Paul (in press).

Rutter, M., 1973, 'Why are London children so disturbed?', *Proc. Roy. Soc. Med.*, 66, 1221–5.

Tyerman, H. J., 1958, 'A research into truancy', *British Journal of Educational Psychology*, 28, 217–25.

Werthman, C., 1967, 'The function of social definitions in the development of delinquent careers', in *Juvenile Delinquency and Youth Crime*, Washington, US Government Printing Office.

Index

Ames, L. B., *see* Ilg, F.
Anastasi, A., 127
anti-school culture, *see* school counter-culture
Armstrong, H., 133
authority, 30–1, 53; *see also* teachers, control

Barth, R., 87, 88, 92
Basic Concept Inventory (BCI), 127–8
Becker, H. S., 29, 204, 206; *et al.*, 134, 143
Bellugi, U. and Brown, R. W., 118
Bernstein, B., 56
Bittner, E., 183
Blumer, H., 7, 88–9
Boocock, S., 219, 223
Bourdieu, P., 194
Braroe, N. W., 183
Brown, R. W., *see* Bellugi, U.
Burns, T., 184
Byrne, D. and Williamson, B., 224

Cassidy, F., *see* McCormick, P.
Castaldi, B., 208
Caudill, W. W. *et al.*, 208
Chanan, G. and Delamont, S., 219
Chittenden, E. *et al.*, 87, 88
Cicourel, A. V., 118, 119, 221; and Kitsuse, J. I., 116, 217, 220
classroom: influence of physical shape, 7, 104, 208–15; interaction, *see* pupils, interaction; teacher-pupil interaction; observers in, 36, 58–60; order, *see* teachers, control
Clegg, A. and Megson, B., 227
Cloward, R. A. and Ohlin, L. E., 206, 217
Cohen, A. K., 206, 217
Coleman, J. S., 219, 224
colleagues, 22, 24, 73, 76, 78
collectivities, *see* groups

conversations, adult-child, 7, 100–2
Cooley, C. H., 69
Corwin, R. G., 219
Coulthard, M., *see* Sinclair, J. M.
Cramond, W. A., 134
Crowther Report, 218
cue-consciousness and examination performance, 6, 143–9
curriculum, 2, 81, 84, 86–96, 133–4; 'hidden', 2, 143
Cutts, N. E. and Moseley, N., 208

Davie, R. *et al.*, 223, 228
Delamont, S., *see* Chanan, G.
deviance, 3–4, 6, 7, 27–31, 47, 48–54, 201–6
Devlin, T., 172–3, 176
'discovery' methods, 6, 133–42
Durkheim, E., 48–50, 52
Dyer, H. S., 219

education, sociology of, 1–2; fieldwork, 55–64; restraints on research, 218
Educational Development Corporation (EDC), 87
Educational Welfare Officers, 220
Englemann, S., 127
ethnomethodology, 4, 33–9, 99
ethogenics, 6, 171–3
examination techniques, 6, 143–9

Featherstone, J., 87
Foster, H. L., 181–2
Friedman, N., 129
Fuchs, E., 208
functionalism, structural, 1, 3, 17–18, 19

gangs, 47
Garfinkel, H., 118, 202; and Sacks, H., 140–1
generation gap, 4, 5, 45, 47, 54

Goffman, E., 29, 102, 109, 139, 141, 165, 179, 181, 203
Goodman, P., 99
Greasers, 46–7
Gross, E., 22
Gross, R. and Murphy, J., 208
groups, 4, 6, 7, 14–18, 51, 53, 190, 199; *see also* pupils, informal groups

Hall, O., 75, 80
Hamilton, D., 134
Hargreaves, D., 152, 161, 217, 219
Hawkins, D., 87
headteachers, 5, 58, 62, 70–4, 76, 79, 80
high-rise flats, 43–5
Holt, J., 99
'hot' and 'cold' medicine, science, 135–42

identity theory, 4, 49–53
Ilg, F. and Ames, L. B., 116
immigrants, 43, 78–9, 189
informal education, *see* open education
injustice to pupils, 58, 174–7, 182–5
Inner London Education Authority, 218
interactionism, symbolic, 1–5, 6, 7, 12–18, 88–9, 217

Jackson, B. and Marsden, D., 56
Jackson, P., 88
Jencks, C., 219
job selection, 3, 188, 191–3, 197
joking, 7, 36, 105, 167, 178–86, 190–1, 193

Kerr, J. F. *et al.*, 134
Killian, L. M., 51
kindergartens, 5–6, 116–25
kinship networks, 4, 41–4
Kitsuse, J. I., *see* Cicourel, A. V.

Klapp, O. E., 121
Kuhn, T. S., 141

labelling, 4, 7, 27–31, 201–6
Lacey, C., 152, 161
'laughs', *see* joking
Lemert, E., 203
lesson structure, 4, 34–9, 104–14
Levinson, D. O., 141
Little, A. *et al.*, 223
London East End, 4, 41–7
Lyman, S. M. and Scott, M. B., 139

McCormick, P. and Cassidy, F., 208
McDill, E. L. and Rigsby, L. C., 220
McHugh, P., 141
Manning, P. K., 4
Marsden, D., *see* Jackson, B.
Marxism, 1, 2, 56, 173
masculine chauvinism, 46, 189
Matza, D., 7, 204–5
Mead, G. H., 88, 205
medical profession, 19–25
medical training methods, 133,
  134–8
Megson, B., *see* Clegg, A.
membershipping, 33–9
Mercer, J. R., 126
Merton, R. K., 52
middle-class attitudes, 44, 188, 190,
  199, 217, 218
Mods, 46–7
Moseley, N., *see* Cutts, N. E.
'mucking about', 6, 7, 165, 179–81
Murphy, J., *see* Gross, R.

Negroes, 27, 181–2
Newsom Report, 227
Nuffield Science, 133

Ohlin, L. E., *see* Cloward, R. A.
open education, 5, 86–96
Opie, I. and P., 99

parents, 5, 68–70, 73–4, 76, 78, 84,
  197, 218
Parlett, M., 143
Parsons, T., 16
Peters, R. S., 87
Phillips, D. L., 141
Phillipson, C. M., 202, 217, 223
placement of pupils, 5–6, 116–25

Plowden Report, 87, 88, 219, 224
Power, M., 218, 219, 224
prefects, 225
principals, *see* headteachers
professions, 3, 19–25
Proshansky, H. M. *et al.*, 209
pupils: attention, 5, 104–14;
  culture, 6, 99, 129, 184, 225;
  see also school counter-culture;
  informal groups, 152–9, 160–1,
  165; interaction, 60, 160–9;
  level of interest, 7, 81, 86–96,
  165–9, 179–81, 183, 184, 188,
  196; own norms and rules, 161,
  173–4, 177, 181–2, 185, 190;
  typing by teachers, 5–6, 7, 120–5;
  see also injustice; placement;
  testing

Rathbone, C., 87, 88, 92
Raven, J. C., 222
Rigsby, L. C., *see* McDill, E. L.
Rockers, 46–7
Rutter, M., 219

Sacks, H., 36, 101; *see also*
  Garfinkel, H.
Schlosberg, H., *see* Woodworth,
  R. S.
school counter-culture, 7, 188–99,
  218
school-leaving age, 177, 188
schools, delinquent, 76–9, 217–29
Schools Council, 218; Humanities
  Curriculum Project, 133
Schutz, A., 129, 141
Science Teacher Education Project,
  133
Scott, M. B., 139; *see also*
  Lyman, S. M.
Scottish Integrated Science
  Scheme, 134
shop-floor culture, 188–91, 193,
  198–9
signification, *see* labelling
Silberman, C., 86, 88
Sinclair, J. M. and Coulthard, M.,
  140
Skinheads, 46–7
Smith, L., 88
smoking, 182–3, 189, 196, 225–8
Snyder, B. R., 143

social class, 6, 53, 76, 152–3, 219
socialization, 44, 98–9
Sommer, R., 208
Spearman, C., 126
streaming/destreaming, 62, 152
Strong, S. M., 121
Stubbs, M., 140
Sudnow, D., 202

Taylor, F. W., 189
teacher-pupil interaction, 2, 5,
  34–9, 59–60, 62–3, 81–5, 104–14,
  182–3, 195
teachers: control, 5, 7, 68–74, 76,
  78, 104–14, 173, 183–4, 188, 195,
  226–8; craftsman, 81–5; effective,
  166–8; new, 59, 63–4, 76–8;
  perspectives, 2, 58–60, 63, 78,
  80; 'soft', 165–8, 174–5, 184;
  transfers, 5, 75–7, 79–80, 223
territoriality, 47
testing of pupils, 5–6, 116–19,
  126–31
Tower Hamlets schools study, 218,
  219, 224
Tropp, A., 57
truancy, 168–9, 189, 218, 220, 228
Turner, R., 53, 55
Tyerman, H. J., 218

uniform, 225, 228

Waller, W., 5, 208
Weber, L., 87
Wechsler, D., 126
Werthman, C., 205, 217
Whyte, W., 88
Wilkins, L., 48–50, 52
Williamson, B., *see* Byrne, D.
Wiseman, S., 57
Woods, P., 202
Woodworth, R. S. and Schlosberg,
  H., 127
work, transition to, 188, 192–4
working-class culture, 7, 41–7,
  56–7, 188–9, 191, 196, 199
Worsley, P. M., 64
Wrong, D., 99

Young, M. F. D., 1
Youth Employment Service, 188
youth subcultures, 4, 45–7